SAINTS

AND

SINNERS

OF
THE
BIBLE

SAINTS

AND

SINNERS

OF
THE
BIBLE

LOUIS ALBERT BANKS, D. D.

Advancing the Ministries of the Gospel

AMG *Publishers*

God's Word to you is our highest calling.

Saints and Sinners of the Bible
Published by AMG Publishers.
6815 Shallowford Road
Chattanooga, TN 37421

Originally published by the author in two volumes.

Print ISBN: 978-0-89957-636-7
ePub ISBN: 978-1-61715-234-4
Mobi ISBN: 978-1-61715-235-1

Cover Design by Daryl Phillips Design

Interior Design and Typesetting by Jennifer Ross

Printed in the United States of America
15 14 13 12 11 10 –Di– 8 7 6 5 4 3 2 1

CONTENTS

PART 2
THE GREAT SINNERS OF THE BIBLE

FOREWORD

In AMG's *Saints and Sinners of the Bible*, Louis Albert Banks presents the lives of these saints and sinners, the decisions they made, and the nature of their character. From these, we are able to learn much more about humankind in general and ourselves in particular.

The stories of the characters of the Bible are more gripping than any novel. More enlightening studies into humanity do not exist. Louis Banks' presentation of these saints and sinners of the Bible will challenge you to faith and righteousness. .

Though originally published in two volumes entitled *The Great Sinners of the Bible* and *The Great Saints of the Bible*, AMG has combined both volumes into one book. In producing Saints and Sinners of the Bible, we at AMG Publishers have made some minor changes to the original work to help make its content more clear to modern readers: We have updated some archaic terms, and we have updated spelling in accordance with how our language has changed over the years; in some cases, unusual forms of punctuation have been simplified to eliminate confusion. Apart from these minor modifications, however, we have remained true to Banks' original work in every way.

Additionally, readers should note that the points of current history mentioned by Banks are from the end of the nineteenth century.

PART 1

THE GREAT SAINTS
OF THE BIBLE

1

THE PIONEER SAINT

*"And Abel…brought of the firstlings of his flock
and of the fat thereof. And the Lord had respect unto
Abel and to his offering"* (Genesis 4:4).

It is the pioneer who makes his mark, often beyond his merits, as compared with men who live in a different period. The pioneer, while in the background of the picture, looms up large as time passes, and he fills the imaginations of the generations that come after him. In the history of our own country there are abundant illustrations of the power of the pioneer not only to make himself strongly influential, but to hold his grip most tenaciously on the institutions which he had a hand in forming and establishing. The hand of the Pilgrim is still on New England, and his influence has affected all the streams of intelligence, social, religious, and governmental, that have gone out from the land where he struggled with hard climate and harsh savages. Go to New York, and the Dutch of New Amsterdam are not hard to trace about the island where they once held sway. The Quaker's broad-brimmed hat and quiet dignity still throw their shadow over Philadelphia, the Creole still meets you in New Orleans, and the spirit of the gold-digger of "forty-nine" will look into your eyes on every street in San Francisco. Great is the pioneer.

Abel was a pioneer in the tribe of the saints. Eve, having had one chance which she lost through the serpent, was given another opportunity in her children. She seems to have felt that there she would achieve great success and win back her lost prestige. So when Cain was born young mother Eve was wild with delight, and said in her rapture, "I have gotten a man from the Lord" (Genesis 4:1) But Cain had a bad kink in him, and it was probably not very long before poor Eve began to suspect that she might have gotten him from another quarter. At all events, when Abel was born she said nothing, but named him "Abel," which meant "vanity." Young as she was, Eve seems to have come to Solomon's conclusion that all was vanity and vexation of spirit.

This shows what poor judges we are of the blessings of life, for in Abel Eve had truly gotten a man from the Lord. So far as we are able to discover, Abel never gave his father and mother a moment of anxiety. From the beginning to the end his life seems to have been sweet and gentle and noble. He was a shepherd, and is the father of the shepherds. We are quite accustomed to think of David as the shepherd saint, but Abel fills that place far more perfectly. David got away from the sheepfold as soon as he could, while he was yet only a lad, and never again went back to it. David's principal career is that of a soldier and a king, if we accept the fact that he was a poet always, from boyhood to old age. Abel, however, was always a shepherd, and it is pleasant to think of him as going out with the first flock of sheep that ever pastured on the hillsides, leading them forth in the early morning of time, a type of the

Good Shepherd who was to come long centuries afterward to give himself as a ransom for the sheep and to be the Shepherd of our souls.

We have no reason to suppose that Abel ever married. He seems to have lived and died without a domestic life of his own, and probably was still a young man when his simple, but pure and honorable, career closed in the first great human tragedy.

Both Cain and Abel were worshipers of God so far as outward ceremony went .Even Cain, evil as he was at heart, would not have dared to omit worship, but took his offerings from his farm and offered them upon the altar. But Cain's heart was wrong; his life was wrong. And as God could not accept Cain he therefore could not accept his offerings, and that was the beginning of Cain's wrath against his brother.

Abel, however, was a worshiper in the truest sense. It is especially recorded that he brought the very best he had in his flock and laid it upon the altar as an offering to God. There is something very suggestive in the way it is stated. The writer says that he "brought of the firstlings of his flock and of the fat thereof" (Genesis 4:4). No doubt we all think the better of Abel because he picked out the fattest lambs to give to God, for there is always a temptation to give to God the lambs that will not sell. Do you think that is too hard? But can you not prove it in your own heart, in your own life? Is not the temptation very strong to use the best we have on ourselves; to spend all that is needed to give ourselves comfort and even luxury, and after we have eaten all the fat, if there is any scrawny old scarecrow left in the flock, to turn that over to God? Such a course dishonors God, and it is degrading to our own souls. How can God be pleased with our offerings when we are so ungenerous and mean in our hearts? When God reasoned with Cain about the danger of allowing envy and sin to dwell in his heart he told him that if he would turn about, and become a good man, would do right, his offering also should be accepted. So we know that it was not because one man brought potatoes and squashes, or cabbages and cucumbers, and the other man brought a lamb, that the one was accepted and the other rejected. No. The whole thing hinged on the character of the man. God will accept your offering if you are a good man. The size of the offering will not count, provided it is your best and behind it is a good heart, and you bring it with love and with a desire to please and honor God.

You will notice that it was the spirit of Abel which pleased God. Abel was a good man and lived a clean, wholesome life, and his life was full of thanksgiving day by day. Whether he watched the sunrise in the morning, or beheld the glow of the sunset at evening, or in the noonday led his flock under the shade of the primeval trees for their rest, or at night looked into the blue vault of heaven at the calm beauty of the stars, his heart went out in gratitude and love to God. Not a lamb in his flock was happier or more trustful in its innocent confidence in its shepherd than was Abel in his glad and happy trust in God. And so out of a full heart, overflowing with gratitude and thanksgiving and inspired by the love that always longs to give the best to the one beloved, Abe; brings the first lamb of his flock, with the fat thereof, and as he lays it upon the altar he wishes he had something better still to put there as a type of the loving gratitude which he feels in his heart. That is why the Lord was pleased with the offering of Abel. So it was when the woman came to the house of Simon, and brought her alabaster box of ointment of great price, and poured it upon the head of Jesus, feeling in her heart that there was nothing too good for her Lord. And when small, greedy souls like Judas complained of the waste Jesus defended the loving deed of the woman. Her great love and the gratitude of her soul that inspired her action were sweeter fragrance to Christ than the perfume of the alabaster. Let us learn from this our great lesson: If we would please God we must be genuine to the very core in our religion; we must do our duty not only with fidelity, but with gratitude and love, which will make our steps quick and our hands skillful and gentle; the whole influence of our worship and service will be glorified by the spirit with which we make our offering.

Abel is a great comfort and a great stay to our faith in the possibilities of human nature. When Eve saw how good Abel was, though living under the shadow of Cain's meanness, she must have thanked God and taken new courage. We look on the Cains of life too much; it makes us suspicious, cynical and we come to feel that all men are envious and greedy and malicious in their spirit. As a recent writer has well said, if we fix our eyes on human baseness and meanness all soon looks black and desperate to us. If, however, we turn to the other side of the shield, if seems as though we have never half appreciated the possibilities for good even among the poorest and the humblest types of humanity. Down in the worst slums of our big cities we find God shining through human rags and tatters, radiating his love in sensibilities tender and true. Up in the midst of a big tenement house, where all about it was squalor and misery and the air breathed the breath of hell, I have stumbled on an oasis in the moral desert where in the little suite of narrow rooms home life was carried on so sweet and wholesome, with such perfect love and self-respect, that it was like a glimpse of heaven blooming at the very mouth of the pit. Indeed, I think we ought to be more impressed with the goodness of mankind than its badness. How the unexpected gentleness of even coarse men and women touches us at times! How beautiful helpfulness seems when it comes from those who themselves need help! I am often impressed with the generosity of the poor, who take from their own backs and bear patiently their own hunger that they may have something to give to the man who is worse off. The masses who live on the edge of doom, who have laid up no reserve for sickness or old age, who know not even how they can afford to die or whether the possibility of decent burial will be afforded them—the courage and practical faith of such as these is the great backstay of our hope in human nature. Their bravery and cheerfulness is the treasure of our time, the reserve moral wealth of mankind.

Yes, if you want to get courage it is the quiet, pure, wholesome man like Abel rather than the dashing, brilliant genius who will give it to you. We must look to the triumphs, unheralded, unsung, achieved every day on obscure battlefields, that have no echo round the globe but tell grandly in the progress of man—"the brave, unflinching life-struggles with adverse conditions; the preservation of pure sentiment and affection; all the elemental and basic virtues saved in the great fight; the spectacle of men, women, even children, loving to give service, even life, for others; self-sacrifice, springing even in noisome places, sweetening and purifying unhallowed spots; the desire to do right because God has set the law of rightness in human hearts." How sublime it all is! And yet it may be illustrated in the next street by some poor old black woman whom the world looks on as a mere drudge, by some helpless cripple, even by some sinful being in a convict's cell. Surely human nature is grand and glorious, and it is a sweet and wholesome thing for us to dig into its gold mine and reveal the treasures which are there. No man lives in vain, though he live lonely and die young, who lives right and leaves a pure record of a loving life behind him.

And that brings me to my last reflection about this pioneer saint of ours. If you want to get the afterglow of Abel's career before your mind you must leap across the gulf of the centuries, and come down to the book of Hebrews, with its roll call of the heroes of the faith. And there you will find Abel lifted into a place of fadeless glory: "By faith Abel offered unto God a more excellent sacrifice than Cain, by with he obtained witness that he was righteous, God testifying of his gifts: and by it he being dead yet speaketh" (Heb. 11:4). Abel's life on earth was very humble and very quiet; he lived in a day without railroads or steamships or cities, a day without telephone or telegraph, ages and ages before printing was discovered; when there were no books or newspapers or magazines in which he could perpetuate himself or leave a record of his faith; but God took care that the perfume of his life should not be wasted, and has wafted it down to our time. And God has put his life in a far more glorious setting than Abel could ever have dreamed of. Though in heaven these thousands of years, he still speaks with a courageous voice to his fellow-men. Mr. Beecher says that when the sun goes below the horizon it has not set; the heavens glow for a full hour after its departure. And when a great and good man departs, the sky of this world is luminous long after he is out of sight. Such a man cannot die out of this world. When he goes he leaves behind much of himself. Being dead, he speaks. How glorious it is to so live that God can lift up our lives, even after we have ceased to live in the human body among men, and make them a vital testimony for goodness and faith that will make the world a happier and sweeter place in which to live!

Let us comfort ourselves with the assurance that the path to nobility which Abel followed so successfully has not been closed. Sometimes in the country, in the woods, we see and old road that has been long overgrown and the trees have fallen across it in the storm, and before you can get over it there must be much taken out of the way. The path between your heart and goodness may be overgrown by thorns and briers, and many a broken tree may be thrown across it, but Christ will help you to clear the way if you will turn your heart toward heaven with the simplicity of an earnest and noble purpose. You may be sure that nothing will ever take the place of goodness. To do good, to be honest and true, to give God the love of a sincere heart, to do your duty with a faithful, loving spirit—nothing can take the place of that. You remember what the psalmist said when he sought to get rid of his sin and make his peace with God: "Thou desirest not sacrifice; else would I give it: thou delightest not in burnt offering. The sacrifices of God are a broken spirit: a broken and a contrite heart, O God, thou wilt not despise" (Ps. 51:16). And I am sure that there are those who hear me who need at this moment to pray the prayer of the psalmist, uttered in that very psalm, when he cries out of a full heart: "Have mercy upon me, O God, according to thy loving-kindness: according unto the multitude of thy tender mercies blot out my transgressions. Wash me thoroughly from mine iniquity, and cleanse me from my sin. For I acknowledge my transgressions: and my sin is ever before me. Against thee, thee only, have I sinned, and done this evil in thy sight…Purge me with hyssop, and I shall be clean; wash me, and I shall be whiter than snow…Hide thy face from my sins, and blot out all mine iniquities. Create in me a clean heart, O God; and renew a right spirit within me. Cast me not away from thy presence; and take not thy holy spirit from me. Restore to me the joy of thy salvation; and uphold me with thy free spirit" (Ps. 51:1–4, 7, 9–12). Your heart may be full of gladness, and all heaven will ring with joy even now, if from the depths of your soul you will give yourself to such prayer.

2

THE FIRST MAN WHO THWARTED DEATH

"Enoch walked with God: and he was not;
for God took him" (Genesis 5:24).

Bret Harte once wrote a book called *Condensed Novels*, the main interest of which was that the great, striking message of the story, with a comprehensive glimpse into its plot and plan, was condensed into a few sentences. The writer took a volume to tell it in the first place, but the critic condensed it into a few words and yet gave its essence. The Bible, above all other books, is a volume of condensed biography. A man who lived 365 years, a year for every day in the year, and whose career was in some respects the most remarkable in the story of mankind, has his biography written in three or four sentences. Less than 100 words in the Old and the New Testaments tell the story of the life of Enoch. And yet they are words full of meaning and say a good deal about him.

Enoch is one of the few men in the Bible story about whom nothing bad is recorded. Some of the greatest men in Bible times, as in our own, have been very unequal and uneven in their greatness. They have what somebody calls "the weakness of their strength." But there are a few men in the Bible, as in our own age, who seem so well balanced in their integrity and nobility of character that we could say of each of them, as we can of Enoch, what Mark Antony said of Brutus:

> "His life was gentle, and the elements
> So mixed in him that Nature might stand up
> And say to all the world, " 'This was a man!'"

Two or three declarations are made about Enoch which open to us a glimpse into the sources of his greatness. They are well worth our study, for they point out to us the open secret of real greatness in any human life. The first tremendous statement made about Enoch is that he "walked with God." That fellowship with God was the secret source of all that was good and great and splendid in the life of Enoch. He lived in a wicked time, in an age that was peculiarly corrupt and evil, and yet in the midst of the wicked men and women who surrounded him his life shone like a star in the night, spotless and clean. The reason was that he drew his strength from his hidden fellowship with God. Men often excuse themselves for living lives far below their knowledge and their occasional desire because of the circumstances which surround them. It is not an uncommon thing to hear a man say, "I know that I do not live as good a life as I should, and my early ideals were infinitely higher than the life I now lead, but no man can live a pure life in my business, or in associating with the kind of men I have to deal with every day." When a man says that, we know that he has no hidden source of power. He is depending on himself and upon worldly supports only. But it is possible for every one of us to have secret power from the very heart of God to help us in gaining the victory over sin.

They are getting ready in California for a most wonderful triumph of modern science and human energy in the industrial world—the conveying of electricity along heavy aluminum cables a distance of 145 miles, to keep the wheels of San Francisco revolving. It is the greatest feat ever accomplished in the transmission of electrical power. California is already well in the lead in the item of long-distance electric power transmission. Los Angeles is supplied with the Promethean energy over eighty-three miles of wire, and that up to the present time has been the longest system by far in the world. In the state of New York, there are the Niagara Falls system of twenty-two miles, and a line from Mechanicville to Schenectady of about twenty miles. This new enterprise, however, will be a great step in advance in man's conquest over nature, or rather in man's adaptation to nature's laws in the acquisition of power. When completed, three bare aluminum wires, on two separate pole lines, running from the natural reservoir of the snowcapped Sierras to San Francisco and Oakland, will more than eclipse every other project of transmission of power, however stupendous. It is an interesting combination that makes this feat possible—a young Polish prince, millions of dollars of American and English capital, twenty billions of gallons of water, and the thunderbolts of Almighty God. Think of sixty thousand volts of subtle, invisible, fierce, invincible, irresistible energy brought down from distant snow-clad mountains to serve human enterprise where cargo-laden vessels and freighted trains meet! This sixty-thousand volts means fourteen thousand horse power, or enough to keep aglow one hundred and eighty thousand incandescent lamps of 16 candle power. It would easily run San Francisco's street railway system and have plenty to spare for factories. It presages the day when steam engines will be discarded and boilers converted into scrap heaps of rusty iron.

That seems to us a wonderful thing; and yet it is insignificant compared to that transmission of power from the heart of God by which a man who has been led captive by his sins is given strength to resist the devil, to break asunder the chain of evil habit, to become a new creature whose thoughts and hopes and imaginations are pure and noble, to live such a life that it can be said of him, "He walked with God."

I want to press this great message home to the heart of any man or woman here who has sought to do good and has been defeated. I want to speak to you who have struggled in your own strength against evil, and in the great wrestling match with your besetting sin have gone to the ground, and your sin has leered in your very face, and shaken its fist in your eyes, and triumphed over you. I bring to you the story of Enoch as a great story of hope. There is power in the God of the lightning and the thunder; there is power in the God of electricity; there is power in the Source of all power that can be transmitted to your heart, as it was to the heart of Enoch, so that you may have victory over every evil thing, no matter how discouraging the circumstances that surround you; so that you may walk with God and have the same testimony that Enoch had, that your life is pleasing to God.

Outside of the Bible no one has interpreted this great message more splendidly than Victor Hugo in his wonderful portrait of Jean Valjean. As Dr. O. P. Gifford said the other day, there are three great characters in Hugo's tragedy—the State, the criminal, and the Christ-like bishop. For nineteen years the State held Jean Valjean between its palms as a boy holds a butterfly, and when the palms were parted there had been no change in character. For nineteen years the State held him a criminal in the galleys as a boy holds the bumblebee in the sweet cup of the hollyhock. And when the penitentiary doors opened and the State parted its fingers, and the criminal buzzed out into society again, the sting was as sharp and the poison as violent as ever. The reason was that character cannot be changed by outside pressure alone.

Jean Valjean went out into the world with his heart full of hate and bitterness, and in that spirit he came to the door of a friend of Jesus Christ. The good bishop, Hugo tells us, had a great heart. He was not a great thinker. He felt that the world was suffering with a great calamity. He felt the fever, he heard the sobbing, of the patient. He did not spend his time trying to find out how sin came, nor why; but he tried to help a little. So he opened the door to this wicked man and welcomed him. While the bishop slept the criminal in the man awoke, and he stole the silver from the bishop's house and escaped. The next morning he was brought back again by the police, and the bishop saved him and sent the police away. And when they were gone he looked into the poor, astonished man's face and said, "Jean Valjean, my brother! I have bought your soul from you. I have drawn it from black thoughts that lead to perdition. I have given it to goodness." And the man redeemed by the words, "My brother," by the quick tear of sympathy, by the Christ in the heart-throb of this large-hearted man, went out to lead a new life. And Jean Valjean became Father Madeline. Away up among the mountains he organized a great industry. And he gave his regenerated life to the building of a Christian community. He saved his money to found hospitals, to care for the sick, to minister to the dying. He was tested in every way possible for a man to be tested, but he triumphed and lived a great, strong, helpful, victorious life. Now, it was the transmission of power from the heart of God to the broken and discouraged heart of Jean Valjean which made that life possible. The God who walked with Enoch revealed Himself to the poor criminal, and he, too, day by day, had the testimony that he pleased God. O my brother, to live without God is to go away from the light toward the darkness. I do not wonder that the sacred writer says that people who live without God are also without hope in the world. As Dr. Hepworth well says, a man no more depends on his heartbeats for physical health than on worship for his spiritual comfort. What a rudderless vessel is on a stormy ocean—the prey of circumstance, the victim of wind and current—that a soul is which has no prayer to utter because there is no one to pray to. But with God as the radiant center of our hopes, and the inexhaustible source of our encouragement and helpfulness, a man may challenge the future without fear.

But the peculiar feature of Enoch's life, that which puts it in a unique class, lies in the fact that he is the first man in the Bible story who thwarted death. He walked with God, and God was pleased with him, "and he was not; for God took him" (Genesis 5:24). A little girl was once talking with another little girl about Enoch. The second little girl had never heard of him, and so the first, who was rich in Bible stories, told her by her mother, made up a version of the story of Enoch which has a very beautiful suggestion in it. Said the little girl to her friend, "God was accustomed to take walks with Enoch, and one day they went farther than usual, and God said, 'Enoch, you are a long way from home; better come in and stay with me;' so he went, and has stayed home ever since." I think that is a better way of putting it than many older theologians would have thought of.

All possibility of the fear of death and the horror of it was taken away from Enoch. Paul, in his letter to the Hebrews, says that as a reward for his great faith and his pure life "Enoch was translated, that he should not see death" (Hebrews 11:5). There is something striking in that phraseology—"should not see death." Some people see ghosts and hobgoblins of death for many, many years before they die. Now, Paul declares that the real sting of death is sin. But Enoch had no such sting, for he lived purely in God's sight; and the way for us to get victory over death is to get rid of sin. With sin banished, with the sweet testimony in our hearts that we please God, death becomes a defeated enemy; it can no longer be anything but the usher that opens the door into the eternal life. The Christian is not seized upon by some policeman. God takes him; Christ comes to receive him. Heaven rings with many bells of welcome, and his friends whom he has loved on earth, and who have preceded him to the skies, crowd about him to receive him into his immortal home. There can be no black and perplexing future to the man or the woman who walks with God in genial, loving fellowship.

One of the strangest propositions to save Galveston, Texas, from future hurricanes comes from France. An artillery expert, who has sidetracked hailstorms and brought rain during droughts by artillery discharges, comes forward with a plan to erect a battery close to Galveston. He says the recent terrible storm which devastated the city and has shocked the whole world could have been rendered harmless if artillery had been used against it as soon as it made its appearance. He would rebuild Galveston as before, and permanently maintain there a battery, with hurricane experts on the lookout day and night. If a West Indian cyclone approached he would fire at it, and, he says, break its back. I am sure that there is power in faith in God, and in the presence of Jesus Christ, to break the back of the very worst storm of grief or trouble that threatens you. Our Christ has "tasted death for every man," and that means that he tasted death for you. It is not needed that you should even taste it again, for Christ drank that cup down to the very dregs. I bring you a message of love from the God of Enoch, who is also the God who "so loved the world that he gave his only begotten Son, that whosoever believeth in him should not perish, but have everlasting life" (John 3:16).

3

AN OLD-TIME PRINCE

"I will bless thee,…and thou shalt be a blessing"
(Genesis 12:2).

Travelers tell us that in all the world there is nothing more beautiful, nothing more refreshing, than an oasis in one of the great African deserts; when after a day and a night or more of barren sand, until it is weary and discouraged, the eye lights on a beautiful patch of green, a luxurious blending of graceful palm, waving grass, rippling springs, pendent fruits, and tropical flowers—an island of verdure, refreshment, and comfort in the midst of a sea of sand. To such an oasis a caravan comes with both man and beast hot with travel, scorched with heat, faint with thirst, and finds food and drink, shelter and rest. The natives call the desert "The Torment," because it is so hard and inhospitable. The oasis is called by the Africans "The Smile of God." What that oasis is to the caravan of the desert a man like Abraham is to the world. Wherever he goes he brings the presence of God in such a gracious and generous and beautiful way that men see God's smile in him.

I want to call your attention to the relation of these two brief sentences which I have chosen for our text: "I will bless thee," and "Thou shalt be a blessing." The two belong together. It is a great shame when a man receives blessings from God—and all we have that is good and beautiful comes from him—and then acts as though they were all for himself and impose no responsibility on the possessor. Such a man insures his own downfall. His blessings become a curse to him, and in the end it would have been better for him if he had never had them. Great intellectual gifts, great musical gifts, great gifts of speech, powers of personal attraction, wealth and position, are only beautiful and splendid when they are received as the gift of God, to be passed on, generously and unselfishly, until the world looking on shall see "the smile of God."

How bright and beautiful the world would soon become if everyone marching under the name of Jesus Christ gave himself completely up to the leading of the divine Spirit, holding all his blessings not for Himself only, but for the world! On one occasion in one of our great cities a thousand men marched through the streets at midnight. Neither moon nor stars appeared in the clouded sky, and the lamps along the street were but as twinkling beads of light which vainly tried to light the gloom of the dull November air. But wherever the possession went, wherever the tramping of their feet was heard, the light, clear, full, and brilliant, lit up the streets and houses, illumined statues, and was flashed back from every window and every gilded sign. Every face shone bright, every form stood clear, and the dull, dark night, right up into the gloom above, glowed and gleamed as with the first sunshine of the morning. The reason of it was that every man carried a pitch-pine torch; each flashed its little measure of light upon the wall of darkness, and altogether they conquered the night about them. So every Christian is to be a light in the world. Each one of us is to bear a torch; indeed, we are to be a torch, helping to dispel the darkness. Let every Christian who hears me determine to so catch the spirit of this old-time prince, who, in the midst of a dark age, dedicated himself to God, that henceforth he will walk among men as "the smile of God," or, as Christ puts it, "the light of the world."

Abraham was born of a family of idolaters, in the land of Ur of the Chaldees. We are not acquainted with the special circumstances which led to his conversion to the true God, but a beautiful legend has come down to us which may be true. This legend says that as the young man lay upon the mountain height, amid his flock at night, there rose a star so brilliant and beautiful in the great arch of heaven that Abraham was filled with the glory of it and said, "This is my god; this will I worship." But, as the still hours of the night passed by, the star sank down and was gone. And he said, "Of what avail is it that I worship my god if it die out in the darkness and I see it no more?" Then above the hills there rose the moon and flooded all the earth with silvery light, quenching many of the stars. And Abraham hailed it, saying, "Thou art fairer and greater than the star; thou art my god, for thou art worthier." But lo, it, too, hastened away and sank in the darkness. Then Abraham cried, "If my gods forsake me, then am I as others that do err!" Soon rose the sun in radiant splendor. It scattered the darkness and his doubts. And he said, "Thou, thou art my god, greater than moon and stars. I will worship thee." But at even the sun sank, and, like the moon and stars, it, too, was gone. Then Abraham was alone; but as he gazed into heaven there came to him the presence of the One behind the star, the moon, the sun—the Maker of them all.

And Abraham cried, "O my people, I am clear of these things. I turn my face to Him who has made the heavens and the earth; He only is my God." Whether the legend be true or not, it must have been in some way like that that God made Himself known to the heart of this young man and led him forth upon his gracious and blessed career.

Let us notice some of the ways in which Abraham's life was a blessing to the world. And I shall not speak of anything that is not of use to every one of us, being within the reach of each of us, and, therefore, it may be God's message to our hearts.

In the first place, he was an altar-builder. Wherever Abraham went, no matter how irreligious the people were, he never failed to build his altar to God. Who can tell how much good Abraham did in that way? His presence in any community was a testimony to the one living and true God. He worshiped God in the sight of the people. He became known to all the East, and is still known to millions of people in that great other side of the world, as "the friend of God." It is possible for us to live in the same way, so that men who know us will think of us as the friend of God. That is what Jesus meant when he said that we should so let our light shine that men who behold our conduct will glorify God, because they will recognize that it is the friendship of God with us that makes it possible for us to overcome the sins of the world and live faithfully before men.

Not only is this true, but we shall make life sacred to ourselves. Wherever Abraham went he consecrated the land by his altars. Robertson says that as Abraham went along he erected altars to commemorate the mercies of God and to remind his posterity that this was really their own land. Here we have that strange feeling of human nature, the utter impossibility of realizing the invisible except through the visible. Churches—what are they built for? To limit God and bind him down to space? Or to explain God to us, to enable us to understand Him, and to teach us that not here only, but in every place, He is present? Consider, then, what the land of Canaan became. Gradually it was dotted over with these stones, teaching the Israelites that it was a sacred land. What these stones did for Israel our memory does for us; it brings back in review our past life. We should remember as we are passing along how precious and sacred it will make the past for us if, like Abraham, we are dotting the days and weeks and years, as they fly, with memorials of communion with God. These are serious questions to ask yourself: What kind of memorials am I setting up along the way to look back upon? When I look back upon them in the future will they make me glad? Will they fill me with thanksgiving? Or will they make me ashamed? God help us to ask these questions in all honesty.

Abraham was not only a man with faith in prayer, but his faith blossomed out in deeds. He lived his religion through the most annoying occurrences of life. All true faith must have that effect. We do not really believe God unless we seek to please Him and do His will. Faith in God is a stalk. The life and the conduct are the branches with shining leaves and fragrant flowers and luscious fruits. As Longfellow sings:

> "Therefore look and believe, for works follow
>   spontaneous,
> Even as the day the sun; for Christian works are
>   no more than

Animate faith and love, as flowers are the animate springtide."

So Abraham showed his faith by his works. He realized
Massey's noble lines:

"One of the chivalry of Christ! He tells us how to
stand
With rootage like the palm, amid the maddest
whirl of sand."

Abraham lived nobly before the world and blessed it
with the presence and influence of a man who could rise
above all selfishness and all meanness in business. When
the herders of Lot began to quarrel with his herders, and
strive was brewing, Abraham in the noblest way said to Lot,
"You and I cannot afford to have quarreling among ourselves. I have not gone out from my people at the call of
heaven, and become a wanderer on the face of the earth,
to live a mean, quarrelsome life. Now, my son, there is
plenty of room. You choose which way you would like to
go, and I will go the other way." If Lot had been as great as
Abraham he would have refused to take the first choice,
being the younger man and owing all his success to his
uncle. But he was a little fellow, to whom a nickel at the
end of his nose looked bigger than a heaven far away, so
he chose the rich pasture lands that stretched out toward
Sodom. And Abraham turned away toward the desert and,
as usual, built an altar to God.

After a little, trouble came to Lot. Four kings came down
on Sodom and Gomorrah, and Lot was gobbled up with
the rest, and not only his flocks and herds, but his family
were carried away by the plunderers. A messenger escaped

in the night and found his way into the desert tenting place of Abraham, and told him the sad story of ruin that had come to Lot. Now, a selfish, worldly man would have said: "It is good riddance to bad rubbish. Lot thought he was very sharp when he picked out the best part of the country and began to make friends in Sodom. He has chosen his bed; let him lie in it. If he had treated me square I would have helped him out, but he was mean to me, and now he can take the consequences." Did you ever hear a man talk like that when a messenger came with a tale of trouble about some acquaintance or relative? But Abraham did for enmity or revenge. No, his big heart only remembered that Lot was his nephew, and that in some sense God had put him as guardian for him, and that he must do his best to save him. So this and that he must do his best to save him. So this great-hearted prince took his trained servants, the first rough-riding cowboys that ever went to war—for this is the first recorded war in the history of the world—and away they went on forced marches toward the enemy. God was with them, nothing could stand before them, and the arrogant and cruel foe was overthrown. Not only Lot and his family were brought back, but also large spoils of war.

The greatness and nobility of Abraham come out in the settling up after the war was over. The king of Sodom was very willing to give up all the spoil to Abraham, and as such things go Abraham would have had a perfect right to it. But Abraham knew that he was God's man, and must keep an unblemished character before all the world, and so he would not touch it. In these days of boodling councilmen, when contracts are put up at auction, and corporations expect to buy their way into franchise and power, it is exceedingly refreshing to look on a man like Abraham and hear him as, standing before the king of Sodom, he says, "I have lifted up mine hand unto the Lord, the Most High God, the possessor of heaven and earth, that I will not take from a thread even to a shoe latchet, and that I will not take anything that is thine, lest thou shouldest say, I have made Abram rich" (Gen. 14:22, 23). Abraham was not going to be rich unless God made him rich. If wealth came to him there must be no smirch on the title, there must be no taint on the money in his wallet. O, brothers, the best thing any Christian business man can do today to help on the kingdom of God is to live like that before all the world.

Abraham was a blessing to the world because wherever he went he was an index finger pointing toward heaven. He lived in tents, but every man who knew him knew that he was getting ready to live in the city of God. He was a busy man, a man with large interests. He had enormous flocks and herds. It was a great caravan wherever Abraham went. He was a prince to be taken into account when men talked of business or of war. But he always had time for his prayers. He never forgot to build his altar unto God. He always did business according to God's law. He lived on earth, but he lived in a heavenly spirit. He tented in the desert, but he had his eye upon "a city which hath foundations, whose builder and maker is God" (Heb. 11:10). All life was sacred and noble and splendid to Abraham, because all life was consecrated by the presence of God and by his own pure conduct. Angels visited him wherever he camped. God talked with him and communed with him in quiet hours. He lived like a prince and wherever he went it was as if "the smile of God" had come that way. He scattered blessings about him with a prodigal hand, and at last he died like a prince and went home to God.

Young man, it is a life like that to which I call you. When I ask you to be a Christian I ask you to live the noblest, purest, truest, happiest life that man can know. I ask you to live like a prince, so that all the blessings that God gives you shall be multiplied into blessings for your fellow-men. The greatest hour of Abraham's life was the one when in his young manhood God called him, and he answered, "I will," to God. The most blessed hour in your life may be now, and hour of supreme crisis, if when God calls you by His word and Spirit you shall respond in the same way. The initiative now is with you. God calls. It is for you to answer. As someone has said, "When the 'I will' of God is met with the 'I will' of your heart, then there is no power in heaven or hell that can thwart or hinder." The only hindrance God can ever know is your will. "Whosoever will may come!"

4

AN EASTERN LOVE STORY

"I being in the way, the Lord led me" (Genesis 24:27).

E liezer had known Abraham a long time. No doubt he had been born in the family, and all his lifetime his reverence and love for the grand old prince, whom everybody admired and held in awe as "the friend of God," had been growing. But it was a sorry time for Eliezer when Abraham sent for him to go courting for Isaac. Poor Eliezer! If Abraham had asked him to drive ten thousand donkeys to market, or go on a mission to open up a treaty with some neighboring tribe, or even to go to war to fetch back a herd of sheep that had been stolen, he would have been at home and would have known what to do. But when Abraham, in the most solemn manner imaginable, made Eliezer put his hand on his thigh and swear that he would go into a strange land where he had never been, and pick out a girl to suit Isaac, I have no doubt the old fellow scratched his head and wondered if he had not lived a little too long for his own good.

If you have never read this beautiful love story in an interested, thoughtful way, such as you give to the most popular book of the season, then you have made a mistake, for here is a condensed love story that in plot and execution is one of the greatest in the world. You can see the nervousness of Eliezer coming out at the very beginning. As soon as Abraham has uncovered to him the delicacy of the mission on which he is to go, a puzzled and scared look comes into his face as he wonders how such a task can be accomplished. He says, "But what shall I do if the woman will not come with me?" I suspect it seemed to him like a wild-goose chase to go expecting that such a woman as he would choose for his master's only son would be willing to follow him back in such an unusual way as this. Then the sublimity of Abraham's faith comes out. He says to his servant, "The Lord God of heaven, which took me from my father's house, and from the land of my kindred, and which spake unto me, and that sware unto me, saying, Unto thy seed will I give this land; he shall send his angel before thee, and thou shalt take a wife unto my son from thence. And if the woman will not be willing to follow thee, then thou shalt be clear from this my oath" (Gen. 24:7–8). How splendidly the confidence of Abraham in God's overwatching providence shines out in this utterance! How much a man misses who lives in a dumb, dead world, in which he imagines things only "happen," and he has only good or bad "luck." Life is made romantic and noble and is exalted beyond measure to the Christian. To such a one angels yet whisper their messages and the "still, small voice" comes to make itself heard. O, brother, this is God's world, and it is a terrible thing to live in it without God. But it is a precious thing to live in this world having the same trustful and happy relation to God that Abraham had, feeling that God's angel goes before you, being assured that God's hand guides and leads you, and that his great purpose is in your life and career. It is to this that I call you when I ask you to be a Christian.

When Eliezer was convinced in his mind and heart that Abraham was not out of his head, but, instead, was following the direction of God in seeking a wife for Isaac who would sympathize with him in his religion, and would not lead him astray into idolatry, he was willing enough to swear the oath asked of him, and immediately set about the preparation for the journey.

I must pause here long enough to say that there would be a great deal more happiness in the world if people were careful, in arranging for marriage, to secure congenial feelings and opinions in religion. It is a bad thing for a man to marry a wife who has no sympathy with his religion, and it is just as bad for a Christian woman to marry a man who will sneer at her worship of God and her love for Christ. If there is any place on earth where religion is necessary to exalt life and make living harmonious and happy it is in the home, and in the intimate relations between husband and wife. A godless home will never be permanently a happy one. Prayer and faith, and the consciousness of God's presence and love, are necessary to glorify and beautify the home and make it what it should be.

But the caravan is starting out on its long journey. When Eliezer had anything on hand to do he believed in doing it at once and in doing it well. So he took ten camels, the very best he could find in Abraham's great flock, and started early in the morning on the road to the city of Nahor, in the land of Mesopotamia. When he reached the outskirts of that town it was late in the afternoon, and he checked his little caravan on the edge of the city, where there seemed to be a fine well of water. In the East the women come out to the wells and carry the water in pitchers on their heads, and Eliezer waited beside the well. I expect his responsibility looked greater than ever, as he appreciated the fact that he had now reached the country where he was to select a wife for Isaac, and felt how utterly unfit he was to make such an important selection. But Eliezer had not lived all his life in the house of Abraham without becoming himself as sincere and devout a worshiper of God as was his master, and so in this hour of his great extremity he gave himself up to prayer. He made his camels kneel down, and then he knelt beside them, and here is the simple prayer he prayed: "O Lord God of my master Abraham, I pray thee, send me good speed this day, and show kindness unto my master Abraham. Behold, I stand here by the well of water; and the daughters of the men of the city come out do draw water: and let it come to pass, that the damsel to whom I shall say, Let down thy pitcher, I pray thee, that I may drink; and she shall say, Drink and I will give thy camels drink also: let the same be she that thou has appointed for thy servant Isaac; and thereby shall I know that thou hast showed kindness unto my master" (Gen. 24:12-14).

Now, I call that a model prayer. Eliezer knew what he wanted, and he prayed for it. He went straight to the point. He did not give the Lord any useless information about anything else. He asked for just what he needed, in a reverent way, and then he stopped. And as he rose from his knees he saw the woman coming to the well. Little did Rebekah know what eyes were watching her as she came gaily along that evening for the usual pitcher of water. There is little chance, after all, for anything valuable in the way of dress parade in this world. Usually the greatest opportunities of life come unheralded and unexpected. We need to be always at our best, always doing the right thing, ever doing the duty that is at hand with a sincere and simple heart, if we are to give God a chance to do the best there is for us. Without the slightest idea that she is on exhibition, Rebekah modestly goes down into the well with her pitcher, and as Eliezer looks on her he falls in love with her for Isaac. He is impressed that this is the woman God intends to be the wife of his master's son. And so as she comes up out of the well he runs to meet her, and with the greatest politeness he exclaims, "Let me, I pray thee, drink a little water of thy pitcher" (Gen. 24:17). And with perfect naturalness Rebekah lets down the pitcher on her hand, and says, "Drink, my lord" (Gen. 24:18). This was a very respectful and modest way for a young girl to address an elderly man who was a stranger. When Eliezer had finished drinking she looked on the tired camels and said, "I will draw water for thy camels also" (Gen. 24:19). Then the lively young girl ran and emptied her pitcher into the watering trough, and to and fro between the well and the trough she went, filling and emptying her pitcher, until the thirsty camels were satisfied.

All this time Eliezer had been studying her. His heart said to him, "God has been good to me and to Abraham. He has filled full the measure of my request. I asked God to be gracious by this sign, and he has. Surely this is God's answer to my prayer." But the devil whispered in his ear and said, "Now, don't be a fool, Eliezer, but wait a while. You don't know whether this girl is the right one or not.

You too easily believe God has answered you. It is only a
curious coincidence. You needn't imagine that the great
God in heaven is listening to servants' prattle." But Eliezer
wisely sent the devil about his business and said to himself,
"I will be true to God. I asked the Lord, and He answered;
I will act upon it." And so when the camels had done
drinking, and Rebekah was about to go back again to her
home, Eliezer asked her to wait a moment, and as she
waited, wondering, he undid the burden of one of the
camels, and took out from his treasures a golden earring
of half a shekel weight, and two bracelets for her hands, of
ten shekels weight gold, and said, "Whose daughter art
thou? Tell me, I pray thee, is there room in thy father's
house for us to lodge in?" (Gen. 24:22, 23). And Rebekah
told him who she was, and that there was abundance of
room and provision for himself and party in her home.
Then as she named the very family from which Abraham
had sent him to select a bride for Isaac, the reverent servant
gave her the rich presents he held in his hand, and bowed
down his head in thanksgiving and worship of God. And
Rebekah must have listened in wonder as he prayed,
"Blessed be the Lord God of my master Abraham, who hath
not left destitute my master of his mercy and his truth; I
being in the way, the Lord led me to the house of my master's brethren" (Gen. 24:27).

Now, by this time Rebekah had stood it as long as she
could without telling somebody, and away she ran to tell
all she had seen and heard to her mother and the folks in
the house, and to show her presents. The man who writes
the story does not say whether she took the pitcher or not,
but I will warrant she did not. Like the woman at the well
of Samaria, who left her water pot behind, she was in such

a hurry to tell the people in town about Jesus, so I am sure Rebekah forgot her pitcher as she ran to tell the news at home. As soon as the news is told there Rebekah's brother Laban comes hurrying out, and with that warm welcome, "Come in, thou blessed of the Lord," brings the man and his whole caravan home with him for the night.

Soon all their wants are attended to, and Eliezer finds himself sitting before a generous meal. Any man who has traveled all day in the hot sun knows what supper means at night. But Eliezer is a remarkable man; when he has business on hand he sticks to it until he is done, and so he looks round upon the circle and says, "I will not eat until I have told mine errand." I wish we all might learn the lesson of fidelity to a great mission that is taught here. Some of you have a duty from your Master, the Lord Jesus Christ, that you have been putting off while you took your time to eat and drink and to clothe yourself luxuriously. You have said, "When I have time I will do it." Surely the servant of Christ ought to be as true as the servant of Abraham. Has God sent you on a mission to some soul? Has God made you feel that some friend or neighbor of yours is desired as a bride for Jesus Christ? Do not, I beg you, ever drink or eat again, never give yourself up to selfishness again, until you have with the utmost fidelity fulfilled your errand.

Then Eliezer opens his heart to these people, and tells them that he comes from Abraham; tells them how God has greatly blessed Abraham and made him rich and powerful. He tells them the story of Isaac, who is now old enough to be married, and how Abraham has honored him by sending him on this journey to find among his own people, who are also worshipers of the true God, a wife for his son. Then he enlarges on the events of the evening, tells about his prayer to God for divine direction, and how, while he was still praying, Rebekah had come to the well, and his prayer had seemed to be answered. And finally, having told all the story he says, "And now if ye will deal kindly and truly with my master, tell me: and if not, tell me; that I may turn to the right hand, or to the left" (Gen. 24:49). Then Bethuel, the father, and Laban, the brother, greatly impressed with the story of God's guidance, answered him: "The thing proceedeth from the Lord: we cannot speak unto thee bad or good. Behold, Rebekah is before thee; take her, and go, and let her be thy master's son's wife, as the Lord hath spoken" (Gen. 24:50, 51). Then Eliezer fell on his knees and prayed to God, and gave thanks to him for his great mercy. My brothers, my sisters, can you not see how much more life's blessings seem when we recognize them as coming from God? Do not imagine for a moment that you detract from the enjoyment of life by becoming truly Christian. No, indeed; the blessings of life are a hundredfold increased in their power to give happiness when we see them as God's gifts. The sweetest way any of us can ever live is in this spirit which Eliezer knew, the spirit of sensitive thanksgiving to the Lord for all life's mercies.

After prayers Eliezer brought forth jewels of silver and of gold and fine and costly raiment and gave them to Rebekah. He also bestowed on the father and mother and brother many rich and costly presents. Then he was ready to eat, and how much happier and more enjoyable was his supper because his mission was accomplished! He must have slept that night the sleep of the just.

The next morning Eliezer greatly astonished the household of Bethuel by saying to them, "Send me away unto my master." They would not hear to this at first, and begged him to wait at least ten days for them to have a farewell visit with Rebekah before he took her away. But Eliezer said, "Hinder me not, seeing the Lord hath prospered my way; send me away that I may go to my master" (Gen. 24:56). Finally they said they would leave it to Rebekah herself, and the girl was called in, and her mother said to her, "Wilt thou go with this man?" And she said, "I will go" (Gen. 24:58). And so the homeward journey, so full of interest to Rebekah, began.

Now, the sermon, all save that you have already gotten in with the story, will last but for a moment. I want to drive the hammer straight at the nail in the text, Eliezer's words, "I being in the way, the Lord led me." God will lead every one of us if we are only in the way to be led. How can we be in the way? We are always in the way when we are doing our duty. What is your duty? Find that, and undertake to do it with an honest, prayerful heart, and you may be sure that God will lead you. Many pray to God to lead them, and then they go their own way, and refuse to do the plain duty which God marks out for them. Eliezer recognized that he would have had no right to expect God's providential guidance unless he had been in the way of his duty. The sinner cannot be guided by God, because he is not in the way of duty. That is what Paul means when he speaks about some people "having no hope, and without God in the world" (Ephesians 2:12). We cannot fight God and be guided by Him at the same time. Some of you are in trouble. Some of you are carrying heavy burdens, and the way is dark before you, and you feel that it would be the sweetest thing in the world if you could just put your hand up into God's and let him lead you safely along the way of life. That is just what God wants to do, and if you will repent of your sins and confess the Lord Jesus Christ, thus putting yourself in the way of duty, God will lead you just as faithfully and just as tenderly as he led Eliezer so long ago. The invitations are generous and full of welcome. Here is one that is wide enough and tender enough for all who are here tonight; it is Christ's own welcome: "Him that cometh to me I will in no wise cast out" (John 6:37). As Rebekah ran to show her gifts to her mother, so do you run into the arms of Christ tonight and put yourself in the way of receiving not only the forgiveness of your sins, but the guiding care of your heavenly father.

Chapter 5

5

THE FULFILLMENT OF LOVE'S DREAMS

"He lifted up his eyes and saw, and, behold, the camels were coming" (Genesis 24:63).

Isaac was nervous and could not rest. Put yourself in his place and see if you do not sympathize with him. Abraham, no doubt, had talked the matter all over with Isaac before Eliezer was sent on his embassage to select a wife for him. I presume it was his taste which selected the precious raiment and the rich jewels that were to clothe and adorn the bride to be chosen for him. And no other heart had been so interested on that morning when that little caravan of ten camels wound its way across the land until it became but a speck in the distance and then vanished away entirely. From that moment it was a mystery and a source of wonder and meditation. In those old days when a caravan was once out of sight it was as completely swallowed up as if it had been on the other side of the ocean. So Isaac could only wait and hope and pray. For a while he tried to make work for himself, and to occupy his mind with the usual duties in looking after his father's interests as the owner of vast flocks and herds and the head of a great tribe of people. But this would not long satisfy a man in Isaac's mood, and so, after he had waited until he thought it possible that Eliezer had had time to fulfill his mission and be on the return, he broke camp in the south country where he dwelt, and left the well of Lahai-roi behind him. Ordinarily the water of the well of Lahai-roi was grateful on his lips, but now he thirsted for the richer wine of love. So he came out on the road, the deep trail cut by the occasional caravans through the centuries of travel, and in the evening he camped by the way to spend the night.

Isaac was in no mood for talking with the rest of his company. In the great emotions of life we are very solitary, and Isaac wanted to be alone. He left the camp behind him and walked forth in the evening twilight to meditate and dream of the wife for whom he hoped and the happy home for which he prayed. O the sweet dreams of youth—dreams of twilight; dreams when the sky is red with the sunset; dreams colored with the purple of the afterglow of departing day; dreams of an innocent heart, of a pure imagination, which forecast a noble fellowship and long for a wider career that is to come with the fullness of manhood! Cherish those dreams. Do not let them die with your boyhood, but be true to them in all the years to come. Men are defeated when their ideals are broken. Men cross the deadline when they no longer dream of the morrow with its solace of love, its inspiration to achievement, and its glory of conquest. Keep your ideals; cherish your dreams; determine to make them good, to bring them to pass. Do this, and when your hair whitens you will be fourscore years young, not old.

Isaac could only bear his uncertainty and wait, for there was no telegraph by which Eliezer could send him a dispatch, announcing his success. There was no long-distance telephone to Mesopotamia by which he could call him up in the Arab tent. There was not even a fast mail train, or a stagecoach, or a postboy on horseback. It was a silent world in those days. The iron had not learned to swim, the steam had not been harnessed, and the lightning had not yet been tamed; but human nature was just the same. Love made men dream then as now, and human hearts grew big with expectancy and hope. And so Isaac waited and dreamed in the twilight, and yet instinctively he walked up the trail of the caravan and not down it, and ever and anon he lifted his eyes the way he knew it must come if it did come. Then suddenly he saw something. He is all excitement in a moment. Do not imagine a quiet, gentle man cannot get excited. There is a deep current running underneath that quiet face; not all the volcanoes explode and belch forth lava. I see Isaac, full of love's dreams and hopes, as he peers with his hand over his eyes out along the trail. At first he thinks it is only imagination, and then he rubs his eyes with his hand, and looks again. Now he knows that something is moving, and, as he watches, the swing and the sway of the camels come into clear vision, and a little later he begins to distinguish the animals, and the peculiar headdress of Eliezer himself, and he knows that the caravan is returning, and he feels pretty sure that so early a return can only mean success. And so he waits with his heart pounding in his bosom.

But there are two sides to this drama. Somebody else is waiting with expectation. Go back to Nahor for a moment. All is stir and bustle about the house of Bethuel. It is a great day, and in many respects a sad day as well as a triumphant one. Rebekah, the beautiful, glad-hearted daughter of the household, is going away today, and going for life. She cannot take an express train next week and come back, stop for lunch, and be home again in the evening to preside over Isaac's dinner. It is a long farewell. The father and mother have passed a sleepless night. Their faces are tremulous as they try to bear their sorrow and send her away with smiles on their lips. Ah, it is a picture with many modern illustrations.

At the World's Fair in Chicago the picture which attracted more attention than any other in the great art gallery, and about which you could always find crowds standing, was the one entitled "Breaking Home Ties." To me there was a deep pathos in the spectacle. I knew that the men and women who looked at the picture so intently had been through the experience portrayed. The boy standing in the foreground, full of hope and courage, saying goodbye to father and mother and brother and sister, brought another picture to their minds, when the blessings of home benediction were in their heads, and lips that are now silent in the grave and eyes that will never flash again on earth were full of kisses and benediction. Some who hear me well remember such scenes, possibly only a little while ago. Every year in multitudes of home these farewell words are said, and these benedictions are received. Happy the boy, blessed the girl, who treasures up in the heart all the tender words and who does not forget the Bible packed away in the trunk that a Christian mother in her love put there to make goodness easier and to lie as a barrier across the path to sin and ruin. Cling to your memory of that tender parting; remember the love and the hope and the ambition for you that are in those true hearts, and vow that by the grace of God you will live worthy of all that love and confidence.

Rebekah's family cover her with their blessings, and away she rides in the caravan that is to take her with rapid step from her home—that is, the old home—and onward to her new home, toward which her heart looks with fluttering hope and confident trust. And at last the long journey is well over, though it is expected that they will camp yet once more before reaching the dwelling place of Isaac. Eliezer, cool-headed and practical, has not taken account of the hotter blood of youth or of the anxiety in the heart of Isaac to see his bride. And so, unexpectedly, the tents of Isaac loom in the distance, and after a little he himself is seen walking toward them. Rebekah sees him also, and she turns to Eliezer with flushed face and quickened interest in her eye and asks, "What man is this that walketh in the field to meet us?" And Eliezer says, "It is my master" (Genesis 24:65). When Rebekah hears that she stops the caravan, and alights from the camel, and takes a veil and covers herself, that she may in the modest manner meet the man who is to be her husband.

It was not a day of quick ceremony, and Isaac must first hear the report of Eliezer concerning the success of his mission. But as that faithful ambassador reported it, with all the oriental picturesqueness, Isaac no doubt wished he would cut it short, and ever and anon turned his eyes with admiring gaze on the girl who was to be his wife. At last, when all the ceremony was done, Isaac, with the gentleness which was a controlling element of his character and with that respect and reverence for womanhood which had been inculcated in him by a noble mother, who was until her death his confidante and his nearest and dearest friend, led Rebekah to Sarah's tent, which had been fitting up for her, and so their home life of wedded love began.

I want to spiritualize this story and let it illustrate to us the wonderful love of God in seeking to win the sinner as the bride of Jesus Christ. The embassage of Eliezer is like that on which God sends a Christian minister now. He is to woo the sinner for Jesus. I never think of that without being humbled and lifting my heart in prayer to God that I may be worthy of this great trust.

The message about Christ which the true Christian minister brings to God's wandering children is God's message. I bring you no message of my own. It is the message of our heavenly Father. He longs for you to share the beautiful life of Jesus Christ, to live a sweet love life with Him here on earth, and afterward to dwell in heaven with Him forever. And as Eliezer went to Mesopotamia with his message from Abraham, to tell of Isaac the young prince and woo Rebekah for his wife, so I come to you as God's servant, to woo you by the goodness of God, by the princely character of Jesus Christ, by the riches of grace the sweet pleasures that are in the life with Him, and, above all, by the tenderness of that love by which He hath redeemed you, to leave the land of sin and come to be the friend in sweetest heart-fellowship with Jesus Christ your Savior.

Abraham sent precious raiment as a gift to the woman whom Eliezer should select for Isaac, that she might come to Isaac properly arrayed to be the bride of so rich and noble a young man. So God gives me authority to promise to you the most precious raiment of character, with which he will clothe you for your journey toward heaven. God does not mean that you shall come home to the skies clad in the seedy garments of your sins or in the filthy rags of your own self-righteousness. But when you accept the offer

I make you, and confess your willingness to give your heart to Christ, He will take from you these vile garments of evil and will clothe you with the precious raiment of righteousness. Ah, how often I have seen that done! I have seen the drunkard put off his drunkenness; I have seen the swearer put off his profanity; I have seen the man of impure conversation put off the vile rags of evil speech; I have seen the man given to anger and malice put away the vicious spirit; I have seen the greedy, avaricious man stripped of his repulsive nature. The drunkard was clothed upon with sobriety, songs and prayer and testimony took the place of oaths, sweet and pure thoughts and noble conduct clothed him who had been immoral, and all the sweetness of brotherly kindness transformed the man of anger, while the miser became generous and open-hearted. O brother, that is what God wants to do with you; He wants to take from you everything that is evil and clothe you with the precious raiment of the kingdom of God.

Abraham sent precious jewels, rich earrings, and bracelets of gold to adorn Rebekah. But more beautiful jewels than ever graced a bride of earth God bestows upon those who give their hearts to His Son. He decks them with patience and kindness and gentleness, He adorns them with hope, faith and love, until the Christian character is the most beautiful known on earth or in heaven. Strange, is it not, that men will cling to their rags of sin when they might be adorned with the jewels that blaze in the light of the city of God?

There were presents also for Rebekah's father and mother and brother; all the household were enriched because of this alliance with the young prince Isaac, of the noble house of Abraham. So there are blessings for all a man's friends when he becomes a Christian. No man ever became a true Christian without becoming a nobler husband, a truer father, and a better man to have for a friend. Many a time a wife has said to me, "Our home has been transformed since my husband became a Christian." I have known many a household where there had been sorrow and strife between husband and wife that was full of love and sweet fellowship after they had given their hearts to Jesus and had been enriched in their souls with the riches of God in Christ.

Abraham sent rich provision in a caravan of his best camels to bring Rebekah home to Isaac. So God sends a caravan of his providential love to bring us on the way toward heaven. "The stars in their courses fought against Sisera," but all the forces of earth and heaven are made to fight in protection of the man who gives his heart to Christ and walks in communion and love with him. Paul after long experience declared, "We know that all things work together for good to them that love God" (Romans 8:28). The God who sent His angel in the night to talk with Paul on the Alexandrian corn ship, and who watched over him in the storm and tempest and brought him safe to land, cares just as much for the man who serves Him now. The God who sent the angels to camp about the path of Jacob on his way home from his wanderings, and who sent the angels with their chariots and horsemen of the upper world to encamp about Elisha at Dothan, will have His angel guards about your path, and so long as you are true to Him no real harm shall befall you.

Isaac went out to meet Rebekah and welcome her to his camp, to his heart, to all that he had. So Jesus says, "I go to prepare a place for you. And…I will come again, and receive you unto myself; that where I am, there ye may be also" (John 14:2, 3).

God help me to woo you tonight for Jesus Christ, your Savior! Isaac had never done anything especially for Rebekah. His only claim was what he could offer to do in the future. But Jesus Christ, when He had all the riches and glory of heaven, came down to earth, and tasted poverty and loneliness and homesickness and hunger and thirst and insult, and died a shameful death upon the cross, that He might buy your ransom. So it is not only for what Christ can do for you, though that is a thousand times more than Isaac could do for Rebekah, but in the name of the undying love which He has already shown for you, that I plead with you to turn away from every sin that defiles, from every thought and deed of wickedness dishonoring to you and to your Christ, and give Him from this hour all your love, all your heart's devotion, all your service.

6

Chapter 6

A PRINCELY WELL-DIGGER

"And it came to pass the same day, that Isaac's servants
came, and told him concerning the well which they had
digged, and said unto him, We have found water"
(Genesis 26:32).

When Mohammed was asked by an acquaintance, "What monument shall I build to my friend?" he replied, "Dig a well." The reply suggests something of what a well means in a country where rain seldom falls and where water is very scarce. The possession of a well in a country like that may mean all the difference between an impossible desert and a place to grow rich with flocks and herds.

Isaac is preeminently the well-digger of the Old Testament time. He began by opening up the old wells his father Abraham had dug many years before. The Philistines had filled up these wells out of spite. They seemed to have been a shiftless, worthless lot, and because they did not have flocks and herds enough to need them they determined that nobody else should use these wells. And so they worked as hard to fill up the wells that added so much to the wealth of the country as Abraham and his servants had worked to open them. How often we see that thing being done! We see men and women working with all their might to undo the good that other people are doing. They do this when they can get no possible good out of it, and their only comfort in it must be to spite somebody or to give pain to some good man or good woman. Many people work harder to live by fraud and sin than they would have to work to live in the most generous and wealthy style if they would devote their attention to honest and righteous pursuits. Many men turn away from a righteous and Christian life because they think the path is hard and full of self-denial. But they are always cheated when they do that. The devil is the hardest taskmaster that ever cracked the whip over a slave's shoulders.

No doubt Isaac took special pleasure in opening up these old wells out of which his father had drank and had received so much comfort. The water would taste sweeter to him because of the memories that associated his father with it. There are plenty of people nowadays who sneer at sentiment and make fun of the imagination; but I tell you, my friend, a man without sentiment and imagination is a poor stick. He is an orange rind without any juice; he is a stale lemon with all the refreshing tart gone. Imagination and sentiment are the great characteristics which lift man up into the higher realm of love. Poor and bankrupt indeed is the man to whom an old well is not dearer because a loved father dug it, or to whom an old Bible is not the more precious because a mother bestowed it as a gift and the name in it was written by her dear fingers.

I was traveling not long ago with a great, strong, broad-shouldered man, a man of large business interests and with a peculiarly clear business mind. He was the very last man you would associate with any sort of morbid or unwholesome sentimentality. But during the day he took out from his valise a little Testament. It was worn with much use, and as he opened it and handed it across to me he said, "Do you know that is the dearest treasure I have on earth?" "Why so?" I inquired. "Ah!" he said, "I never take it in my hand but I see my little girl, a bright, laughing, happy, bewitching child of ten years of age, as she brought it to me on the morning of my birthday ten years ago, and as she put it in my hand she said, 'There, papa, I want you to carry that with you when you travel, and every time you take it out to read in it you will remember the little girl at home who loves you so.'" The tears came in the big man's eyes as he continued: "A month after that I was a thousand miles away, when I received a telegram from my wife which said, 'Come home quick. Lucy is very sick.' I hurried home; it seemed to me the trains never went so slow. Death had outrun them, and my little darling had left her farewell kiss with her mother for me. Now," he said, "you know why I love that little Testament. Every time I take it up I see her dear face again, and it seems to be looking happily at me out of the gate of heaven, and I read it, and try by God's help to do the square thing, because of the little girl who loved me so."

Do you think that man was any the less a man because of that atmosphere of sacred sentiment in which he lived? O no; he was infinitely more the man because of it. Do not be ashamed of the old wells that the father dug. Be proud of them, and open them up again if they have been filled with worldliness or sin.

There is that old well of family prayers. I expect some of you have let it get filled up, and if you have I am sure it has had a very withering effect on your Christian experience. A quaint old writer offers this prescription, "To produce spiritual indifference add to five minutes only of prayer fourteen hours of worldliness and nearly ten of torpor." I beg of every man or woman here who is carrying on a home life to give the daily Scripture reading and prayer the right of way. I never can thank God enough for the dear old well where my childish lips drank the sweet, cool waters of faith and trust in God, at the family altar. If I can give my boys and girls as precious a memory of home religion, so that it will be with them, as it has been with me, a well of living water to refresh the soul in every time of trial and famine, I shall feel that I have left them an inheritance that is better than any of the riches of the world. O if the old well has been packed full of the earth of worldliness, dig it open again, and let the water of spiritual life have a fair chance to bless and refresh your hearts and characters.

There is an old well of praise to God—the well that bubbles up with confidence that God has His arm around you, and that He cares personally for you. What sweet water it was; how sweet it is yet to all who keep that well fresh! Have you gotten to the point in your indifference and worldly wisdom that you are inclined to sneer at that simple-hearted, singing, confident faith that your mother had, that led her to give God praise for every little blessing that came into her life? If so, you are getting poorer instead of richer. Better dig that old well open again. There is great happiness in it. My wife moved me to tears the other night when she told me what she heard our little girl, seven years old, singing as a little improvised song to herself, after she had gone to bed in the dark. It was sort of whistling to keep her courage up. She sang, "My father loves me, and I do not need to be afraid, because my father loves me." And the little voice rang all the changes on those words, and at last she dropped asleep with them on her lips. No wealth, no culture, no position or power in the world can make any man happy unless he is able to lie down at night amid the threatening storms that gather about every human life and sing with his thoughts uplifted to God what the little girl sang about her father, "My Father loves me, and I do not need to be afraid, because my Father loves me." It is only that sort of trust and the thanksgiving which it arouses in the soul that can make us truly happy. If we have that feeling we can sing at our work. Our great ambitions may fail or succeed, but we shall be able to sing just the same. Paul Laurence Dunbar puts it well in his simple song:

> "A song is but a little thing,
> And yet what joy it is to sing!
> In hours of toil it gives me zest,
> And when at eve I long for rest,
> When cows come home along the bars,
> And in the fold I hear the bell,
> As Night, the shepherd, herds his stars,
> I sing my song, and all is well.
> "There are no ears to hear my lays,
> No lips to lift a word of praise;
> But still, with faith unfaltering,
> I live and laugh and love and sing.
> What matters yon unheeding throng?
> They cannot feel my spirit's spell,
> Since life is sweet and love is long,
> I sing my song, and all is well.
> "My days are never days of ease;

I till my ground and prune my trees.
When ripened gold is all the plain,
I put my sickle to the grain.
I labor hard, and toil and sweat,
While others dream within the dell;
But even while my brow is wet,
I sing my song, and all is well.
"Sometimes the sun, unkindly hot,
My garden makes a desert spot;
Sometimes a blight upon the tree
Takes all my fruit away from me;
And then with throes of bitter pain
Rebellious passions rise and swell;
But—life is more than fruit or grain,
And so I sing, and all is well."

It did not always go easy with Isaac. God's blessing was with him all the time. When he sowed in the fields he got a hundredfold, and his flocks and his herds multiplied rapidly. But he grew rich so fast that the Philistines were scared about him, and they crowded him out of the country. And as he went he dug wells for his flocks. The first one he dug the Philistines strove with him for it, and he named it Esek, which means "strife," and he moved on and let them have it. And the next well he dug they were still more bitter in their contention, and he called that well Sitnah, which means "Hatred," and turned it over to them like the other. And then he moved away into another part of the country, and he digged a new well, and had gone so far away that they did not seem to be longer afraid of him, and so they let him alone in the possession of this well, and he called the name of it Rehoboth, which means "Room," and he gave as his reason for naming it that, "Now the Lord hath made room for us, and we shall be fruitful in the land"

(Genesis 26:22). And here the Lord appeared to him in a special manner, and renewed to him all the promises that had been made to Abraham, that in him and his family should all the nations of the earth be blessed (see Genesis 26:24, referring to Gen. 12:3). And the Lord led him still farther away from the Philistines. And now the Philistines began to fear because they saw Isaac no more. They feared that in the new land to which he had gone he would soon grow so great and powerful that he would come back and take vengeance on them for their unkindness. So Abimelech, the king of the Philistines, took with him his chief officers and paid a visit to Isaac, and negotiated a treaty with him. And they swore an oath together that there should be peace between them forever. And these visitors were scarcely out of sight when Isaac's servants came running to him with the good news that they had struck water in the new well which they had been digging, and Isaac in the peace and happiness that had come to him called the well Shebah, "the oath," and the city was named Beersheba, which, interpreted, is "The Well of the Oath."

I am sure there is some message here for us. It is not enough for us to be satisfied to simply open up the old wells dug by our fathers. We must press forward to the new duties and the new privileges of our own time. It is not enough for the Christian church to stand behind the walls the fathers built and sing "Hold the fort!" No, indeed; we have our new duties, our new opportunities, with the new life of our own time, and we must open the new wells that are needed for the salvation of men.

There is another suggestion here, and that is, we must not be discouraged and give up because one well of happiness is closed to us and we cannot have everything exactly our own way. When the well of Esek had become impossible Isaac moved on and dug the well Sitnah. And when he was crowded away from that he did not despair, but pressed forward and dug the new well Rehoboth. We must learn from this that life is not to be considered as finished and all our career spoiled because one of the wells of happiness is covered up, or because we may be meanly or cruelly crowded away from our just rights to happiness in some particular direction. No, indeed! The story of every great career shows that triumph has not come without many disappointments and defeats. And it also shows that men and women who will not be defeated, but who are crowded out in one place only to dig a new well in another, will after a while find room for themselves, and God will lead them, and will bless them with fruitfulness and peace.

And, finally, there is one lesson that everyone here who is not a Christian ought to learn tonight—that is, that perfect peace and contentment of life can never come to you until you yield yourself to be guided of the Lord and draw water from your Beer-sheba, your well of the oath. God has given us his oath that if we will forsake our sins and give him our hearts we shall have this perfect well of peace: "God, willing more abundantly to show unto the heirs of promise the immutability of his counsel, confirmed it by an oath: that by two immutable things, in which it was impossible for God to lie, we might have a strong consolation, who have fled for refuge to lay hold upon the hope set before us: which hope we have as an anchor of the soul, both sure and steadfast, and which entereth into that within the veil" (Hebrews 6:19). Some of you have been drinking the waters of uneasiness. Your heart has had no rest. You have been crowded out of one place, and then another, and it has seemed to you that the whole world was against you. Turn from your sin and give your heart to God, and he will give you tenting room beside "the well of the oath," where your heart shall have peace.

And God will not only give you peace, but he will give you the well-digger's joy of being a great blessing to others. It is a terrible thing for a man to feel that his staying away from Christ may be the means of keeping someone else away until he is lost forever; but it is a sweet thing to feel that you have given to drink the water of life to others as you have passed along on your journey.

A tender incident of Mr. Moody's last homeward journey is told by Mr. Paul D. Moody. When the train pulled into Detroit it was over an hour late. Unless at least half of this time should be made up, the Eastern connection at Niagara for the through Boston train could not be made. As the train was standing in the station at Detroit, waiting for the signal to start, the engineer, a grizzled old veteran of the rail, came back along the train until he reached the special car.

"Whose car is this?" he asked one of the party who was standing outside.

"It's a special, taking Mr. Moody to his home," was the reply.

"Where has he been?" came the question.

"He has been holding meetings in Kansas City, where he was taken ill, and now we are taking him home. We are about an hour late, and if we don't make up the time we won't make the proper connection for Boston."

"Look here," said the engineer, his voice choking as he spoke; "fifteen years ago I was led to Christ by Moody, and

I have lived a better and a happier life ever since. I didn't know Moody's car was on tonight, but if you want me to make up the time for you I'll do that. Just tell Mr. Moody that one of his friends is at the throttle, and then hold your breath."

As soon as the train got clear of the city the engineer pulled open the throttle, and it is said that he made the fastest time ever made over his division. Including stops, he ran one hundred and thirty miles in exactly one hundred and thirty minutes. Connections were made all right, and when the party in the special awakened the next morning they were on the Boston train.

What a precious comfort it must have been to Mr. Moody to know that there were thousands of men and women all over the world who felt in that way concerning him! My friend, give your heart to Christ now, and begin the preparation of some refreshing cordial like that for your comfort in life's closing years.

7

A FRIENDLESS PRISONER WHO TURNED OUT WELL

"Joseph's master took him, and put him into prison,
a place where the king's prisoners were bound; and he was
there in the prison" (Genesis 39:20).

A case was on trial in a Kentucky courtroom. An old man of somewhat shabby appearance had just given important testimony; and the lawyer whose cause suffered by his statements strove in every way to confuse and trip him, but in vain. The witness stuck to his story, and did not lose his temper, in spite of the irritating manner in which the cross-examination was conducted.

Finally, in the hope of breaking down the credibility of the witness, the lawyer at a venture asked, "Have you ever been in prison?

"I have," replied the witness.

"Ah," exclaimed the attorney, with a triumphant glance at the jury, "I thought as much. May I inquire how long you were there?"

"Two years and three months," answered the witness,

quietly, with a manner that was interpreted by the lawyer as indicating chagrin at an unexpected exposure.

"Indeed," said the delighted lawyer, feeling his case already won, "that was a heavy sentence. I trust the jury will note the significance of the fact. Now, sir, tell the jury where you were confined."

"In Andersonville," replied the old man, drawing himself up proudly.

There was a moment of silence. The jurors looked at each other; and then the courtroom rang with cheers which the court officers were powerless to check, and in which some of the jury joined. It is scarcely necessary to add that that lawyer lost his verdict.

Joseph's prison experience was as honorable as that.

Many of you remember how Joseph came to have a master—this young prince of the house of Jacob, the great-grandson of the mighty Abraham. His brethren, moved by envy and jealousy, had seized him one day on the hills of Dothan and sold him to a merchants' caravan which had brought him down to Egypt. And one morning in the proud capital city of the Pharaohs there was a big auction of slaves in the marketplace. Among that crowd of wretched creatures was Joseph the dreamer. He is worn with hard usage and sorrow, but there is something about him yet that is kingly and splendid. There is something in the pose of the head, in the faraway look in the eyes, in the air of genuineness and self-respect, that attracts attention.

Can you bring that slave auction back to your eye so that it is real again? It is not a pretty sight, I know; but perhaps it will do you good to see it. There they are, the half-naked, shrinking men and women, to be examined and poked about and speculated on, like so many cattle from the prairies or so many pigs from the sty. Jeering, blasphemous men catch a woman by the hair, or chuck her under the chin, or make her open her mouth and show her teeth, as they get ready to bid; and others look about among the boys and the men, talking over their good points or picking out their defects as a man would a horse he is about to buy for his stables. And yet these were men and women with love and fear and hope and longing in them, such as you and I know. Ah, a slave market was a terrible place! In his young manhood, when Abraham Lincoln was running a flatboat, he saw a slave market one day in New Orleans; saw such things there as I have been hinting at here. The brave heart of that backwoods youth rose up within him in indignation. A great hate of the institution which permitted the slave market took possession of his soul. He clenched his fist until the nails cut into the flesh, and through his gritted teeth he said, "If ever I have a chance to strike that thing I shall hit it hard." The time came God gave him a chance, and he struck the slave market to the death in America.

Among the people who were interested in the slave market that morning so long ago was a man named Potiphar, and important man, who lived in a palace. Potiphar wanted a house servant. I do not imagine the selection was very important to him; he had no hope of getting a man in that slave market who would soon carry his own purse and be chief steward of the palace. He probably wanted somebody to attend to the door, or wait on the table, or do some work of that kind. Potiphar's eyes lit on Joseph. Now, Joseph was a handsome young fellow. Among his other gifts the Lord had given him a beautiful figure and an attractive face, and when your eye lighted on him once it looked back again. Besides, there was about him a certain gentleness, a certain thoughtfulness and refinement, that caused Potiphar to think he would make a good servant for his house. So when the bidding began Potiphar bid the highest, and Joseph went away with him to live in his palace.

Now, we have not time to follow Joseph through all the details of his experience. But it is interesting to note that this young slave soon won his master's confidence and trust, and we know that to have done that he must have been a cheerful, pleasant-spirited man in his new place. If he had gone about grumbling and fretful and peevish he never would have been promoted in the house of Potiphar. The greatness of Joseph's nature comes out right there, that while he was in a very hard position—a highborn youth forced to be the slave of a man of a foreign country—he did not grow morbid or vindictive, but gave himself to his new task with that genial good will which won the confidence of everybody about him. It is a great thing to live in what somebody has called "the golden temper." It is the cheerful man or woman who gets on under difficulties.

There was another very important point which, no doubt, had a great deal to do with Joseph's cheerfulness, and that was, "The Lord was with him" and favored him. A man can do great things if God is in his heart. But I want you to take note that Joseph did not go lounging and loafing around the palace of Potiphar, depending on the favor of God to carry him through. If he had done that you and I would never have heard of him. Instead, he set himself to work and made himself necessary to Potiphar. I will tell you, young man, there is one thing you can always depend upon as a foundation to promotion, and that is, make yourself absolutely necessary to your employer or to the people who are associated with you. The man who is possessed with a desire to be valuable to other people is always sought after.

Josh Billings was in a New York office one day when an overdressed young man entered. After a few moments' conversation the celebrated humorist said, "Young man, may I ask how long you have worn that collar?" referring to a collar of prodigious height, of which the youth seemed very proud.

With considerable self-satisfaction the young man responded, "Why, a week."

"Well, I want to say," drawled Josh Billings, "that a man who can wear a paper collar for a week ain't good for anything else."

And the man of wit cut deep in that sentence into the causes which lead to many a failure. I see failures every day coming to men because they are not willing to pay the price for success. Real triumphs are bought at great price— the price of self-denial, the price of invested energy, the price of hard work, the price of bloody sweat. Even Christ the Lord could not triumph on any other condition. The Lord helped Joseph indeed, but first and last Joseph won because he responded to the help of the Lord. He got on in Potiphar's palace because he did more work than anybody else there. And you can get on in the same way.

But in the midst of Joseph's success, which soon brought him to be his master's confidential and trusted secretary, there came the serpent with temptation—temptation at the most delicate and subtle for a man in his position. I shall not enlarge on that particular temptation. Go read it again in these chapters. It was a temptation which in one guise or another comes to every young man and young woman in Cleveland, the temptation to buy present happiness, present preferment, present friendship, at the price of honor and a good conscience. Whatever the temptation may be, whatever sin it may be one is lured toward, that is, after all, the essence of all temptation. And I want to call your attention to the two strong anchors that held in Joseph's case.

The first refuge of Joseph was his personal honor. Joseph said, "I cannot prove treacherous to my master. He has trusted me, and I have accepted the trust. He leaves everything in my power; he believes in my honor, my manhood. How can I prove recreant to this splendid trust he has put in my hands? I will not do it! I will not soil my honor!" You may laugh as you will about the old ideas of chivalry, and about the extravagance and errors that grew up around its ideas of honor, but I tell you it is a sorry day for any young man when he comes to have no keen and careful sense of his personal honor as a man. It is a bad thing, a fatal thing, when you come to care more for what other people think of you than for what you think of yourself, what you know yourself to be. The true man can stand everything in the way of misunderstanding from the outer world if he consciously goes to bed every night as an honest man.

But I want you to notice the second, and, after all, the greatest, stronghold of Joseph, and that which made him impregnable. It was his keen sense of personal accountability to God. For Joseph to yield to this temptation was to sin against God; it was to break God's law. And it is with an agony of real feeling that he cries out, "How then can I do this great wickedness, and sin against God?" (Genesis 39:9). Joseph had a wholesome idea of sin. There is a modern idea about sin which is the ax at the root of the tree that is cutting down many a fair young life. It is the idea that expresses itself on this wise: "God is too good, He is too merciful, He is too loving, He is too kind, to punish the poor sinner." What a devil's logic that is! Reflect on it for a moment. Because your mother is so gracious and gentle and longsuffering you will presume on her goodness and outrage her most sacred and tender feelings. The true logic is that goodness should lead us to repentance. Because God has been good to us and has favored us with his mercy, therefore we should draw back with horror from breaking His commandments and sinning against His goodness. My young friend, I tremble for you from the bottom of my heart if the keen edge of your fear of sin is being rubbed off. Your safety lies in your fear of sin and in your keeping alive a keen sense of your personal accountability to your God.

Well, Joseph stood square and solid and firm, and the result was that he went to prison. And there we have the same story over again. Some men are like a rubber ball— the harder you throw them to the ground the higher they will bounce. Joseph was that kind of a man. He was superior to circumstances because his force of character was great. God's favor was with him in the prison as it had been in the palace. God never deserts a man because he is down. And God have mercy on us when we are mean enough to do it! Joseph rose in the prison from the same causes that elevated him in the house of Potiphar. He made the best of things. It was all a mystery to him His heart was heavy and sore. But he did not go around making everybody else blue. No. He communed with God there in the prison. The people were astonished at his good cheer. Like the Christ of whom he was a type, he "had meat to eat that they knew not of" (John 4:32).

It is stated that one of the hottest regions on the earth is along the Persian Gulf, where little or no rain falls. At Bahrein the arid shore has no fresh water, yet a comparatively numerous population contrives to live there, thanks to the copious springs which break forth from the bottom of the sea. The fresh water is got by diving. The diver, sitting in his boat, winds a great goatskin bag around his left arm, the hand grasping its mouth. Then he takes in his right hand a heavy stone, to which is attached a strong line, and thus equipped he plunges in and quickly reaches the bottom. Instantly opening the bag over the strong jet of water, he springs up the ascending current, at the same time closing the bag, and is helped aboard. The stone is then hauled up, and the diver, after taking breath, plunges again. The source of the copious submarine springs is thought to be in the green hills of Osmon, some five or six hundred miles distant. So Joseph, too, had his hidden fountain of prayer and communion with God that sustained him and comforted him and kept his hope and his dreams alive. And the rulers of the prison came to have confidence in him, and as the years passed he came to be the head of everything there, next to the keeper of the prison himself. His kindness and his good will won also the confidence of the prisoners, so that they brought their troubles and their mysteries to him to solve.

It was the helpful spirit of Joseph that led to his great triumph. Through God's grace to him he interpreted the dreams of some of the king's prisoners who were with him in the prison. You may see in that an illustration of how important it is that we do not allow the disappointments or hurts of life to break down the high dreams of our hearts for a noble career. If Joseph had done that he never would have been prime minister of Egypt. If he had allowed himself to become doubting and despairing, and when the prison door closed on him had said to himself, "It's all over with me now. That's the end, the ruin, and overthrow of my dreams. I shall die here like a dog forgotten of everyone"—if Joseph had said that, that would have been the end, no doubt. And if he had been in that spirit when these disgraced officers of the king came to him with their dreams he would have turned upon them in sour and morose way and said "Don't you believe in dreams. They will only get you into trouble. I had my dreams once. I know what stuff dreams are made of. I have seen the sun, the moon, and the stars bowing down to me. I have seen all the sheaves of the fields bowing down before my sheaf. And now see me here, a disgraced slave in a dungeon. It was my dreams that brought all this on me. Beware of dreams!" But Joseph did not talk that way; he was superior to all that. And though in prison, he cherished the dreams of his youth and believed that God would somehow yet bring them to pass.

My friend, do not allow anything to destroy the dreams which God has given you of a pure and noble and victorious life. Cling to them, no matter how hard the circumstances that surround you, and you will be growing worthy of them even in the hard prison of trial. Like John Bunyan,

Joseph grew to be a greater man in prison than he had been in freedom, and God is making better men and women of many of us because of the hard circumstances that imprison us and restrain us and develop all sides of our nature. Cherish your ideals; cling to the noblest dreams God ever gave you of manhood and womanhood, and strive by his grace to realize them.

But someone says, "Your advice is good for men and women who are in the prison of trial wrongfully, because of their fidelity, like Joseph; but what good is it to the man who is in the pit, whose feet are deep in the mire, through his own fault, because of his own folly?" I bless God that even to you I have a message of hope. The God who stood by Joseph is the God who gave Jesus Christ to come to earth and suffer and die in your stead, that "by his stripes" you may be healed. It is Christ's own estimate of His mission that He came "to proclaim liberty to the captives, and the opening of the prison to them that are bound" (Isaiah 61:1). Are you a captive to evil habit? Are you bound by fetters of appetite or passion? Christ comes to set you free. His message to you is one of deliverance, and He longs to throw the doors wide open and let your soul go free to realize your sweetest, noblest dreams of a good and a glorious life.

8

A SAINT WITH A CROOKED PATH

"The Angel which redeemed me from all evil..."
(Genesis 48:16).

M any a man has had occasion to use an old proverb which says, "If my foresight were as good as my hindsight I would get along better." A man's judgment about life is worth more after he has had experience than it is when he is just starting in. Jacob had had much experience, and had lived through a long and varied career. He had known poverty and hardship and exile, and he had enjoyed riches and power. He had tasted deeply both of the cup of love and of grief, and now he was getting close to the end of the journey of his human life on earth, and he sent a messenger from Goshen, where he spent the last quiet years of his life, to tell Joseph, his favorite son, who was then the premier of Egypt, that he wished to have a last talk with him before he died. Joseph took his two sons and hastened to the bedside of his dying father. How such a picture brings it all close to home to us! At first glance this old story of Jacob and Joseph seems afar off, and we wonder what there can be in it to interest us now, but this little touch of human grief makes us all kin. There are some of us who have had the telegram that told that father or mother was sick, and we remember how slow the train seemed to go. Though it were the fast express, it seemed to crawl with a snail-like pace, so anxious were we to be with our loved ones. And so Joseph went with his boys, hoping to see his father's hand upon their heads in blessing. When he came into the room where his father was Jacob made a last effort to be propped up in bed to receive them. Joseph said to his father, "They are my sons, whom God hath given me in this place." But the old man could not see across the room, for his eyes were dim with age and he said, "Bring them, I pray thee, unto me, and I will bless them" (Genesis 48:9). And Joseph led the boys near unto his father, and he kissed them, and tenderly embraced them. And the dear old man, full of gratitude and thanksgiving to God, exclaimed to Joseph, "I had not thought to see thy face: and, lo, God hath showed me also thy seed" (Genesis 48:11).

God had been better to Jacob than all his fears, and how often that is the case! We cannot see very far into the future, and we are anxious over little things, and we fret and chafe under our restraints and the discipline which is necessary for us; but all the time God is planning our good. Jacob for years had never dreamed of seeing Joseph again, and now he has not only had these years of joy in Joseph's prosperity and honor, but he has seen his children also.

There is nothing sweeter, I think, than to see the joy and the gladness of a noble father, or of a great-souled, self-sacrificing mother, in the children who have come to positions of trust and confidence and are performing the work of life with honor. It always does my heart good to hear an old man speak about his son in terms which show his just pride in him, and I never fail to taste the deliciousness of it when I see a mother's cheek glow with pride and happiness when someone speaks of some honored person in her presence and she turns with bright eyes to say, "That is my son," or, "That is my daughter." O young men, young women, it is a noble thing to so live in the world, and to so perform your work among men, that you will bring joy and honest pride to those true hearts that watched over your childhood and threw the shield of their love between you and so many of the dangers and hardships of youth.

After Jacob's burst of thanksgiving for God's goodness to him he put his hands on the heads of Joseph's boys and uttered the words which I have chosen for our text, "The Angel which redeemed me from all evil, bless the lads" (Genesis 48:16). And so here we come to our real theme, which is that saintly as Jacob is now, coming to old age justly honored by everybody, at peace with God and with man, his very presence a benediction, it has not always been so with him. He is a saint, but a saint with a crooked past. The angel of redemption was very necessary in Jacob's case. There seems to have been a crooked streak in Jacob. He was about as tricky a young Jew in his early days as one would be likely to find anywhere. If you had been around the place on the day when he tricked Esau out of his father's blessing you would have thought that there was poor timber in that young fellow out of which to make a saint.

Recall the story for a moment: Isaac feels that he is getting close to the end of his active career, and he desires to bestow his blessing upon Esau. And so he tells Esau, who was a great hunter, to go out into the hills with his quiver and bow, and kill a deer, and bring home the venison and make him savory meat, of which he was particularly fond, that he might eat and give him his blessing before he died.

Isaac was a good judge of something good to eat, for the man who does not delight in the taste of broiled venison, cooked in the open air, has yet something of the physical life enjoyment to learn, and has my pity. It is delightful to see an old man who has lived so simply and plainly, so naturally, that in his old age he has a hearty zest and appetite for the viands that delighted him in his youth. One of the wages of dissipation and gluttony is that it robs a man of those natural and wholesome tastes of the body. One of the blessings of a pure and cleanly life is the coming to old age with the body still alive to the possibility of enjoyment. Nothing is sadder than to see a man debauching this wonderful instrument of pleasure—the human body. I saw a man the other day, not yet middle aged, and yet he had so sinned against his body that it was no longer a musical instrument full of harmonies, but an instrument of torture more terrible than the horrible contrivances of the Spanish Inquisition. One of the incidental blessings of a righteous life is that it keeps the body as wholesome as the soul.

Now, all this plan of Isaac's would have gone well if it had not been that Rebekah overheard about the venison hunt and the blessing that was to follow. Rebekah loved Jacob better than she did Esau, and she wanted the blessing for her favorite son; so she told Jacob about it, and commanded him to go at once into the nearest herd of goats and get two fat kids, from which she could make the savory meat which his father loved. Then she says, "Thou shalt bring it to thy father, that he may eat, and that he may bless thee before his death" (Genesis 27:10). Rebekah was a tricky woman, and Jacob took to it naturally. He does not raise any objection on the ground of the proposition being wrong; his only fear is that he will get caught at it. He argues with his mother, "Esau my brother is a hairy man, and I am a smooth man; my father peradventure will feel me, and I shall seem to him as a deceiver; and I shall bring a curse upon me, and not a blessing" (Genesis 27:11,12). But the mother urged him and sent him away. Jacob got off on the wrong foot. If he had taken the ground that it was wrong to deceive his father he might have saved both his mother and himself from evil. But it was all a question of whether he should be caught or not.

It may be that I am speaking to someone who has come to have that low idea of right and wrong. You do the right thing when you think you will be detected otherwise, and when you think you can do the wrong thing that is pleasant and not be found out you do it without much compunction of conscience. You have somehow got it into your head that if you can break the law of God and feel sure that it will always be covered up it is a small matter. Sin uncovered to the light of day, so that it brings immediately shame and disgrace and punishment, seems a terrible thing to you. But a sin covered and hidden away seems a matter of little importance. My friend, if that is coming to be your position you are in terrible danger of eternal disaster. Sin is not a mere matter of policy. It is a breaking of God's law, and its wages is death. No matter though it be hidden from human eyes now, you may be sure that it is already found out in the most serious quarter. God knows about it. He is not deceived for a moment. And your own conscience has a record of it, and God can call it to the front at will in such a way as to make you shudder and start back with horror. The discovery of sin is not the worst thing; it is the fact that you are a sinner, that you have broken God's law. Henceforth there is no place on earth safe for you, for you cannot go anywhere where you will get out of reach of God.

Urged by his mother, Jacob hurried out to the goatherd and brought back the two kids, and Rebekah with her own hands prepared the tempting dish for Isaac. Now, Isaac was blind, and on this Rebekah depended for the success of her scheme. She took Esau's clothes and put them on Jacob, and as Esau was a hairy man she put the skins of the goats on Jacob's hands, and upon the smooth of his neck, and sent him into the presence of Isaac. When he came to Isaac he had to begin to lie almost at once. Isaac was dozing, and when he heard the noise he roused up, and said, "Who art thou?" I can see Jacob cringing under it, like a boy who has started to go in swimming, standing on the edge of the stream in the spring when the water is cold. But he reasons that he is in for it now, and so he lies to his poor blind father, and says, "I am Esau thy firstborn; I have done according as thou badest me: arise, I pray the, sit and eat of my venison, that thy soul may bless me" (Genesis 27:19).

"How is it that thou hast found it so quickly, my son?" (Genesis 27:20).

The depths to which a man will sink when he has once started at lying is revealed in Jacob's answer. It is God's blessing he wants through Isaac's lips, and yet he brings God's name into his falsehood as he replies, "Because the Lord thy God brought it to me" (Genesis 27:20).

Isaac was a little suspicious. The ears of blind people get to be keen; and though Jacob talked as near like Esau as he could, it did not sound right to his father, and so the cautious old man says, "Come near, I pray thee, that I may feel thee, my son, whether thou be my very son Esau or not" (Genesis 27:21).

Jacob thought he was discovered then, and, trembling, expecting every minute to be detected, he drew near in silence. Isaac felt him over and said, "The voice is Jacob's voice, but the hands are the hands of Esau" (Gen. 27:22). And, still suspicious, he put Jacob straight to the test: "Art thou my very son Esau?" (Genesis 27:24).

That was more than Jacob had bargained for. He had expected to act a lie, but now he is compelled to tell one straight out, again and again. And yet, after all, it is as great a sin to act a lie as to tell one. You will note here the evolution of sin. Jacob went before his father expecting to act out in silence one lie, and in order to carry it through he was compelled to tell three lies directly. A man who tells one lie, or acts one, may be very sure that on an average he will have to tell three more to get out of it. And then he will be like Jacob; he will not get out of it, but will get the deeper into the quagmire of falsehood. There is a highway of holiness and truth upon which a man may walk without difficulty, but on either side of it there are the quicksands of falsehood. The only safety is in the simple, honest, genuine truth.

Jacob carried his point, but only for a little while, for Esau came back after a little and discovered to get vengeance on his brother. He let it get whispered around that as soon as Isaac was dead he would kill Jacob. And to save his life Jacob was sent forth an exile and a wanderer from his father's house.

There is no attempt in the Bible to palliate sin. There is not the slightest effort made to cover up Jacob's tricky conduct or to whitewash his character. He has sinned, and his exile, with all its loneliness and sorrow, is the immediate consequence. But, mean and despicable as he was, God still loved him, and sent His angel of mercy to speak to him in the visions of the night, and to assure him of God's willingness to forgive him and redeem him from this low plane of life into which he had fallen. And story of Jacob's life for many years is the story of a man constantly under conviction of sin, ever and anon recognizing God and His mercy, and yet falling back again into his old dishonest conduct, until at last, in a great crisis hour, there comes to Jacob the conviction that only in the power of Almighty God to transform his nature is there the possibility of his redemption from this rotten spot in his heart. He throws himself upon God's angel, and declares that he will never let him go until he receives that blessing. In this struggle he is victorious. His name is changed. God's angel tells him that his name shall no more be Jacob, the supplanter, the crooked man who cannot be trusted; but his name in the future shall be Israel, because as a prince he has had power with God and man, and has prevailed.

It is the Angel of redemption that makes the story of Jacob one of possible hope and comfort and blessing for us. It is idle to tell a man of his sins of the certain punishment of sin unless you can point him to the fountain where his sin and uncleanness may be washed away. The Angel who redeemed Jacob, mean as he was, from all evil, and who brought him finally to a character that was gracious and pure and noble, can do the same thing with you.

Four years ago last month I was living in Brooklyn, New York, and became acquainted with a man who had fallen

into very grievous sin and had suffered for it as had Jacob.
I appealed to him as I appeal to you now, to turn from his
sin and throw himself on God's mercy. I begged him to surrender himself completely to Jesus Christ. Finally he did
so, and the other day I received this letter from him, written
on the anniversary of his conversion. I have received one
on each anniversary of that occasion. This is what he writes:

"This is an anniversary night with me. I hardly know
what to write. Charles Wesley must have felt as I do tonight
when he wrote:

> "Where shall my wandering soul begin?
> How shall I all to heaven aspire?
> A slave redeemed from death and sin,
> A brand plucked from eternal fire,
> How shall I equal triumphs raise,
> Or sing my great Deliverer's praise?"

"The best, the most satisfying, year of my Christian life
ends tonight. Better than this, however, the Almighty arm
is still mine to lean upon. 'The path of life' is open before
me; 'fullness of joy' is in his presence, and I have access
through faith in Jesus Christ; 'pleasures for evermore,' free,
limitless in every respect; no condemnation; justification;
and peace with God."

What a blessed thing it would be for you if you could
write a letter like that! The mercy of God is a surely within
your reach as it was within the reach of this man, and he
will send his Angel to bring you out of the City of Destruction, and across every Slough of Despond, to the Cross,
where your burden shall fall away, and you may start with
joy on the heavenly path.

Chapter 9

THE SECOND VIOLIN

*"And Miriam the prophetess, the sister of Aaron, took a
timbrel in her hand; and all the women went out after her
with timbrels and the dances. And Miriam answered them,
Sing ye to the Lord, for he hath triumphed gloriously:
the horse and his rider hath he thrown into the sea"*
(Exodus 15:20, 21).

Miriam was always second violin to Moses in the
family music, whether at home in childhood or
on the broader stage of national affairs. Some
people suffer by being the relatives of great men, being thus
always overshadowed and held back from the proper degree of appreciation which they might otherwise win for
themselves. Others are greatly helped by being associated
with great characters, for they catch some of the glow reflected from the greater sun. Miriam was a large personality
in herself, yet I am inclined to think she gains more than
she loses by being the sister of Moses. The family of Amram
turned out well. Aaron, Miriam, and Moses were the three
lights in Israel throughout the days of the exodus. Moses
was the great man of the trio, and one of a dozen great men
in human history; but Aaron and Miriam were valuable

seconds. Aaron had a weak backbone, but he had an eloquent tongue, and the Lord made good use of it.

Three pictures of Miriam are given in the old Bible
story. The first one has the river Nile for a background. It
is in the days when Egypt had been stirred with fear because the Israelites multiplied so rapidly, the politicians
foreseeing the day when they would be in the majority and
might seize control of the country. The Egyptians lived luxuriously and wickedly, until they had very small families
and increased but slowly in population; but the Hebrews
were plain and simple and frugal in their habits of life, and
great families of children thronged their humble firesides.
And so the cruel edict went forth that every boy born
among the Hebrews should be destroyed. But it is very
hard to carry out a law which runs athwart human nature
like that. It was at this time that Amram, who had two children already, Aaron and Miriam, was in deep perplexity
because there was born into the family a little boy babe.
They hid him until that was no longer possible, and then
the mother with all a mother's ingenuity devised a scheme
by which she hoped to save her child. She made of bulrushes a little ark large enough to hold a baby, so carefully
made that it would not leak, and she put the child into
this and carried it down to the edge of the river where the
water was quiet and still, and put it out among the reeds
at a place where Pharaoh's daughter was accustomed to
come every morning to bathe in the river. It was a shrewd
scheme, worthy of a mother, and it worked well. After a
while the maidens came down from the palace, and the
princess, seeing the dainty little ark of bulrushes, had it
brought to her, and when she opened it, and the little
child cried, her heart was touched with pity, and she did

exactly what Mrs. Amram believed she would do—she decided to save the child's life. But God is always better to us even than our dreams, for the princess not only decided to save the life of the child, but she determined to adopt him for her own son, thus insuring for him great opportunities and privileges.

And here Miriam comes in. Miriam was a bright, wide-awake little girl at this time, and she had been stationed as a sentinel to see what became of the baby. When she saw the kindness of the princess she came running up with a child's dash and impulsiveness, and inquired if she could go and hunt a nurse for the babe. And when told to go Miriam had no trouble in finding one. She knew a certain Mrs. Amram who had a child the same age, and who, having sent her child to sea in an ark of bulrushes that morning, would be very glad to take another in his place. And so it was that Moses came to have a good nurse who was greatly devoted to his interests, and who saw to it that he was brought up reverently to fear the true God.

We know nothing of Miriam's history between this time and the time when she appears as a leader of hundreds of thousands of women in singing a song which Moses had written, celebrating the deliverance of the Israelites from the Egyptian army on the shore of the Red Sea. A long time had passed away. Moses grew to be a young man, and then was forty years in exile on the slopes of Mount Horeb, herding the flocks of Jethro, his father-in-law, before he came back to lead the hosts of Israel out of Egypt. So the bright-eyed little girl who had watched on the banks of the Nile the fate of her baby brother is now gray-haired and old, but her strength is unabated, and she still has a voice full of music and power. We cannot tell what story full of pathos, and possibly of tragedy, with all the notes of love and hope and sorrow in it, is covered up by those years of silence which have left Miriam without a mate and a flock of her own; but here we find her with the Red Sea behind, with victory in the hearts of the people, and, as usual, playing second violin in the orchestra to Moses' first.

The occasion is most picturesque and splendid. Some six hundred thousand Hebrews—not an army, but a great retreating multitude of men, women, and children—were on the borders of the sea, with the mountains on either hand, and behind them the pursuing army of Egypt, led by the cruel, revengeful Pharaoh, with his war chariots and his veteran soldiery, determined on their destruction. They were in a pocket—the sea before them, the mountains to the right and left, and the enemy behind. Help could only come from one quarter, and that was from above.

Possibly I speak to someone here this evening in just that situation. The Red Sea, full of threatening trouble and impassable difficulty, rolls its troubled waves at your feet. Mountains of opposition too high for you to scale rise on either hand. Behind you is the enemy. And the devil whispers in your ear that there is no way of escape. You are ready to cry out against God, against your friends, against circumstances, even as the children of Israel cried out against Moses. But there was one way of help for them, and there is for you; the way up into heaven into the heart of God is still open. In their great emergency God came to the deliverance of these people, and if you will cry out to him reverently and earnestly, as Moses did, he will come to your help. He opened a path before them through the sea. I do

not know how he did it. Some say it was done by a great
wind, which blew the water down into one end of the sea
until there was dry crossing. I don't know whether that was
so or not. What I am sure of is that my God, who holds the
winds in His fist and the seas in the hollow of His hand,
can make a promenade through the sea for his children
whenever he wishes.

The pillar of cloud which had guided the Hebrews by
day, and which had changed into a pillar of fire by night,
stood behind them that night as they marched through the
sea. The Egyptians, with that folly which always pursues
men when they are on a sinful course, thought this cloud
which had settled between them and their victims furnished a splendid opportunity to come upon them un-
awares, and so they pressed forward. The cloud was so
dense that they could not see the children of Israel, but
they could hear their voices and the murmur of the great
host, and so they pressed forward, expecting soon to be
upon them. They thought every moment to break through
the cloud and fall upon their prey. And all the night the astonished and amazed army of Pharaoh pursued after the
Hebrews, always seemingly just within reach of them, and
yet so strangely hindered by that dense cloud that they
never came upon them. Finally, when the Hebrews are all
safe across the sea, the pursuing army sees the cloud suddenly transformed. "It becomes a column of fire as high as
heaven, shooting forth lightning and shaking the earth
with mighty thunders. To them it seems as if some awful
eye were looking upon them out of the darkness, blazing
with infinite anger and striking them through with strange
fear. Chariot horses break the ranks and dash against each
other in wild confusion. Wheels are entangled with wheels

and torn off, while the frantic war horses drag the scythe-armed axles over dismounted charioteers and trample prostrate soldiers alive into the mire. The archers and the spearmen are pierced with their own weapons. While the lightning flames and the thunder rolls, and the host of men and horses are struggling together in fear and madness and agony, two mighty waves come crashing over them from opposite directions, and when the shock has subsided and the sea is calm Pharaoh and his host, the pride and the glory of Egypt, are no more." In the morning when the sun rises the light of day reveals strange driftwood to the eyes of the escaped Hebrews. The shore is lined with floating chariots and dead horses and the bodies and the trappings of a drowned army.

The sublimity of the occasion inspired Moses to produce a great song of triumph. If you will bring back all the circumstances of the occasion it cannot but impress you as in your imagination you hear the great chant of a multitude singing:

> I will sing unto the Lord, for he hath triumphed
> gloriously:
> The horse and his rider hath he thrown into the
> sea.
> The Lord is my strength and song,
> And he is become my salvation:
> This is my God, and I will praise him;
> My father's God, and I will exalt him.
> The Lord is a man of war:
> The Lord is his name.
> Pharaoh's chariots and his host hath he cast into
> the sea:
> And his chosen captains are sunk in the Red Sea.
> The deeps cover them:

They went down into the depths like a stone.
Thy right hand, O Lord, is glorious in power,
Thy right hand, O Lord, dasheth in pieces the
    enemy.
And in the greatness of thine excellency thou
    overthrowest them that rise up against thee:
Thou sendest forth thy wrath, it consumeth them
    as stubble.
And with the blast of thy nostrils the waters were
    piled up,
The floods stood upright as an heap;
The deeps were congealed in the heart of the sea.
The enemy said,
I will pursue, I will overtake, I will divide the spoil:
My lust shall be satisfied upon them;
I will draw my sword, my hand shall destroy them.
Thou didst blow with thy wind, the sea covered
    them:
They sank as lead in the mighty waters.
Who is like unto thee, O Lord, among the gods?
Who is like thee, glorious in holiness,
Fearful in praises, doing wonders?
Thou stretchedst out thy right hand,
The earth swallowed them.
Thou in thy mercy hast led the people which
    thou hast redeemed:
Thou hast guided them in thy strength to thy
    holy habitation" (Exodus 15:1-13).

Then Moses has a vision of the effect which this mighty deliverance will have on the people round about, and it gives him great courage for the future. And so he continues to sing:

"The peoples have heard, they tremble:
Pangs have taken hold on the inhabitants of

Philistia.
Then were the dukes of Edom amazed;
The mighty men of Moab, trembling taketh hold
    upon them:
All the inhabitants of Canaan are melted away.
Terror and dread falleth upon them;
By the greatness of thine arm they are as still as a
    stone;
Till thy people pass over, O Lord,
Till the people pass over which thou hast
    purchased.
Thou shalt bring them in, and plant them in the
    mountain of thine inheritance,
The place, O Lord, which thou hast made for
    thee to dwell in,
The sanctuary, O Lord, which thy hands have
    established.
The Lord shall reign forever and ever"
    (Exodus 15:14-18).

And here Miriam rose to the occasion as she had long ago, when she saw the princess looking into the ark of bulrushes on the banks of the Nile. She gathered the women, and, leading them with her timbrel and her own powerful voice, they went forth in solemn dance and triumphant note to sing this hymn. It is a great thing to be able to write such a hymn, and it is also a great thing to have the courage and inspiration and faith to sing it after it is written.

The third picture in the story of Miriam I can treat only too briefly. A year passed away, and a difference of opinion arose between Aaron and Miriam on the one hand, and Moses on the other, because of the latter's marriage. Miriam and Aaron did not like Moses' wife, and that led to controversy. In the discussion they became envious of Moses, and said, "Hath the Lord indeed spoken only by Moses? Hath he not spoken also by us?" How natural it was for Miriam to fall into that kind of a sin! Was not Moses the baby she had seen in the ark of bulrushes? Was he not the little baby brother? Had she not watched over him and mothered him? Was he not many years younger than she? Surely Moses was more likely to be wrong than she, and she was envious of the leadership that was given to him, and so it led her into sin against God, and the leprosy, white and blighting, came upon her. And the people, in fear and dread, thrust her outside the camp, where she wandered in the depths of despair. Then it was that Moses' heart broke before the Lord. He could not go on and leave Miriam there to die a poor leper in the desert and the wilderness. He would not break camp, but stayed to pray, and day after day he called out to God from the depths of his great heart, "Heal her now, O God, I beseech thee." And the Lord heard Moses in the prayer for his sister, and no doubt her own broken-hearted and repentant prayer had also gone up to the ear of Heaven, for her sins were forgiven, her leprosy was healed, and she was brought back again before the people marched forward toward the promised land.

It may be that I speak to someone now who has been as closely associated with the people of God as Miriam was, and yet has fallen into sin, and is knowing tonight the backslider's leprosy and leanness of heart. If so, I want to assure you that Jesus Christ your Saviour is interceding for you, and Christians are praying for you, and the voice of God is speaking in your heart and conscience, calling you back again to the home of your soul. Do not refuse to heed that voice. Someone sings:

"One great Voice august
Is speaking always in this world of men;
Speaking direct – no need of word or pen –
Mystic and yet so clear!
"Do you hear a Voice
Calling sweetly, softly through the years:
Through the wrong and sorrow, through the
    tears
Of a wasted life?
"Have you heard a Voice
Resonant in times of hot, mad sin,
When the chalice of the heart within
Dripped with poisoned wine?
"Have you heard a Voice
Whispering sadly as the soul stooped down,
Groveling to some baseness – its fair crown
Dimmed and blurred with shame?
"Have you heard a Voice
Calling gladly as the soul arose,
Patient and strong, brave to endure all blows
In this world's strife?
"Have you heard a Voice
Looking up to heaven with quiet smile,
Feeling some omnipotence the while
Bearing up the life?
"'Tis the Voice of God,
Sweet, appealing, as in Eden's grove;
Sternly warning in his righteous love,
'Tis the Father's Voice.
"Aye, the Father's Voice,
Calling ever, always, through the years,
Through all wrong and sorrow – through all
    tears –
Calling children home!"

Chapter 10

10

THE FIVE WISE VIRGINS OF THE OLD TESTAMENT

"And the Lord spake unto Moses saying, 'The daughters of
Zelophehad speak right: thou shalt surely give them a
possession of an inheritance among their father's brethren"
(Numbers 27:6, 7).

These daughters of Zelophehad are the five wise virgins of the Old Testament story. Plucky girls they were, too. Zelophehad had five daughters and no sons. I suppose he was disappointed about it, because there was more premium on boys in those days than there is now; but it would take very bright, lively boys to balance off such girls as these were. Now, Zelophehad died young, and left these daughters with their own way to make in the world, and though a girl counted for more in Israel than among any other people at that time, yet it was a warlike age and the world was young, and when the daughters of Zelophehad listened to the talk about the dividing up of the land of Canaan when it should be conquered they found that everybody took it for granted that all their hopes of an inheritance died with the father, and as there was no boy in the family the name would die out from among the honored families of Israel. Now, today it is a matter of course that if a father dies his inheritance will pass to his children—to the girls just the same as to the boys—but I want you girls to remember that the first precedent ever laid down in any law book that started the world toward this era of equality in the matter of inheritance is this very decision that was brought about by the daughters of Zelophehad. No woman ought to ever forget that the Bible is the charter book of woman's equality and open opportunity to equal privilege of honor in the world.

Now, the daughters of Zelophehad thought the matter over, and they called a council and put their five heads together. Let us look at them a moment. We may have a fair photograph of them, even though they lived so long ago, through their names. In the old days names meant something. Among the simple people in a plain age children are named because of certain characteristics, and so names fit better than they often do in these days. There sit the five girls in council. Mahlah is the eldest and has the place of honor, though she is not so strong as the rest. She was a frail, delicate little baby, and the parents were afraid they would not be able to bring her through the teething time, and so they called her "Mahlah," the sick one. But who has not noticed that often it is the frail and delicate child, the one who has to be sheltered and protected lest the wind blow too coldly or the burden press to heavily, that is dearest of all in the family circle?

Next to her is Noah. I suspect she was a restless child, all activity. The name of Noah was used also for boys. It had in the early times two meanings directly opposite to each other—"rest" and "motion." I asked a woman what it ought to mean in this girl's case, and quick as a flash she said, "When given to a man it meant rest, and when given to a woman it meant motion."

Then there was Hoglah. A graceful girl, quick, alert, every action or attitude one of beauty. So lively and animated was she in her childhood that somebody said one day, "She's as quick and pretty as a partridge," and so ever after she was "Hoglah," the partridge.

On the other side of her was Milcah, the lawyer of the family. She was a precocious child, and could talk when she was a year old. She was always asking questions, and it never did to tell her, "Just because," for an answer; she always had to know the reason of things. She never believed a thing was right because it had been going on that way. She wanted a better reason. So they called her "Milcah," the counselor, the wise girl.

There is only one more, Tirzah. Now, Tirzah was not a genius in any way, yet she was the most popular of the lot. She was not nearly as longheaded as Milcah; she was not so beautiful and graceful as Hoglah; she was not so quick as Noah, and there was nothing of that delicate, indescribable charm of the frail body and the spiritual nature which marked Mahlah. She was just a good, wholesome girl who was always good-humored and cheerful. So they called her "Tirzah," the pleasant one. You could never get her out of sorts. When the bread wasn't baked well, and the meat was tough, and everybody else had the blues, Tirzah was pleasant. She was incarnate sunshine in the household.

Now, the photograph is before you. See the group gathered together. What shall they do? They are to be left without any inheritance in the new land. Canaan will mean

nothing to them, for they will have to be servants to their
relatives, the drudges in their uncle's household, or dow-
erless brides among their richer comrades, unless they can
secure justice. Then it was that Milcah, the long-headed,
came to the front. She said: "There is no reason why we
should be left out just because we are girls. I do not believe
God intended that a girl should not have as fair a show in
the world as a boy. Now I'll tell you what we'll do: the next
time the council meets, when Moses and the priests and
the elders and the great men of the congregation meet together to decide these puzzling questions, we five girls will
march in and lay our appeal before Moses." This proposition perhaps took the breath away from the others at first,
and their hearts fluttered with fear. It is such an unusual
thing, and was so certain to be criticized. But finally they
decide to do it, and the next time the council is in session
they appear. Mahlah, who usually, as the eldest, is in the
lead, drops behind now, and Milcah, the long-headed,
comes to the front, and before Moses and the leaders of the
people the five daughters plead their own case. Every eye
is on them. Moses is chairman of the meeting. Eleazar, the
priest, sits beside him, and gathered about are the princes
and all the congregation. And this is their plea: "Our father
died in the wilderness, and he was not in the company of
them that gathered themselves together against the Lord in
the company of Korah; but died in his own sin"-that is, he
had never failed in his loyalty as a good citizen of Israel.
Whatever sins he had were such as attach to humanity, in
personal ways, and he had never been guilty of anything
that would cause his inheritance to be turned away from
his family. And then Milcah puts her question, "Why
should the name of our father be done away from among

his family, because he hath no son? Give unto us therefore a possession among the brethren of our father."

No doubt there was consternation in the council. Not a voice was raised in their behalf. It is surprising that some hard-headed old crank did not get up and rebuke their audacity in thinking of such a thing. Possibly some young fellow, attracted by the wise Milcah or the graceful Hoglah, felt a moving of his heart to speak a word in their defense, but when he saw the frowns on the older faces he kept his seat. But Moses was a man of remarkably open mind and heart, and he told them that this was a new question, to which he had given no study before, and he would take it before the Lord and pray about it, and find out what ought to be done. The girls were happy then, for there was no cant about Moses. When Moses talked about taking a thing before the Lord it did not mean that he would consult his own prejudices and decide to suit himself, but it meant that Moses would seek the will of God and fearlessly carry it out.

Now, when Moses went to the Lord with the question the answer was, "The daughters of Zelophehad speak right: thou shalt surely give them a possession of an inheritance among their father's brethren; and thou shall cause the inheritance of their father to pass unto them" (Numbers 27:7) And then the Lord continued to direct Moses that in the future every such case should be settled with the same fairness and equality of justice. So you may drive that stake down, that there is a "Thus saith the Lord" directly in the face of all this assumed aristocracy of sex which deals with a girl's work and wages and rights not by what she does, but by her sex.

There is a great demand for continued agitation to
arouse public sentiment to justice in this matter. You can
go into many of the great dry goods stores and the great
manufacturing houses, as well as into the government bu-
reaus, where both men and women are employed in doing
the same kind of work and you will often find there where
the woman is equally as valuable as the man as a worker
she is discounted in her wages from twenty-five to fifty per
cent because she is a woman. She is paid not according to
her work, but according to her sex, which is a crying injustice, and is the source of great sorrow and trouble in the
world. Women ought on every opportunity to stand out for
equal rights and privileges for all women. The daughters of
Zelpohehad by their brave act made a brighter day for every
Hebrew girl who was left to fight her own way as an orphan
in all the years to follow. So no woman ought to be indifferent to injustice toward other girls or women because she
herself happens to be hedged about by kindly circumstance. She should have the public spirit to stand out
bravely for the rights of all women. The working women
of this country, who are having ever-increasing opportunities for toil and ever-improving wages and justice, owe a
great debt of gratitude and honor to such women as Lucy
Stone and Susan B. Anthony and Frances Willard, and
many other noble-spirited women who, against every conceivable kind of opposition, fought a battle not for themselves alone, but for all women through all time.

The brave women, many of them delicate and shrinking
and timid, who are to-day making the fight for woman's
right and privilege and duty in citizenship, centralizing in
the governing power of the ballot, are doing a great service
to womanhood and humanity. It is idle to say that women

should not share in the government because they are not as well fitted to bear arms in war as men. What a slight percentage of men are ever needed to bear arms as soldiers compared to the great army of nurses and physicians and teachers and mothers and multitudes of others before whose heroism any brave and wise soldier will doff his military cap! No brave man who knows the story of humanity will ever speak lightly of women's heroism.

Lady Henry Somerset says that the bravest deed she ever saw occurred on a boulevard in Parks, where a sister of charity was walking with some children. There seemed to be an excitement down the street. The little sister listened for a moment, and then, turning to a flower-woman, she asked: "Of what are they frightened? Is it a runaway horse? Keep close to the parapet, my children."

"No, no, sister," said the woman, gathering up her pots and drawing them closely around her; "they say there is a mad dog."

"A mad dog! A mad dog! Will he bite, my sister; will he bite?" cried an elder girl. "Will he come our way? I remember on our farm a boy was bitten, and he died. O my sister, hasten" Where can we go to escape so terrible a fate? Presently the crowd began to thicken and two or three panic-stricken women came running down the boulevard. "He comes!" they cried. "He is biting right and left; we shall none of us escape!"

"What imbeciles women are!" shouted a burly man as he hastened his footsteps and made for the nearest bridge.

The crowd had almost dispersed; it took but a moment to drive them, panic-stricken, from the street.

The sister hesitated. Around her clung the tiny children,

too young to be able to run with any speed and too numerous for her to be able to disperse them quickly. And then in an instant a dog came toward them, his tail between his legs and white froth hanging from his mouth. It seemed as if the animal was more frightened than the human beings who had fled before it. Almost before it reached the place where the children stood it began to snap right and left, and then dashed toward the pavement.

The little sister stood for a moment, and then as though a sudden inspiration came to her, without an instant's hesitation she went straight to meet the dog as it approached.

The animal ran toward her, yapping and snapping and snarling as it came. Down bent the gray figure and the white cap as she knelt upon the flagstones; and after a short, fierce struggle two plump little hands were forced down the animal's throat.

Two gendarmes, puffing and heated from a long pursuit, came where she was; and when they saw her action the men turned pale and murmured under their breath, "She is lost."

The sister looked up into their faces; the color had gone out of her round cheeks; she was almost as white as her cap. "Save the children!" she said; "save the children!"

But their answer was a heavy blow from the back of a sword on the head of the animal, which fell dead at their feet.

The crowd gathered round with the wonderful celerity with which men and women will collect when danger is over.

"What heroism!" said the men.

"What courage!" said the women.

But the sturdy form swayed a moment, and then the little bleeding hands were clasped together as she leaned upon the parapet for support.

A cab drove up, and the nun was taken to the nearest hospital.

The hospital nurse told Lady Henry Somerset the end: "Ah, the little sister! It was the bravest thing a women ever did; or for the matter of that a man either. She lay here so quiet when her hands were dressed, and so faint, and the doctors would not let her move because they wanted some days to elapse in order to see what effect the virus had taken. She was so patient, and yet so gay, she made all the sick people in the ward smile – it seemed like God's sunshine when she was there. But the convulsions took her on the fifth day, and again and again they racked her poor little body until it was a living death to behold her. After the paroxysms she would look up and say, 'I am glad I saved the children—such young lives, so much before them, so many to love them—tell them I am glad I saved them.' But the suffering was not to last, for the good God knew that she could bear no more, and she went to her reward."

And do you tell me that a womanhood which has filled history with women capable of heroism like that deserves to be shut out from rightful privileges in the government of a free people? No, indeed! God is saying to us today, "The daughters of the Woman's Christian Temperance Union speak right; thou shalt surely give them an inheritance in the civil life of their people, among their brethren." Everything that is good will feel the touch of our obedience to God in that respect. Public schools, public libraries, boards of control of hospitals and asylums, city councils, street cleaning, water inspection, milk inspection, every interest involving home thoughtfulness, carefulness for life, and the purity and cleanliness of childhood, every pure interest, will be refreshed and encouraged and blessed by the infusion of womanhood into an equality with men in government.

On the other hand, every vicious thing—the brothel, the gambling hell, the liquor saloons, the prize fight—every vile interest that preys upon the community, dreads the day and pools all its powers to stay the coming of the time when womanhood shall come to its own in equal privileges and duties of citizenship.

I call upon every woman to take note that these women were reverent, and their reverence for God and their faith in the triumph of Israel in Canaan led them to make this brave appeal to Moses, and through him to God who did them justice. I do not wonder that Christianity makes an appeal of peculiar to women. Indeed, I marvel to see a woman who is not a Christian. When I think of what Christianity has done for women, how it has always been her friend and her defender, lifting from her shoulders the burden of injustice and steadily opening the path to influence and power, I marvel to see a woman who does not love and honor and serve Jesus Christ her Saviour with all the loyalty and devotion of her soul. If you have never yet confessed the debt of gratitude you owe to Christ you ought to do so here and now. And for the same reason ought every man to serve and honor Jesus; for whatever lifts up woman lifts up man. Women cannot be low and narrow and mean and men be high and noble. Tennyson never said a truer thing than when he declared that "they sink or rise together."

I call for your gratitude to Christ, the Elder Brother, the Friend, the Saviour, who is able to lift every burden from your shoulder, to banish every cloud from your sky, and lead you forth on an ever-brightening pathway to the skies.

Chapter 11

THE PROPHETS IN THE PEWS

"And there ran a young man, and told Moses, and said,
Eldad and Medad do prophesy in the camp. And Joshua
the son of Nun, the servant of Moses, one of his young
men, answered and said, My lord Moses, forbid them.
And Moses said unto him, Enviest thou for my sake?
Would God that all the Lord's people were prophets, and
that the Lord would put his Spirit upon them"
(Numbers 11:27-29).

No picture in the life of Moses makes the largeness and nobility of the man stand out in more splendid outline It was in the days when the children of Israel were on their pilgrimage through the wilderness to the promised land that two young men, Eldad and Medad, brothers probably, came into a rich experience of divine grace. What it was that brought them to a deeper consecration to God than they had known before we know not; we only know the fact that these men came into a clear and glorious consciousness of the divine presence, and their hearts were so moved by the Spirit of God that they went out among the tents and preached and prayed and sang and bore witness to the glorious truth which God had made known to them. Now, all this was irregular; they were not licensed or anointed prophets; they had never attended the school of the prophets and had no authority from the elders or from Moses to preach. No wonder somebody was stirred up over it. There is an element in human nature which is always disturbed by anything new. In many people it is overcome and controlled by a breadth of mind and soul which will not yield to its power, but in many others it has full sway.

The surprising thing, however, is that a young man should have been so incensed at the preaching of these two brothers. It is natural for youth to be progressive, and a nation is poor indeed when its young men are conservative. "Old men for counsel and young men for war" is a proverb born of the fact, noted throughout all history, that it is the young man, with the fresh eye and the quick imagination, the alert look, the daring soul, the hopeful, buoyant spirit, who, as a rule, is quick to see the wrong that is in the community, to feel the necessity for reformation, and to have the courage and divine recklessness to fight and if need be to die joyously for a good cause. The great wars are fought by boys, and youth is usually at the forefront in anything that promises a blessing to humanity. So it makes us sick at heart to see this young man running to report Eldad and Medad. Young men ought to care more for real earnestness and divine enthusiasm than for all the red tape in the world.

We confess to still more surprise, when this young fellow comes into the camp to tell Moses about the two men that dare preach without license, that it is Joshua, Moses' private secretary and close friend, who is afterward to become the great general and leader, who sides in with the young fellow, though he is a young man himself, and craves permission of Moses to go and put a stop to this irregular preaching. The answer of Moses, however, shows us that it is not mere conservatism, not love of form and ceremony and regularity, which moves Joshua; it is rather his devotion to Moses, his desire to keep Moses at the head of everything, which prompts his attitude. You see that cropping out in Joshua's language. That phrase, "My lord Moses"—how unusual it sounds in the Bible!—suggests Joshua's attitude toward Moses. He had a lofty idea of the character of Moses, but he was young and unseasoned in his wisdom, and thought he could protect Moses' greatness by restraining people who threatened to be his rivals.

This explanation of Joshua's folly makes him very close of kin to us today. Have we never had temptation to be envious at another man's success? If not for yourself, has there never been a gnawing at your heart because another seemed to eclipse your friend, the hero of your admiration and love? We all know that that kind of envy is very common, but it is just as foolish now as in the days of Joshua. You can never preserve your own greatness or make evident the superior greatness of your friend by putting yourself or him in a glass case and allowing no rivals. No, indeed; both we and our friends must take our chances in the open field of earnest endeavor. Someone has said—it sounds like Carlyle—that the way to greatness is an open secret, and it is for anyone who would be worthy of it. If Moses is to lead he must lead because he is greater, nobler, and purer than anybody else. And it is folly for us today to cherish in our hearts for a moment any sorrow or envy at the good which has come to another; rather let us rejoice at all the good that comes to men in this world, and rejoice still further that the path to everything that is good is open to ourselves and to everyone whom we love.

But both the young talebearer and Joshua who seconded him met with a bluff rebuke at the lips of Moses. Moses is too great to be caught in any such trap as that. Moses says in substance: "Eldad and Medad are prophesying, are they? Preaching, you say; telling people of the love of God, bearing witness to the Holy Spirit who is come into their hearts; telling people that the God who led us across the Red Sea will stand by us through all our trials and bring us safe into the promised land at last. Well, what hurt will that do the people?" "O but," stammers the young fellow, taken aback at the way Moses receives his news, "you know they are not licensed; they have never been to the school of the prophets. They have no right to hold meetings and to preach as though they were regular prophets."

Then I see Moses, as he looks hopefully and sadly in the young man's face, and says: "I would God we had more such men as Eldad and Medad; I would God all the people of Israel were of the same spirit as these men. I have not noticed that we were in any danger of being too religious. I think we need not be afraid of there being too much spirituality in the camp. I hope the Lord will call every citizen of Israel to be just such a prophet, and that the Lord will put his Spirit upon them!"

Now, in order to understand Moses' attitude, let us consider for a moment what a prophet was in that day. If you study the lives of Elijah and Elisha and the other prophets you will find that the idea of the mission of a prophet being only to foretell some great event hidden in the mysteries of the future is a mistake. Where the prophet foretold one thing he witnessed to God in 100 instances. His great mission was not to "foretell," but to "tell forth," to the people the message of God to them and call them back from their sins to righteousness. The prophets were men who feared God with that loving fear which made them dare the most wicked kings rather than displease him. They were men who hated evil. They dressed in sheepskins of the desert and lived on the food that ravens would bring them, when they might have been clothed in silk and fed at the king's table if they had been willing to wink at wickedness. They were men genuine and sincere to the very core. They loved the truth, and they bore witness to the truth everywhere. They had a clear vision of spiritual things. They were the conscience of the day. In times of materialism, when men were given over to lusts of the flesh, they kept their eyes clear to behold spiritual realities. Elisha at Dothan, when his young friend saw only the hosts of the Syrian army gathered about to capture them, saw with the clear eye of the prophet that God would not desert him. He saw that the mountain was full of angels and that the chariots and horsemen of heaven where his defense. Now, Moses wished that his people were of that sort, and I have prolonged this introduction in order that we may come to clear ideas and reflect intelligently upon the needs of such prophets in the pews of modern churches.

If the world is to be saved they must be prophets in every home, in every store, in every circle of human living where Christ has his followers. Christians are called to be prophets. Wherever they go they are to bear witness to the truth of God, to the fact that Jesus "hath power on earth to forgive sins." Wherever the Christian goes there must be something about his conversation, his attitude towards men, and his spirit that will make man to feel and know that to him spiritual things are real, that he was living in this world with an eye of hope, beholding, like Abraham, "a city which hath foundations, whose builder and maker is God" (Hebrews 11:10).

O how the world needs such prophets! Modern society needs such prophets. Much of modern social life is built up and carried on with a perpetual appeal to the flesh. It is eat and drink and be merry, and try to forget that there is such a thing as death in the world. The world is given up, largely, in social circles, to a wild, passionate race after luxury and fashion. The man or the woman who can waste the most money, in a way that will appeal in the most sensational manner to the jaded appetite, the half-deadened lust, the satiated imagination, and is in many circles the most popular society leader of the hour. And too often Christian people, and people whose breadth and intelligence and knowledge give hope of better things, are caught in the net of this silly and wicked competition. In the midst of this whirl of folly how great is the need of a revival of real Christianity, and infusion of men and women who are prophets of God, who will demand that society must be genuine, must be sincere, must be built upon a basis of truth and noble character, must stand for doing honor to goodness and for the rebuke of impunity and evil! Prophets of this sort might sometimes have a reward of banishment and martyrdom such as many of the old-time prophets knew, but they would also have the blessing of God and the certain glory of heaven. One thing is sure, that Christian men and women are called upon to stand as God's prophets in every social circle where they may move, and must be as true to God in society as in the home and the church.

We need such prophets in business circles. Every little while we are told that business in these modern days is honeycombed with insincerity and dishonesty. We are assured that in almost every department of food preparation there are shams and humbugs and frauds. Now, I am no pessimist; I do not join with the people who believe that the former days were so much better than these. There have always been deacons—and men who were not deacons—who sanded the sugar. But none of us can doubt that in this time of intense and desperate struggle for material success, when men and women are measured so largely by money and display, there is a constant and terrible pressure toward what is called "sharp dealing," which in business parlance means dishonest dealing; that there is a lack of genuineness, a lack of sincerity and honor, in many business transactions. Now, I say that in such a time there is a great demand that Christian men and women in business shall stand in their place as the prophets of God; loving the truth, clinging to the truth, whether they lose money or make it by so doing; hating evil and dishonesty; always keeping an eye on the fact that the riches of this world perish, but the gold of heaven is eternal. We need men and women who go through the realm of business life with characters so genuine and pure, and lives so true and generous, that every man or woman who deals with them feels the strength and the courage of their Christian character. There are no such pulpits today as the pulpit occupied by the railroad presidents, the men who sit in places of power in the great manufactories, the rulers in the counting rooms of the great banking institutions and in the mammoth mercantile houses. Here is the place where the prophets of God can do untold and lasting good.

We need prophets of God in politics. No Department of human life has been given over to the devil in so large a degree as politics. And yet it is in politics that government is born, and upon which the great mass of the people are largely dependent for the measure of happiness and peace in which they live. Multitudes are dependent for the influences which make or unmake them, both physically and morally, on the issues that are born and have their victory or defeat in political life. The greatest scandal of the Republic, and that for which we need to be most ashamed, is the way political affairs have been given over to the baser elements of the community, or the still deeper shame that many men who bear the name of Jesus Christ, and who are more or less true to him in home and social and business circles, seem to throw the standards of godliness in Christianity to the winds when they go into politics, and, however they may live otherwise, in politics they cannot be told from the heathen with whom they associate. Now, the man who is true to God as his prophet cannot but see that a thing cannot be morally wrong and yet be politically right. What is wrong for you to do as a man is not right to be done by a political ring or a political party. Political success cannot without sin be bought at the cost of corruption. If the Christian men of this country would stand in political circles, in caucus, in primary, in convention, and in public office with clear eyed and earnest hearted devotion to the standards of Jesus Christ, so that men everywhere would say, "this man is God's man; in office or out of it he is God's man," Christianity would without doubt control the governmental forces of life in modern America. The liquor saloon would die, the gambling hell would be abolished, the brothel licensed by police blackmail could not exist, and iniquitous combinations of politicians and money sharks growing rich on the duped populace would be dispersed. America would rise to a new birth of righteousness if the Christian men of the nation would stand unflinching in politics and in office as the prophets of God.

Let us not excuse ourselves from being God's prophets because, it may be, we move in social circles that do not belong to the "Four Hundred," do business in a narrow way, and have no other political force them to cast a poor man's ballot. It is of such prophets that we are studying. Who ever heard of Eldad and Medad before the day that there earnestness and enthusiasm for God and righteousness brought them to the notice of Moses and of the people? Let each man and each woman, in his or her place, be God's prophet. Fear God, hate evil, love the truth, keep the eyes open toward heaven, live in fellowship with Jesus Christ, courageously defend and bear witness to Christ's standard of righteousness everywhere, and whether your name is known widely or narrowly you will be God's true prophet, and he will see to it that your fidelity and faithful service are a blessing to the world.

12

MRS. ACHSAH OTHNIEL'S WEDDING PRESENT

"And Caleb said unto her, What wouldest thou?
Who answered, Give me a blessing; for thou has given me
a south land; give me also springs of water. And he gave
her the upper springs, and the nether springs"
(Joshua 15:18, 19).

Caleb is one of the finest characters in the Bible. He is one of the few men in this book of hero tales on whom there is no discount. He is a stalwart, honest character, a man who obeyed God without question, who never feared to do his duty, and never turned his back on an enemy.

Caleb was one of the spies whom Moses sent into the promised land to find out concerning the fertility of the country, and also the character of the inhabitants and the possibilities of the capture of its strongholds. There were 12 of the spies, and they all came back loaded down with fruits and bringing great stories of the richness and fertility of the country. But they had also seen the giants, the sons of Anak, and they were the biggest men their eyes had ever beheld, and 10 of the spies were frightened out of all their courage. They declared they felt like grasshoppers in the presence of the huge Anakim, and that it would be folly for Moses to take his untrained soldiers against such giant warriors. Then it was Caleb stood up with Joshua and declared that by the help of God they were well able to go forward and possess the country. Caleb never felt like a grasshopper in the face of any man. He was a man of big heart and strong soul. There may have been giants with larger bodies in those days; but when it came to the question of manhood Caleb was in the front rank of the giant men of his time.

Forty years later, after the cowards had had a chance to die off, Caleb came back, and under the leadership of his friend Joshua was present at the overthrow of Jericho and helped by his prowess to capture the land he had been longing to enter for 40 years. When he came to divide up the country Caleb, who is now eighty-five years old, instead of asking for some quiet, well-watered valley, where he might be hedged about on all sides by friends and not have to fight to hold his possessions in his old age, went to Joshua and begged as a special privilege that he might be given part of the country that had not yet been captured. There was one mountain on which the huge sons of Anak had lived for generations, and where their strongholds were; when the Israelites had come into the country they had given these mountain giants a wide berth, and they remained in possession of their territory. But on Caleb's eighty-fifth birthday he came to Joshua and begged that he might have a chance to carve out his own plantation up there in the mountain. It makes the blood run fast in a man's veins to read the courageous words of the grim old soldier. He stands there before Joshua and says: "I am this day fourscore and five years old. As yet I am as strong this day as I was in the day that Moses sent me: as my strength was then, even so is my strength now, for war, both to go out, and to come here. Now therefore give me this mountain, whereof the Lord spake in that day; for thou heardest it in that day how the Anakim were there, and that the cities were great and fenced: if so be the Lord will be with me then I shall be able to drive them out, as the Lord said" (Joshua 14:10–12).

Of course Joshua was very willing to give old general Caleb a chance to whip the giants, who were the one great nightmare left to bother him. Naturally there were plenty of people who wanted the easy places, and it was a great relief to Joshua to be able to satisfy the man who had the greatest claim of all by giving him an opportunity to go and whip the common enemy and capture a possession for himself.

We may well believe that Caleb let no grass grow under his feet in his attempt to capture his mountain inheritance. He drove the giants from one town to another, and finally they seem to have made their last stand in a strong town called Kirjath-sepher. It was there that Sheshai and Ahiman and Talmai, the children of Anak, the three most famous giants of their day, made their last stand.

Now, Caleb had a daughter whose name was Achsah, and no doubt there were plenty of young fellows who were suitors for her hand. Naturally it would be a desirable thing, from a business point of view, to be the son-in-law of so great and famous a man as Caleb. It may have been that Caleb was bothered a good deal in this way, and undertook to kill two birds with one stone when he made his remarkable proposition. This was that he would give his daughter Achsah in marriage to the man who captured Kirjath-sepher, the stronghold of the giants. That was rather a strong proposition, and was likely to eliminate the suitors who were of the sort that would be peculiarly objectionable to a man of Caleb's temperament. Caleb was not the kind of man who was likely to take to a milksop for a son-in-law. We can well believe that that rugged old soldier would have rather buried Achsah any day then to have seen her wedded to a coward, and so I imagine I can see the grim smile on the old gray-headed warrior's face as he conceived this scheme for testing the mettle of his daughter's lovers.

Suitors were perhaps scarce after that, but the list was by no means entirely exhausted. There was a young man named Othniel, a nephew of Caleb, who was as brave a man as his uncle. Othniel loved his cousin Achsah, and when he heard the old man's announcement a smile of joy glowed on his face. He tightened his girdle, sharpened his spear, looked well to the edge of the sword, and gathered his soldiers for a campaign against the giants. The details of the battle are not given us. All we know is that Othniel overthrew the Giants, captured the famous stronghold, came back and bore away his bride in triumph.

But Achsah was a long-headed young lady, and had no idea of starting in the world empty handed. So she spurred Othniel up to ask his father-in-law to give him a large farm as a dowry with the bride, and Caleb, having found a son-in-law after his own heart, was disposed to be generous, and granted the request. They seem to have gone out at once to look over the new possessions, Caleb being with them, when Achsah so that there was still something needed to perfect her future plantation. So she alighted from the beast on which she was riding and bowed low before her father. The genial old general asked what she wished. Her answer was, "Give me a blessing; for thou hast given me a south land; give me also springs of water. And he gave her the upper springs and the nether springs (Joshua 15:19).

Now there are three or four things which impress me very much in this beautiful story. The first is that the best things of life are personal, and must be won by struggle. The thing that costs nothing is not usually highly-valued. That which is bought at personal risk and sacrifice becomes precious to him who has struggled to obtain it. I think we have every reason to believe that in these days, when many young people start in to live in the midst of luxurious surroundings, beginning where their fathers and mothers left off—people who have been born with a gold spoon in their mouth and have never known hardship or economy or sacrifice—are also failing to know the real joy and blessing of that loving fellowship which can come only to those who have in sympathy and love fought a common battle against the odds and won a victory which belongs to them both. I think it is the height of unwisdom for a young man to aim to get rich before marriage, so that he will be able to give his wife a fine mansion and every luxury. Two young people who love each other and have good health, where the man has a fair position with opportunity for promotion, are equipped for marriage, and if they have in them the true mettle of manhood and womanhood they will make their own way in the world.

But this truth applies not only to marriage. It is always true that you must do most for yourself. Parents make the great mistake of bringing up children to think that somebody else must do everything for them. On the contrary, they ought to be brought up to do for themselves everything that they can do. Your success or your failure in life will depend more on your own courage, your personal pluck, the kind of manhood or womanhood that is in you, than upon any circumstances that could be thrown about you. Strongholds of giants of the best fields of opportunity for any young man who has hte pluck of an Othniel to back him for the campaign.

Another suggestion in this story pleases me very much, and that is the side light it throws on that word of God which declares that He "pitieth His children" like a father. In Caleb's treatment of his daughter and her husband you have an ideal father. He has thrown these young people on their self-reliance, he has put Othniel through a terrible test, he has made him show the true soldierly qualities which are in him; but when he has done his part, how gracious old Caleb is to these two young folks who warm themselves in his smile!

So God demands of us, His children, that we shall do the best there is in us. We must, so far as we can, work out our own salvation; we must carve out our own career. God will not do for us what we can do for ourselves; but when we had done that, how gracious He is! He will not only give us what is necessary, but He will cause us to abound. See how Caleb treats his daughter. She does not claim it as a right, but asks it as a blessing. She admits that her father has already done everything that could be expected. He has given her a fine plantation, the great wealth always calls for more. And so she reminds her father that this is a south land which he has bestowed upon her, a land warm and genial, it is true, but because of that a land where the sun falls down with full force, and where a great deal of water will be necessary. And so she says, "You have given me such a splendid field; now give me springs of water." And Caleb rises at once to the occasion and bestows upon her not only the upper springs, which doubtless were the ones she had expected, but the nether springs also, which he did out of pure love for her, and to cause her delight to abound and overflow. And is not that the way God treats us? Is He not always giving us more than we ask? We come to the Lord with a deep sense of remorse because of our sins and we cry out to God for forgiveness, and He not only forgives us, but He causes to spring up in our hearts mountains of living joy, that flow on and on, increasing in the volume of gladness through all the years to come. The psalmist must have had some thoughts of this in his mind when he exclaimed, "the voice of rejoicing and salvation is in the tents of the righteous." Do not imagine that in urging you to become a Christian I am thinking only of saving you from guilt, sorrow, and from punishment. No, indeed. I'm thinking also of your soul's health and joy. Sin is not only wicked; it is a sickness, a loathsome disease that takes away the true gladness and beauty of life I know men of great wealth and culture and with abundance of friends whose life is yet one daily struggle for health. There can be no joy and delight in the other blessings of life if the ever waiting pain is threatening at the door. And so in even a stronger sense is it true that sin makes joy impossible. It is the good man, a good man, who has been forgiven of God, was conscience has had the sting of remorse removed, whose soul has been cleansed and sweetened, that rejoices in spiritual health and knows the real joy of living.

Come to God in humble repentance and faith, pleading the name and the merits of Jesus Christ in their behalf, and he will not only give you the upper springs of salvation from your wicked habits and from the evil mastery of sin, but he will give you also the nether springs, that will beautify and make glorious every day of the years to come. You are not able to conceive how much the blessing of God can add to the power of your life to be helpful and beautiful, in adorning the blessing the life of mankind. No one can tell what possibilities for goodness and blessedness there are in you until God has opened the gracious fountains of life in your heart.

13

THE YOUNG MEN WHO WHIPPED THE GIANTS

*"The mountain shall be thine;…for thou shalt drive out
the Canaanites, though they have iron chariots, and
though they be strong"* (Joshua 17:18).

The children of a great man are likely to feel their importance. Ephraim and Manasseh, the sons of Joseph, naturally thought they amounted to a good deal because the name of Joseph's stood alongside that of Moses as the greatest modern Hebrew of that day. The whole nation owed everything to Joseph. There was about the whole story of Joseph enough of the romantic and picturesque to make a national hero of him. His sale into slavery when he was a boy, and imprisonment in Egypt, his signal fidelity to God, through whose mercy and grace he had come to be Prime Minister of the greatest nation of the world at that time, had every element of romance and heroism about Joseph had been the father of the nation. It was on account of Pharaoh had permitted them to come down into Egypt as in time of famine, and it was through his influence that they had gotten a footing in the land. It is natural that these sons of Joseph and their descendents should feel that they deserved a good deal of courtesy and respect in settilng up the new land of Canaan., They had always been treated with a good deal of consideration, and when that has happened for a while it comes rather hard to just stand around like other people. Now, these tribes and Manasseh and Ephraim were not satisfied with the division of the land; they had received their allotment with the rest, but they thought they ought to have more, and so they came to Joshua. Their spokesman, speaking for the whole, said, "Why hast thou given me but one lot and one portion to inherit, seeing I am a great people, forasmuch as the Lord had blessed me hitherto?" (Joshua 17:14). But Joshua was equal to the occasion. He was not only a brilliant soldier, but he was a very shrewd man, and so he turned on these ambitious men very graciously and said, "If thou be a great people, then get thee up to the wood country, and cut down for thyself there in the land of Perrizites and of the giants, if Mount Ephraim be too narrow for thee" (Gen. 17:15). They had thought about all this, but there were great difficulties in the way, and they reply to Joshua, "The hill is not enough for us: and all the Canaanites that dwell in the land of the valley have chariots of iron, both they who are of Beth-shean and her towns, and they who are of the valley Jezreel" (Joshua 17:16).

Then Joshua, who had been parrying with them rather playfully hitherto, replied to them in an earnest and serious manner. Said he, "Thou art a great people, and hast great power: thou shalt not have one lot only: but the mountain shall be thine; for it is a wood, and thou shalt cut it down: in the outgoings of it shall be done: for thou shalt drive out Canaanites, though they have iron chariots, and though they be strong" (Joshua 17:18).

There you have our theme: if you want a larger field, a nobler career, you must whip the giants which are in the way. It will seem easier to do it, choice assures a mean and narrow life. The only way to a great and noble manhood is to whip out the giants which stand in your path. The devil will seek to make you cowardly, and will assure you that chariots are two strong and the giants are too large for you to wrestle with; but he is a liar, and the fact remains that if you will go forth bravely in the strength of God you shall destroy the giants and conquer a glorious career for yourself. The devil a great deal of bluffing in this world. A great many of his giants prove to be poorly armed and helpless when attacked by a determined man.

At a certain monastery in southern France the visitor is proudly told the story of the exploit of a monk who was once one of the inmates of the convent. The monks belong to a mendicant order and send out one of their members periodically on begging excursions. Many years ago one of these monks was coming back to the monastery, his purse well filled, when he was attacked in a corner of the wood by a highwayman, who pointed a pistol at his head. The monk, being entirely unarmed, at once surrendered, crying for help, and tossing his purse to the thief, who put it in his coat.

"Ah," gasped the monk, "take it! take it! But what a wigging the prior will give me if he thinks I made no resistance. If you are a highwayman of the fine old school you will do me a favor."

"Certainly," said the thief. He was anxious to deserve the compliment. "Anything you wish. What is it?"

"I want to prove to the prior that I defended myself

heroically against your attack. Won't you please shoot a few holes through that coat?"

He pulled off his cloak and threw it down. The thief courteously pointed the pistol at it and pulled the trigger. There was no report.

"What's the matter?" asked the monk.

"I must own to you," said the highwayman, "that I possess no such commodity as gunpowder."

"Well, you are an unusual highwayman. Then please slash the coat a little with your dirk."

"I am also destitute of a knife," said the thief. "I have no weapon of any kind. I attack none but cowards and fools."

"You do, eh?" exclaimed the monk. "Then I guess I'm as good as you. Come on."

He fell upon the thief and smote him hip and thigh. When he had made quite sure that he had beaten the wretch into unconsciousness he repossessed himself of the purse and went on his way to the monastery.

And many of the devil's giants with which he makes the souls of men to tremble are like that. They are cowards, and easily whipped, when confronted by a brave man. There is no giant which you cannot destroy if you have on the whole armor of Christ, being armed with the sword of the Spirit and taking the shield of faith.

One of the giants which most young men have to deal with is laziness. Perhaps you would not all confess it, but I imagine there is that in nearly every one of us which makes us dread to tackle a hard job. These sons of Joseph dreaded the giants, and dreaded to undertake to drive them out, because of their strength. It was a great task, and they thought if Joshua would take pity on them and give them a territory from which all the enemy had been driven, even if it were not quite so valuable, they would rather have it. But Joshua was their truest friend. He would not allow them to give place to their laziness. You may depend upon it that the men and women who demand of you that you shall be at your best, and live worthy of yourself, are much better friends than those who flatter you for what you already are. If Joshua had only wanted to curry favor with them and gain popularity he might have let them go on the lazy path; but he was too great and noble a man for that. He knew that they were able to do what seemed impossible to them, and only in so doing could they develop their own strength. So I say to you, young men, that there is before you a path which looks easy, and every lazy bone in you aches to take it, but it is the path to shame and disgrace. It will lead you to a mean end. There is another path which calls for self-sacrifice and courage and requires that you shall do your very best and fight for every inch you make; but it is a path that leads upward and onward, and if you take it you will be a much larger and more splendid character ten years from now than you are today.

Another giant which confronts the young men of our day is extravagance. I don't know whether that was the trouble with these young men or not; it is quite possible that it was so. Joseph's sons had had a very different bringing up from the other families of the Hebrews. Their father had been prime minister of Egypt. They had been brought up in a palace, and had lived on the best food and worn the best clothing in the land. It is very natural to suppose that they had formed habits in life which, compared with the other families of the Hebrews, were very luxurious and extravagant, and no doubt their descendants were cast in a similar mold. They could not easily get along on the same territory as the other families. If that were so, Joshua took the right course with them, for he proposed to make them earn their own living. He says, in substance, "You think you are a great people; so be it. If so, then you are able to whip the giants that stand in the way of your enlarging your estate. Drive them out, and you will have all the room you need." One of the great giants, nowadays, which is carrying young men down to ruin is the desire to live beyond their means. Within the last few weeks there have been an unusual number of cases of bank clerks and trusted employees who have gone down in wreckage, and when the story came out it was found that extravagance in life—fast horses, fast friends, and fast habits—has swept them away from the path of honesty and manhood. A man who earns only fifteen dollars a week can never be honest and spend twenty. And the beginnings of dishonesty ordinarily begin with extravagance in living. Let every young man beware of starting on that path.

There is another giant in the shape of physical appetite and passion. We might call him the giant of self-indulgence, whether it be drink, or avarice, or lust. No giant is slaying so many as this one. A man was found dead in one of our hotels the other night, and beside his bed there was an empty whisky bottle, the shameful scepter of a giant that slays 100,000 men a year in this country alone. No doubt the beginnings of that man's ruin were among friendly surroundings. Possibly it was at the table where well-dressed women and bright men made gay repartee and where the serpent hid his fangs in the wine goblet. Or it may have been in the little circle of young fellows beginning to have their beer together just for the sake of jolly good company. There seemed no harm, no danger, all were so gay and hopeful and strong. But little by little the giant of self-indulgence got control until the end was despair and death. Are some of you going that road? Are you playing with the giant? Remember he has cast down many wounded, and hell enlarges itself to take care of his victims.

There is only one power that will enable you to whip all the giants that rise up in your nature and in your life, and that is the power of love in Jesus Christ. Love is the mightiest conqueror in the world. Senator Chauncey Depew, the great after-dinner speaker, says that the strangest dinner he ever attended was on Christmas night, a few years ago, in New York. A woman well known for her philanthropic work in New York City was the hostess, and she had as her guests the hungry and homeless men who nightly form what is known as "the bread line" outside of a bakery on Broadway, waiting for the bread that is there distributed. The woman who arranged for the dinner invited Mr. Depew to come and make a speech to those who partook of it. It was her idea that a little after-dinner speech would make the dinner more of a success, and she described the good that might be done in the way so strongly that he agreed to attend.

The dinner was at night, and the great orator made up his mind to be as careful about his dress as though he were going to a dinner at the Mansion House in London. He put on his dress clothes, embellished with a boutonnière, and arrayed in this style he went to the dinner. Mr. Depew says that nothing ever made quite such an impression on him as the sight of those men as they ate that dinner. In the row

of faces about the table it did not take a student of crimi-
nology to pick out those whose criminal instincts had for
years been dominant, and in their hardened features it was
almost impossible to read what feeling that dinner or his
appearance produced. All ate ravenously, and what struck
Mr. Depew very forcibly was the lack of conversation. In
fact, the great majority of the men seemed to prefer to eat
in silence. Now and then a word would be passed, but it
was generally in an undertone.

After a while it came time for him to speak. While they
were eating it had begun to dawn upon him that the task
was a hard one, and when he got up to speak he felt that
this was only too true. Although they had eaten well and
their inner man had been satisfied in a measure they had
not known for years, if ever before, yet the look given the
orator by every man at that dinner appeared to be one of
resentment and defiance. His first words failed to change
in any face the sullen look which it wore, and as his eyes
swept over that strange assemblage absolutely no sign of
animation was visible on any countenance before him. He
wondered, as he never had in any previous effort, how he
could interest those men who sat looking at him so silently
and so sullenly.

At first everything fell flat. Then he tried some humorous
little things, full of wit and good cheer, but the first story
produced no impression. There was the same sullen look
upon the faces, which seemed to portend danger should the
owners of them meet him under different circumstances.
But as he persisted in the same kindly spirit, by the time he
reached the end of the second story he saw that some were
listening to him in a way that really denoted interest. One

or two smiled, but there were others whose faces there was absolutely no sign of interest, but, instead, the defiant look of the anarchist for one whom they regarded as a traditional enemy.

He told a third story. It, too, was lively and humorous and breathed good will. When he finished it some of those before him were laughing outright and others were smiling. He only saw a few who were still silent; one in particular, because he had noticed his eyes continually fastened on the speaker from the moment he came into the room. As they began to thaw out Depew became more at ease and more determined to conquer them all. He talked on subjects suggested by the season, and he found all of them were listening attentively, and the next story he told was followed by a laugh that sounded like music after the somewhat ominous silence which had seemed to linger over that strange feast. Even the most sullen man of all, and the one who had been watching him so vengefully, laughed now with the rest, a rasping laugh that he heard above the others, but hard as it was it betrayed unmistakable enjoyment.

Mr. Depew talked an hour to those men, the strangest and the hardest audience he had ever had in forty-four years of speech-making. He had just opened his heart to them in kindness and good fellowship, and given them the very best that was in him. When he had finished he made up his mind that he would shake hands with them as they passed out. He stationed himself near the door, and each man took the hand he proffered, and they shook hands. If the faces in which he looked were strange the feelings of their hands was even more so. Some of them grasped his hand firmly and spoke their thanks, while others had a hesitancy about it. In his shirt front he had a diamond of large value, given to him by Cornelius Vanderbilt. He saw nearly everyone look at it, drop his eyes, and pass on.

Finally, along came the man whom he had noticed as the most sullen of all. He had lingered behind, and Depew had felt that his eyes were on him all the time. He was the typical anarchist, and incarnation of hate against society. Hate in him, as his face showed plainly, had so long been the ruling passion that it had almost obliterated all others. Depew put out his hand, all the time looking into his eyes, for somehow he felt that it was this man, if any, who would do him harm. His hand closed on that of Mr. Depew in a way that made him think it was to render him powerless. For a moment the man hesitated, while Depew was on this guard, prepared for anything. Then he said, "Chauncey Depew, I made up my mind when I saw you here tonight to kill you, but you've captured me."

The great orator says he has never seen that man since, but he has no reason to believe what he said was untrue. The good will, the good cheer, the sincere kindness of heart, the atmosphere of human love, had conquered the giant, the devil, in him for the time being.

Now, what Chauncey Depew did in that man for a while Jesus Christ is able to do permanently in every man and woman in the world. The sins of your heart may be too powerful for anything else to break down, but the divine love in Jesus Christ can conquer them. I am sure I am speaking to some who are conscious of sin, and who know that there is no hope of salvation save in the mercy of God.

Come to him in Jesus' name, and you shall know his mercy in the slaying of all the giants that oppress you.

It is said that in the time of Napoleon one of his officers was accused of disloyalty and was apprehended. His daughter prepared a petition. One day when the emperor entered Paris she approached with her petition. The emperor was struck with her looks and the earnest words she used in presenting the petition, and he read it. He said, "I will inquire about it." In a day or two her father was liberated. Two or three years afterward that same officer was involved in some scheme against the emperor and was again arrested. The daughter came again with a petition. The emperor saw the petition, but did not take it. He said, "Child, you came to me before for your father, and I granted your request; I cannot grant it again." "Sire," she said, "my father was innocent then, and I asked for justice; now my father is guilty, and I ask for mercy."

We have sinned against God, we are too guilty to ask for justice; but we may come in Jesus' name and ask for mercy, and we shall not be turned away empty.

14

A SOLDIER'S DREAM

"And when Gideon was come, behold, there was a man
that told a dream unto his fellow, and said, 'Behold, I
dreamed a dream, and, lo, a cake of barley bread tumbled
into the host of Midian, and came unto a tent, and smote
it that it fell, and overturned it, that the tent lay along.'
And his fellow answered and said, 'This is nothing else
save the sword of Gideon the son of Joash, a man of Israel:
for into his hand hath God delivered Midian, and all the
host.' And it was so, when Gideon heard the telling of the
dream, and the interpretation thereof, that he worshiped,
and returned into the host of Israel, and said 'Arise; for the
LORD hath delivered into your hand the host of Midian' "
(Judges 7:13-15).

It was a hard time in Israel. They were under the control
of the Midianites. These miscreants would come down
every time one of them began to get ahead a little, and
steal his sheep or his oxen, and either steal or destroy his
crops. It was a very disheartening state of affairs. In their
great sorrow they repented of their wickedness and began
to cry out to God for help. And one day Gideon, the son
of Joash, was threshing wheat in a little cave up on the side

of a hill. It was as hidden a place as he could get, for he feared the Midianites might see him. And while he worked, meditating on the sad condition of his people, the angel of the Lord came and sat under an oak tree nearby, and as Gideon looked at him in astonishment the angel said, "The Lord is with thee, thou mighty man of valor. " But Gideon said out of the fullness of his heart, "O my Lord, if the Lord be with us, why then is all this befallen us? And where be all his miracles which our fathers told us saying, 'Did not the Lord bring us up from Egypt? But now the Lord hath forsaken us, and delivered us into the hands of the Midianites" (Judges 6:12-13).

Then the Lord through the angel told Gideon to go forth, and he would make him the savior of his people. But it was very hard for Gideon to believe that he had been chosen for so great a work. He argued with the Lord. He said, "My family is poor in Manasseh, and I am the least in my father's house" (Judges 6:15). But the Lord assured him that He had really chosen him, and that He would be with him and give him power to come off conqueror over his enemies. Gideon was a very cautious man, and he feared there was some mistake about it. And he said to the angel, "If now I have found graced in thy sight, then show me a sign that thou talkest with me. Depart not hence, I pray thee, until I come unto thee, and bring forth my present, and set it before thee" (Judges 6:17-18). The angel told him He would wait, and Gideon went into his house and made ready a kid and some unleavened cakes of flour. "The flesh he put in a basket, and he the broth in a pot, and brought it out unto him under the oak, and presented it. Then the angel said to him, "take the flesh and the unleavened cakes and lay them upon the rock, and pour out the broth" (Judges 6:19,20). When Gideon had done as he had commanded the angel reached forth the staff that was in his hand, and touched the flesh and the unleavened cakes, and there rose up fire out of the rock and consumed the flesh and the bread. Then the angel vanished.

When Gideon was sure that he had been really talking with an angel he was afraid it meant that he was going to die. Possibly some of us now who call ourselves Christians live such earthly and unspiritual lives that we would be just as badly frightened if we thought God had really answered one of our prayers. But Gideon cried out to God, and said, "Alas, O Lord God! For because I have seen an angel of the Lord face to face" (Judges 6:22).But the Lord in His compassion and kindness said to him, "Peace be unto thee; fear not: thou shalt not die" (Judges 6:23).

Gideon was so greatly impressed that he built an altar on the spot, and called it Jehovah-shalom—"the Lord send peace."

That night the Lord moved him to enter upon his work, and he took an ox and went and hitched it to the altar of Baal and pulled it over, and he cut down the grove that was sacred to the false god, and then he built another altar to the true God and offered sacrifice there.

Let us learn from this that the very foundation of a good life is to make peace with God. Tear down the altars of false gods, cut down everything in your life that is of the evil one, set up the worship of God instead; that is the beginning of a Christian life. That much you can do here and now. You have been going after other gods. You have worshiped money, or passion, or appetite, or pleasure, and God has been driven out of His place in your heart and life. Your enemies have brought you into bondage to them, until you are mastered by wicked habits. The one way to get freedom is to tear down the idols and build an altar to God. It is not a perplexing thing to do. The way is very plain and simple— as simple as it was for Gideon to hitch his ox to that heathen idol and pull it away and then take some loose stones and set up an altar for the Lord and make his sacrifice there. Christ has made the sacrifice once for all for you. But you may come tonight and accept the sacrifice that Christ has made. How plain the way is marked out in the Scriptures! "If we confess our sins, he is faithful and just to forgive us our sins, and to cleanse us from all unrighteousness" (1 John 1:9). There is something for us to do. God has opened the way for our salvation, and now it is for us to pull down the false altars and to bring the worship of our hearts and the confession of our lips to Christ.

The Midianites scented danger. They saw that something was wrong, and that the people were getting altogether too bold when Gideon dared to tear down the altar of Baal. So they gathered together a great army and came and pitched their tents in the valley of Jezreel. They thought they would have an easy campaign; but the Spirit of the Lord came upon Gideon, and he blew a trumpet which, like the midnight ride of Paul Revere in the days of the Revolutionary ancestors, stirred the people everywhere, and they gathered round Gideon to fight for their freedom.

But Gideon was new to the business, and he was a timid man about assuming responsibility, and so he cried out to God, "If thou wilt save Israel by mine hand, as thou hast said, Behold, I will put a fleece of wool in the floor; and if the dew be on the fleece only, and it be dry upon all the earth besides, then shall I know that thou wilt save Israel by mine hand, and thou hast said" (Judges 6:36, 37) So, sure enough, the next morning the fleece was wet with dew. Naturally, Gideon was very anxious about it, and he rose early to see the result of his prayer, and he found the fleece so wet that he, in wringing it together in his hands, squeezed a bowlful of water out of it. You would have thought he would have had no doubt after that; but the man longed to feel absolutely certain he was being led by God, and so he prayed again and said, "Let not thine anger be hot against me, and I will speak but this once: let me prove, I pray thee, but this once with the fleece; let it now be dry upon the fleece, and upon all the ground let there by dew." And God did so that night: for it was dry upon the fleece only, and there was dew on all the ground" (Judges 6:39, 40).

Now, Gideon's mind was made up. He believed he had been called of God to fight his country's battles. So he led the people forth and pitched them in battle array. But the Lord said to Gideon that he had such a large army that if they went forth to battle then and were successful they would think it was their own strength and skill which won the battle, and in their pride they would return again to their wickedness. The Lord knew it was better for the people to feel that it was God who helped them. Therefore at the command of God Gideon went among the people shouting, "Whosoever is fearful and afraid, let him return and depart early from Mount Gilead." And there returned of the people 22,000, and there remained 10,000 (Judges 7:3). It beats all how many people leave when you let the cowards go. But the Lord said to Gideon, "The people are yet too many; bring them down unto the water, and I will try them for thee there: and it shall be, that of whom I say unto thee, This shall go with thee, the same shall go with thee; and of whomsoever I say unto thee, This shall not go with thee, the same shall not go" (Judges 7:4). So Gideon brought the people down to the stream of water, and the Lord said to him, "Everyone that lappeth of the water with his tongue, as a dog lappeth, him shalt thou set by himself; likewise everyone that boweth down upon his knees to drink" (Judges 7:5). The reason of that was evident. If a man was selfish and self-indulgent, and cared more for getting a good drink of water than he did for being alert and ready to fight the enemy at a moment's notice, when he came to the water he would fling himself down on the ground, throwing his weapons down by his side, and bend down to drink. But if he was very careful he would keep weapons in hand, and would drink by lifting a handful of water at a time. Now, when Gideon came to let the selfish ones go home 9,700 more left him, and there were a bare 300 earnest, self-sacrificing soldiers who thought more of the success of the campaign than they did of satisfying their own thirst. So Gideon was left with the 300 men who waited for the night.

But Gideon needed heartening up before he would be ready to do his best, and so the Lord said to him, "Arise, get thee down unto the host; for I have delivered it into thine hand. But if thou fear to go down, go thou with Phurah thy servant down to the host: and thou shalt hear what they say; and afterward shall thine hands be strengthened to go down unto the host" (Judges 7:9-11). So Gideon thought he would be the better for hearing something, and he slipped through the darkness toward where the enemy was encamped. As he came out on the hillside, and could look far up and down the valley in the dim light of the night, it seemed to him that his enemy was like grasshoppers for multitude, and he had never seen so many camels together in his life. But he crept up close to one of the outer tents, and he heard two soldiers talking together. One of them had been asleep, and he was telling the other his dream. He said that he dreamed that a barley cake came tumbling down the hill from where the Israelites were, and rolled through the army until it struck a tent, and smashed it flat on the ground. I think he was rather inclined to laugh at it, but the man he told it to was frightened. He said, "There is something more than a funny dream in that. That barley cake is the sword of Gideon, and your dream means that God has delivered our army into the hands of Gideon." When Gideon heard that through the darkness he was so happy he could scarcely keep from shouting. He did worship God as he lay there on the ground, and then he went back to his little army and said, "Arise; for the Lord hath delivered into your hand the host of Midian" (Judges 7:15). Then he gave to every man a trumpet and an empty pitcher with a little lighted lamp inside it. And he said to them that they were all to do just as they saw him do. When he blew his trumpet, then the whole 300 of them stationed here and there around the entire army of the Midianites were to blow their trumpets; and when he struck his pitcher and broke it so that the light shone out, then every man along the line to the right and left of Gideon was to do the same thing. So they went forth to the battle. Slowly, silently, they crept up until they got close. Then Gideon blew his trumpet, and every man along the line blew the trumpet. The Midianites, feeling secure, were sound asleep, and when every man heard a trumpet close to his tent, and rubbing his sleepy eyes, saw lights coming, they thought there was a company of men behind every light and trumpet. And so a great panic filled the hearts of the Midianites, and they became an easy prey in the hands of Gideon.

This story has in it a great message. You and I can win the great battle of life only in the strength of God. Our strength is cowardice and selfishness when left alone. But God is able to take the small remnant of good there is in us and give us the victory. He delights to have mercy upon us, and he cares as much for your winning the battle of life as he did for Gideon. It may be that you have been whipped and defeated again and again, until you are like the Israelites in the days of Gideon. You have lost all hope of being good, and you are so discouraged about yourself that you are almost ready to give up and to live and die without hope and without God in the world. But the God that came to Gideon's relief will come to yours if you will ask him, and he will have mercy upon you. No matter how sadly you have been defeated, he can give you the victory.

Rev. Charles Garrett was once in Leeds, England, and preached an earnest sermon on "He delighteth in mercy." About a year afterward, he was in Leeds again. At the close of the service a workingman came up to him, with his face shining, and, taking the preacher's hand in his, gripped it like a vise.

Said he, "Well, now, I am so glad to see you. You don't know why I am so glad to see you."

Mr. Garrett said, "Tell me."

Said the man, "Do you remember preaching on 'He delighteth in mercy?'"

"Yes, I remember it."

"Well," said the workingman, "I was there, and my father was there. My father was one of the worst drunkards in England. He broke my mother's heart with his cruelty, and my sister Jane was so ill-used that she died young. At last the home was broken up. I could not live with him any longer. I had not seen him for months. When I came to the chapel I saw him sitting in the front seat. I made up my mind to follow him to his home in a cellar, where I saw him cowering over a few embers burning there. His head was in his hands. When I spoke he started and turned around. His eyes were red with weeping. He said, 'O Bill, I am so glad you are come.' I said, 'What is the matter, father?' He said, 'Well, I have been to the chapel tonight, and I saw you there. I heard Mr. Garrett talking about "mercy's roll."' He sobbed like a child; then he said, 'As Mr. Garrett was talking I thought about my poor wife's name was on that roll, and Jane died and left us, her name is there, and your name is there, and mine is not. O what must I do?' I said, 'Did not Mr. Garret say the roll is not finished? There is room for another name.' He said, 'But mine is such a black name.' I said, 'Try it.' We knelt down together and O how he cried to God for pardon! And by and by God heard him; he turned to me with his face lit up, and he said, 'O my lad, my name is on mercy's roll. I feel it is there, and the clouds are all gone, and my God is reconciled.'"

And the man went on to tell Mr. Garrett: "I am living with father at home now; we made it up all right. He is happy as the day is long."

My friend, let me bring you the simple question, "Is you name on mercy's roll?" If not, I pray you have it put on tonight!

15

A WOMAN'S WILL

*"And Ruth said, 'Entreat me not to leave thee, or to return
from following after thee: for whither thou goest, I will go;
and where thou lodgest, I will lodge: thy people shall be my
people, and thy God my God" (Ruth 1:16).*

The Bible is a book of life, and it is true to life. God's
dealings are alike in nature and in history; hills follow valleys, light follows shadow, beauty and sublimity stand over against each other. So in the Bible we
have the book of Judges, full of war and tumult; and the
book of Samuel, full of more war and tumult. Men hate
and steal and life and kill until the heart is sick with the
havoc which sin has wrought among men. But right between these two books, as a beautiful valley full of flowers
and fertile fields and with a gentle brook singing down
through the meadows that is often found between two
mountain ranges, is the book of Ruth, a wonderful story
of love and of holy character, filling all that part of the Old
Testament with it fragrance.

All the world of literature has praised this beautiful story.
Voltaire, the infidel, wrote about it with great enthusiasm,
and called it "a gem in oriental history." Headley gives it

as his judgment that fiction has never written so truthful and beautiful a tale—one which, while it reaches and subdues the heart, leaves no stain that would soil an angel's purity. No novelist has ever been able to paint so lovely, so perfect, a character as this simple story reveals to us. From the time Ruth appears before our gaze, in the fullness of her young womanhood, under the shadow of a first great sorrow, to the last, when we leave her in a triumph surpassing her fondest dreams, she seems endowed with every virtue and charm which render a woman attractive.

The background of the story is told in a few simple and effective sentences. Naomi's husband, Elimelech, was a man of wealth living in Bethlehem; but the famine came down on the land, and to get food for his wife and two sons he moved to the land of Moab, where he found abundance. The boys grew up and married Ruth and Orpah, and then the father died. In the course of a few years the two young men died also, and then Naomi, broken-hearted and poverty-stricken—for the wealth of the family had taken wings and flown away—determined to go back and die in her native land. Her last interview with her daughters-in-law, in which she prayed that the kindness and love which they had shown her sons might be repaid to them of God, is very touching. At first they both were inclined to go with her, and no doubt the good woman from her own personal standpoint would have been glad of this; but she did not wish them to go without counting up the cost, and so she gave them the reasons why it might be better for them to remain. They would be going among strangers, and might be met with unkindness, and she would have no power to protect them. In their own land they had relatives and friends who loved them and would care for them. Orpah was convinced by these reasons, and, after graciously and lovingly kissing Naomi, turned back to her old home. Ruth, however, still clung to the elder woman. Naomi declared to her that it was and act of folly and madness to follow the sad fortunes of one whose life was behind her and whose only hopes were in the grave, and she urged Ruth to go back with Orpah. But Ruth was one of those gentle, timid, modest women whom the slightest harsh breath would shock, and yet where her heart was interested she was as brave and determined as a lion. She might be as fragile as a willow in some things, but when you touched her affections, and the power of her will to abide faithful to them, she was like the oak that has faced the storms of a thousand years. She would not go back. During these ten years of association with Naomi Ruth had come not only to love that good woman for her own sake, but she had come to feel that Naomi's religion was true, and that her God was the one true God. If Ruth had had no religious convictions she would no doubt have gone back with Orpah; but the Spirit of God had taken hold upon her heart, and she felt that her opportunity to know more of God and to worship him was all bound up in Naomi. Hence, with loving fidelity, she threw her arms about Naomi's neck, and sobbed forth one of the most famous sentences in the world of literature: "Entreat me not to leave thee,...for wither thou goest, I will go; and where thou lodgest, I will lodge: thy people shall be my people, and thy God my God: where thou diest, will I die, and there will I be buried: the Lord do so to me, and more also, if aught but death part thee and me" (Ruth 1:16, 17).

There was no answer to such an appeal but to fold Ruth to her heart and thank God for giving her the rare blessing of such affectionate devotion. And so the two women turned their faces toward Bethlehem.

I have not the time to follow the rest of the story, and tell how Ruth, to support herself and Naomi, went into the harvest as a gleaner, put all her pride and the habits of her former wealthy associations aside, working as a common peasant in the fields; of how her beauty and the nobility of her character shone forth even in her humble toil; of her marriage to the rich and powerful Boaz, and her becoming the ancestress of David and of the Christ. Honors of which Ruth could not have dreamed waited beyond the choice which she made on that morning in Moab, when she chose for time and for eternity not only the land and the people but the God of Naomi. Our purpose is to note the power of the will to choose the path we will follow. God has made us so like himself that this kingly power of choice belongs to us. Some of you who hear me are standing, as did Ruth and Orpah, where the ways meet and diverge. You may see the path of goodness, the beauty and the glory of the Christian life, as Orpah saw Naomi and the land of Bethlehem, as something lovely and to be desired; and yet, like her, you may turn back—turn back with tears, possibly, and with the kiss of regret, but yet fail to decide for Christ and goodness and heaven. Dr. Talmage says there are many people like Orpah, who know how to weep, but they do not know how to pray. Their fineness of feeling leads them into the friendships of the world, but not into communion with God. They can love everybody but Him who is the One altogether lovely. All other sorrow rends their hearts, but they are untouched by the crown of thorns and the cruel agonies of the cross of Christ. Good news fills them with excitement, but the glad tidings of great joy and salvation do not greatly stir their souls. They have a certain anxiety to do what is right, and yet they rob God of his most precious jewels. They are grateful for the slightest favors of their neighbors and friends, and yet they make no return to Him who was smitten in their stead, and who counted out in drops of his own blood the price of their redemption. They would weep at the door of a prison, at the sight of a wicked captive in chains, but have no compassion for their own souls, over which Satan, like a grim jailor, holds the lock and key. Will you be like that? Depend upon it that every time God's Spirit speaks to your soul and you grieve the Spirit you are hardening you heart and taking away from yourself something of the will power to choose the noblest things. If God has given you a heart that is warm toward Christ, that has something of gratitude and love springing up toward him, I beg of you that you will give way to it, for only in action will it grow into something greater and more splendid. Someone sings:

> "Dig channels for the streams of love,
> Where they may broadly run,
> And love has overflowing streams
> To fill them every one.
> But if at any time thou cease
> Such channels to provide,
> The very founts of love to thee
> Will soon be parched and dried.
> For thou must share if thou wouldst keep
> That good thing from above;
> Ceasing to share, you cease to have,
> Such is the law of love."

I am sure some of you who are listening can recall many good impulses to righteousness, many visions of the nobler life, that have failed to ripen into any holier choice, into any supreme and dominating purpose in your life, because you have given your impulse, your awakening gratitude, your aroused love, no channel in which to run. That is the glory of an open confession to Jesus Christ. It shares with all men the new light that has come to your soul, and what might have been only a transient and temporary emotion swells up into a living fountain of purpose when you have thus bravely committed yourself to follow Christ.

We ought to have suggested to us by our theme this evening the great truth that a right choice has often more of blessing in it than can be seen from the start. At the beginning of Ruth's pilgrimage with Naomi all that she could see ahead was that she would have the fellowship of her dear friend and the protection and blessing of Naomi's God. All the rest was dark and full of mystery; but when Naomi's God had become Ruth's God all things began to work together for good to her, and her path opened and brightened with every year. Every good thing she could imagine came to grow and blossom and bear fruit in her life. That is possible to everyone who will choose Christ and follow him.

Several years ago some of the admirers of Shakespeare purchased the cottage in which the great poet was born, and, wishing to do something delightful in memory of him, they planted in the ground surrounding that cottage all the flowers that Shakespeare had mentioned in his dramatic poetry. Now, Shakespeare was a great lover of the old English flowers, and so the traveler is charmed with the great variety of the old-time flowers which adorn the place with their loveliness. There they are, the peony, love-in-idleness, the oxlip, the freckled cowslip, the nodding violet, the red rose, the musk rose, columbine, woodbine, brier, and many others, making a very dainty and sweet garden.

But there is a spiritual garden, far more beautiful and fragrant than that, possible to every human soul. It is a garden where the flowers of the Spirit, dear to the heart of Jesus Christ, may grow and bloom and fill the world with their sweetness and beauty. I could not begin to name all their varieties, but some of the old standbys, the dear old flowers of heaven, are love, joy, peace, longsuffering, gentleness, goodness, faith, meekness, temperance, patience, courage, truthfulness, kindness, hospitality, tenderness, and so on and on—flowers that bloom in lowly hearts as luxuriously as in kingly souls; as fragrant in a cottage window as in the garden of a palace; breathing forth, wherever they blossom, the sweetness of heaven. To choose Christ is to choose all this, for it is Christ in the heart, dominating and ruling the thoughts and affections, which makes heaven here and hearafter. I call you to this noble choice.

16

THE SHEPHERD WHO WHIPPED CHAMPION BRUTE

"This day will the Lord deliver thee into mine hand"
(1 Samuel 17:46).

Thais is one of the old stories which are always new because they pulsate with human life. Goliath of Gath was the champion brute of that brutal age. The poor wretches of our time who are trying to get a chance to pummel each other into unconsciousness for so much cash would be pygmies compared with Goliath. He could take any two of them, one in each hand, and crack their heads together until the empty drums would rattle. For forty days Goliath, exulting in his giant strength, towering aloft above all other men, had gone forth before the army of Saul and defied them to send some other brute out to fight him and let the fate of the two armies depend on that. Saul was none too good to do it, but he had no one to send who would have any chance with the giant. Then it was that David, the shepherd lad who had grown up among the hills of Bethlehem, came down to the army on an errand for his father. He was only a boy in a sheepskin coat, but the Spirit of God was with him, and up among the hills, watching with a shepherd's love over his flock, he had grown up reverent and pure and had come to know God and to trust in him with all his heart.

When David saw the giant come forth with his blasphemy and defiance he was not scared, but he was shocked that the army of the Lord should flee from before this wicked and sinful man, and so he offered to go himself as God's messenger to destroy the enemy of Israel. Saul was at first disposed to laugh, and then, when he grew serious, he offered him is own armor; but David's trust was not in such things. He knew that the giant was far more than a match for him in physical strength. If he were to overthrow him and save his people it must be by going forth in his own natural way and trusting the result to God. So David took his shepherd's sling out of his pocket and chose him five smooth stones out of the brook, and with his sling and his shepherd's staff went out to meet the giant. When Goliath saw him coming he was very angry. He considered it the worst insult he had ever met that he, the champion giant of the whole earth, should be asked to fight with this puny boy, who anybody could see was only a shepherd from the hills. It was too much for the big brute's temper. He raged and foamed at the mouth. "Am I a dog," he said, "that thou comest to me with staves?" And the Philistine cursed David by his gods, and said to him, "Come to me, and I will give thy flesh unto the fowls of the air, and to the beasts of the field."

I suppose Goliath thought, when he raged like that, that David would be frightened out of his wits and take to his heels; but he had reckoned without his host, for the ruddy, fair-haired boy spoke up as sweet as a chirping robin and said: "Thou comest to me with a sword, and with a spear, and with a shield: but I come to thee in the name of the Lord of hosts, the God of the armies of Israel, whom thou has defied. This day will the Lord deliver thee into mine hand; and I will smite thee, and take thine head from thee; and I will give the carcasses of the host of the Philistines this day unto the fowls of the air, and to the wild beasts of the earth; that all the earth may know that there is a God in Israel. And all this assembly shall know that the Lord saveth not with sword and speak; for the battle is the Lord's, and he will give you into our hands. And it came to pass, when the Philistine arose, and came and drew nigh to meet David, that David hasted, and ran toward the army to meet the Philistine. And David put his hand in his bag, and took thence a stone, and slang it, and smote the Philistine in his forehead, that the stone sunk into his forehead; and he fell upon his face to the earth. So David prevailed over the Philistine with a sling and with a stone, and smote the Philistine, and slew him: but there was no sword in the hand of David. Therefore David ran, and stood upon the Philistine, and took his sword, and drew it out of the sheath thereof, and slew him, and cut off his head therewith. And when the Philistines saw their champion was dead, they fled. And the men of Israel and of Judah arose, and shouted" (1 Samuel 17:45-52).

Now, this old battle, though it was fought so long ago, has many a valuable lesson for the youth of today. This battle was fought in the valley of Elah, but just such battles are being fought in these modern cities every day. David obtained salvation for himself and for his people, and in this story any young man or young woman here who confronted with the giant of sin may learn how to obtain his or her own salvation.

In the first place, you may get the suggestion that you must go forth to obey the Lord just as you are. Saul wanted to cover David with armor, but David knew that that would only be a hindrance to him, and so he took it off and went in his simple shepherd outfit. There is no use in your trying to fix yourself up with some armor of self-righteousness that you may help the Lord whip the devil. Come just as you are. It is the Lord's battle. The Lord is able and willing to give you salvation. Break off all sins at once by giving yourself up to do God's will. Sometimes a man thinks it is brave to try to do a part of the Lord's work himself before his obeys God. But the bravest thing a man ever did about sin was to turn away from it with all his heart and give himself up to do just as God would have him do.

Jared Fuller tells the story of a young man named Kay in an Eastern city who enlisted in the regular army. He was quickly sent West, and was soon a marked man, because he was evidently well educated and had come from a home of refinement and good breeding. Everybody wondered how he had come to enlist in the regular army. He soon became a model soldier, never failed in his duty, and rode like an Indian; but he never talked about the past.

There was one peculiarity about young Kay – he was the only man in the entire battery who did not drink whisky. One day one of his comrades set up a jug of liquor in the barracks, and the boys invited Kay down to see what was going on. But when he smelled the liquor he turned and fairly ran to his quarters.

"That boy will make a mighty poor soldier," declared the grizzled old sergeant. "If he runs away from a jug of rum that way what would he do in the face of the Indians?"

One day the major called Kay and said to him: "Kay, I wish you would ride down to Rockville for me."

"Yes, sir; I'll be glad to do it, sir," he responded, quickly.

"Very well. There's a packet to go to Bob Higgins, the express agent."

"Where will I find him, sir?"

"Well, just go into Casey's saloon and sit down. He'll show up in the course of the afternoon."

Kay, who had stretched forth his hand for the envelope, drew back. "I beg your pardon, major, but will it not be all right if I leave the packet with the bartender?"

"No. Higgins must give you a receipt. There's money in it."

"I – I –" stammered Kay.

"What's the matter with you, man?" exclaimed the major, testily. "Don't you want to go?" The major had a temper of his own, and Kay knew it, as all the regiment did."

"I should be glad to go for you, sir. But can't I meet Higgins somewhere else, sir?"

"You'll not be sure of finding him elsewhere," returned the major. "What's the matter with Casey's? Are you afraid to go there?"

"Yes, sir; I am," said Kay, slowly. "It was liquor that got me enlisted for three years. I didn't know what I was about, sir, or I'd never have joined. My people don't know where I am. My mother thinks I'm dead. You'll excuse me, sir, but if your request isn't an official command I shall have to ask you to let me off."

"Humph!" exclaimed the angry major. "A pretty excuse,

indeed. You may go. I'll find a more accommodating and less cowardly man."

Kay had a hard time after that for a while, but an incident soon happened with gave him his proper level. A salute was to be fired in honor of a visiting general, and Kay was one of the firing squad of seven. The charge used for the great gun was fifty pounds of powder, and each charge was enclosed in a woolen bag. One load did not discharge, and the sergeant ordered it pulled out of the cannon. As the bag came out officers and men were horror-stricken to see that one corner of the bag had ignited! The bag fell to the round and for an instant – the passing of a breath – there was a deathlike silence; not a man of the firing squad stirred. Then, with a single bound, like the leap of a panther, Kay was upon the bag of powder. With his bare hands he rolled it upon the sward and smothered the deadly spark, and, while the others stood trembling and amazed, he made his work sure by plastering the singed wool with damp earth. Then he arose, hastily brushed off his blouse, and stood at attention again. But in those few seconds of time Kay had arised from the position of coward to that of hero of the battery.

You may always depend upon it that the man who is most afraid of doing wrong will be brave enough on other occasions. We should run from sin to God. Jesus taught us to pray to God, "Lead us not into temptation," and it is great folly for a man to pray that prayer in the morning and then go unnecessarily into associations which he knows will tempt him to sin.

Another lesson for us to learn here is that if God gives us work to do, and it is hard work, and work which we have not the power to do in our own strength, we are not to wait and haggle over it, but run toward it with all our might in the strength of God. What a buoyant and encouraging picture it is to see that young shepherd boy, with the red roses in his cheeks, as fair and gentle-looking as a girl, running forward to meet the giant, never doubting what the issue will be because he is going in the strength of God to fight the Lord's battle! Some of you are interested in the salvation of someone else; don't put it off. Work for their salvation at once; concentrate your whole thought and attention to it, and pray for them. Go at it, as David did to fight the giant, saying in your heart, "The battle is the Lord's, and he will give it into my hands" (1 Samuel 17:47).

Bishop Warren tells the story of a young man in Cincinnati who was a prodigal son. Wandering in his half-inebriate dissipation along the street, he heard a sound of singing coming out from a chapel He entered, seeking shelter as much as anything else. The preacher was earnestly exhorting men to flee the wrath to come; his soul was set on fire of God, and that prodigal son was smitten with a sense of sin so that he could not bear the burden, and staggering down the aisle, fell upon his face before the altar. They did not send for a physician; they did not try to revive him. Their spiritual souls knew what was the trouble; they gathered round him, and with souls earnest as life sent their faith into the skies. He joined his, and arose a Christian. That very night he wrote a letter to his mother, of course; and in a few days back came the answer. He saw the familiar handwriting. Turning it over to open it – it was sealed after the custom of the times with a black seal – he tore it open with trembling fingers, and read with bleared eyes: "Dear Son: Just at the time when you say God smote you with a sense of sin your poor father's soul sent out of the

body with the agonized cry, 'God be merciful to my son!'"
That soul, so earnest that it could not stay in the body, sent
its cry up to heaven. And down to earth, five hundred miles
away, God smote that young man with a sense of sin. I am
afraid we go to heavy-footed to our work. Let us go to it
with gladness and enthusiasm and concentrated devotion,
and men will be saved.

Let me press one other thought home on your hearts,
and that is that God is just as much interested in you as he
was in David. He wants to give you the victory. He loves
you and longs to save you. Though you have wandered
away so far and your heart has been so ungrateful, he still
loves you and sends to you these invitations to come home.

Have you ever read Ian Maclaren's beautiful story – I
think one of the most tender of them all – "The Transformation of Lachlan Campbell"? You remember how Lachlan's daughter, Flora, having no mother to guide her, went
astray and wandered into the far country. Then one day, in
the little kirk-session, Lachlan rose and himself moved
that Flora's name be struck off from the roll. But one who
herself had learned many things in the school of suffering,
Marget Howe, went to find out Lachlan in his darkened
home. And when she came to the cottage she found Flora's
plants laid out in the sun, and her father watering them
on his knees, and one that was ready to die he had sheltered with his plaid from the wind. When Lachlan took
her into the cottage, and showed her what he had done,
how with his own hand he had crossed out Flora's name
from the family Bible. But Marget could see that the hand
that held the pen had wavered, and the ink had run as if it
had been mingled with tears. Then a letter was written bid-

ding Flora to come back, for her father loved her, And mourned for her, and would not be comforted. And that very night Lachlan took some of his stern Puritan books, and made of them a stand near the window, and set the lamp upon it, and every night its light fell upon the steep path that climbed to Flora's home. And one day she came, and again the old Bible was brought out, while Lachlan, with bowed head, told her what he had done. "Give me the pen," said Flora; and when Lachlan lifted his head this was what he read:

> Flora Campbell,
> Missed April, 1873.
> Found September, 1873.
> "Her father fell on her neck and kissed her."

That was just like a father, and yet no father ever missed and waited for his child as God misses and waits for you. He, too, has a family record which he keeps in heaven. Your name is written there with all the rest of his children, and if tonight you will come back from all your wandering he will write underneath your name "This my son [or my daughter] was dead, and is alive again; he [or she] was lost, and is found."

Chapter 17

17

THE EMPTY SEAT
AT THE KING'S TABLE

"David's place was empty" (1 Samuel 20:25).

A sarcastic but brilliant literary man once said, "If the Lord will take care of my friends I will charge myself with my enemies." This was his keen and caustic way of saying that a man's best friends often bring trouble upon him by the very overflow of their affection and devotion. David might well have adopted that language if he could have foreseen the trouble that was to come to him from the enthusiastic reception with which the people met him as he came back with Saul's army after the overthrow of Goliath. That heroic and splendid deed had made him the hero and the idol of the nation. The people went wild over him. Saul at first joined in the praise; he made David captain of his guard, and heaped honors upon him. But as they came back to the national capital when the war was over, and the great procession came out to meet them, David's friends and admirers did a foolish thing. As the king and his guard passed through the long lines singing women, with their tabrets and other musical instruments, chanted the praises of the heroes, and one singing choir would say, "Saul has slain his thousands," and another down the line would take it up and cry, "David has slain his ten thousands." Now, that was all very nice for David, but Saul did not see the wit of it. He turned to Abner, his chief general, and said, "That's pretty cool, isn't it? They have ascribed unto David tens of thousands, and to me they have ascribed but thousands. That young fellow is getting on pretty fast. He'll be wanting to be king next. There is nothing left but that to add to his glory."

If Saul had been himself as he was in his nobler and younger manhood, he would have no doubt have thrust out this jealousy and envy and looked at the matter with a larger vision; but Saul had sinned against God, and the chief glory of his manhood, the assurance of the divine presence with him, had already disappeared. Down in his heart he felt that he was a doomed man, doomed by his own folly and sin. And so as David grew in popularity, and Saul could not help but confess he deserved it, his wrath grew more fierce against David. If David had committed some follow, showing that he was no better than Saul, Saul might have forgiven him; but David acted wisely, and Saul, looking on, saw that the Lord was with him, and that alarmed him. At first Saul was angry at David now and then; but nothing grows more rapidly than hatred when once given a chance in the heart; and so, the historian says, after a time Saul came to hate David continually. Twice when David was with him he threw a javelin at him; but David was young and active, and on both occasions he managed to leap out of the way and escape with his life. He saw, however, that Saul was determined to kill him, and when the great annual feast came he knew there was only one way to save his life, and that was to keep away from that feast. And so it happened that David's place was empty. It was not empty because David was a coward. The whole nation knew he was the bravest man of them all. But it was empty because David was no fool and would not needlessly thrust his head into the lion's mouth.

Right here is a good lesson for multitudes of young men of our own time. There are good many seats that you would better leave empty for the safety of your own manhood. Where perils threaten, and duty does not call you, let that chair alone. Many a bright and brave young man has gone down before the enemy of souls because he thought it looked cowardly to keep out of danger. Many men become drunkards that way. Young men nowadays know very well the danger and folly of strong drink, and know that the only wise and safe course is to let it alone. And yet they are possessed with the idea that it is cowardly and unmanly to sign a temperance pledge or to make or sustain a total abstinence resolution. It would be just as fair to say that David was a coward because he did not thrust himself into a certain death by going to Saul's feast. It is a manly, a wise, a brave thing for a man to stand aloof from the tempting feast to which he cannot go without degrading himself or putting himself in peril of being caught in the net of an evil habit which may work his destruction. When the wine is to pass around let your place at the table be empty. That empty seat is a pledge of your honor and best manhood.

Let your place be empty when the associations are to be skeptical and irreverent; when the guests are to talk lightly and sneeringly of holy and sacred things; when the honor of womanhood is to be lightly bandied from lip to lip; when the salacious song is to be sung; when the stories or the conversation are to be such that they would bring a blush to the cheek of your mother or your sister. Then, for the sake of your manhood and your character, let your seat be empty. No man can touch pitch and not be defiled. A snail cannot crawl across your carpet and not leave a trail of slime. You cannot handle charcoal without being soiled. Neither can you hear sneering comments on goodness or about the Bible, impure stories, or witticisms turned with blasphemy, and not be degraded in the very fiber of your inner soul. Depend upon it that to associate with evil, and thus allow to be cherished in your heart and mind evil thoughts and imaginations that will change your whole manhood will in the course of time make you an entirely different being. Remember this that the wickedest monsters the world has ever seen have many of them had a boyhood and youth as innocent and pure and noble as was your boyhood. Change was wrought by the associations of life, the banquet of life to which they seated themselves. In one of the galleries in Florence there are two busts of that monster of iniquity, the emperor Nero. The first is of a sweet child, a gay and a happy young lad, and the face is beautiful and charming. It is a pleasure to look upon it. The second is that of a youth who has abandoned himself to his passions, and the lines that indicate it are as plain to the observer as the furrows in a plowed field. The face repels you, and you turn from it in disgust. And if you could have a third picture, you see Nero after he is ripe in sin, your repulse and disgust would deepen into horror. If you do not wish to become a man of impure heart, of low and vulgar mind, then I beg you, in God's name, let your place be empty at the club or room or anywhere where such men congregate and hold their feast.

But there is another King who has made a feast, and I am here tonight to urge you to accept his invitation to it. God has spread a feast of mercy and salvation. Everything is ready, and every man or woman who has already accepted an invitation to that feast of divine love is authorized to extend the invitation everywhere and to cry in the ears of each friend, "Come, for all things are now ready." Some of you have been invited many times, and yet your place is empty. Some of you were brought up in Christian homes. Your father and mother were guests at the heavenly feast, and when you were a little boy they consecrated you to God by their prayers. It was their fondest hope that when they had finished their career on earth you might be ready to take their place and keep the family name at the feast. Some of their chairs are empty.

In my study are three photographs which have impressed me very deeply. They were given to me two or three years ago by a young man, and amateur photographer, and they represent to him a story that is very sacred. Each picture is an interior view of the same little old country sitting room with its great stone fireplace and broad stone hearth. In the first picture the fire is burning in the fireplace, and the crane hangs there over the flames. On the one side of the fire in his rocking chair is the old gray-haired father with his newspaper, and sitting across on the other side is the white-haired, gentle mother, busy with her knitting. That was a picture the young man took when he came away from home. He was here in American for a few years, and went back to pay a visit, and he took another picture. This time one of the rocking chairs is empty. On one side of the same old fireplace the old mother still rocks and knits. She looks a little older and little wistful, but sweet and gentle as of yore, and across the fire is the empty chair, for the old father has gone home. The year before the pictures came into my hands my young friend had been back again in the old country and take another picture. The old fireplace with its hanging crane was just the same, but the fire had died down, and only ashes were there, and both the rocking chairs were empty. O the pathos of those empty rocking chairs! Some of you have a story like that in your hearts. Isn't it time for you to sit in the empty chair at the feast, and fill out the prayers of those saints of God who loved you so, and who have now taken their seats at the table in heaven!

Is there any good reason why you should not do this? I am sure there are some of you who have been brought up in Christian homes who are very close to the kingdom, and yet your place there is empty. All your sympathies are with the Christian church. You thoroughly believe that Jesus Christ is the Savior of men, and you are pleased to know of the advance of his kingdom. You are glad when other men give their hearts to the Lord, and yet you stand there lingering at the door, looking on at the feast in a vague way, though with a longing in your heart. There is your empty seat. Why do you not go and fill it?

Rev. Mark Guy Pearse tells me how he was walking down the street one day with a man just of your type. This gentleman had a few weeks previously met with a very severe accident. As they talked together of it, and of his narrow escape, Mr. Pearse said gently, "And what if it had been as it might have been?"

"I think it would have been all right," said he. Then he waited for a minute or two, as if wanting to say something more, yet as if afraid.

"You know," said he, "I never professed to be a Christian or anything like that; but the morning the accident happened, as I was going down to my business I was thinking of those words, 'Simon, son of Jonas, lovest thou me?' I did wish with all my heart that I could answer as Peter did, 'Lord, thou knowest that I love thee.' I felt very sad that I could not. Then it came to me, Well, if I cannot say so much as Peter, could I not turn them round a little and find something easier? So I began to think that there was one thing that I could not say. I could not say, 'Lord, thou knowest that I do not love thee,' and I found some comfort in that. At last I got bold enough to look up and say, 'Lord, thou knowest all things; thou knowest that I *want* to love thee.' Well, then I began to think about his great love to me; I thought of his life, of his words, of his cross, and almost before I knew what I was doing I looked up and said, 'Thou knowest that I *do* love thee!'"

"And yet you don't profess to be a Christian?" said Mr. Pearse. "Then you ought to."

And so I say to you that you are wronging your divine Lord, you are wronging your Christian acquaintances, you are wronging the men and women about you who so greatly need the comfort and the saving help of Jesus Christ, you are robbing yourself of infinite blessings by not publicly taking your seat at the Lord's table before all the world. Christ asks of you that open confession of your faith, your gratitude, and your love, and you ought to obey and please him this very hour.

But I am sure if I had a chance to talk with you quietly and personally, face to face, there are some of you who would say, "I do long to be a Christian, I would gladly sit down at the King's table; but I am so unworthy, and I am afraid that if I did accept the invitation I should only bring shame on the King and on my fellow-guests by falling away again into sin."

Well, let us seriously inquire into that. How did you get your unworthiness? Was it not because you took your life out of God's hands? It was worthy enough in your child-hood, in your sweet and innocent youth, as it came from God. Your heart turned to him in prayer and confidence and trust as naturally as it turned toward your mother. What has become of that innocence, that worthiness? Ah, you have blotted it out by your sins.

Velasquez, the great Spanish artist, once painted a por-trait of the king, his master, and was so satisfied that it was a masterpiece of his brush that he signed it in full. But the critics attacked the painting severely, and the artist, in cha-grin, painted the figure over until it was completely effaced. Then he altered his signature into the words, "Velasquez unpainted this." Ah, it is your own hand that has un-painted the image of God that was yours in the innocency of childhood.

But this very fact ought to show you the way of salva-tion. Your sin and sorrow have been that you have gone away from God. Your salvation can only lie in coming back to God and taking your empty place at the feast of his love. "Ah, but how can I come back, sinful as I am? I am not fit to come." Well, if you want to know what Jesus thinks about that go to the story of the prodigal. He was all rags, all hunger, all unfit. He had no way to make himself fit. What did he say when he came home? This was what he said: "Father, I have sinned against heaven, and in thy sight, and am no more worthy to be called thy son" (Luke 15:21). Strange, isn't it? He said just what you do. For the meaning of all that was just this: "I am unworthy to live at your home as your son." But listen! It is now the father's turn to speak, and he doesn't speak to the boy at first at all. "But the father said to his servants, Bring forth the best robe, and put it on him; and put a ring on his hand, and shoes on his feet: and bring hither the fatted calf, and kill it; and let us eat, and be merry: for this my son was dead, and is alive again; he was lost, and is found. And they began to be merry" (Luke 15:22-24). The empty seat was filled again. O brother, sister, come home and take your place at the King's table, for he is not only King, but Father.

Chapter 18

THE FLOWERS WHICH BLOOM IN THE DESERT

"Let him alone, and let him curse; for the Lord
hath bidden him. It may be that the Lord will look on
mine affliction, and that the Lord will requite me good
for his cursing this day"
(2 Samuel 16:11, 12).

Some flowers grow in the desert which do not grow anywhere else, flowers which only hard and trying exposure can bring to their bloom. Out on the great sandy sagebrush plains I have seen the most dainty and beautiful flowers, beautifying and glorifying the desert by their color and their fragrance. Up above the snow line, on bleak mountain sides, in little patches where the reflection of the sun from the bare surface of a rock or from a strip of lava had melted the snow and ice, I have seen flowers as delicate and beautiful as any that bloom in tropical gardens. Humboldt picked a blossom that was growing in a little cup of lava where the rain had changed a handful of dust and ashes into soil on the very edge of the smoking, burning hell of the crater of Vesuvius.

All this shows that every part of God's universe is struggling to blossom, and that he means kindness in deserts and bleak mountain summits and wild volcanic eruptions as certainly as in spreading uplands and wide-sweeping fertile valleys. They are all a part of one great plan formulated by infinite wisdom and love. In our text we see David the king driven into the desert place of his life. It was not the first time that David had been in the desert, but it was the worst of all. It is hard to imagine a more heart-breaking trial than that through which the old king was passing. The sorrow that comes to a father's heart from a thankless child is bitter indeed. No wonder Shakespeare makes one of his characters cry,

> "How sharper than a serpent's tooth it is
> To have a thankless child!"

It must have been peculiarly hard to endure the taunts and scoffs of outsiders at a time like that. As the king came along with his company to cross over the Jordan, Shimei, one of the hill men, who had long hated David because he himself had been one of the strong defenders of Saul, thought this was a good time to pour out his wrath on the head of the humiliated king. And so he came down from the hills with insults and epithets and curses. To show his contempt he cast stones at David. David's attendants, full of wrath and indignation, wanted to put him to death from his insults. One of them said, "Why should this dead dog curse my lord, the king? Let me go over, I pray thee, and take off his head" (2 Samuel 16:9). But David would not hear to it; he bore the indignity with patience, and in the language of our text his reasons are made clear. The king felt that this dark experience through which he was passing was not the mere byplay of some arbitrary fate. God was in it, and if God was teaching him a lesson, then no doubt Shimei's curses were a part of that teaching.

It is often wise to take heed seriously and candidly to what your enemies say about you. A man who is wise enough to get good out of his enemies is a hard man to whip. He will feed and get strong on the desert sand. Our enemies furnish a soil for that beautiful and fragrant flower of *humility*. Our friends and admirers never help us much on that line. Many a man is spoiled of the best life possible for him because he grows altogether in the rich, deep loam of appreciation. The soil is so rich that he runs all to stalk, and the grain does not develop. As the old folks used to say on the farm, he is like potatoes planted in the wrong time of the moon; he runs all to top and there are few potatoes in the hill. Many people are spoiled by the lack of that cultivation of humility which comes to the truly genuine person who listens to see if God has a message for him in the curses of his enemies, in the bitter epithets of the people who do not like him, even more eagerly than he heeds the kind of flattering speech of friends. David felt something of this when he said, "Let him alone, and let him curse; the Lord hath bidden him" (2 Samuel 16:11). Among all the obsequious courtiers nobody had made David look on the seamy side of his life with the same care and heart-searching fidelity to which Shimei's curses forced him. And out of that soil there grew a blossom which was very beautiful. David became more gracious, more forbearing, more patient, more forgiving, and had less self-sufficiency and haughtiness about him than before. If you want to see the full result of David's campaign in the desert on David himself, you must wait until he comes back in great triumph after the death of Absalom. They built a ferryboat to carry him across the Jordan, and when he landed on the other side the first man he met was Shimei, full of tears and repentance, with his face in the dust. The same man who wanted to kill him when they were going out, to punish him for his meanness and treachery, wanted to wreak vengeance on him now. But David would not do it. Perhaps he felt that unwittingly Shimei had done him a good turn, and he opened his new reign with an act of forgiveness that was one of the most splendid and beautiful things in all the career of David.

There is a certain largeness of vision that comes to us in trouble and severe trial that we can never know while we live under the soft, warm skies of prosperity. The desert develops the inner resources of men and women. Who believes for a moment that young Schwab, who is at the head of the greatest financial movement of the twentieth century, with a salary of a million dollars a year under the age of forty, would ever have come to such a position of power if his boyhood had been hedged about with softness and ease and luxury? It was because he was poor, because life was a desert, because in the desert of poverty the eye must be quick and alert, the ear sensitive, the brain alive to every opportunity, the whole boy and man self-reliant, that there was developed that robust manhood which brought into play all his talents and gave him the courage and the daring and the large business horizon which made the greatest financial success possible.

The same story may be read everywhere. The desert of trial and sorrow, with its exposure to the sharp cutting wind and to the fierce beat of the sun, gives men a proper appreciation of the relative value of things. Great trouble clears the air, and we see the folly of fretting over little things. With Absalom treacherous to him, David felt that the curses of Shimei were like the buzzing of a mosquito. Why should he turn aside to fight a sand fly when this great trouble was to be met? So it is if we live our lives reverently, and take the desert places as coming from God as surely as do the rich valleys and fertile fields of life, there blooms for us in the desert the lily of *wisdom*, which enables us to discern the difference between what is small and insignificant and what is of great moment.

David found another flower which blooms in the desert of trial. That is the flower of *faith*. When everything goes to suit us, when there are no heavy burdens to bear, no perplexing trials to meet, we walk by sight, not by faith. The noblest faith is a flower of the desert. Faith has her birth in tears. Faith is a sun that shines when all other suns are blotted out. Faith is a silver lining for the blackest clouds. Men who have never faced blinding storms in their experience, who have never known severe trials that tested their metal, know but little of the rich compensations and the hidden treasures of the Christian faith. It was in the desert that Abraham "looked for a city which hath foundations, whose builder and make is God" (Hebrews 11:10). It is this kind of faith about which one of our hymn writers sings:

> "A faith that shines more bright and clear
> When tempests rage without;
> That when in danger knows no fear,
> In darkness feels no doubt;
> "That bears, unmoved, the world's dread frown,
> Nor heeds its scornful smile;
> That seas of trouble cannot drown,
> Nor Satan's arts beguile."

In this bitter experience David had to walk by faith, and his faith rose to meet the occasion. See the silver star that shines out through the black cloud: "It may be," cries the psalmist-king, "that the Lord will look on mine affliction, and that the Lord will requite me good for his cursing this day" (2 Samuel 16:12).

Another flower that blooms in the desert is that of usefulness. A flower counts for more in the desert that anywhere else. A dainty little moss blossom a hundred miles from a cultivated garden, surrounded on every side by bleak wastes, is a thing to rejoice over more than the most beautiful roses or the most gorgeous lilies in a garden that is prodigal with them and where everything is conductive to their growth. And so it is the flower of the desert that testifies with most power to God's immanence in his world and his constant purpose to bless mankind. It is in the desert places of trial that men and women come to great power and usefulness. Their lives send forth more fragrance of sympathy and love there than in any hothouse of material success.

A striking and beautiful illustration of this fact is found in the story of the early Christians. Before Jesus went away he talked with his disciples and sought to prepare their minds for the trials and persecutions through which they would have to pass. He told them plainly that there was ahead of them a time of war, of bitterness and cruelty, and that they should know what it was to be persecuted and to be cast into prison for his sake. But, said Jesus, with encouragement, "It shall turn to you for a testimony." What did that mean but that the best and purest flower of usefulness would bloom in their days of persecution? And how gloriously the prediction was realized! How true it was that

Paul's prison-ship became a mighty pulpit from which he preached Christ. The dungeon of Philippi, in the midst of the desert of their most cruel sufferings, became illuminated with the very glory of heaven, turning into a testimony that broke down hardened unbelief, and Paul and Silas left behind them in that jail a very garden of the Lord. These flowers of usefulness and blessing sprang up wherever Paul went. Flowers sprouted and bloomed in the Sahara-like desert of Nero's palace, until Paul could write to his friends and give them the love of "the saints in Caesar's household" (Philippians 4:22). And throughout all those early days, wherever men and women were persecuted and abused and put to death for Christ's sake, the flower of their testimony bloomed so fragrantly that it charmed and baffled the heathen world. Let us not lose the great lesson. The dark days have their value. The years of greatest trial are often years of greatest usefulness. Bunyan is immortal only because of the years that were spent in Bedford jail. Our sick beds are often God's opportunity to make our lives blossom like the rose. Times when we are misunderstood, when we are betrayed, furnish a chance to show what Jesus Christ can do for a man in the desert. Men who would not look at a Christian testimony under any other circumstances will look at that lonely flower in that strange place and believe in God. It is God's world and not the devil's. Let us give ourselves up to be his children, to love and serve him without reserve, and we shall be able to complete with full confidence William Bathurst's beautiful hymn from which I quoted a moment ago:

"Lord, give us such a faith as this,
And then, whate're may come,
We'll taste, e'en here, the hallowed bliss
Of an eternal home."

19

A YOUNG MAN WHO SLEW A LION ON A SNOWY DAY

"Benaiah the son of Jehoiada, the son of a valiant man,
of Kabzeel, who had done many acts,…went down also
and slew a lion in the midst of a pit in the time of snow"
(2 Samuel 23:20).

B enaiah was one of the noblest and bravest of that little group of heroic souls who gathered about David in the time of his exile. He was not only a brave and strong man, but he came of a family of that sort. His father was a notable man, and his grandfather had been known as a valiant man. Supreme courage was characteristic of the family, and Benaiah not only kept up the honorable name of his race, but set the banner on still higher ground. That ought to be the lofty ambition of every one of us.

It is a splendid thing to have a Christian father and mother; to be brought up in a home that is reverent with prayer, tender, and sympathetic with love, and noble with high and pure ideals. Many young men do not appreciate how much they owe to a Christian home until they have gone out from it and feel its lack. Then it comes back on them with a great rush of feeling that they have robbed themselves immeasurably in not appreciating to the fullest extent the privileges and blessings of a home on which the benediction of God has rested. It is a shame for a man to grow up in such a home and then go away and live so recklessly and sinfully as to bring disgrace on the teachings which were given him at his mother's knee. If we were born of pure and noble parents, whose Christian consecration surrounded our childhood with holy influences, we should seek to be worthy of that training and to do honor to our parents by lifting higher than ever, if possible, the banner of a noble life which they have put into our hands.

Benaiah especially showed his courage in that he lived bravely under difficulties. He had done some splendid and heroic things before. He had once been compelled to meet in battle two giant men of Moab, and he overcame both of them. He had once been beset by an Egyptian with a spear, while Benaiah had only a staff, but by his courage and the spirit that was in him he managed to take the spear out of the Egyptian's hand and destroy him with his own weapon. But all these struggles were in the hot excitement of personal human combat and did not involve the determination required to go down into a pit and meet a lion face to face. Many a man who would fight a lion out in the open, where there would be a possible way of escape or a chance to get help if overmatched, would not go down alone into a pit to such a conflict. Many another man who would fight a lion on a bright sunshiny morning would want to be excused in a time of snow, when it was cold and chilly. But Benaiah seemed to have felt that the best time to fight a lion is when you can get at him, and so on that cold, snowy morning when he heard the lion roar he went down and slew him.

The devil is always trying to make men believe that some other time there will be a better opportunity than now to overcome the enemy of their souls, who goes about "like a roaring lion, seeking whom he may devour." And so men get into the habit of putting off the fight until they get settled down into evil ways. The brave, manly way is to live up to the light we have, and when we find out the sin that besets us to go straight for it in God's name and kill it. The fact is if we do not slay our sin it will slay us. It must be a fight to the death. Benaiah knew when he went down into the pit that day that down there in the snow one of them had to die; either his own blood or the lion's would redden the white snow that morning. And so it is with you. If you do not slay the lion that confronts you it will overcome and destroy you; but if with courageous front you face your enemy in the strength of Christ you will find that you are more than a match for him and that he will give way in terror.

A poor bagpiper in a European village had been playing at an evening's performance, and his friendly employers presented him with a basket of food in addition to his wages. His way home lay across a broad heath, and when he had reached the middle of it a wolf, scenting from a distance the provisions in the poor fellow's basket, rapidly and furiously approached him. The man's terror did not deprive him of his presence of mind, and he quickly took out a large piece of meat and threw it to the animal, which as he expected, stopped to devour it. Meanwhile, he fled with his utmost speed; but the wolf with invigorated appetite followed rapidly the weak, almost fainting, and breathless fugitive. Finding that the fierce beast was quickly gaining ground upon him, he next drew out a good-sized cake from his little store and threw it in the animal's way as he again approached. His voracious foe, having paused as before to gorge the dainty offering, again pursued. A small fish was all that remained in the basket. As the wolf drew near for the third time the miserable man drew forth with a heavy heart and cast it to his greedy and savage enemy, and again he renewed his fight with ever-increasing speed, for his hope now lay in his safe arrival home, as the goal was almost gained. But the wolf was again at his heels, and as nothing remained to secure its further delay he was overcome with alarm, and saw no chance of escape. He was about to resign himself to his fate when, casting a last despairing glance at his old faithful companion, the bagpipes, a happy idea struck him, and as a last effort he hugged the instrument and blew a most sonorous blast; when lo! The affrighted wolf, tucking his tail between his legs, scampered off with the speed of the wind. "Ah, you vagabond thief," cried the piper, "if I had thought of that skirl o' the pipes would ha' contented ye I would ha' saved my meat, my cake, and my fish!"

How many men and women pursued by wolfish sins and lusts fling out to them here and there along the path of life all the sweetest joys of the soul? Peace, quietness of conscience, and possibility of communion with God, the sweet assurances of a home in heaven – all these are flung away to the vicious beast, which only pursues them the more relentlessly; but whenever a man, driven desperate or grown wise, turns on his enemy with a blast of prayer or song, sounding the trumpet of the Gospel of Jesus Christ, his enemy is gone in a moment. He realizes then the truth of what James said, "Resist the devil, and he will flee from you" (James 4:7).

Benaiah went alone to his struggle; but you need not go alone, for Jesus Christ your Savior has fought the great battle for you, and if you will go in his strength you shall have his precious fellowship all the while. Some hesitate about becoming Christians because at the doorway there are repentance and self-denial and struggle. They fail to appreciate that beyond the self-denial and the struggle are the glorious victory and the noble peace. Benaiah could not have safety from the lion nor the sense of victory over him unless he first killed him. The danger, the fierce struggle, must come first. But afterward it was safety and victory.

Henry Ward Beecher used to say that if he should speak of a garden only as "a place fenced in" you would have no idea of his clusters of roses and pyramids of honeysuckles and beds of odorous flowers and rows of blossoming shrubs and fruit-bearing trees. And if we should say of a cathedral, "It is built of stone, cold stone," what its gorgeous openings for door and window and its noble spire? So if you regard religion as a matter of repentance and self-denial only you stop at the fence and see nothing of the beauty of the garden; you think only of the stones and forget the marvelous beauty into which it is fashioned.

Christ calls upon every one of us to come out openly in fight against our sins, pledging ourselves to be his friend and soldier. Strange that people should so often hesitate at that vital point. You say to me, "I know that my sin is wrong; I know that it is right to be a Christian; I feel sure that every motive referring to my own happiness or to the gratitude which I owe to God and to Christ my Savior would leave me to make and open confession of Christ; but I hesitate at making so public a profession." But is it not noble and brave and manly to make a public profession that stands for right? When Abraham Lincoln felt that the time had come to issue the proclamation emancipating the salves he called his cabinet together. He told them that the time for all doubt and hesitation had passed, and the time had come to announce emancipation as the declared policy of the government. Then in a low and reverent voice the great Lincoln added, "And I have promised my God that I will do it." The Secretary of the Treasury, Salmon P. Chase, who sat near Mr. Lincoln, heard but indistinctly the low-voiced utterance, and inquired, "Did I understand you correctly, Mr. President?" Then speaking louder, so that all might hear, Abraham Lincoln replied, "I made a solemn vow before God that if General Lee should be driven back from Pennsylvania I would crown the result by the declaration of freedom to the slaves." The great man was not ashamed to commit himself to do what he felt to be right. So I beg of you that you rise up to the dignity of your manhood and your womanhood and publicly renounce your sin and confess Christ as your Savior. Do not be kept back by any difficulties in the way. Jesus invites you, and he will bring you off more than conqueror through his great love.

Dr. F. D. Power relates how in a time of spiritual awakening in a certain town the foreman of a factory became anxious about his soul. They pointed him to Christ as the sinner's only refuge, but he still halted. At length his employer wrote a note, asking to see him at six o'clock, when he left his work for the day. He came promptly, holding the letter in his hand.

"Do you wish to see me, James?" asked his employer.

He was astonished and held up the letter.

"O I see you believe I wanted to see you, and when I sent you the message you came at once."

"Surely, sir," said James.

"Well, see; here is a letter sent you by one equally in earnest," said his employer, holding up a slip of paper.

The man took it, and read slowly, "'Come-unto-me-all-ye-that-labor.'" His lips quivered, his eyes filled; choked with emotion, he asked, "Am I just to believe that, in the same way I believed your letter?"

"Just the same way," was the answer. "If you receive the witness of men, the witness of God is greater."

Take Christ at his word now, no matter what difficulties stand in the way, no matter how hard the battle looks beforehand. Accept Christ's invitation and come to him. He will give you victory, and you shall have peace.

20

GOD'S RAVENS

"And the word of the LORD came unto him, saying,
Get thee hence, and turn thee eastward, and hide thyself
by the brook Cherith, that is before Jordan. And it shall be,
that thou shalt drink of the brook; and I have commanded
the ravens to feed thee there" (1 Kings 17:2-4).

When wicked men govern the people have a hard time. Israel in the hand of Ahab was bad enough; but Israel in the hand of Ahab, after Ahab had become a puppet in the hand of Jezebel, was worse yet. Many a bad man is held back from being his worst because he has a good wife; it is hard on the wife, but better for the people over whom he may have authority. But Ahab was bad from the beginning, and when he went courting he seemed to want to show the greatest disrespect and defiance of God that it was possible for him to do, and went to the court of Ethbaal, king of the Zidonians, who was a fierce worshiper of the idol Baal. Ethbaal had a notorious daughter named Jezebel. She was a fascinating young woman, but utterly unscrupulous, and also a zealous worshiper of Baal. She would have nothing to do with Ahab, king though he was, unless he forsook is religion and became a worshiper of idols.

Ahab, however, had no religion except in form, and he threw that off at her demand, and they were married. Ahab was weak and mean, and Jezebel was mean and strong. Both were bad at heart, but Jezebel was much the stronger character and held the whip hand.

Under the influence of such a court things naturally went from bad to worse in Israel. Idol worship was encouraged on all sides. Ahab built altars to Baal, and the people groveled in wickedness. The historian of that day says that "Ahab did more to provoke the Lord God of Israel to anger than all the kings of Israel that were before him" (1 Kings 16:33)—and that is saying a good deal.

Ahab and Jezebel lived in an ivory palace and made great display of wealth. The priests of Baal were arrayed in gorgeous vestments, and the scenes of worship in the idol groves were surrounded with all the glory of military splendor. Every voice seemed to be hushed and silenced except the voices of the courtiers, who applauded anything the king did, no matter how wicked it was.

But have you never noticed in the summer, when all is stillness, that up in the mountains, or out over the lake or the ocean, a thunderstorm will be brewing that will suddenly burst into the midst of the most quiet day and fill all the sky with its blackness and shake the earth with its thunder? So it was in the days of Ahab. There was a young man watching all this wickedness from a distance—a big, strong, broad-shouldered young countryman, who feared God, the true God, and was devoted to his service. He watched this wickedness with a troubled heart and with great indignation. He prayed to God day after day to interfere and save his native land from the utter ruin into which the wicked king and queen were leading it.

At last God sent him as his messenger to the court of
Ahab. I see him as he comes down from the hills. He is a
man accustomed to the outdoors and the desert, broad-
shouldered, with a great shock of black hair, having a huge
garment of sheepskins girt about him and carrying a great
staff with which he walked. As he came striding into the
town, and went onward toward the grove of Baal where the
royal worshipers were gathered, many a young dandy of a
courtier and many a young beauty of the higher class cast
a look of scorn at this rude sunburned man from the
desert. But little did Elijah care what they thought or what
they said. He had a mission from God, the God who made
heaven and earth, and he had only one thought, and that
was to fulfill this mission. On he strode, and I imagine the
little street boys gathered about and ran to keep up to see
what this strange man from the hills meant.

Suddenly he burst upon the royal assembly. Before anybody could interfere he took his stand before Ahab and
Jezebel as they sat in their magnificence, and with flashing
eyes he lifted his sunburned face to the king and said: "As
the Lord God of Israel liveth, before who I stand, there
shall not be dew nor rain these years, but according to my
word" (1 Kings 17:1). And then, while everybody is excited
and astonished, and Ahab sits with whitened cheek and
jaw dropped down from fright, with Jezebel startled and
angry, but confused, the man turns and is gone. Before anybody has wit enough to try to stop him he has disappeared
as completely as if the earth had opened and swallowed
him up.

It had been a brave and splendid thing to do, and yet
Elijah had done it simply and naturally, because he was

supremely conscious that he was God's man, and that whether it pleased the king or not he must do the will of God. God was more real to Elijah than was Ahab. That is the secret of great courage. If you want to be free from the slavery of little things and have the courage to overcome all mean cowardice, then you must give yourself completely to do the will of God. The man who is with all his heart the servant of God will not fear the face of man. Some of you fear to become Christians lest you fall out by the way through the sneers or the opposition of wicked associations or friends; but this man-fearing spirit will disappear when, like Elijah, you can say that you stand daily in the presence of the living God.

Now, the God who called this man to go on his mission always takes care of his messengers when they obey him, and so the Lord said to Elijah, "Get thee hence, and turn thee eastward, and hide thyself by the brook Cherith, that is before Jordan. And it shall be, that thou shalt drink of the brook; and I have commanded the ravens to feed these there" (1 Kings 17:3, 4). I want you to note that God's ravens already had their orders. God had made full preparation to care for his prophet. It reminds me of what David says in one of the psalms concerning the goodness which the Lord has laid up for those that do his will. All along the way of life, if we are doing our duty, we may be sure that God has given orders ahead that things shall work together for our good. But we can make no such claim unless we are doing our duty. The path of duty is the guarded path along which angels are stationed as sentinels and to which ravens have their orders to bring food to God's faithful servants.

Now, Elijah believed God, and so he at once started to the brook Cherith exactly as the Lord had commanded, and the ravens brought him bread and flesh in the morning, and bread and flesh in the evening; and he drank of the brook. I want you to take notice that God feeds his people well. Prisoners are sometimes fed on bread and water, but God gives his people a meat breakfast as well as a meat supper. You never saw a man yet who was doing his whole duty as a Christian, for whom there was only one great question—"How can I order my life so as to please God, and do the very best of my ability the work he has for me?"—you never saw a man like that who went poorly fed. Such people always bear testimony that God is a good provider. He may feed them in unusual ways, but he feeds them well. Krummacher, in his life of Elijah, says: "Who else was it but the God of Elijah who delivered a poor man out of his distress, not, indeed, by a raven, but by a singing bird? The man was sitting early in the morning at his own house door, his heart heavy and his eyes filled with tears, for he was expecting that day an officer to come and distrain him for a small debt. While sitting there a little bird flew through the streets, fluttering up and down as if in distress; then suddenly it flew in at the good man's door and perched itself on an empty cupboard. The good man closed the door, caught the bird, and set it in a cage. Presently someone came and knocked at the door. 'It is the officer,' thought the man, in great fear. Timidly he opened the door; there stood the servant of a lady who lived near, asking if he had seen a bird fly into his house. At once the man gave up the bird, and it was carried away. A few minutes afterward the servant returned, bring the message, 'My mistress sets a great value upon this, and is much obliged to you, and she requests you to accept this with her thanks.' There was put into his hand the very amount that he owed; and the good man sang to the God of Elijah a sweeter note than the bird."

Hepworth Dixon, in a book entitled *Her Majesty's Tower*, tells an interesting story of Sir Henry Wyatt, who was once wrongfully imprisoned in that famous jail. He was shut into a cold and narrow room, where he had neither bed to lie on nor clothes sufficient to warm him nor food enough to sustain life. Wyatt left a little account in his private papers, in which he declares that he would have starved there had not God, who had sent a crow to feed his prophet, sent to him a cat both to feed and warm him. While he was waiting there in hunger and cold one gloomy day a cat came down into the dungeon to him, and purred and rubbed herself against his knee in great friendship, as though she was offering herself as a companion in his loneliness. He was very grateful to the cat, laid her in his bosom to warm him, and by making much of her won her love. After this she would come every day to him through a little opening in the upper part of the tower far beyond his reach, and when she could get one would bring him a pigeon. He complained to his keeper of his cold and short fare, but the keeper assured him that he was only obeying orders and dared not give him any better. "But," said Sir Henry, "if I can provide any wilt thou promise to dress it for me?" The keeper had no idea he would be able to provide anything, and so he good-humoredly answered: "I many well enough. You are safe for that matter." But upon being urged again he promised and kept his promise, and cooked for him from time to time such pigeons as the cat provided for him. Sir Henry Wyatt afterward, in his prosperous days, always made much of cats, and there is not a picture of him anywhere but with a cat beside him. The knight with his faithful cat, pigeon in paw, is one of the interesting pictures in the South Kensington Gallery of Portraits.

Many of you who hear me could tell stories out of your own experience which have just as clearly marked the care and love of the God of Elijah in your behalf as these which I have related. Every true Christian who commits his way unto the Lord and does his duty prayerfully day by day is able to sing with David, "Thou preparest a table before me in the presence of mine enemies: thou anointest my head with oil; my cup runneth over" (Psalm 23:5).

What an infinite mercy it is that I may come to you who are sinners against God, and who are conscious that you merit only condemnation for your past conduct toward him, and invite you to be reconciled to God, and promise you the forgiveness of your sins if you will repent of them and ask pardon in the name of Jesus your Saviour. The God who fed Elijah, and who cares for the hunger of the bodies of his people, cares still more for the hunger of the soul. Christ says, "Blessed are they which do hunger and thirst after righteousness: for they shall be filled" (Matthew 5:6). Think of it!—filled with righteousness. You who have been dogged by your besetting sins, and have tried to do right and failed again and again, bring your hungry souls to the mercy seat and let their hunger cry out before God. He will feed you with the spirit of uprightness, and you shall have a meal that will make you strong to do right.

Why should you go hungry and restless in spirit when God is so willing to feed you, and has made such abundant provisions for it? In the square in Venice lying in front of St. Mark's Cathedral, when the clock strikes twelve at noon, "the doves of St. Mark" gather in great flocks from all parts of the city and settle down in the square to be fed. And this is the story they tell about it: A generous woman passing one noonday across the square saw some birds shivering in the cold, and having some bread with her, she scattered some crumbs among them. The next day, at the same hour, she scattered some more bread among them, and it grew to be a custom with her which continued for many years, until she died. But she did not forget her birds, even as death approached, for she provided in her will that a certain amount of money should be set apart, the income of which should be used to keep up the same practice; and now, at the first stroke of the bell at noon, the birds begin to come there, and when the clock has struck twelve the square is full of them, and they are never disappointed. Jesus Christ gave his life upon the cross to provide for our salvation. He is the Bread of Life, sufficient to feed every poor hungry soul on earth; and the more hungry you are, the more pressing is your need, the more hungry you feel yourself to be, the more certain the feast. The doves of St. Mark are only certain of being fed at noon, but it is always high noon at the mercy seat. Whenever a poor sinner, hungry for pardon and rest and peace, come to the mercy seat, bowing low at the cross in repentance and faith, Christ is there to feed the soul; not scantily, not barely enough, but with a great feast of pardon and forgiving love that causes the soul to overflow with joy and gladness.

21

THE CONVERSION OF A MAJOR GENERAL

"And he returned to the man of God, he and all his
company, and came and stood before him: and he said,
Behold, now I know that there is no God in all the earth,
but in Israel: now therefore, I pray thee,
take a blessing of thy servant" (2 Kings 5:15).

Naaman was the most popular man in Syria. He was the great general of the country. There is no hero like the military hero to seize the imagination of the multitude, especially when the country is constantly beset with enemies. We have just seen something of it in our own country. A man who was a physician with the rank of captain three years ago, through a chance to show the heroic metal that was in him in the Spanish-American War, is now governor-general of Cuba, a brigadier general in the regular army, and if he survives a few years will be at the head of the United States army. And the people look on and rejoice at these honors. Across the sea our British cousins have recently been heaping their honors on Lord Roberts for his victories in South Africa, and wherever he appears he is a lion of the hour. It was something like that with Naaman. In a great war, when the existence of his country was seemingly at stake, Naaman had risen to the occasion and had proved himself to be a great general. So great was his victory that he was called "the deliverer" of his native land. The king and all the people honored him.

And yet I presume Naaman was one of the most unhappy men in all Syria. It is one of the sad thoughts that give us pause as we walk up and down the street to know that back of many a face which is like a mask there is raging a tumult of passion or grief, or a heart that is sinking in despair, though the bold front gives no indication of it. We learn to know that behind the doors of many a mansion of wealth there is hidden in the closet a skeleton whose grisly presence robs every feast of its joy and banishes comfort from every heart dwelling within those splendid walls. So Naaman, honored by the king, honored by the people, living splendidly, going forth surrounded with a guard of honor whenever he appeared, was yet a broken and a grieving man because "he was a leper." The most deadly disease known to mankind had laid its hand on him; there was no hope of cure; there was only a looking forward to loathsome death. And ever and anon, in spite of his efforts to throw it off and forget it, that horrible specter would force itself on Naaman's attention.

Well, when things get at their worst something happens. How often it is that God interfere in our behalf just at the place where help seems impossible! The sunlight came into the darkened chamber of Naaman's life by a very interesting chain of circumstances. A roving detachment of the Syrian army, a small band of scouts, had captured a little girl from among the people of Israel. She was a little slip of a thing, but she was bright and intelligent, and though she was a captive there was so much spirit and cheer about her that Mrs. Naaman took a great fancy to her, and concluded she would like to have her for her own maid. Naturally, that brought her into very intimate association with the wife of the great general. Some girls in her case would have been so utterly beaten down at the sad plight in which they found themselves that they would have been of no good to anybody; but this little maid plucked up her courage, and, though a prisoner in an enemy's country, thanked God it was no worse, and tried to make the place where she was a sweeter place to live in because she was there. How much wiser that is than to give ourselves up to despondency because things have gone harshly with us! No matter how hard the place in which we find ourselves there are always two ways open to us. One of them is to mediate and muse on our own misery, refuse to look on anything hopeful, and make ourselves a weight rather than a help to everybody that comes in contact with us. The other way is the way of this little girl who was Mrs. Naaman's maid—to say to ourselves: "True, things have gone wrong; I am a captive to circumstances that are very uncomfortable, but I cannot make it any better by grieving over it and giving up to gloom. It is God's world yet; he means good to me, and the best thing I can do is to look on the bright side of things and try to gladden everyone I meet by my good cheer. Whether I stay here for a long or short time, it will be better if I make it helpful and pleasant to those who are about me." Such people are always a benediction wherever they go.

So one day the little maid from Israel looked up with a quick flash of sympathy in her eyes when General Naaman went out and left them alone, and said to her mistress in the quaint language of the time, "Would God my lord were with the prophet that is in Samaria! for he would recover him of his leprosy" (2 Kings 5:3).

That night when Naaman came home his wife said to him, "My little girl that I picked out from among those captives is an Israelite, and, do you know, she said a strange thing today."

"What was that?" grunted the old officer, thinking about the affairs of the day more than the gossip of his wife's sitting room.

"Why, after you went out today she seemed to be troubled about your affliction and she said to me that she wished you could see the prophet in Samaria, for he has power to recover people even from leprosy."

But poor Naaman had no faith in it, and as he went to bed he said to his wife: "The silly child no doubt thinks her prophet can do a good deal more than he can perform. There is only one cure for leprosy, and that is death." The old man turned over with a sigh and tried to seek refuge in sleep. But he did not sleep well, and again and again the remark of the little maiden came back to him.

The next day when he was having an audience with the king, Naaman referred to the little girl's remark, and the king's attention was at once caught by it. Naaman was very important to him; he did not know how they ever were going to get along without him, and he wished his favorite general might be cured. So the king at once said: "We can't afford to let any chance go by. The little girl may be right. You get ready, and I will write a letter to the king of Israel, which to take to him, and we will see if there is anything in it."

So General Naaman got ready. He took with him a large sum in silver and gold, and splendid garments, which were in those days often used in the place of money. And he made the journey, ending up at the palace of the king of Israel, to whom he brought the letter of the king of Syria. Now, when the king of Israel read this letter he was alarmed. "He rent his clothes and said, Am I God, to kill and to make alive, that this man doth send unto me to recover a man of his leprosy? Wherefore consider, I pray you, and see how he seeketh a quarrel against me" (2 Kings 5:7).

Somebody from the palace went to Elisha, the man of God, and told him about it. Then Elisha sent a message to the king in which he said: "Wherefore hast thou rent thy clothes? Let him come now to me, and he shall know that there is a prophet in Israel" (2 Kings 5:8).

The king was greatly relieved when he got that message, and hurried Naaman away to the prophet. So in his splendid chariot drawn by beautiful horses, and with a great retinue, as befitted a general, Naaman drew up at the prophet's humble door. Pretty soon a man came out with the message, "Go and wash in the Jordan seven times, and thy flesh shall come again to thee, and thou shalt be clean" (2 Kings 5:10).

Military men are not famous for having patience and easy tempers, and Naaman was no exception to the rule. He was red-hot in a moment. He had expected some dramatic performance. He imagined the prophet would come down and stand over him, with something in his presence to indicate supernatural power, and strike his hands over the leprous spots and make them well again. But to send out a messenger with what seemed to him an insulting message like that was more than he could stand. He drove away swearing he had had enough of Israel. "Fools! do they think I am so dirty that the rivers of my own land cannot wash me clean, that I need to come over here and wash in Jordan? I'll get out of this town as quick as possible"—and away he drove.

When the first halt came, however, some of his servants who had been with him a great while and loved him much reasoned with him about it. They said to him: "Pardon us for intruding on you our thoughts, but it seems to us you are not acting with your usual wisdom in this matter. We are sure that if the prophet had told you to do some very hard thing, such as going on a long journey to bathe in some spring in some distant mountains, or if he had told you to go back home and get many times as much money as you bought, or to take some miserable medicine that would have been agonizing to use, you would have submitted to it at once, so great is your desire to be healed. Why not try it all the more because it is simple and easy? It will not hurt you to go down and bathe in the Jordan, even if it does no good, and if it should turn out true, what a glorious thing it would be to go home strong and well again!"

As Naaman's anger cooled he saw that these men were talking good, solid sense, and so he ordered the driver to turn around and go back to the Jordan. When an impulsive, high-strung man like Naaman really starts to do a thing he does it well. So he went down into the Jordan and dipped himself seven times, very carefully, according to the saying of the man of God, and as he came up out of the water the seventh time his heart leaped, and then almost stood still for joy, for lo! every leprous spot was gone; his

flesh was soft as a child's, and he felt the thrill of new
health and strength coursing through his veins.

Naaman was not only healed of his leprosy at that moment, but he was at once convinced that the prophet was
indeed a man of God, and that it was divine power which
had healed him. He saw that his gods at home must be all
false gods. He was not only healed in body, but he was converted in his heart's love and adoration to the God of Elisha. He drove back at once to where Elisha lived. He did
not wait for the prophet to come out to him; he went in to
the prophet. All his pride and self-will were gone. And he
took all his company with him as witnesses, and as he
stood before Elisha he said, "Behold, now I know that there
is no God in all the earth, but in Israel: now therefore, I
pray thee, take a blessing of thy servant" (2 Kings 5:15). Elisha would not have his money, but he went away declaring
that even though he was compelled as an officer to attend
the king in the worship of false gods his heart would ever
worship the true God.

I am sure this story ought to be the message of salvation
to some of you who hear it. You have been smitten with the
leprosy of sin. Its spots of defilement are upon you. Ever
and anon you are forced to confess it. Your conscience rises
up to condemn you, and you hear God's word with trembling when it so steadily declares, "The wages of sin in
death" (Romans 6:23). There has never been discovered a
way that a man can get rid of his sins except through divine
help. If you were to succeed in making money up to the
wildest dreams you have ever cherished it would not relieve
you of the burden of one sin. If you were to win a position,
and achieve honor and power beyond your highest ambi-

tions, it would not purge your guilty conscience of one single sin. Neither wealth nor power nor education can save a man from his sins. "There is none other name under heaven given among men, whereby we must be saved" (Acts 4:12), but the name of Jesus Christ. The power that was exerted to make the water of Jordan work healing to Naaman will be exercised again if you will obey the Lord Jesus Christ. If you will confess your sins, and forsake them, with faith in Jesus, the power of Almighty God will blot out your transgressions, cleanse your heart of evil, give you new hopes and purposes, and make you fresh and strong again to live a pure life.

Do not be so unwise as to do what Naaman was tempted to do—turn away from God's message because it seems so simple. Rather all the more take hold upon salvation because it is within your reach.

Salvation is within your reach, but you must act first. There is abundant provision through Jesus Christ for the forgiveness of your sins, but as Naaman could not have his cure without obedience to the message from the prophet, so you cannot find salvation except through obedience to Jesus Christ. Will you obey him tonight? God help you!

Chapter 22

THE HORSES AND THE CHARIOTS OF THE SUN

"And he took away the horses that the kings of Judah had given to the sun, at the entering in of the house of the Lord, by the chamber of Nathan-melech the chamberlain, which was in the suburbs, and burned the chariots of the sun with fire"
(2 Kings 23:11).

Chrysostom, speaking of the zeal of Peter, said that he was like a man made all of fire walking among stubble. Josiah was like that. He was at once a king and an earnest and good man who feared God and sought with all his power to purify his kingdom. As England through the long reign of Queen Victoria has had the benign and wholesome influence of a good queen whose life has been pure and noble, so for thirty-one years the Jewish people had the example of a king who "did that which was right in the sight of the Lord,…and turned not aside to the right hand or to the left" (2 Kings 22:2).

His land was honeycombed with idolatry, and Josiah sought to crush it out. Among other evidences of their degradation he found, just at the entering in of the house of the Lord, a stable kept for an idolatrous use; the horses that were kept there being holy horses, given to the sun. Old Matthew Henry says scornfully, "As if he needed them, who rejoiceth as a strong man to run a race!" Some say that these horses were led forth in pomp every morning to meet the rising sun; others that the worshipers of the sun rode out upon them to adore the rising sun. It would seem more probable that they drew the chariots of the sun, which the people in their vanity and wickedness worshiped.

Now, Josiah, in undertaking to destroy this idolatry among the people, rightly believed that it was important to take away everything upon which the imagination of the people centered. And so he took away these horses of the sun, and took the chariots of the sun and burned them with fire, leaving nothing to remind the worshipers of their idolatry. Here we have suggested a very important truth— that sin has its great fortress in the imagination. Men first begin to sin in the imagination. That is the way the serpent caught Eve. He declared to her that if she ate of the forbidden fruit she would become wise like a god, and great realms of interesting and wonderful knowledge would be opened to her. Her imagination ran riot. She had not cared about the forbidden fruit before, but now as she looked at it she began to long for it, and it seemed more desirable than anything else. If she had gone away about her business, and sent the serpent away with a blow on the head, the fatal spell would have been broken; but instead of that she allowed her imagination to conjure up wonderful dreams of the delights of that strange wisdom which the devil had promised. Thus little by little that evil imagination came into power, and she was overcome and destroyed.

All sin is like that. Men and women of today are led away by the evil one in just the same way. The imagination is set at work, and there is a glamour and fascination of evil upon which the mind acts. Josiah knew that. He knew that every time those horses—no doubt the most beautiful and fleet that the wicked kings of Judah had been able to find in all the land—were driven forth in the morning to meet the sunrise, or at evening to catch the glow of the sunset, the flashing rays falling on their arched necks and reflected back from the gilded chariots, it threw a spell, a fascination, over the people who looked on; and people said: "It is a beautiful worship; it is so much more picturesque and attractive than the sober worship of God in the house of the Lord. Surely there cannot be any wrong in it when it is so beautiful and fascinating." So they were led on until they became idolaters, and their idolatry led them into brutal self-indulgence, and they gave themselves over to sins that would have horrified them when they first became fascinated by the beautiful procession of the horses and the chariots of the sun. Josiah was wise, and laid the ax at the root of the tree, when he burned the chariots of the sun with fire, and took away the horses from the gaze of the people. So I say to you, if you want to get rid of your sin you must destroy its citadel in the secret place of the imagination.

Paul says that it is the very essence of the mission of Christianity in the world to pull down evil imaginations. Sin never can be destroyed otherwise. "With the heart man believeth unto righteousness; and with the mouth confession is made unto salvation" (Romans 10:10). No mere formal renunciation of sin will ever effect the reformation of anyone. If you long to be rid of the power of sin there is just one way open, and that is to renounce your sin in your heart, to give your heart over to new tenants.

Suppose Josiah had said: "It is not a good thing for these people to see these beautiful horses driven out to meet the sun, and to look on the golden chariots, with their uniformed drivers, flashing back the sunlight. All this is a temptation to them to turn their minds away from the true God. Still, it is not a good thing to destroy property; so I will have these horses shut up, and the chariots stored away, where they will be out of sight." Would that have met the case? Would it have had the same effect on the people? No, indeed. The people would have said, "O well, this is just a little spasm of reform; Josiah has shut up the horses, and stored away the chariots; but after a little while they will be brought out again, and things will go on as before." But if he had done like that he would have acted exactly as many people act now. Perhaps some of you have been acting in that way. It has been forced home upon you that you have been breaking the law of God, and that you are under condemnation. It may be that the death of a friend, or some sudden and terrible tragedy that has come, seemingly as a judgment upon sin, to yourself or to someone else, has aroused your conscience and given you a look into the deep and dreadful depths of your own evil heart. You have been made to look at the possibilities of evil into which your sin might lead you, and as the disciples of Jesus at the last supper shuddered when told that one of them would betray the Master, so you have shuddered and drawn away and said in horror: "Am I to do a thing like that? Is my career to end in that drunkard's grave, or in that disgraced and shameful way? God forbid!" And you have turned away with a determination to make a change in your conduct; you have said to yourself, "I must do differently. I must call a halt. I am going at too rapid a pace." But while you have said that, and have meant it, too, you have really done nothing to break with your old associations, and all the old fellowships still hold their grip on the secret forces of your imagination and life. You have said, "I will not do this sin anymore," but you put nothing in its place to crowd it out and hold the fortress of your soul against it.

There is a story in the Bible of a devil who was cast out from a man's heart. And that evil spirit went up and down the earth and found no rest, and after a while he had a longing to see the old house where he had lived so long, and went back, expecting to find that his place had been taken up. In the deep recesses of his devilish heart he had no hope of getting back. He never thought of the man being so foolish as that. But when he went back, to his astonishment, the old house from which he had been driven forth was swept and garnished and fixed up for a tenant, but it was empty. Then that demon went away in ghoulish glee, and hunted up his boon companions, and got seven other devils more foul and degraded than himself, and they entered in and had a big revel and debauch, and the owner of that house and that heart was worse off than ever before. Are you getting ready to reenact that sort of a story in your life? That is exactly what you are getting ready for if you are comforting yourself with the fact that you have made good resolutions not to give way again to your besetting sin, and that for a week, or a month, or even a year, you have kept the door barred against it. I assure you that there is only one way by which you can really overcome the enemy of your soul, and that is by breaking with your sin forever and giving your heart over to Christ and righteousness. Josiah burned the chariots of the sun in the most public way possible. Everybody knew the testimony of the king against this vile idolatry. If you have determined to give up your sin I beg of you to make your confession of sin and your witness of your acceptance of Jesus Christ as public as that. Christ asks this of you because there is no real chance of salvation without a real committal of yourself to God and an open and final renunciation of your sins. The way to keep your heart a safe fortress against your sin coming back again is to invite Jesus Christ to come into your heart and live there, to sit at the head of your table, to be master of your conversation, to choose for you your associations, so that his will is supreme in all that you do. If you do that the devil of your besetting sin, when he comes back to lurk about the old place, will see a sight that will send a chill of dismay and despair to his evil heart. He will see Christ sitting by your fireside; he will hear your songs of praise to God for his infinite love and grace; he will hear your prayer to God for help, and he will see that every door is padlocked and bolted threefold strong by prayer and praise and fellowship with Jesus Christ your Saviour. There is a fortress the devil can never take.

In Christ's name I give you his loving invitation to burn everything that holds you back, destroy the wicked imaginations which are ruining you, and open your heart in welcome to the Saviour who comes with infinite gifts of salvation and forgiveness in his hands.

23

THE MAN HE MIGHT HAVE BEEN

*"And when Jesus came to the place, he looked up, and saw
him, and said unto him, Zacchaeus, make haste, and come
down; for today I must abide at thy house. And he made
haste, and came down, and received him joyfully"*
(Luke 19:5, 6).

*"But God said unto him, Thou fool, this night thy soul
shall be required of thee: then whose shall those things be,
which thou hast provided?"* (Luke 12:20).

Recently I read a very interesting story of a man getting on in years, a very sharp, shrewd business man
who had grown hard and selfish and narrow and
mean as he grew old, who was sitting at dinner after the
rest of the family had gone out for the evening. He had
made a trade that day and had gotten the long end of the
bargain by a rather shady transaction, and was congratu-
lating himself on it. As he sat nodding over a bottle of wine
at the close of dinner the servant brought him a card, and
while he fumbled for his glasses to get a look at the card
the visitor came into the dining room. The old merchant
looked up and saw the face of a man he was sure he had

known before, a face which he instinctively liked. He shook hands with him warmly, not caring to ask his name, thinking it would come to him in a moment. He took his friend into the library, and they talked of old times. The visitor knew all his family and his schoolmates, and all his early hopes and aspirations, and the old man was deeply touched as the talk went on. Finally the visitor told him that he was married to a woman whom the old merchant had himself loved in his early boyhood, but from whom he had turned in his ambition to get money rapidly. He said his wife and daughter were with him only a few blocks away, and the merchant must come with him to call on them. He did so, and spent the most delightful evening of his life. Again and again he was touched to tears in his enjoyment of the music and the conversation. He found his visitor to be a distinguished man of letters, whose honored literary pseudonym was on everybody's lips, but whose writings in his hard race for wealth he had had no time to read. When he went home in the evening his visitor accompanied him to the door, and back into the dining room where he had found him, and then took leave of him by calling his attention to the card he had given him, which bore the merchant's own name. His parting words were, "I am the man you might have been." The hard-headed business man, being suddenly aroused, found it had all been an after-dinner dream.

But it is a dream with a message. This nobler man whom the old man had so admired, and whom he felt to be so superior to himself, was the man he might have been if he had been turned aright at the critical point of his youth or young manhood. Failing then, he had taken the other path, which led to a hard, selfish, sensual old age, and surely nothing can be more terrible than that.

I have coupled Zacchaeus and the rich fool together because the rich fool shows what Zacchaeus escaped. He is the man Zacchaeus might have been at the end, if he had not met Christ and had his life transformed and changed by that divine influence. Zacchaeus was going on in the same evil way, although Zacchaeus's farm was of another sort than that of the rich fool. It was a political farm. He was a tax-gatherer, and blackmailed the men with whom he did business. He had become rich, but he found his riches did not bring him peace. His poor, hungry heart would not be fed on that kind of food, and there was a longing there that would not be satisfied.

About this time Christ came on his last journey to Jerusalem. The news spread through the town, and Zacchaeus was very anxious to see him; and being a little, short-legged fellow, he climbed up into a tree for a better view of the man the fame of whose goodness and the news of whose miracles of healing and mercy had spread through the land. As Christ drew near Zacchaeus feasted his eyes on that wonderful face. Many artists have made that face impressive on canvas, helped only by their imagination and their art; but what must it have been to see the Christ? What a privilege to look upon the face upon which sin had never cast a shadow; a face reflecting the glorious light of the countenance of God; eyes full of infinite tenderness, more compassionate than any father's, more tender than any mother's, and yet as innocent as a child's. When Zacchaeus looked into those eyes heaven seemed to have come down to earth and to stand rebuking him for all his sin, and yet inviting him to forgiveness and eternal hope.

Jesus saw his need, and responded to it at once. He had no time to spare. He was on his way to Jerusalem and to the cross. He would never be in Jericho again. He would only have time to stop there for dinner, and then go on. His only chance to lift Zacchaeus out of the mire and the clay of his worldly, corrupt life was that hour. So Jesus said, "Zacchaeus, make haste, and come down; for today I must abide at thy house" (Luke 19:5). Zacchaeus' heart was in his throat. He felt that here was the chance of a lifetime. I imagine he almost fell out of the tree, for he made haste and came down joyfully and led Jesus away home with him. We do not know what they said on the way. The people who looked on were angry. And some of the rich society folks who are ever ready to run after any newcomer who is popular and make him the lion of their dinner parties, however little they may care for his principles or his work, said, "H had gone to be guest with a man that is a sinner." But when Zacchaeus and Jesus got home, and had had their talk out, Zacchaeus stood before him and said to him, "Behold, Lord, the half of my goods I give to the poor; and if I have taken anything from any man by false accusation, I restore him fourfold" (Luke 19:8). And Jesus said unto him: "This day is salvation come to this house, forsomuch as he also is a son of Abraham. For the Son of man is come to seek and to save that which was lost" (Luke 19:9, 10). How Zacchaeus' life must have blossomed and become beautiful and gracious from that day! Perhaps in after years, when he saw some rich old man coming to the end of life, all selfish and mean and wicked and ready to hear the doom of the rich fool pronounced on him, Zacchaeus said to himself: "I had a very narrow escape from being just that kind of an old man. I was getting ready for just that sort of a miserable end. But one blessed day—ah, what a day that was!—Jesus Christ came through Jericho on his way to Jerusalem. It was his last journey; he was on his way to the cross on which he died for us all. And he came to my house and broke bread with me at my table, and his love broke my heart. He made my meanness and my dishonesty seem so horrible that I repented of my sins. Since that day a peace and a joy that I never knew before have illuminated my soul. It was Jesus Christ that saved me from living the life and dying the death of the rich fool.

This ought to raise some very serious questions in all our hearts. On what path are we traveling? If we go on to the end as we are now faced, will the end be peace or will it be disaster? A young man is now in our city jail awaiting trial and sentence for a confessed murder—a man under twenty years of age, with life utterly blighted and blasted, as an ear of corn might be smitten by the hot, poisonous breath of a simoon. There is something very suggestive in the picture of that young fellow wringing his hands and sobbing and crying out in his bitter agony, "When I left home I was an innocent boy, and now I am a murderer!" Suppose when this young fellow ran away from home and gave himself up to evil associations and sinful ways he had gone into Christian associations and been touched by influences that would have brought him to give his heart to Christ and live a life of uprightness and honor. What a different youth would be wearing his name tonight! Take the picture of any man here, twenty years of age, who loves God, who seeks to serve Jesus Christ, and who is giving faithful service somewhere for his daily bread, who has written a loving letter home to his mother this afternoon, and is looking forward to an honorable and a pure career; and then go down yonder to a jail, and in the darkness of that cell with its iron grating, where a poor, despairing youth of the same age waits with dread and horrible fear the coming doom, and take a flash light of that scene, and put them side by side, and you will see the difference that Jesus Christ and his righteousness can make in a human life.

I doubt not that within this great company of young people there are some of you who need to meet with Jesus Christ, and get an uplift out of the sin into which you are sinking, as much as did Zacchaeus or this young man who has fallen into such terrible disaster. Christ is able and willing to lend you all his strength and power, to bear you into a new life that will be full of safety and honor.

James Buckham, in the story of "Waukewa's Eagle," preserved the legend of an Indian boy who found a young eagle that was wounded. He nursed it back to strength and health, and it became as strong as ever and flew away into the great abyss of the sky. But that young Indian boy found a year later that his kindness had been a good investment. It was the salmon season, and Waukewa was enjoying to its full the sport of spearing the silver-sided fish. One glittering salmon after another he threw into his bark canoe. So absorbed in the sport was he that he did not notice when the head of the rapids was reached and the canoe began to glide more swiftly among the rocks. But suddenly he looked up, caught his paddle, and dipped it wildly into the swirling water. The canoe swung sidewise, shivered, held its own against the torrent, and then slowly, inch by inch, began to creep upstream toward the shore. But suddenly there was a load, cruel snap, and the paddle parted in the boy's hand, broken just above the blade! Waukewa gave a cry of despairing agony. Then he bent to the gunwale of his canoe and with the shattered blade fought desperately against the current. But it was useless. The racing torrent swept him downward; the hungry falls roared tauntingly in his ears. But suddenly a shadow fell across the canoe. Waukewa lifted his eyes and saw a great eagle hovering over, with dangling legs and a spread of wings which blotted out the sun. Once more the eyes of the Indian boy and the eagle met, and now it was the eagle who was the master! With a glad cry the Indian boy stood up in his canoe, and the eagle hovered lower. Now the canoe tossed on that great swelling wave which climbs to the cataract's edge, and the boy lifted his hands and caught the legs of the eagle. The next moment he looked down into the awful gulf of waters to its very verge. The canoe was snatched from beneath him, and plunged down the black wall of the cataract, but he and the struggling eagle were floating outward and downward through the cloud of mist. The cataract roared terribly, like a wild beast robbed of its prey; the spray beat and blinded, the air rushed upward as they fell. But the eagle struggled on with its burden. He fought his way out of the mist and the flying spray. His great wings threshed the air with a whistling sound. Down, down they sank, the boy and the eagle, but ever farther from the precipice of water and the boiling whirlpool below. At length, with a fluttering plunge, the eagle dropped on a sand bar below the whirlpool, and he and the Indian boy lay there a minute, breathless and exhausted. Then the eagle slowly lifted himself, took the air under his free wings and soared away, while the Indian boy knelt on the sand, his shining eyes following the great bird till he faded into the gray of the cliffs.

That may be only a legend, but all it suggests is more than realized by every young man who, caught in the current of evil and being swept ever nearer the cataract of ruin, will reach out his hand to Jesus Christ as his Saviour. He will not only bear you up and away from danger, but he will remain with you through life, be your comforter, your friend, your counselor, and share with you the burdens of life. In his divine friendship you will find that life's hardest yoke is easy and its heaviest burden light.

I beg you to note that the suggestion of the importance of the immediate acceptance of divine mercy. If Zacchaeus had put Christ off until some other day salvation never would have come to his house. It was that day, or not at all; and no one of us has wisdom to know whether still other opportunities will come to anyone here. This much we know, that "Today is the day of salvation." You may come now. Another time is not necessary, for this is all-sufficient. O I would that Jesus Christ would come walking into the chamber of your heart tonight, and that with the eye of your soul you might look down into those wondrous eyes of the Saviour and hear him saying to you, as he said to Zacchaeus, "Come, I must abide today at thy house" (Luke 19:5). And if you do hear that voice I beg of you to have the wisdom of Zacchaeus and respond at once to the divine call. Come joyfully, hearkening unto what Christ has to say to your soul.

24

A BRIGHT MAN WHO NEEDED MAKING OVER

"Jesus answered and said unto him, Verily, verily, I say unto thee, Except a man be born again, he cannot see the kingdom of God" (John 3:3).

Nicodemus was a bright man and a man of good social standing and high political position among his people. He was more than that, for he had a desire to be a good man. I suppose there are a good many politicians who have more such desires than they get credit for. Down deep in the human heart God speaks to men again and again. No man ever goes in silence to disaster without having had warning upon warning of danger. God hangs many a signal lantern along the road of the evildoer to warn him back from the dangerous path.

Nicodemus was a high-toned man in every way. He was a man of thought and seriousness, and when Christ came he had taken a great deal of interest in his work and had seen enough of it to make him believe that Christ was a teacher come from God and that more than mortal power attended him. In the daytime the people thronged about

Christ, and there was very little opportunity for quiet conversation. So one evening Nicodemus sought out Jesus for a good talk. He began by stating his own idea of Christ. He did this in the most complimentary way, and we are a little surprised at first that Christ responds with a direct statement regarding his own personal need of being born anew. But we have only a part of the conversation, and we do not know how much that John regarded as merely introductory is omitted. No doubt Nicodemus followed his complimentary remarks concerning Christ with some sort of inquiry as to the conditions of salvation. And John, regarding the answer of Jesus as the most important part of the conversation, begins with that. In the most solemn manner Christ makes the strong declaration, "Verily, verily, I say unto thee, Except a man be born again, he cannot see the kingdom of God" (John 3:3). There is no doubt that Christ meant Nicodemus himself in this case, and Nicodemus evidently understood the statement to be personal. A man may have a well-cultivated head and heart which has been refined and influenced by his youthful training and education, and yet need to be "born again" in the purpose of his living. Christ saw this great need in Nicodemus. Lest there be some mistake about it, he repeated it during the talk: "Ye must be born again!" Nicodemus had no power in himself to bring about this great transformation, but there was power in Christ. Jesus was able to bring that wind of the divine Spirit which would carry away every evil thought and purpose and renew the soul with a new life, rescue it from all its old perils and slaveries, and start it forth upon a new voyage of existence.

I am sure that I speak to some this very hour who recognize that that is your own need. You need to catch a new zest, a new appetite for goodness. You have fallen into a rut of selfishness or of some besetting sin, and you need the power not only to get out of the rut, not only to cease to do evil, but you need to be renewed in your soul, so that you shall be able to enjoy what Goldsmith calls "the luxury of doing good."

Not long ago a great storm raged in the harbor of Marseilles, France. A passenger steamer had been driven on to a bar by the tremendous fury of the waves. The ship was threatened with destruction. Many deeds of heroism were performed in determined efforts to make some connection between the shore and the threatened vessel. But in all the harbor there was not a craft equal to such an emergency. There were tugs there that could weather an ordinary storm, but they could not live in such a sea as beat upon the apparently doomed ship. Finally, there came an admiralty tug from Toulon, a boat which had been built for this very sort of thing, and the rescue was soon accomplished. So there are men and women who have been stranded by the raging waves of appetite and passion, and unless they can soon be gotten off the reefs they will be only ruined hulks, poor wreckages of men and women. One of the most pitiable things in life is to see the efforts made from a worldly standpoint to rescue people from the damaging results of their sins. The philosophies and educational systems of men are not equal to the emergency. But there is one who is equal to it. Across the darkness, cutting the waves, is a strong Swimmer. The Lord Jesus Christ is equal to the occasion. He is able to come to the stranded soul and bid a man hope again. He who put hope into the heart of Nicodemus, and sent Mary Magdalene away with a comforted soul, is equal to the emergencies of men and women today.

Christ promises, if we will yield our hearts to him, a complete and perfect rescue. It is not a mere promise that men may be able to live a little better than they have been living, but there is the great and splendid assurance that Christ will so transform our hearts that we may absolutely cease to sin, and sin shall lose all its power over us, and we shall do that which is right. This wonderful figure of the new birth used in this story is no stronger than many other figures used in the New Testament to assure our hearts concerning the absolute transformation of the soul which God promises to us if we fully accept this salvation in Jesus Christ. Paul says in one place that through Christ we may become dead unto sin, but alive unto God. What a strong figure that is! If a man is dead to a thing it can have no power at all over him.

The story is told of Dr. Nathaniel Emmons, who used to be pastor of the Congregational Church in Franklin, Massachusetts, that he made an agreement with Dr. Samuel Hopkins, who was a pastor in Great Barrington, that the survivor would preach the other's funeral sermon. Soon after this arrangement was made each of them set to work to prepare the sermon in the event of his friend's decease. But the years went on, and the manuscripts accumulated dust in their studies, and it looked as though neither of them would ever be used. When both were very old men they met one day and recalled the arrangement of their early manhood, and concluded to meet and read over their respective tributes. That must have been an interesting occasion, when the two old, white-haired men sat down to read the eloquent words which they had prepared in early life as a eulogy upon each other's lifework. One of them— we are not informed which—led off in this strange preaching match. As he proceeded with the introduction of his funeral sermon, and read out the glowing paragraphs of admiration and eulogy, his friend broke in with the exclamation, "Come, come, you are putting it too strong."

"Ah!" cried the other, "be still. You have no right to interrupt."

"No right!" cried his friend, "of course I have the right."

"Well, but do you not remember that you're dead?" said the reader of the sermon.

Dr. Meyer, who recalls the story, says this is the best illustration he has ever seen of what Paul meant when he said, "Reckon yourselves to be dead indeed unto sin" (Romans 6:11). There was the bright, witty old man, strong and hearty, listening to the words of warm affection, the generous epitaph on the consistent life and devoted ministry; but for all that he had to reckon himself to be dead. He might hear the words, but he might offer no remarks.

Now, the promise of God to us in Jesus Christ is that we may be so completely born again, renewed in our hearts, transformed in our purposes, that we shall be dead to the old sins that have hitherto had power and mastery over us. What a blessed promise! Would it not be a blessed thing, my brother, if you could be dead to that appetite for drink? Would it not be a gift from heaven if you could be dead to that dynamite-like temper of yours? Would it not be a blessed thing if you could be dead to that jealous, revengeful spirit? Would it not be a victory worth having if you could be dead to the evil lust that allures you from God and right living? Would it not be something to shout over if you could die to all these temptations to sin that have been too strong for you and have been leading you handcuffed on the way to hell, if you could be dead to them, so that you could see them, but make no answer to them? And that is just what God promises us—that if we will repent of our sins, and turn away from them, and take Jesus Christ to be our divine Lord and Saviour, he will make us anew and we shall become "new creatures in Christ Jesus." There is no case too hard for Christ to conquer.

Mr. Mullen, the evangelist, was one day driving on the South Side of Chicago when he met a tramp going the same way. He stopped him and said, "Don't you want a ride?"

"Yep" was the reply.

"Jump up here. Get in."

Turning abruptly to the tramp, he said, "Why aren't you a Christian?"

"I am a Christian. I am a Catholic."

"O I don't care what church you belong to."

While the man looked at him in astonishment softly came these words: "Don't you know that David said, 'I have not seen the righteous forsaken, nor his seed begging bread'? I you were the seed of Jesus Christ you would never have to beg bread. Why don't you be a Christian? Come now, tell me."

Tears came to the man's eyes.

When he asked the tramp if he had had any dinner he said, "No."

"Will you come with me and have some? I am going up here to my boarding house, and you can come there with me if you want to go and get a good dinner."

Upon reaching the boarding house they went into the dining room and sat down at the table, where the conversation was on Christ and how he died for sinful men. But the man, being a foreigner by birth, probably to avoid this annoying conversation, said that he could not understand very well. So a German Bible was procured at a minister's house who lived nearby. And in there, where they afterward went, the man broke down, got down on his knees, and cried before God. Neither the minister nor Mr. Mullen could understand what the man was saying, but God was dealing with him, and as verse after verse was shown him and he was told to read it the conviction deepened on his heart and conscience. Soon the man straightened up and cried out, "Light, light, light!"

"The Light of the world" had illuminated that poor, sinful heart, and from that hour he lived a new life, a transformed life, in Jesus Christ. From a tramp and a beggar he became a manly Christian man and a good citizen. The conversion of this man started a fire of revival about that boarding house, and one young man converted there is now in the missionary field, and another is an earnest and successful minister.

Brother, there is power in Jesus Christ to save your soul, power in him to blot out your sins, to renew your spirit, to create in you a clean heart, and to send you forth to a pure and noble life.

25

THE PEACE WHICH IS BORN OF LOVE

"They…began every one of them to say unto him, Lord, is it I?" (Matthew 26:22).

"He then lying on Jesus' breast saith unto him, Lord, who is it?" (John 13:25).

The differing attitudes of soul which prompted these two questions in apparent at a glance. The first question is born of uncertainty concerning one's own heart and relation to Christ. The disciples had been following Jesus for three years, all but one of them growing in their love and confidence through all that time. If you had asked any one of them anywhere if he was Christ's friend you would have had a very pronounced affirmative. You could have had a fight out of Peter any time by suggesting that there was in him the making of a traitor to his great Master. But to protest under ordinary circumstances the integrity of their devotion and love was a different thing facing the gentle but heart-searching eyes of Jesus Christ and listening to that sad and terrible sentence from him, "Verily, I say unto

you, that one of you shall betray me" (Matthew 26:21).
They knew Jesus well enough to know that he always spoke
to truth, and every word went straight to their hearts. It
brushed away any spirit of boastfulness or pride in their
own strength of character. Each man looked into his own
soul and shuddered at the possibilities of evil that might be
lurking there. They could imagine no sin so horrible as to
betray their loving and gracious Lord to his enemies, and
yet one of them was to do it. They sat there with white,
drawn faces and sorrowfully asked, one after another, "Lord,
is it I?"

Now, all this time John was sitting next to Jesus, as
usual, for the intimacy between Jesus and John was recognized by all the group of disciples to be closer than that
between Jesus and any of the others. John, with that tender
sympathy of love which the evident sadness of Christ
aroused in his heart, had laid his head on the bosom of
Jesus, and looked up into his face with unutterable love.
Poor fellow, he could not do anything else, but he could
show his love, and he could not have done anything that
would have pleased Christ more. While they were all in a
suspense that was agonizing Peter signaled John that he
should ask who it was. Everybody knew it was not John,
and John knew it himself, and therefore he was the man
to ask the question. And John lying there, with his head
on Christ's bosom, safe and secure in that warm nest of
love, sure of his standing ground with Jesus, said, "Lord,
who is it?"

Here, then, is our theme. The supreme pledge of the
heart's peace is in personal love for Christ and in the sweet
assurance that we are surrounded by the love of Christ forever. Peace is the diving gift, and can only come through

love. The apostle says, "The Lord of peace give you peace" (2 Thess. 3:16). Peace, like every other heavenly grace, is to be had as a gift. You may work yourself into worry, but you never can work yourself into peace. Jesus said to the weary and the heavy laden, "I will give you rest;" and again, to those who were troubled and sorrowful, "Peace I leave with you, my peace I give unto you" (John 14:27). You cannot buy it, you cannot be educated in it, you must receive it as a gift. An old Scotch drover once said to Robert Bruce, the famous Edinburgh preacher, "I'se gie thee twenty cows to gree God and me." But not twenty cows, nor twenty kingdoms, could purchase an agreement between you and God. Twenty universes would not be price enough. The only ransom money that will be accepted in such an agreement is "the precious blood of Christ." Christ died for us for love's sake, and the only agreement of your soul with God that can bring you peace must be on the basis of mutual love.

We are all seeking peace, and yet how far astray we go in our search. We look to the material surroundings, which can never give us anything but temporary happiness, and for the most part will not be able to do that. I am never surprised at finding a man despondent about himself and about the world who has no source of peace except in material things. It is the upward look that beholds the hills of peace.

Harry Voorhees' father was a member of Congress, and Harry often spent hours at his father's desk or on the floor of the House. One morning Mr. Voorhees remarked fretfully, "What abominable weather! I can't work; it's too gloomy and dull here."

The little boy looked at the beautiful stained glass just over his head in the colored ceiling and said, cheerfully,

"Papa, you forgot to look up. See how red and pretty it is, and so light!"

"You are right, little man, I did forget!"

If John at that last supper looked about him at the sorrowful faces of his friends it was all gloomy and dark, but when he looked up into the face of Jesus it was light with hope.

There is no folly so serious in the conduct of our lives as to allow anything to separate us from the assurance of Christ's love. That is a wise piece of advice give to us in the New Testament which says, "Keep yourself in the love of God" (Jude 1:21).

A gentleman called to inquire about the condition of a friend who had been thrown from his horse, and during the conversation the sick man said: "As I rode in in the morning I found a wire in the park, and I said 'I must have that wire removed.' But at night I rode back, never thinking of the wire; the horse stumbled, and so I am laid on my back."

Is there a wire, ever so slight, in the road of your daily life, that is likely to be a foe to your peace? Take it away at once. Keep the track clear between your heart and God.

In a recent book on Abraham Lincoln by General Charles Collis a beautiful story is told of that great man's belief in prayer. General Sickles had said to him after Gettysburg, "Mr. Lincoln, we heart at Gettysburg that here at the capital you were all so anxious about the result of the battle that the government officials packed up, and got ready to leave at short notice with the official archives."

"Yes," he said, "some precautions were prudently taken, but for my part I was sure of our success in Gettysburg."

"Why," asked General Collis, "were you so confident? The Army of the Potomac has suffered many reverses."

There was a pause. The President seemed in deep meditation. His pale face was lighted up by an expression General Collis had never observed before. Turning to the general, he said: "When Lee crossed the Potomac and entered Pennsylvania, followed by our army, I felt that the crisis had come. I knew that defeat in a great battle on Northern soil involved the loss of Washington, to be followed, perhaps, by the intervention of England and France in favor of the Southern Confederacy. I went to my room and got down on my knees in prayer. Never before had I prayed with such earnestness. I wish I could repeat my prayer. I felt that I must put all my trust in Almighty God. God has often been our protector in other days. I prayed that he would not let the nation perish. I asked him to help us and give us the victory now. I felt that my prayer was answered. I knew that God was on our side. I had no misgivings as to the result at Gettysburg."

I thank God that it is not only reserved for great occasions like that and for great men to know that sweet assurance of heart that prayer is answered and that God's divine love overshadows us. No, indeed; the humblest soul may know and feel that blessed confidence and safety.

It is the supreme glory of this perfect love between our hearts and the heart of Jesus, such as John knew, that our relation with the Lord is thus freed from all stiffness and formality, all slavish fear, and there pervades our hearts like an atmosphere a sweet confidence as simple as a child's. And that is Christ's supreme definition of a Christian heart. He makes the child's heart, the child-faith, the ideal toward which our hopes must turn. We ought to keep the sweet and gentle frankness of childhood through all our lives in our prayer.

A mother had taught her little girl to pray for her father when she offered up her petitions to the Lord. Suddenly that father was removed by death. Kneeling in her sorrow at her mother's side for an evening prayer, her voice faltered, and, glancing into her mother's eyes, she sobbed: "O mother, I cannot leave him out. Let me say, 'Thank God I had a dear father once,' so I can keep him in my prayers." How sweetly the dear child honored her father by her tender love! And how perfect and simple her thought toward God!

Brothers and sisters, here is a path of peace. If we hold ourselves in that attitude toward our heavenly Father, then we may be sure that the Lord of peace himself will give us peace always by all means. We shall have happiness sometimes, but peace always; health sometimes, but peace always; prosperity sometimes, but peace always; friends sometimes, but peace always. And, after all, that is the greatest gift, the noblest experience, that one may know in this or in any world.

This perfect peace, born of a perfect love toward Christ, will give us the right attitude toward our fellowmen. I think one of the saddest predictions in the Bible is that made by Christ where he tells us that some people will come up to the very judgment expecting to get into heaven and explaining that while on earth they had borne the name of Jesus and done many things in his name, and our divine Lord will have to say to them, "I never knew you" (Matthew 7:23). It is one thing to bear the name of Jesus and to express admiration and praise for him, and another thing to so love him that you love all his brothers and sisters and are possessed by his spirit and purpose, so that you go out arm in arm with him "to seek and to save that which was lost" (Luke 19:10).

When Philip P. Bliss, who became such a famous singer afterward, was a young lad on the farm he was bringing home the cows one evening, and passing a house occupied for the summer by a rich family from the city, he heard for the first time in his life the sweet tones of a piano. You can imagine what it meant to that boy to whom music was more than food. Music floated down to his ears through the open doors, and the boy listened like one in a dream. It seemed to him that he could not live without seeing the wonderful instrument capable of producing it. He drew near the house, and glancing through the window, he caught a glimpse of the rich furnishings of the parlor; but he had eyes only for the grand piano, from the ivory keys of which the white, slender fingers flying over it brought out such delightful sounds, which mingled with the voice that sang, with the purest tone he had ever heard, "Jesus, Lover of my soul." One verse followed another till the hymn was ended, and the young lady arose from the piano.

Like one in a dream, the barefooted boy stepped forward through the open door into the room, saying shyly, "Please, won't you play 'Tell me the old, old story'?" The boy's face was radiant with the joy that filled his heart. He never dreamed of refusal. You can imagine his astonishment, therefore, when the girl shouted in anger, "Get out you beggar! How dare you enter a gentleman's door, tracking the dust of the street over the carpets, and leaving the print of your dirty bare feet wherever you step?"

Frightened at the girl's threatened violence, Philip tried to explain that it was the sweetness of the music that made him forget himself; but with increasing rage she commanded him to go, declaring that any further delay would necessitate setting the dog upon him.

"Sic, Bull! sic!" began the young woman, whose handsome face was not positively repulsive through its disfiguring frowns.

"How ugly she is! And I thought her so beautiful," Philip said to himself, after he was safe in the lane out of danger from the savage dog. "I don't see how she can sing 'Jesus, Lover of my soul,' one moment, and then the next act as if—well, as if she did not mean it," added the puzzled boy, as he drove the cows homeward.

It is a terrible thing to bear the name of Jesus, and sing the songs of the Saviour, and offer him the praise of our lips, while in our heart there is no fellowship with him. How empty is all such profession and service! But the perfect love that "casteth out fear" also casts out selfishness and brings us into harmony with the spirit of Jesus.

There is a beautiful story of James Usher, that once when he was traveling in Scotland he came to the parsonage of Samuel Rutherford, the famous old Scotch preacher, and, being a young man, Usher was subjected with Rutherford's children to the evening catechism. To the question, "How many commandments are there?" he answered, "Eleven," to Rutherford's astonishment and indignation. "An' how do you mak that oot, young mon?" To which Usher made reply, "'A new commandment I give unto you, that ye love one another'" (John 13:34).

The eloquent and scholarly Prince Wu, the Chinese

ambassador, calls a halt even at the Golden Rule, and says that it is impossible for a man to live up to that. But, thank God, there are multitudes on earth and in heaven who can bear testimony that it is not only possible to love others as we would have them love us, but to rise far above it to what somebody has called the Diamond Rule, which is, as it fell from the lips of Christ, "I would that ye love one another as I have loved you" (John 13:34). There is only one way to do that, and that is to abide in the resting place which John enjoyed with his head on the bosom of Jesus. If we keep close to Christ, and his love abides in us, filling our thoughts and purposes as the rich blood of the vine pours itself out into the branches, finding its harvest at last in the great purple clusters of grapes, the spirit of Jesus Christ possessing all our thoughts, all our affections, all our ambitions, shall cause us to be fruitful trees in the garden of the Lord, under whose shadow men shall find rest, and on the branches of which there shall hang precious fruit for all men.

26

A POLITICIAN WHO LOST HIS INFIDELITY

"What must I do to be saved?" (Acts 16:30).

Julius Lockup was a successful ward politician in the old Roman town of Philippi. We do not know just what kind of struggles he had gone through to get to be the chief jailer of the town, but knowing something of politics, we are sure that Julius had had his share of experience. He was a Roman, and therefore opposed from every standpoint to the new religion which Paul and Silas brought into the country. And when those earnest and enthusiastic preachers set themselves against the peculiar wickedness of the city of Philippi, and got into trouble, Julius was glad of it. It is astonishing how quick a man can get into trouble if he will fight the special sins that are alive in the town where he lives. A man can fight sin in the abstract, and thunder against it with all his guns, and sinners deep-dyed will speak well of him; but when he begins to open up on the particular sins that are destroying the souls and bodies of men and women in his own town it is like stirring up a hornet's nest.

Now, it seems that the particular sin of Philippi at this time was spiritualism, and there was one popular medium who was attracting a great deal of attention. She was a poor, silly tool in the hands of cunning and shrewd scoundrels who were filling their pockets by her pretended divination. When Paul and Silas came to attract a good deal of attention in the town this woman followed them about from day to day, and called out after them, until Paul finally rebuked her and silenced her, and she ceased to tell fortunes any more. The flow of money into the coffers of her masters stopped, and then there was a row.

Spiritualism of every sort and kind has always been the foe of Christianity. It could not be otherwise, for it is one of the most arrant frauds and humbugs of every time. It seems to me that our own city at this time is peculiarly cursed with these lying imposters who are robbing the silly and the ignorant by their pretentions to tell the secrets of God and unravel the mysteries of the future. They are all frauds, without a single exception, and it is a shame that they are permitted to carry on their nefarious exploits. It is not only that they rob the people of money; they rob them of what is far more important—of all intelligent faith in God—and prejudice them against the Church and against Christ until it comes to be very rare to find a person who has been drawn away after these frauds who afterward becomes a sincere and happy Christian. I say with all the earnestness of my heart to everyone that is tempted to visit one of these trance mediums, or clairvoyants, or whatever they may call themselves, to give them a wide berth.

Now, when Paul had stopped this business the men who lost money by the reform immediately had Paul and

Silas arrested and brought them before the magistrates. Then they stirred up a mob to come and scare the magistrates so as to make them do what they wanted, and the magistrates, being of the low, time-serving, politician sort, a good deal like some of our police judges nowadays, were anxious to make a great show before the crowd, and so they tore off the clothes from Paul and Silas and commanded the constables to beat them publicly, and after they had beaten them with as many stripes as they thought they could give them and leave them alive they were taken to the jail and turned over to Julius Lockup, and he was ordered to take good care of them.

Now, it is not a very hard job to keep safely a man who is suffering as Paul and Silas were, and if anything could appeal to the heart of Julius it would seem that their poor, bloody backs would have aroused his sympathy. But Julius was hardhearted, and so he said, "O yes, I will keep them safe enough," and he took them and put them in the inner cell; and, not satisfied with that, he thrust their feet into the stocks, so that they should be denied the poor relief of changing their position and giving a little ease to their pain. I do not know whether Paul and Silas asked for anything better or not. It would have been like Paul to have stood square on his rights in the matter; but if he did he got short shift from Julius, who locked the door on them, and left them without anything to eat and without further care.

I have often imagined what happened that night, before the singing began, in that inner dungeon. It has occurred to me that sometimes that perhaps Silas was inclined to be down-hearted and have the blues, and the singing came about through Paul's trying to cheer him up. I have imagined that after Julius went away, and his heavy footfall died out, and all was quiet, Silas said faintly, "Paul, how long do you suppose this will last? I don't feel as though this could be endured very long."

Then I have heard Paul say with a cheerful tone, from which all trace of suffering was excluded, "These light afflictions, which are but for a moment, shall work out for us a far more exceeding and eternal weight of glory" (2 Corinthians 4:17).

Then poor Silas said, "But the hunger in my stomach and the pain in my back are right here now, and the eternal life seems so far away tonight."

"O Silas," said Paul, "do not permit yourself to be deceived by the devil. The things which are present are only temporal, and last but a little while; but the things which are unseen and spiritual, they shall endure forever. Don't you worry, Silas; our heavenly Father, and our Saviour, and all the holy angels are watching over us. You and I are not whipped so long as we are not separated from Christ. They can't separate us from Christ with a cat-o'-nine-tails. I have been thinking it all over, and I am persuaded that neither death, nor life, nor angels, nor principalities, nor powers, nor things present, nor things to come, nor height, nor depth, nor any other creature, shall be able to separate us from the love of God, which is in Christ Jesus our Lord" (Romans 8:38, 39).

And then, to get Silas' mind off his trouble, Paul says, "Let's pray around." And so he prayed. It must have been a wonderful thing to hear Paul pray, and how he must have poured out his soul that night!

Before he got through praying the heart of Silas had taken fire, and he prayed with almost as much fervor as Paul. They forgot everything so completely that they were carried out of themselves, and prayed so loud that the other prisoners, and Julius Lockup, the jailer, heard them at their praying.

When Julius heart it first he sneered, "Those fellows are making a big show of their religion tonight." But before they got through there was a sort of thrill about it that went to his soul. Down in the bottom of his heart he thought, "It must be a sweet thing to believe in a God in so real a way that it makes one pray like that." And his own empty, wicked life seemed more barren to him than ever.

When they got through praying Paul said, "Silas, let us sing something." What do you suppose they sang? I have always believed they sang the Twenty-third Psalm. And with jubilant voices—for their hearts were now full of ecstasy, and their poor, blood-stained bodies were forgotten—they poured forth their confidence and trust in the Shepherd God. I don't know just what rendering Paul used, but it could not have been so very unlike that of James Montgomery, and at the midnight the jailer was astounded to hear, in voices that sounded as though they were having a good time,

> "The Lord is my shepherd, no want shall I know;
> I feed in green pastures, safe-folded I rest;
> He leadeth my soul where the still waters flow,
> Restores me when wandering, redeems when oppressed."

When Julius head that his mouth dropped open and his eyes stood out. "If that don't beat anything I have ever heard," said he. "If they call that dungeon, with their feet in the stocks, 'green pastures,' I wonder what it would take to make a desert? I don't like this thing. There is something strange and uncanny about it. Those men are hungry, and their backs are bruised and bloody, and they are in a most uncomfortable position; and yet they are praying and singing as if they were at the top notch of joy. I have handled a good many thousand prisoners in my time, but I have never known men to act like that. I have heard men moan, and I have heard them curse and swear, but I have never heard them pray and sing and rejoice at midnight in that inner cell." And the more he listened the worse Julius felt. He began to reflect on himself. At last he muttered, "They must be a pretty good sort. Poor souls! I might have made it a good deal easier for them. It was pretty hard, sticking their feet into the stocks, when they were in that fix. If they had cursed me I could have slept soundly on it, but to have them take it like this breaks me all up. What if their religion is true? Suppose these men tell the truth, and there is one great and true God, and all the Roman gods are false? Suppose Jesus Christ, who was crucified at Jerusalem, was sent to be the Redeemer of the world, as they say; what condemnation have I heaped on my head by treating his ministers in this brutal way! I wonder what they mean by singing that their Lord redeems them when oppressed? Do they think they are going to get out? Do they imagine their Lord will come and set them free? If that should happen I would lose my head." By this time Julius was mightily stirred within his conscience, and feared he knew not what.

Then, suddenly, there was a mighty earthquake. The walls of the prison reeled to and fro like a drunken man, and every prison door in the jail flew open. That earthquake seemed to have a bunch of keys at its girdle. The prisoners, most of them, stunned and startled, came rushing together in the common hall. Not only the doors opened, but the stocks gave way, too, and Paul and Silas came with the rest.

Poor Julius was in despair. He supposed the prisoners would now all escape, and knowing he would be disgraced and beheaded, he drew his sword to take his own life. But Paul shouted to him in a voice full of good cheer and authority, "Do thyself no harm: for we are all here" (Acts 16:28). That very moment Julius believed. He was not very sure about his creed yet, but he was sure these men had the key to eternal life, and he came running, and fell at their feet, and cried out, "Sirs, what must I do to be saved?" (Acts 16:30).

Now Paul was at home. He knew just how to deal with a man in that condition, and Silas was not a whit behind him, and with one accord they cried out as one man, "Believe on the Lord Jesus Christ, and thou shalt be saved, and thy house" (Acts 16:31). And they went right on and held and inquiry meeting with him, and with all the rest of the people in the jail, and many gave their hearts to the Lord.

It is interesting to note the first effect it had on Julius. He wanted to do something kind and generous to Paul and Silas. He would not let them baptize him until he had done what he could to relieve their needs. He got water and washed their stripes. Ah, I can see him at it. His jailer's uniform is on him, but now full of repentance and how tender is his face! A few hours ago he could look on their bruises with a mocking leer, but now they move him to tears. That is one of the blessed influences of Christianity. It humanizes the heart. It makes us tender and sympathetic. If you show me a man who does not get more tenderhearted and whose sympathies are not deepened by his becoming a Christian, I know there is some awful mistake about his Christianity. We cannot really believe on the Lord Jesus Christ without coming into sympathy with his brothers and sisters.

We know nothing of the future story of Julius Lockup. I hope he was a faithful man of God while he lived, and if so he has long since gone to his reward, and for 1800 years has enjoyed the glories of heaven. I bring this message to you tonight. I am sure it ought to be God's message to many of your souls. You have been refusing Jesus. You have thrust him into the inner prison. When men have tried to win you to the Lord you have put their feet into the stocks of your hardhearted indifference. But in spite of all that, again and again, the Christian message comes to your soul, and Pilate's old question, "What shall I do with this Jesus who is called Christ?" is thrust upon you for answer. This is the last Sunday night in the old year when you will have a chance to answer the question. It may be for some the last Sunday night on earth. It may be my last opportunity to give you the invitation. I thank God for the privilege now. If any heart is rising up under this story with the query of the old jailer, "What must I do to be saved?" I can only answer in the language of Paul and Silas, "Believe on the Lord Jesus Christ, and thou shalt be saved."

27

THE POWER HOUSE OF THE SOUL

"Now then it is no more I that do it,
but sin that dwelleth in me"
(Romans 7:17).

"I labored more abundantly than they all: yet not I, but the
grace of God which was with me"
(1 Corinthians 15:10).

"...nevertheless I live: yet not I, but Christ liveth in me"
(Galatians 2:20).

A short time since I had the opportunity of spending a forenoon looking over the greatest tin manufacturing plant in the world. I followed the material from the time it came in, only huge lumps of steel, until it passed through all the processes of the black pickle and the white pickle and had come out of the boiling tin bath a beautiful plate, shining like the sun, in which I could see my face as in a mirror. Everywhere I went there was evidence of tremendous power in the movements of machinery and the transportation of material. I saw no visible source of it, but its results were manifest in every department. Finally, I said to the gentleman who was with me, "I should like to see the power house where all the power manifest here is generated." And he took me away from all the noise and confusion of machinery that was capable of moving hundreds of thousands of tons, carrying out all the process by which that great mill did its work, in to a modest little structure where two great engines, quietly, without any noise, generated the power to carry on the immense plant. It was very impressive. The man who controlled those engines in the power house could stop all the machinery among the acres of buildings outside by a single movement of his right hand. They all depended on him for power.

Now, it is something like that, in the higher realm of the soul, that Paul is talking in these verses which I have selected to suggest and illustrate our great theme. Sin has come like an invader into the human heart and captured the power house of the soul. There is a longing desire in the man, because he is a child of God, to do right; but the evil engineer who has charge of the power house and is master of that fateful lever of the will makes him do evil when he would do good. Now, there is no superficial way by which a man can escape from this terrible condition. He can only escape by routing and casting out the sin which has come to have mastery over the power house of the soul. It does no good to adorn the power house. That will not change the control of the power inside. So it is that neither education, nor culture of any sort, nor wealth, nor any kind of circumstances can make a sinful heart clean and pure. It is not circumstances; it is the man himself who is at fault. So long as a man is wrong in himself nobody can help him but the God who can transform the heart and drive sin away from the control of the human will. As Christina Rossetti sings:

> "God strengthen me to bear myself,
> That heaviest weight of all to bear,
> Inalienable weight of care.
> "All others are outside myself;
> I lock my door and bar them out,
> The turmoil, tedium, gad-about.
> "I lock my door upon myself,
> And bar them out; but who shall wall
> Self from myself most loathed at all?
> "If I could once lay down myself,
> And start self-purged upon the race
> That all must run! Death runs apace.
> "If I could set aside myself,
> And start with lightened heart upon
> The road by all men overgone!
> "God harden me against myself,
> This coward with pathetic voice
> Who craves for ease and rest and joys:
> "Myself, arch-traitor to myself;
> My hollowest friend, by deadliest foe,
> My clog whatever road I go.
> "Yet One there is can curb myself,
> Can roll the strangling load from me,
> Break off the yoke and set me free."

The saddest thing about the tragedy of sin is when men and women silence the voice of the Spirit in their hearts and consciences until they fondly imagine that because they do not break into frequent outbursts of sinful acts therefore they are not sinners. If there are any who hear me who are thus lulling themselves into sleep on the very edge of the volcano, I can only pray God that his word may awaken you and his Spirit convict you until you shall see your heart with its spirit and purpose and motive mirrored in God's truth.

Rev. F. B. Meyer says that he was once paying pastoral calls when he dropped in on a washer-woman who had just put out a line of clothes. He congratulated her because they looked so white. So, very much encouraged by her pastor's kind words, she asked him to have a cup of tea, and they sat down. While they were taking the tea the sky clouded, and there was a sudden snowstorm; and as the preacher came out the white snow lay everywhere, and he said to her:

"Your washing does not look quite so clean as it did."

"Ah!" she said, "the washing is right enough; but what can stand against God Almighty's white?"

O my friend, you that are prone to be proud of your own self-righteousness, how do your motives, your thoughts, your imaginations, your selfish desires, look against "God Almighty's white"?

Henry Ware says sadly:

> "It is not what my hands have done
> That weighs my spirit down;
> That casts a shadow on the sun,
> And over earth a frown.
> It is not any heinous guilt,
> Or vice by men abhorred;
> For fair the fame that I have built,
> A fair life's just reward;
> And men would wonder if they knew
> How sad I feel with sins so few.
> "Alas! they only read in part
> When thus they judge the whole;
> They cannot look upon the heart,

They cannot read the soul.
But survey myself within,
And mournfully I feel
How deep the principle of sin
Its roots may there conceal,
And spread its poison through the frame,
Without a deed that men may blame."

Now, there is just one way to salvation, and that is to change the control of the powerhouse of the human heart. So long as sin rules there there will be no permanent change in you. Cast sin out, and put Jesus Christ in control, and every good thing is possible to you. There is an old Eastern story of Osman, a poor man with a rich soul, who dwelt at the gate of King Schiraz, and he so loved and lived the precept of the Koran that all sufferers went to him for help instead of the king. King and beggar died, and went to the gates of paradise. [In the story] the royal beggar entered, and the beggar-king was shut out. "I knew all the way along how this would be," said King Schiraz, "but after I once began to love myself more than my God and my neighbor I could not find the wonder-touch which would change my character." Thank God, the wonder-touch is Jesus Christ. He who when on earth could touch the ears of a deaf man and make him hear again; could touch the eyes of the man that was born blind and cause him to see; who could take by the hand a woman whose frame was racked with fever and the fever would depart; he who could touch the leper and make him whole; he who could touch miserly Zacchaeus and make him honest and generous; he who could touch a man tormented by devils and send him forth loving and noble, has the power to touch the sinful soul and make it clean again; power to speak to the man who is "dead in trespasses and in sins" and cause him to come forth to a new life.

This is the transformation that Paul had undergone. While sin lived in the power house of his soul and controlled the lever of his will he went wrong; but when, on that wonderful day on the road to Damascus, the heavenly voice spoke to him, and cried out, "Saul, Saul, why persecutest thou me? It is hard for thee to kick against the pricks" (Acts 9: 4, 5), and Paul surrendered and cried out tremblingly, "Lord, what wilt thou have me to do?" (Acts 9:6)—from that hour Paul was a new man; and the reason he was a new man was that there was a new engineer in the power house of his soul. Sin was cast out, and Jesus Christ came in to dwell in the holy of holies of Paul's inner life. So completely was he given up to do the will of God that he could say with all sincerity, "Nevertheless I live; yet not I, but Christ liveth in me" (Galatians 2:20). And when he talks about his work, which was the marvel of all the early Christian centuries, he can say, "I labored more abundantly than they all: yet not I, but the grace of God which was with me" (1 Corinthians 15:10).

My friends, if you would escape the bondage of sin, if you would have freedom from the evil masteries of the flesh, yield your hearts completely to Jesus Christ. It is useless to cry out to God for help while you refuse to do what he asks of you. The old Roman historian tells us that Pharnaces, while still in revolt against Caesar, send to him a golden crown. Caesar sternly refused the gift. "Let Pharnaces," said he, "return to his obedience." God cannot recognize your gifts so long as your heart is in rebellion against him. No man is rich enough to buy off God. God wants your love, your devotion; and nothing less than that is honorable to you or to God. The Civil War was not ended until, at Appomattox, General Lee surrendered his army to General Grant, saying, as he looked up to the banner of the Stars and Stripes floating overhead, "We will never take up arms against the old flag again." And there can be no harmony between your soul and God until with penitence you exclaim with David, "Against thee, thee only, have I sinned, and done this evil in thy sight" (Psalm 51:4). We must not only come to Jesus, but sin must be cast out. "You say that you have come to Christ," said John Bunyan; "then tell me what you have come from?" Sin must be renounced and Christ welcomed. These are the two great factors of salvation.

Do that here and now, and you will make of this time an epoch that will be forever dear and precious to your souls. You will always hereafter know what William Hunter meant when he sang:

> "There is a spot to me more dear
> Than native vale or mountain,
> A spot for which affection's tear
> Springs grateful from its fountain.
> 'Tis not where kindred souls abound,
> Thought that is almost heaven,
> But where I first my Saviour found,
> And felt my sins forgiven."

28

THE STENOGRAPHER TO WHOM PAUL DICTATED HIS LETTERS

"I Tertius, who wrote this epistle, salute you in the Lord"
(Romans 16:22).

S
ir Joshua Reynolds painted a picture of the famous Sarah Siddons in the character of the Tragic Muse. The portrait was a great success, and pleased both the artist and the public. The soul of the theme was so embodied on the canvas, and the poetry so incarnated in pose and expression, that many persons were strongly affected in contemplating it. The great artist assured the gifted Mrs. Siddons that the colors would remain unfaded as long as the canvas would hold together, and gracefully and gallantly added, "And to confirm my opinion, here is my name; for I have resolved to go down to posterity on the hem of your garment." Accordingly, his name appears on the border of the drapery. So Tertius comes down to us from the past, and will go on to the future, so long as the Bible is loved and honored among men, on the margin of Paul's letter to the Romans.

It is not possible for us to speak with certainty as to what caused Tertius to write this little salutation; but I think we may be reasonably sure, from our knowledge of human nature, of what would lead him to do it. In that day there were very few Christians, and they were lonely in the cold, pagan world, were persecuted and abused, and were frequently called upon to give up their lives for their faith. Such a condition of things would cause them to have a strong fellow-feeling with each other. Their sympathy one with another would be very tender and genuine. Now, Tertius did not know a Christian in Rome. All those people were strange to him, and they did not know there was such a man. But Tertius, lonely, homesick for love and fellowship, puts in this little love note on the margin, saying, in substance ,"I, Tertius, Paul's stenographer, who wrote down this epistle from his holy lips, I, too, am a Christian, and I salute you in the Lord. You don't know me, and I don't know you, but we both know the Lord, and I think you will like to know when you read these words of Paul that it was a faithful Christian hand which wrote them down for you."

I think there is a good message in that for us. Do not forget, if you are not a Christian, that when you are asked to become a friend of Jesus you are invited to become a member of a great family of brothers and sisters who are bound together by a common love for Jesus Christ. I know Christians are only human, and now and then hypocrites get into the Church and feign a Christianity which they do not possess, and many others live imperfect lives who are honestly trying to do right; but despite all these "flies in the ointment" this brotherhood of Christians the world over is the richest and sweetest human fellowship on earth, and if you come into it you will find that it hedges you about for good and that it inspires and encourages you by the warmth of its sympathy. I wish all of you could have heard, and especially you who are not Christians, what a number of us heard in the prayer meeting last Friday night. A young man arose in that meeting, and with voice choked with emotion and eyes wet with tears told this story: Some eight months ago, in youthful folly, he was led to leave a good home in a far-distant State, and to break away from school and become a wanderer with "a show," in circumstances which brought him constantly into evil temptations. After four months of such a life he came to this city and this church. I had the privilege of shaking hands with him at the door. It seemed good to him to get a warm handshake of welcome. It made the sermon more palatable afterward, and the young man said that all the sermon seemed spoken entirely for him. He determined then and there to separate himself from the things that tempted him and to begin a humble and earnest Christian life. He did so. He put himself into the Christian fellowship of our young people. Honest employment was secured for him, and life has grown sweeter for him every day. He wrote to his father and mother and told them about it, and those fond hearts that had been mourning him almost as if he were dead were filled with joy. And what he came to say to us at the prayer meeting was that he was now going back to his home and to school, and ever anticipation ahead of him was one of happiness; but he shuddered to think what might have happened instead if he had not come at the time he did into the warm, loving fellowship of the Church. My friends, if I speak to any lonely hearts tonight, hearts that feel the need of a good, safe, true circle of friends, I want to urge upon you the importance of taking Christ as the first great Friend of your life, and thus finding the doorway of welcome into the great brotherhood of

Christ's friends to which Tertius, Paul's Christian stenographer, belonged.

Another thing about Tertius is suggested by this little sentence in the margin. It shows him to have been a young man who was not ashamed of his work. He could not have composed such a letter as this to the Romans, but he could transcribe it, and do it in a nice, neat way, to that it would be easy to read, and give Paul's grand utterances a fair chance to be a blessing to those to whom the letter was addressed. He seems to have been a man who loved his work and rejoiced ion it. His work to him was worth more than the wages he got for it. He surely never would have become rich as Paul's stenographer. If a young fellow were hunting a fine place, so far as salary was concerned, he would not have picked out for his employer a despised Christian minister of that day, when Christians were the most unpopular people in the world. But he loved the work, and he liked to have a hand in it. He did it for love's sweet sake, and that is the way to do our work if we want to get the best effect of it on ourselves. All work that is honorable and needs to be done may develop a large manhood or womanhood in us if we perform it in the right spirit. No profession or business is high and noble enough to keep the labor connected with it from becoming the most vulgar slavery if it is performed in the slavish spirit. And no work is so humble or so seemingly unimportant but that if it be done in a spirit of fidelity to duty, with an ambition to do it in the ideal way, it may become beautiful and noble service that shall have its constant influence in enlarging and beautifying the character of the one who does it.

Another important suggestion in this little story is the

fact that Tertius, as Paul's stenographer, though he is only written in the margin of Paul's letter, and this one sentence is all there is about him, is yet a link in the great chain of salvation which has been such a blessing to millions and millions of people. Every one of us who does his work well and faithfully becomes a link in the great chain of human good. Paul could not get along without Tertius. I suppose Paul had weak eyes, so that it was utterly impossible for him to confine himself to writing his own letters and sermons. If it had not been for Tertius and others like him this letter to the Romans and the rest of Paul's wonderful thoughts would never have been written. None of us can tell where the good result of any honest, faithful work ends. If may be a link in the golden chain that shall wrap the whole world closer about the feet of God.

Dr. Harwood Pattison recently wrote a most interesting essay on what he calls "the Chain of Life." I can only give you a skeleton of it, but it suggests a line of thought that is exceedingly comforting and encouraging. He tells the story of Richard Sibbes, who was a good man in the old Puritan days. So good was he that people called him "Heavenly Richard Sibbes." And witty Thomas Fuller declared that he was "most eminent for that grace which is most worth, yet costs the least to keep it, namely, Christian humility." Well, "Heavenly Richard Sibbes" wrote a little book called *The Bruised Reed*. It breathed forth his confidence in the strength of Jesus Christ which comes to sustain the weakest people who trust in him. That is the first link. A peddler got hold of some of these little books and went selling them door to door. He sold one at the house of Richard Baxter. Baxter was a young fellow, and he picked up this *Bruised Reed* and read it, and it seemed to have come to him in just the nick of time. It caused him to open his heart to Christ, and he became a happy Christian. Now, Richard Baxter became a famous preacher and writer whose life was a great blessing to the world. Under the impulse he got from *The Bruised Reed* he wrote a little book entitled *Call to the Unconverted*, a most powerful appeal to sinners to be reconciled to God, and there is the second link in our chain. About the time there was a young man in England, a cultivated, moral, nice fellow with pleasant surroundings, but whose heart was hungry and restless and unsatisfied. One day, somebody told him about Richard Baxter's new book, and he got it and became wonderfully charmed with it. It led him to the Fountain of Life, where he drank deeply of the living water and slaked all the thirst of his soul. Philip Doddridge in turn became one of the world's greatest benedictions. He is one of the noblest of our hymn writers. He it was who wrote "How gentle God's commands!" "Grace! 'tis a charming sound," "O happy day that fixed my choice," "Awake, my soul, stretch every nerve," and multitudes of others that the whole world is singing in every denomination of Christians. How many hymns were inspired by his reading of Baxter's *Call to the Unconverted* I do not know, but it is certain that it stirred him up to write his book *The Rise and Progress of Religion in the Soul*. If he had never done anything but that he would have been immortal. Thousands and thousands have been converted because of that book. So there is the third link in the chain. In 1784 the most brilliant young man in England, a friend of Prime Minister Pitt, was going on a journey with a friend. They were going for a leisurely tour on the Continent. They were looking up some books to take with them. The young man picked up Doddridge's *Rise and Progress of*

Religion, and asked his friend what was its character. His friend, though not an experimental Christian, had heard the book well recommended, and said, "It is one of the best books ever written." So the young fellow took it with them to read on their journey. That young man was William Wilberforce, the fame of whose statesmanship will live forever in the abolition of British slavery. Wilberforce and his friend read Doddridge's book aloud, the one to the other, and so mightily did it affect them that they were both happily converted while on their journey and returned to England devout Christians. It was Doddridge's book, and the Christian experience that came through it, which made Wilberforce the mighty champion of the slave. There is our fourth link. As Wilberforce pushed forward his great reformation he in turn wrote a little book called *The Practical View of Real Christianity*. The publisher did not want to publish it, because he said people would not read that kind of books; but he was mistaken, for the first edition ran out in a few days, and it has been doing well ever since. And it unites us with our one other link. In the year 1819 there was a young Presbyterian minister in Scotland who was prostrated by a long and dangerous illness. He was famous for his eloquence, but, despite all that and his profession, he had not yet come to know Christ in the pardon of his sins. As he was creeping back again to health after his illness Wilberforce's book fell into his hands. It took hold upon his soul. He read it, pondered it, prayed over it, and was transformed into a new man. That man was Thomas Chalmers, whose flaming earnestness and marvelously spiritual ministry stirred all Scotland and brought multitudes to Christ. What a chain of life that is! And yet in the ordinary walks of life such chains of influence are being made up all the time. If we are faithful to God, if we live clean and pure lives, if we do our work with brave and honest hearts, we may be sure that God will know how to fasten our link into the chain and make us a great blessing to our fellow men.

There is one other suggestion worth of our serious thought. What will you be remembered by? Tertius had his chance and took it. So long as the name of Paul fills a place in the heart of humanity Tertius will be remembered, and there will be a sweet taste in the mouth of men as they think of him. He was a worker for the Lord, doing his duty as Paul's secretary, doing it lovingly for Christ's sake, and he is remembered by it and for it. For what will people remember us after we are dead? Will they remember us for our avarice, as they remember Judas? Will they remember us for our drunkenness? Shall we be remembered for our quarrelsome disposition, or our selfishness? Or shall we, like Tertius, be remembered because of our devotion to Christ, our brotherly or sisterly spirit of kindness and good will? There is no time to lose; none of us can tell when the chapter will be made up. If we are to be remembered for good character and good deeds and a true spirit we must be putting them into our work now.

No doubt I speak to someone who is sad at heart because sin has already gotten the victory over you, and you feel that you have failed to do your work well in the sight of God, and that you are under his condemnation. I want to bring you the happy message, a message that Tertius had written in this very letter as it fell from Paul's lips, "I am not ashamed of the gospel of Christ: for it is the power of God unto salvation to everyone who believeth" (Romans

1:16). Let me give you another message which Tertius had written down: "The wages of sin is death; but the gift of God is eternal life through Jesus Christ our Lord" (Romans 6:23). It may have been such messages as that which led Tertius to become a Christian in the first place. And perhaps it was because he felt so grateful to Paul for having led him to Christ that he stood by him, though no doubt he was offered work that paid more money. Paul could not pay as much salary as some other people could have paid him, yet it paid better in the long run, for how richly has Paul endowed Tertius for all eternity!

"The message is sweet, and I am tempted to become a Christian," says someone, "but I fear I should hold out." Let me give you another message which Tertius wrote as Paul spoke it to him. Paul had been dictating a letter to the Romans about how he had been whipped and stoned and abused for the Gospel's sake, and then he says: "In all these things we are more than conquerors through him that loved us. For I am persuaded that neither death, nor life, nor angels, nor principalities, nor powers, nor things present, nor things to come, nor height, nor depth, nor any other creature, shall be able to separate us from the love of God, which is in Christ Jesus our Lord" (Romans 8:37-39). Surely that must cover your case. The devil tries to make you think that you are in peculiar circumstances, where even with the Lord's help you could not live a Christian life, but that is one of the meanest lies.

Dr. Webb-Peploe, the English preacher, had a call one evening from a woman who had been greatly impressed in his meeting. But she said that she was a peculiar person, that her circumstances and temptations were so very, very peculiar that she could not expect Christ would give her power to overcome them.

"Well," said Mr. Peploe, "suppose you tell God so." Whereupon he began to pray, asking her to follow him, both speaking aloud: "O God, I thank thee for all thy promises of overcoming power in Christ; but my circumstances and temptations are so very, very peculiar that I find them too strong for Christ to help me. I am sorry he is not stronger to meet my case, but my case is so very, very peculiar I cannot expect to find his help sufficient."

"Why do you not say this after me?" inquired Mr. Peploe, as he noticed that the woman had soon become silent as he continued to pray.

"Why, that is rank blasphemy," she answered.

"Just so," said he; "but this is only your thought put into words, and why is it worse to say this to God than to think it of him? Now let us," he added, "try another approach to God: 'O God, I thank thee for all thy promises in Christ of overcoming power, and that, though I am a peculiar person, and my circumstances are very, very peculiar, and my temptations are very, very peculiar, thy grace is very, very peculiar, and abundant to meet my very, very peculiar needs, and very, very peculiar difficulties, in a very, very peculiar degree.'"

She saw the truth, and embraced it, and went home rejoicing in her soul. I bring you God's message tonight, and pray that you may hear it unto eternal life.

29

THE MAN WHO LIVES AT SATAN'S SEAT

*"And to the angel of the church in Pergamos write;
These things saith he which hath the sharp sword with two
edges; I know thy works, and where thou dwellest, even
where Satan's seat is: and thou holdest fast my name, and
hast not denied my faith, even in those days wherein
Antipas was my faithful martyr, who was slain among you,
where Satan dwelleth"* (Revelation 2:12, 13).

Pergamos was at that time the most important and famous city in all Asia, and naturally there was where Satan made his seat. He had his headquarters nigh to the sources of power. The minister of the Christian church in Pergamos, called here "the angel of the church in Pergamos," is given a very high commendation for negative goodness. He has resisted all provocation that would lead him to deny the faith in Christ. Not even when Antipas, who seems to have been a famous martyr for Christ, was put to death, and the storm threatened his own destruction, would this preacher deny the faith that had become his. But while he was negatively good, and held steadfast to the name of Christian, his aggressive qualities did not seem to be equal to his defensive armor. He was all right to stand a siege, but he was not a success at storming breastworks; for though he had remained steadfast and faithful himself, and there is no indication that he had gone over to any false doctrines, yet the Lord declared that he had a few things against him because some of the people in his church held to false doctrine and had been led into sin, and the implication is that if he had done his duty in faithfully making war on these evil things this condition would not have existed. It is not enough to be good in a negative way; we must be a positive, earnest, Christian force.

The message, which I desire to bring to you, however, is a different one, and is suggested in the Lord's description of Pergamos as Satan's seat. Satan still makes his headquarters in the city, and while we may find evil in the country, and in the town and village, it is still true that the large city is peculiarly Satan's seat of power. Every vicious and evil thing of our time congregates in the large cities. That vilest of abominations, the liquor saloon, penetrates to the town and to the country as well, but it is always to some extent on its good behavior in thinly populated regions. It is in the large city that the saloon becomes the hotbed of every form and kind of iniquity. The liquor saloon has become peculiarly the incarnation of all that is devilish in modern life. The saloon is no longer simply one man selling liquor to another, accursed as that is of God; but it is usually a single trap among a multitude owned by some giant corporation which joins with the liquor business every form of vice and immorality. Gambling, lust, and often robbery join hand in hand around the liquor saloon, all inspired and nourished by the one fountain of iniquity. If we could look into the hearts of suffering women and ruined men in this city our own hearts would break with pity and horror.

The story is told of the police court in one of our large cities that one morning a tall, fine-looking woman was brought in, and waited the usual questioning. There was something so piteously desperate in the prisoner's appearance, and her great haunted eyes had such a look of anguish, that the judge, accustomed to all sad sights and sounds, hesitated before asking with unwonted gentleness, "What is your name, my woman, and where were you born?"

"My name is Aleen Burne, yer honor, an' I were born in Aberdeen, off the Scotland coast land."

"And you are charged with striking a man?"

"I am, yer honor."

"And you meant to?"

"I did, indeed, yer honor. He's kilt me, yer honor."

The woman spoke with a low, impassioned wail which caused respectful attention.

"McGinnis testifies that he never laid a hand on you," returned the judge.

"He stabbed me to the heart, yer honor."

"Stabbed you! Suppose you tell me about it."

"I will. Ye might no ken wha' it is, yer honor, to hev one bonnie laddie, an' none else. I lef' the guid father o' my lad sleeping in the kirkyard, when I brought my wee bairnie to this land. For many a year I toiled in sun an' shade for my winsome Robbie. He growed so fine an' tall that he were ta'en to a gentleman's store to help. Then this man McGinnis set his evil eye on the lad. I was forced to pass his den on my way to an' fra' the bread store, an' he minded 'twas mesel' hated the uncanny look o' the place. An' one morn', as I passed by, he said I needn't be so grand about my b'y, he were no above ta'en a sup of the liquor wi' the rest. I begged my chiel by the love of God to let the stoof alone. Me Robbie promised to bide my wishes; but the man McGinnis watched o' the nights when 'twere cauld and stormin', an' gave the lad many a cup o' his dreadful drinks, to warm him, he would say. I got on my knees to me bairn, and prayed him pass the place no more, but to gang to hame by some other road. Then I went mesel' to the mon, an' p'raps ye ken, yer honor, how a mither wud beg an' pray for the bone o' her bone an' flesh o' her flesh; but he laughed me in the face. Last night, yer honor, the noise at me door frightened me; I runned wi' all me micht to sees wha' were the trouble, an' me Robbie swayed in the room, an' fell at me feet—he were drunk, yer honor! Then McGinnis poket his face in a the door, and asked, 'Wha' think ye now, Mistress Burne?' Did I mean to strike the mon, yer honor? An' I could, I'd a-struck the breath fra' his body. Ye'd better keep me wi' lock an' key till me gloom dies out; but, O jedge, jedge, I wish mesel' an' me lad there were in the kirkyard aside the guid father! They tell me if I could prove the mon sold liquor to the bairn under age the law could stop him. I tell ye, jedge, there's naught but God's vengeance can stop his ilk. It's well enough to arrest the mither as strikes the mon as ruins her bairn, but wait ye till the Lord Almighty strikes—aye, wait ye for that!"

And yet that story is not a shade blacker than stories I could tell out of lives which have come under my observation in the last two years. O what a sacrifice of young men on the altar of strong drink in this city! Every year they come up from the country, strong-bodied, clear-brained, temperate in habits; and they come here, where Satan's seat is, and temptations to stimulants strike them on a new side; and, with all the old influences of the home life that has defended them and held them back removed, they drift into the current of dissipation and are swallowed up and destroyed before they know their danger. Young man just beginning to tipple, taking your moderate glass now and again, in God's name be warned. A brother minister told me last Monday that a man came to him half drunk and in despair a few days ago, and when asked how he got into such a condition, the man said: "I went to hear a certain minister speak, and he said there was no harm in taking a drink of liquor now and then, if a man did not take too much; that the only harm was in taking too much. And I thought I could follow his advice and be a man, and show that I was not afraid, and I tried it, and I have not been sober for a month. All my savings of several years' hard work are gone, my position is lost, and I am a broken and ruined man." God have mercy on men of influence and position who hang out the false lights that lead young men to wreck character and soul on the coast line of these cities where Satan has his seat!

Satan has his seat in these modern cities in many business circles, and often from the time a young man comes to the city he is tempted constantly to forswear his honor and integrity to get on in business. Young men say to me sometimes, "There's no use talking; a man cannot be a Christian and get on in my business." Now, I tell you that a man has no right to have a business where it is essential for him to lie and cheat and sell his soul to the devil in order to succeed in it. If you have a business like that get out of it. No man is worse swindled than he who exchanges his honor and his manhood for financial gain. Keep your record clean. The man who gets started on a path of dishonesty soon finds that the path before him is all downhill and more slippery than glass. Get out of that path. Fly from it even if, like Lot in getting out of Sodom, you have to leave it all behind. Better to do that and escape with your soul than that you should go down in that hell of dishonor.

Satan ruins many in these cities under the guise of amusement and pleasure. Pleasure that does not flow from a pure source is always ruinous, and for men and women to get into the idea that they are simply living to be amused, to get pleasure from the senses, is fatal to the development of a good or pure life. It is the hour when a man is off duty, when he is away from his work, that is often most fatal to him. Show me young men or women who in their hours of recreation seek to improve their minds, to enlarge and ennoble themselves, and to prove helpful and beneficial to others, and I will show you growing lives that have all noble possibilities before them. But there are in this city multitudes of young men and women who have been working hard for five years, some of them for ten years, who have spent every cent they could make in the theater or the ballroom or in worse dissipations. After all these years what have they gained from their coming to the city? They have lost the freshness and the youthful glow and much of the vitality which they brought with them from the country or the little town, and they have gained nothing but weariness and disgust, a hardened heart, and a load of sin that they have no power to shake off. It is a terrible thing to be broken down by the enemy of your soul when he fights like a lion; but how contemptible it seems when a man is eaten of the moths and worms of silly pleasure and dissipation!

But while Satan's seat is in the city, and upon every hand he has his agencies and influences at work to entrap unwary souls, Christ is in the city also. He is the same Christ who stood above the city of Jerusalem where Satan had his seat, and looking down upon it wept, and cried, "O Jerusalem, Jerusalem, thou that killest the prophets, and stonest them which are sent unto thee, how often would I have gathered thy children together, even as a hen gathereth her chickens under her wings, and ye would not" (Matthew 23:37). He is the same tenderhearted, loving Christ tonight, and if you will come to him in the midst of these temptations to evil he will impart to you strength to live a pure and a noble life, even where Satan's seat is. As Daniel went into the den of lions and was not harmed, as Joseph passed through the palace of lust and came out unscathed, as the Hebrew exiles went through the fiery furnace without the smell of fire upon their garments, because the form of the Fourth was with them, so there are thousands of young men and women today who pass through the temptations and snares of life of the city with thoughts clean and wholesome, with ambitions pure and noble, and with character and life unspotted from the world.

It is to such a life that I call you. Christ is able and willing to stand by you as a wall of defense, sticking closer to you than a brother in the midst of all the trials of life. Many a time young men have said to me, "I was alright so long as I was at home with my mother. When I went home every night, and met her kiss at the door, and looked into her pure eyes across the table, it was easy to keep my life clean and wholesome. If I had stayed there I never would have gone astray. But I came away from home, and I was lonely and homesick, and it seemed to me that nobody cared; and when I went wrong there was nobody to be hurt by it; and so it was that I lost my grip upon myself." O brother, give your heart to Christ, and it will not be a lone fight anymore. Never was mother so devoted to her boy as Jesus Christ will be to you, and in his fellowship you shall have strength to overcome all your foes.

30

THE HONOR OF A GENTLEMAN

"And he said unto them, When I sent you without purse,
and scrip, and shoes, lacked ye anything?
And they said, Nothing" (Luke 22:35).

David Livingstone was once surrounded by foes in the heart of Africa. His enemies were more than a hundred to one, and they seemed bent on mischief. So far as any human foresight could see he was to perish there alone without even an opportunity of letting the world know how he died. The sun was going toward the setting, and it appeared to him to be the last time he should see it on earth. He went into his tent, took up his well-worn Bible, and turned to the words that Christ gave to his disciples as a last love message before his final ascension into heaven: "Go ye therefore, and teach all nations…teaching them to observe all things whatsoever I have commanded you: and, lo, I am with you always, even unto the end of the world" (Matthew 28:19, 20). Livingstone closed his Bible and said, "That is the word of a gentleman, and he will never break it." He went to bed as usual and slept in peace. The next day he was able to peacefully settle all his difficulties with the enemies and went on his way rejoicing.

The story referred to by our text is somewhat similar. Christ had sent forth his disciples two by two, and then had had a preaching campaign, and came back to report. He had sent them forth without money, and without any visible means of support, and yet he had promised to be with them and stand by them; and now some time after he appeals to them to say whether it be true that he has kept his word, and with one accord they declare that his honor as a gentleman has never failed.

That is the message I bring to you tonight. God calls to every one of you, in whatsoever place you are, to turn from every sin and confess Jesus Christ. Christ comes to you with this stirring appeal, that he has given his life for you, and he asks for your confession, your open friendship, and your publicly avowed testimony for him. It is surely a very strong appeal. Nobody else has ever laid you under such obligations as Jesus Christ.

Henry Clay was at one time considerably distressed by a large debt due to the bank. Some of his friends heard of this and quietly raised the money and paid off the debt, without notifying Mr. Clay. In utter ignorance of what had been going on, he went to the bank one day, and, addressing the cashier, said, "I have called to see you in reference to that debt of mine to the bank."

"You don't owe us anything," was the reply.

Mr. Clay looked inquiringly, and said, "You don't understand me. I came to see about that debt which I am owing the bank."

"You don't owe us anything."

"Why! How am I to understand you?"

"A number of your friends have contributed and paid off that debt, and you do not owe this bank one dollar."

The tears rushed to Mr. Clay's eyes, and, unable to speak, he turned and walked out of the bank.

But that is a very faint image of what Christ has done for you. You were in debt to the law of God beyond all your ability ever to pay; but Jesus Christ came and paid your debt with his own blood, and now he appeals to you to give your heart and life to him.

But there is the most wonderful thing about it, and that is what I want to impress tonight especially: Christ promises you, on his honor as a gentleman, that if you give your heart and your service to him you shall not only get a hundredfold more in this life, but in the world to come you shall have eternal life. He promises to stand by you in every emergency and bring you off victorious. He promises to give you his peace. And he will keep his word.

The day before he died Richard Baxter said to two of his friends who visited him: "I have pain; there is no arguing against sense. But I have peace; I have peace." So it shall be with you in the great storms that come upon you. A few years ago a terrible storm swept along the Massachusetts coast, and the next morning there was a rumor that Minot Lighthouse had gone down. The next day the keeper was on the street in Boston, and someone said to him, "We thought the lighthouse had been wrecked." He replied, "It was the mightiest storm that ever I have known; the waves were the highest; but in all the storm the lighthouse never shook." It is the universal testimony of those who have given their hearts fully to Christ, and have kept his commandments, that he has never failed them for a moment. Winifred Iverson, studying this text, brings the promise out very clearly in a little song:

> " 'Lacked ye anything, my follower?'
> Jesus asked his love-thrilled band,
> 'When I sent you forth defenseless,
> Poor, and homeless, o'er the land—
> Lambs, where wolf-fangs gleamed blood-red?'
> 'Nothing, Lord,' they said.
> " 'Lacked ye anything, beloved,'
> Jesus asks us even now,
> 'When I led you through the desert?
> As ye stepped, remember how
> Fullness seemed so far away?'
> 'Nothing, Lord,' we say.
> " 'Lacked you anything, beloved,
> When, with speech so poor and weak,
> As ambassadors I sent you,
> Heaven's high interests to seek;
> Lacked anything that day?'
> 'Nothing, Lord,' we say.
> " 'Lacked ye anything, beloved?
> Hath there failed one word of mine—
> Anything of lovingkindness,
> Tender mercy, grace divine;
> Any good thing on your way?'
> 'Nothing, Lord,' we say."

Another thought is suggested to me in our study, and that is that Christ offers to take poor sinners who are in the same condition as were those disciples, without anything to recommend them, without any resources of their own, and if they will give their hearts to him and serve him he will send them forth with his divine guarantee to be with them and to stand by them and to bring them off more than conquerors through his great love. Christ takes a poor sinner who is utterly bankrupt in a spiritual way, and deals with him as I have known men to do with miners who had lost all they had in the early days on the Pacific coast. Sometimes a well-to-do man would take a prospector who had not a cent in the world and was utterly unable to help himself, and buy him an outfit, including all the provisions and tools and clothing he needed, and send him out on a prospecting tour into the mountains. They used to call it "grub-staking" a man. Christ takes a man whose sins have defeated him, and whom nobody else will believe in or trust, and he "stakes" him, and sends him forth with new courage to dig for the gold of manhood.

Mark Guy Pearse tells a story which came under his own observation. It was a beautiful Sunday morning in June. A minister of kindly and gracious heart, passing down the road to church, met a man dressed in his working clothes, who, when he saw the minister coming, put his hand to his cap and drew it down over the side of his face; that eye was badly blackened, and the other was bloodshot, and the face was cut and bruised. It was plain enough that he had been in some drunken brawl. The sympathetic minister paused and said in his most kindly way: "Good morning, good morning. This is a lovely morning isn't it? A delicious day."

The man only grunted a reply. The minister continued: "Yes; a day, this, when it is really a pleasure to live, isn't it? Earth and heaven so full of beauty—the very birds praising God. A beautiful day, indeed!"

"Ugh!" grunted the man.

"Well," continued the minister, in a voice full of kindness and good cheer, "I hope you will enjoy the day. When everything is so full of gladness it is a sad thing if we men and women can't praise God, isn't it? Good morning."

This time the grunt was so savage that there was no mistaking the man's anger, but the minister paid no attention to it, and walked on his way.

The man who had been so worsted in the drunken brawl went a little way farther and flung himself down under a hedge and tried to sleep. But he could not get out of his mind what the Christian man had said to him.

"'Delicious day,' indeed!" he grunted to himself, kicking out angrily. "A pretty thing to say to the likes of me! 'A delicious day'—when a fellow has not a bone in his body that isn't aching, and when his head is fit to split, and his throat is all fire! Ugh!" And he kicked again. " 'A delicious day,' I dare say when a fellow has had to go without breakfast, and dare not show himself at home, and does not know where he's to get a bit of dinner from!" And he ground his heels savagely into the bank. " 'A delicious day'—very!— when a man has been mad enough to drink the week's wages, and his wife and children have hardly anything to eat and only rags to wear, and go breaking their hearts and crying their eyes out, as miserable as they can live. 'A delicious day,' indeed! Ugh!" And thrusting his hands deep into his empty pockets, the miserable fellow got up out of the hedge and slouched along the lane.

The birds were singing, and the sound of the church bell swelled across the valley. The bees, laden with honey, were diving into the flowers, and the gaily painted butterflies hovered about him. Still the voices kept up the song, "A beautiful day—a delicious day," and he could not escape it.

"'A delicious day!'" he began again to himself. "Yes, I

dare say it is for that man. He left a happy home this morning. He does not need to go sneaking along, ashamed to be seen. He has not made anybody's heart ache—and has not given anybody the chance of making him ache all over," he added, grimly. "He is doing some good in the world, helping to make folks better and the world brighter. It must be easy enough to have a fine day all the year round when a man lives like that. But look at me. Nobody is ever the better for anything I do or say, but there's plenty that are a great deal worse."

He lay down again under the hedge, but after thinking a while he started up, muttering to himself: "Whose fault is it that the day is not delicious for me? Why, my own, of course. It's no good putting the blame anywhere else. There is only one man that can end the misery, and that is the man who began it. And end it I will!" he cried, striking his heel again deep into the hedge. There was silence again for a little while, and again he exclaimed aloud, talking to himself: "A fool, of course, I am to be making a day like this miserable for myself and everybody, undoing the very shining of the sun, and contradicting the very singing of the birds, and setting myself against the flowers and the fields, getting out of joint with the world. A fool I am, and a fool I have been. But I won't be a fool any longer!"

He got up and started for the little cottage where he lived. He hoped he might step in unnoticed, but his wife stood on the doorstep. As soon as she saw him she set her white lips together and planted her hands—-long, thin hands they were—on her hips, and then proceeding to relieve herself of the feelings that had been gathering for hours.

"You've come, have you! And a pretty face you've brought with you, too! Well, it is a comfort to see that you've got what you deserve. A pretty sight you are for a day like this! And a fine day you've made for those who look to you to keep 'em, too, but who would be a deal better off if they had never seen you. Call yourself a man, much less a husband and father, which is libel on the beasts to say so! I wonder God Almighty lets a slouching thing like you go darkening a day like this."

Watching his opportunity, he managed presently to slip past his wife into an inner room. Turning the key in the door, he was safe. Then he lay down and had a long sleep. No sooner was he awake than there came back again those voices: "A beautiful day—a delicious day." Yes, he would be a fool no longer. The days should be delicious for him, too, and those about him, as well as for other people.

He washed himself and made himself look as decent as he could, and then came forth to his wife and children. No word of love had they heard for many a day, and they turned as if to make sure that it was really he as he came up to his wife and put his hand tenderly on her shoulder. "Lass," he said, "I've been an awful fool, and I am sorry." The touch of kindness and the word of tenderness at once melted the wife's heart. She said nothing, and looked down as if to keep her eyes from saying anything. "I've just been a fool; but I won't be any more, by God's help." He could say no more; and his wife could say nothing. That night he went to hear the minister preach who had spoken so kindly to him in the morning, and then and there he gave his heart to God, and at the foot of the cross, where Bunyan's Pilgrim lost his burden, the poor drunkard lost his guilt and sin. So into that black hell of a drunkard's home there came the sunshine of the presence of Jesus Christ—the sunshine that drove away the sin and the guilt and the sorrow, the sunshine that brought good cheer and good company, and left a family ready to say on a June morning, "It is a delicious day!"

I bring you Christ's loving message this night. I pledge you this honor as a gentleman that he will keep his word with you. Bring him your heart, repent of your sins, do his will, and he will throw about you the endowment of his love.

PART 2

THE GREAT SINNERS OF THE BIBLE

31

EVE'S DIALOGUE WITH THE DEVIL

"Now the serpent was more subtile than any beast of the field which the Lord God had made. And he said unto the woman, Yea, hath God said, Ye shall not eat of every tree of the garden? And the woman said unto the serpent, We may eat of the fruit of the trees of the garden: but of the fruit of the tree which is in the midst of the garden, God hath said, Ye shall not eat of it, neither shall ye touch it, lest ye die. And the serpent said unto the woman, Ye shall not surely die: for God doth know that in the day ye eat thereof, then your eyes shall be opened, and ye shall be as gods, knowing good and evil. And when the woman saw that the tree was good for food, and that it was pleasant to the eyes, and a tree to be desired to make one wise, she took of the fruit thereof, and did eat, and gave also unto her husband with her; and he did eat" (Genesis 3:1-6).

Some people have quibbled over this story and raised a laugh by calling it the snake story, and by many kindred allusions, but there is no reason for being troubled at the idea of God choosing to speak his message in an unusual way, or in his permitting the incarnation of the evil spirit in the form of a serpent. Nothing in the Bible is harder to believe than are the actual occurrences of our own times. If the destruction of the Spanish fleet at Manila without the loss of a single life on the part of the Americans, or the destruction of Cervera's fleet of swift, modern war ships with the loss of but one life on the part of their enemies, had happened four or five thousand years ago, and been recorded in the Old Testament, what derision the infidels would have flung at the story! I can imagine Ingersoll having a lecture on the mistakes of Dewey or Sampson fully as witty and scornful as his diatribe on "The Mistakes of Moses."

It does not make the least difference to us whether this dialogue between Eve and the serpent is a literal historical occurrence or whether it is a poetical portrayal of the drama by which sin became a dark and real fact in human life. Its message to us is exactly the same in either case. One thing is sure, the picture is true to life; and it is full of graphic illustrations, valuable to the men and women who are living now, and upon whom the devil is making attacks as subtle and deceitful as those by which he accomplished the overthrow of Eve.

The devil makes his first pass at Eve by insinuating against God's goodness and generosity. What an ingratiating question it is! "Can it be possible," says the serpent, in substance, with a sardonic smile, "That your God has shut off a part of the garden from you and commanded that you shall not eat of every tree of the garden?" Eve's fatal blunder was that she did not thrust his vile suggestion back into his very teeth and end the conversation then and there. If she had been as loyal to God as an old Scotch woman I have heard about, the story would have had a different ending. This old woman was in hard circumstances, and having no bread she knelt on the floor of her little cabin, built close against the rocks of a mountain side, and prayed for some. A roguish boy of the neighborhood, chancing to pass that way, heard her voice and listened at the door. He hurried home and quickly returned with a loaf, ran up on the rocks, and so upon the cabin roof, and tossed the bread down the smokeless chimney. It rolled from the empty fireplace to the chair beside which the old woman still knelt, earnestly praying. There was a moment's pause, and then she was loud in her thanksgiving to God for the speedy answer to her prayer.

"Ye need na' be thankin' the Lord for it," the youngster shouted down the chimney; "I brought it."

"Ah, my laddie," cried she, from below, "it was the Lord that sent it, even if the devil brought it."

But Eve was not thus loyal at heart. She begins not to state clearly the divine goodness, but to weakly apologize for the Lord, and ends her sentence by showing her own doubt both of God's goodness and of the sincerity of his warnings. The fact is that Eve was all ready for the serpent when he came. She had herself been looking on the forbidden tree with rebellious longing, and had been so taken up with desire for the forbidden fruit that she had forgotten to be grateful for the beauty and fragrance and food that hung from every other bough of every other tree in the Garden of Eden. A great many people slander the devil by trying to throw on him the brunt of all their sins, but St. James says: "Every man is tempted, when he is drawn away of his own lust, and enticed. Then when lust hath conceived, it bringeth forth sin" (James 1:14, 15). So the beginning, after all, of Eve's ruin was in her own ungrateful imagination, where she had permitted these rebellious thoughts to lie until they were like dry tinder waiting for the devil's match.

Eve left out a most important and significant word in stating God's permission to "eat of the trees of the garden," and thus detracted much from the generous character of the provision which God had made. But when she came to speak of the warning of the Lord against eating of the forbidden fruit, she put in words of her own to make the prohibition seem more hard and severe. From Eve's statement, "But of the fruit of the tree which is in the midst of the garden, God hath said, Ye shall not eat of it, neither shall ye touch it, lest ye die" (Genesis 3:3) one would think that God had utterly shut up the tree, guarding it with the most extreme jealousy and rigor, when the only prohibition was against eating of the fruit—which would bring sorrow and death. How often we hear people talking the same way now; as though God had given us appetites and desires which were never to be gratified, which are only to be resisted, and intimating that man's only chance for happiness lies in the violation of God's commandment, when the truth is that God has marvelously adapted us to the world in which we live, and in the wholesome and right gratification of our desires there is always peace and happiness; the prohibitions of God's law are only signal lights that tell where are the dangerous rocks upon which our souls may be wrecked.

But Eve also shows, in her answer to the serpent, that she is beginning to doubt the sincerity of the divine warning.

The declaration of God had been: "Thou shalt not eat of it: for in the day that thou eatest thereof thou shalt surely die" (Genesis 2:17). But after Eve has begun her parley with the tempter her version of this clear and simple statement is, "Ye shall not eat of it, neither shall ye touch it, lest ye die." "Lest ye die!" This is what she substitutes for "In the day that thou eatest thereof thou shalt surely die." "Lest ye die!" How different is that from the other statement. The first is sure death; the second is a bare possibility of something happening. Thus Eve was getting ready for the bold on-slaught of her enemy which was to insure her destruction. She had lost her vantage ground by not flinging the lie in his face when first he began to slander her heavenly Father.

A few years ago a young Englishwoman crossed the Atlantic to marry a young man in New York city to whom she had been betrothed in England, and who had come to this country two years before to engage in business. She was to marry him at the home of a friend of her mother's with whom she was staying. During the time she was making up her wedding outfit he came to see her one evening when he was just drunk enough to be foolish. She was shocked and pained beyond measure. She afterward learned that he was in the habit of drinking to excess. She immediately stopped her preparations and told him she could not marry him. He protested that she would drive him to distraction, promising never to drink another drop. But her answer was: "I dare not trust my future happiness to a drunkard, I came three thousand miles, and I will return three thousand miles." How much better it would have been had Eve only said to the advances of the tempter: "No. I will not trust my future happiness to a slanderer of God." But, instead, she parleyed with him, revealing to him the brooding thoughts of ingratitude and rebellion which she cherished secretly, until we are not astonished at the bold, brazen declaration of the serpent in reply: "Ye shall not surely die!" And when Eve had so far yielded to the fascination of sin that she could hear God's word declared false and still remain in conversation with the person who uttered the declaration, she was ready to take the fatal step from which there was no retraction.

Notice Eve's conduct then: "And when the woman saw that the tree was good for food, and that it was pleasant to the eyes, and a tree to be desired to make one wise, she took of the fruit thereof, and did eat, and gave also unto her husband with her; and he did eat" (Genesis 3:6). How did Eve see that it was good for food? Was it some new discovery she had made? Or was it that she had come to look at it through the devil's spectacles? Isaiah says: "Woe unto them that call evil good, and good evil" (Isaiah 5:20). Association with such people always means deterioration. Eve had conversed with Satan until God's commandment seemed to her to be a lie, and the lies of the serpent seemed to be the truth.

Hear the message, you who need it! Some of you remember when the simple word of God, as stated in your mother's Bible, was law and gospel to you. When God said, "The wages of sin is death," you never doubted it for a moment. When God said, "Look not thou upon the wine when it is red, when it giveth his color in the cup, when it moveth itself aright. At the last it biteth like a serpent, and stingeth like an adder" (Proverbs 23:31–32), you had no doubt that it was heaven's truth; a merciful warning to keep your feet from a dangerous path. There was a time when the declaration of God's word that the house of the strange woman is "the way to hell" seemed certain fact. There was a time when the declaration of the divine word which says, "Be not deceived; God is not mocked; for whatsoever a man soweth, that shall he also reap" (Galatians 6:7) seemed as natural a truth as the growth of the wheat crop on your father's farm. What has wrought all this change? How is it that you are so indifferent and reckless of these statements now? Is it because you have discovered them to be untrue? Ah! you know that is not the case. The devil pays the same wages now as in the days of Eve. The adder in the wine has not lost its sting. The house of lust has not closed its back door into hell. The fields of the soul have not lost their fertility to grow harvests according to the seed sown. What has wrought the change? Is not the true answer this: that you have parleyed with the old serpent, that you have hardened your conscience, that you have played fast and loose with your better nature, until you are beginning to call evil good, and good evil?

Peace went out of the garden as sin entered it. Two vagabonds, in fear born of their sins, hid themselves from the presence of God. The garden ceased to be a paradise when sin came to possess their hearts. Truly has some poet written:

> "If sin be in the heart
> The fairest sky is foul, and sad the summer
>   weather,
> The eye no longer sees the lambs at play together,
> The dull ear cannot hear the birds that sing so
>   sweetly,
> And all the joy of God's good earth is gone
>   completely,

If sin be in the heart.

"If peace be in the heart
The wildest winter storm is full of solemn
   beauty.
The midnight lightning flash but shows the path
   of duty,
Each living creature tells some new and joyous
   story,
The very trees and stones all cast a ray of glory,
If peace be in the heart."

But someone says: "The battle is past, and I am defeated. The sin is already in my heart, and when I would do good the evil more than masters me and leaves me in sad bondage." The same God who brought a message of hope to Eve in the midst of her despair authorizes me to bring you a message of salvation if you will forsake your sins. There is no way you can regain your lost innocence but by giving up your sins and accepting pardon through Jesus Christ.

A little child was one day playing with a very beautiful and precious vase, when he put his hand in through the slender mouth and could not withdraw it. He ran to his father for help; but he, too, tried in vain to get it out. They were talking of breaking the vase, when the father said, "Make one more effort; open your hand and hold your fingers out straight and close together as you see me doing, and then pull." To the astonishment of the family the boy said, "O no, papa, I couldn't put out my fingers like that, for if I did, I would drop my penny." That was the secret of his trouble—he had been holding on to his penny all the time. Some of you are like him. You would like to be good;

you want to be a Christian; but there is some secret sin that you are cherishing, and are not willing to let go. You will never get out of the devil's clutches until you open wide your hand and let go all your sins. As you value your peace, your nobility of character, your immortal life, give up your sins now and forever!

32

THE FIRST COWARD
IN THE WORLD

"And the Lord God called unto Adam, and said unto him,
Where art thou? And he said, I heard thy voice in the
garden, and I was afraid, because I was naked; and I hid
myself. And he said, Who told thee that thou wast naked?
Hast thou eaten of the tree, whereof I commanded thee
that thou shouldest not eat? And the man said,
The woman whom thou gavest to be with me,
she gave me of the tree, and I did eat" (Genesis 3:9-12).

There is no accusation that will so quickly bring the hot blood of indignation to a man's face as to be called a coward. Perhaps it is because cowardice is the badge of sin. Sin was the source of cowardice in the world. Adam had no fear until he was conscious that he had broken God's law and brought himself under condemnation. He had no fear of the animal world before that. He was master over all the beasts of the field. He gave them their names, and he was put in possession of them. His fear was born of his sin. His intelligence, his power to reason, which was intended to give him control over all living creatures on the earth, was thwarted when his sin made him a coward.

An Arabic legend which has but recently come into our language tells how a noble young lion burned with a desire to travel over the world.

"Why," asked his mother, covering him with caresses, "why do you wish to leave me? Are you not happy here? Take care, my child; beyond these vast solitudes that make your empire you will meet, among other dangers, the most terrible of all your enemies—that formidable being they call man!"

At last, tied of this warning and taking counsel of his courage alone, the young heir to the kingdom of beasts took leave of his mother one day, saying: "I fear nothing; I am young and strong; I am as brave as my father was before me; and if I see this creature called man—well—he shall see me!"

He departed. The first day he perceived an ox in his road. "Are you man?" he asked.

"No," replied the peaceful creature, chewing his cud; "he of whom you speak is my master; he yokes me to the plow, and if I move too slowly for him he urges me on with a steel point with which he probes my flesh. It is called a goad, I believe."

The young lion walked off pensively. The next day he saw a horse hobbled in a field. "Are you man?" asked the fierce traveler.

"O no, my lord," cried the trembling horse. "I am his servant; I carry him on my back. When I do not go at the speed he desires he belabors my flanks with a sort of star-shaped wheel covered with pointed blades."

Shaking his mane fiercely, the young lion resumed his course, gnashing his teeth and asking himself, in impotent rage, who this being could be who made all things submit to his caprice, his force, his will!

A short time after that he met an animal of enormous size who seemed gifted with indomitable strength. "This time I cannot be mistaken," he approaching it. "You are man, are you not?"

"You are indeed wrong. I'm an elephant, and he whose name you have just spoken is my lord and master. I carry him on my back when he hunts the tiger."

On hearing these words the young lion hurried on, more and more perplexed.

Suddenly a hollow sound, occurring at regular intervals, startled him from his reverie. The noise seemed to come from the depth of the wood. He advanced and saw a great oak tree, in a clearing, tottering to the ground, felled by an instrument in the hands of a being whom the lion did not at first even notice. Addressing himself to the tree he asked: "Are you man?"

"No," replied the giant oak, sinking slowly down; "I am dying of the blows his hands have rained upon me."

Then for the first time the lion deigned to look at the being of whom the oak had spoken. But at the sight of a creature so paltry and frail he roared disdainfully: "How can this be! Is it you my mother fears so, and of whom she warned me? Was it one of you who dared approach my father? Is it you from whom they have told me to flee?"

"It is I," replied the woodsman, simply.

"But, you poor creature, you are feebleness itself! My name alone should make you pale with fear, and I could bring you to earth with one blow of my paw!"

Not deigning to respond at first, the man cut a deep gash in the trunk of the dying tree, and turning to the young lion said: "I seem feeble to you. Look at this oak tree, straight and tall, and full of pride in its mighty strength; nevertheless it is felled to the earth. It is not my feeble muscle with which I conquer you; it is mind! That makes me your master! You doubt it still? Put you paw in that groove, if you dare," he added, pointing to the crack he held open with his ax.

At the words "if you dare," the young lion obeyed without hesitation. The woodsman tore away his ax still wet with the sap of the tree; and the great beast was a prisoner.

"Well—and now; am I man?" asked the woodsman, gravely. "Am I your master?"

Crushed by such boldness, the lion bent his head in silence to acknowledge his defeat. As soon as he was liberated he stretched himself on the moss and began, sorrowfully, to lick his bleeding paw. The man bent over the vanquished beast and bathed the wound carefully, then went on his way, his ax swung over his shoulder, without saying a word or even turning his head.

The lion followed him with his eyes until he was lost to sight. Filled with shame, his confidence in his power and courage shaken, two great tears dimmed his eyes, and raising himself wearily he made his way slowly back to the desert. "From that day," says the old legend, "a lion has known it is useless to attack a brave man."

But man's supremacy over the universe was lost by his sin, and he is only slowly winning it back as he is escaping from the cruel bondage of iniquity, which made him first a coward and has held him since a slave.

The first result of Adam's sin was that it made him fear to meet God. Before that he had talked with God face to face. His supreme joy was in the perfect freedom and welcome which he felt in the divine presence. He had done always those things which were pleasing to God, and he rejoiced in the sunshine of God's pleasure. But the moment he has sinned against God he begins, cowardly, to hide himself—an indication of the unwisdom which comes to us through sin, as God was the only One who could forgive him, and thus bring peace to his heart. The wise thing would have been for Adam to go searching after God, crying aloud through the trees of the garden, "My God, I have sinned against thee! Where art thou?" But his sin drives him into doing just the opposite of that. He foolishly tries to hide himself from God, hoping to escape the results of his sin. And so it is not Adam seeking after God, but it is God who searches after Adam, and calls aloud, "Adam, where art thou?"

Are there any here who are trying to hide from God? Your sins have made you a coward—you dare not lift your shamed eyes into the light of his face—so you are seeking to cover up your transgressions and find some escape from your misery in that way. But there is no escape by covering up sin. David found sin thus covered to be like "a fire in his bones," and many a modern sinner finds himself a smothered volcano of burning conscience, which he vainly tries to crush out. We cannot escape from the law of God; neither can we escape from his questioning. David thought this matter all out, and said: "There is not a word in my tongue, but, lo, O Lord, thou knowest it altogether. Thou has beset me behind and before, and laid thine hand upon me. Such knowledge is too wonderful for me; it is high, I cannot attain unto it. Whither shall I go from thy Spirit? or whither shall I flee from thy presence? If I ascend up into heaven, thou art there. If I make my bed in hell, behold, thou art there. If I take the wings of the morning, and dwell in the uttermost parts of the sea; even there shall thy hand lead me, and thy right hand shall hold me. If I say, Surely the darkness shall cover me; even the night shall be light about me. Yea, the darkness hideth not from thee; but the night shineth as the day: the darkness and the light are both alike to thee" (Psalm 139:4-12).

I think many people do not appreciate that the very worst thing sin ever does for us is to bring about this separation of the soul from God. Adam no longer enjoyed the presence of God. Instead of the feeling of a son for his father, he became vagabond in feeling before a word had been said to him by way of punishment of his sin. Sin carries with it the pledge of its own punishment. The real vagabondage of sin begins the moment it is committed, in the sense of separation from God. The deepest sinners, and those who are in the greatest danger of eternal disaster, are not always those whose sins bring them under the shame and disgrace of the fellow-men. Surely the New Testament idea of it, as set forth by Christ himself, is that the worst sinner in the world is the intelligent and, it may be, refined and cultured man or woman who lives without God, and whose life of indifference and selfishness is a perpetual defiance to God. Christ said that the publican and the harlot were more likely to press into the kingdom of God and be saved than these self-sufficient people who have washed the outside of the platter but whose hearts give him no love and no devotion. Think for a moment what that means: that the drunkard, or the outbreaking and disgraced sinner whose name is pilloried by social condemnation, is more likely to be saved than some man, like yourself, who lives prudently and carefully so far as the ordinary requirements of society are concerned, but lives prayerless and selfish, refusing to give to God affection and service; that a poor, lost woman of the street has more chance of salvation than many a woman who would draw back her skirts from the contamination of her touch, but who sins against light and intelligence and hardens her heart against the wealth of God's love poured into her home and her life.

Dr. Horton says that the position of such people is the same as that of Lucifer, son of the morning, who fell from heaven because he was to himself a god. Such a man is the supreme sinner against God. And the awful fact is that such sinners are so common in our day, and so difficult to reach with the plain and simple truth of God's word. I long to do my whole duty by any of you so situated who hear me at this hour. I do not bring against you any railing accusation. I do not speak in the spirit of accusation, but with a brother's hand draw aside the fig-leaf apron of excuses you are making, and seek, for your soul's sake, to show you the nakedness of your sin before God. You have not lifted your club against your brother, like Cain; you have not fallen into drunkenness, like Noah; nor lost the glory of your strength through lust, like Samson; but, like Adam, you have yielded to the seductive temptations of a sin that has separated you from God. You may still say your prayers, but they have lost their meaning. There is in them no conscious approach of your soul toward God in loving confidence and trust. In your better moments, when conscience has the right of way, you know yourself for what you are—a sinner shrinking from the condemnation impending because of transgression.

There is just one hope, and that is to stop hiding and come back, in the name of Jesus Christ, to the God against whom you have sinned. None plead his name in vain, and no other name has power to cancel your debt; "for he hath made him to be sin for us, who knew no sin" (2 Corinthians 5:21). And we have the promise that, "if we confess our sins," instead of covering them, "he is faithful and just to forgive us our sins, and to cleanse us from all unrighteousness" (1 John 1:9). The way of confession is the way of salvation.

A young civil engineer of western Kentucky, who assisted his father in his business of railroad prospecting and surveying, had contracted intemperate habits. His work from place to place threw him into the society of loose men much more than his father seemed to be aware of, and being a generous convivial fellow, he paid for his popularity by copying their indulgences.

His dangerous appetite and his occasional fits of dissipation were so shrewdly concealed that his parents were kept in ignorance of them for two years—until he was twenty years old. They were worthy people and constant churchgoers, the father being choir leader and the mother a soprano singer.

Once, while the young man was employed on a section of road forty miles from home, it became necessary to "lie over" from Thursday noon till Monday. His father would be detained till Saturday, reaching home in time for the choir rehearsal, but the son returned at once and went to a liquor saloon to commence a three days' "spree."

The saloon keeper understood his case too well, and kept him hidden in his own apartments. When his father returned, expecting to find the boy at home, a surprise awaited him. Trouble began when the question, "Where's Harry?" informed the startled mother that he was missing.

For the Sunday evening service she was to sing a solo, and by special request—because she sang it so well—her selection was to be the hymn, "Where Is My Wandering Boy?"

It seemed to her impossible to perform her promise under the circumstances; and when, on Sunday morning, a policeman found Harry, the certainty was no more comforting than the suspense had been; but she was advised that he would be "all right tomorrow morning: and that she would better not see him until he 'sobered up'."

Toward night Harry began to come to himself. His father had hired a man to stay with him and see to his recovery, and when he learned that his mother had been told of his plight, the information cut him to the heart and helped to sober him.

When the bells rang he announced his determination to go to church. He knew nothing of the evening program. He was still in his working clothes, but no reasoning could dissuade him, and his attendant, after making him as presentable as possible, went with him to the service.

Entering by a side door, they found seats in a secluded corner, but not far from the pulpit and the organ. The house filled, and after the usual succession of prayer, anthem, and sermon the time for the solo came. It was probably the first time in that church that a mother had ever sung out of her own soul's distress:

"Oh, where is my wandering boy to-night,
The child of my love and care?"

Every word was to her own heart a cruel stab. The great audience caught the feeling of the song, but there was one heart as near to breaking as her own. She sung the last stanza,

"Go for my wandering boy to-night,
Go search for him where you will,
But bring him to me with all his blight,
And tell him I love him still.
Oh, where is my wandering boy?"

Just then a young man in a woolen shirt and corduroy trousers and jacket made his way down the aisle to the choir stairs with outstretched arms, and, sobbing like a child, exclaimed, "Here I am, mother!"

The mother ran down the steps and folded him in her arms. The astonished organist, quick to take in the meaning of the scene, pulled out all his stops and played "Old Hundred"—"Praise God, from whom all blessing flow." The congregation, with their hundreds of voice, joined in the great doxology, while the father, the pastor, and the friends of the returned prodigal stood by him with moist eyes and welcoming hands.

The wayward boy ended his wanderings then and there. That moment was a consecration and the beginning of a life of sobriety and Christian usefulness.

Some wanderers may be here to-night. Will you no openly confess Christ as your Saviour? Today is the day of salvation!

33

THE SINNER CROSS-EXAMINED

"Why is thy countenance fallen?" (Genesis 4:6).

God is the great Questioner. He alone in all the universe has at once the right and the power to interrogate every intelligent soul to the very depths of its thought and being. Every man entering upon any course of conduct should take into consideration the fact that it will not go unquestioned. He may defy or elude the questioning of his fellow-men, but he cannot put aside the heart-searching inquiries that will come from God. Adam hid in the Garden of Eden and sought to shelter himself from the discovery of his sin, but through the trees of his despoiled paradise there came the ringing question, "Adam, where art thou?" The question was personal, and he had no trouble in finding out who was intended. When Elijah had fled away in cowardice from the wrath of Jezebel, and had for a time forgotten his mission and his work, hiding in the cave in the mountains, the voice of Him who had called him to be a prophet sought him out with the probing question: "What doest thou here, Elijah?" That was a question which could not be put aside, and which had to be answered.

When Paul was on his way to Damascus, full of hate and bigotry, and was suddenly surrounded and overwhelmed by the glare of that light in which the noonday glory seemed insignificant, he was met by the appeal from the crucified but now risen Christ, "Why persecutest thou me?" Paul had authority—reaching to dungeon and rack and cross—over the disciples of Jesus, but the Christ himself he could not put aside, and his question had to be answered. Cain was no exception to this rule. He had, at the point where our text occurs, done no overt act of enmity against his brother. He had lifted no club to strike him, and doubtless in his heart no purpose had yet formed to destroy the life of Abel. But God, who sees and judges the thoughts of men, beholds the falling countenance and the bitter envy that is behind it, and faces Cain with a question that goes to the root of his sin when he asks: "Why art thou wroth, and why is thy countenance fallen?"

Depend upon it, we shall, each of us, have to meet the same kind of questionings. We are not our own. We do not belong to a lawless world. We are not the children of chaos. We are the creation of infinite wisdom and love, capable of lofty deeds, and we cannot recklessly throw away our splendid inheritance, dragging ourselves in the gutter of moral and spiritual bankruptcy, without facing heart-searching questions from the very throne of God. How merciful it is that the path to ruin is thus made thorny and hard! We quote the proverb, "The way of the transgressor is hard," many times with a tone of regret, as though it were a hard saying and an undesirable fact, but there is nothing which more plainly shows the love and merciful provision of God. We should be grateful that it is not easy to do wrong and keep on doing it. As Christ said to Paul, "It is hard for thee to kick against the pricks" (Acts 9:5) so God has set many a pricking thorn in the path that leads away from peace into the darkness of sin. Happy are they who regard these merciful warnings!

The fact that Abel's sacrifice was accepted while Cain's was rejected is by no means proof that Abel was a pet of the divine heart while there was prejudice against Cain. While the sacrifices seem similar in many ways, the spirit of the two men made them as different as light and darkness. Cain brought his offering, as a matter of form or ceremony, out of a bad and wicked life. His heart and conduct were alike evil. He did not bring his offering in the spirit of the poor publican, who smote upon his breast and said, "God be merciful to me a sinner," but rather as a matter of religious display. As Joseph Parker says, Cain was the sort of a churchgoer who could go to church and make his offering and then be in a spirit to kill his brother as soon as church was over. I fear we have much of that sort of churchgoing yet; men who attend the public worship, unite in its songs of praise, giving outward deference, as Cain did, to the worship of God, who yet go away to politics or business or social engagements on Monday with nothing in their spirit or conduct to indicate that their character has in any way been affected by the Sunday's service. To join in public worship on Sunday and go from that to cheat in business, or like in politics, or be revengeful in social life on week days, is to reincarnate the spirit of Cain in modern life.

Abel's worship was very different. He was a good man not alone on days of sacrifice offering, but on all days of the week. He came to the worship in humility, bringing the very best of his flocks as a sacrifice for his sins. The man who brings only formal service to God does not bring the best, but the poorest, of all his possessions. Abel brought the best he had in a grateful and loving spirit. Cain, in a spirit of vulgar display, brought the poorest he had, with a greedy, selfish heart behind it.

We ought not to count it such a hard thing to give God our love and affection, for from our babyhood it has been the only gold that would pass in the highest exchange. What true mother would compare for a moment the most insignificant gift which came from a child obedient and loving with the rich gift of another that was flung with contempt from a wicked, willful heart? I recently saw a company of children out gathering wild flowers, when suddenly one of the little flock proposed that each of them should gather a bouquet for mother. They set about it with a will. The older children brought home very respectable bouquets, made up of a diversity of flowers, and they were received with smiles of appreciation, for love was in them all; but the baby had plucked a few ragged pieces of clover that had seen their best days, and now and then a weed that his chubby fingers could break, and brought the ugly little bunch of half-withered plants, with a smile of heavenly innocence and love that illuminated his beaming face, exclaiming, "Baby gathered the f'owers for muvver!" And I noticed that, while all the bouquets were received and cared for, those the mother seemed to appreciate most and treasure longest the baby's faded clover and worthless weeds. He had brought the very best he could. No wonder that God, who made a father's and a mother's love, and whose heart is the center of every perfect feeling of sympathetic relationship, rejoices in him who brings his offerings with the loving spirit of a son.

Cain's spirit is evidenced by the effect produced upon him by the divine refusal to accept his offering and the appreciation of Abel's sacrifice. He was not wounded at the heart because his own offering did not please God; he was too selfishly indifferent to the divine favor for that; but the thing that rankled in his bosom was that Abel was marked for approval, while he, the pretentious and self-sufficient Cain, was discounted. This was the cause of his anger, and this it was that made his countenance fall into the ugliness of envy and hate.

How tenderly God reasoned with him, reminding him that the path of religious prosperity and happiness was as wide open to him as it was to Abel, and that if he would turn over a new leaf and begin to do well, bringing his offering out of a good heart and in a right spirit, he too, would be accepted. But the other alternative was put just as clearly: that if he continued to do wrong, and nurtured in his heart the envious, revengeful spirit which now possessed him, still greater sin waited at the door in the near future.

The word translated in our version "lieth" is a very strong, vital word, which is well translated "coucheth" in the revised version. There it reads: "Sin coucheth at the door." So Cain did not go on to do murder without warning. If at the voice of God he had turned about then, with sincere repentance, how different would have been the story! But he brooded over Abel's happiness and success until thy seemed to be the cause of the sharp proddings of his wicked conscience. So, when at last, in a sudden outburst of passion, he rose up and slew his brother, his awful sin was the wild beast which God had warned him was couching at the door of the envy and anger which he cherished on the day his sacrifice was rejected.

I doubt not this is just the earnest, heart-searching message needed by some of you who are listening to me. Your sin is in its beginning; it has not yet entered upon the open, outbreaking, disgraceful epoch of its history. It is as yet an evil picture in the imagination, only the shadow of a purpose that haunts you like a specter in your worst hours. In your better moods you thrust it aside for the devil that it is, and will not admit it to be a possibility. But it returns again and again, and every time the temptation has added force. There is a demonlike attraction in sin. While we revolt against it and look back upon it with remorse, yet every time it is yielded to, or even considered in the secret chambers of the imagination as a possibility, it lures the soul with ever-increasing, magnetic force. The only wise course is to thrust the sin aside at first, by the help of God. He is as willing to give us power to rule over it and put it under our feet as he was to give power to Cain, who rejected the divine aid, or to Abel, who accepted it.

It seems to me no more bitter ingredient can enter into the poisoned cup of sin, which the unrepenting sinner is forced to drink down to the dregs, than the conviction that the final disaster which overthrew the life was a wild beast which the sinner himself chained at his door and fattened for his own destruction. You could hardly believe the story of the folly of a man who would chain a fierce, bloodthirsty tiger at his own door, ready to tear him in pieces when he should pass out from his home; and yet God says in this warning to Cain that that is exactly what a man does who persists in purposing and doing evil: he is chaining at the door of tomorrow or the day after a still greater sin, which will rend him in pieces. His greed and selfishness and envious anger seemed to Cain, no doubt, very harmless kinds of sins, as they doubtless seem to some of you. He did not see that lying at the door, only a few days away, was murder, with its haggard face and assassin-like fingers. Would to God I had the power to stand before any man or woman here who has a rotten spot of self-indulgence, or greed, or rankling envy, growing in the soul, and could open your eyes to show you at the door of the future the horrid sin into which this will grow, and the possible shame and ruin to which it may bring your unhappy soul! If I could do that, there would be many who would turn this very hour from a life of evil to a life of doing well.

Remember, God does not ask impossible things of us. In its great essentials the Christian life is a very simple thing. It is to cease to do evil and begin to do well, and that not in your own strength. Pardon waits for you if, with the humility and simple-heartedness of Abel, you will turn away from your sin and accept the divine aid for a pure and upright life. You do not need to bring the firstling of the flock to be slain upon an earthly altar, for Christ has become "the Lamb of God that taketh away the sin of the world" (John 1:29). His blood has made atonement for you. You can bring the best you have: your open confession, your humble service, your loving obedience. Such a decision would turn many a Cain-life, with its approaching doom, into an Abel-life, brightening in the smile of God, which illuminates a path that will shine brighter and brighter unto the perfect day.

34

NOAH, AND THE TRAGIC STORY OF THE MAN WHO BUILT THE ARK

*"And God said unto Noah, The end of all flesh is come be-
fore me; for the earth is filled with violence through them:
and, behold, I will destroy them with the earth.
Make thee an ark"* (Genesis 6:13, 14).

*"And the Lord said unto Noah, Come thou and all thy
house into the ark; for thee have I seen righteous before me
in this generation"* (Genesis 7:1).

*"And Noah went in, and his sons, and his wife, and his
sons' wives with him, into the ark"* (Genesis 7:7).

"And the Lord shut him in" (Genesis 7:16).

*"And every living substance was destroyed which was upon
the face of the ground, both man, and cattle, and the
creeping things, and the fowl of the heaven; and they were
destroyed from the earth: and Noah only remained alive,
and they that were with him in the ark"* (Genesis 7:23).

The warnings of the Bible are as full of mercy as its invitations and its promises. God always deals righteously with his children. The way of sin is made hard, and dark, and full of forebodings, while the "path of the just is as a shining light, that shineth more and more unto the perfect day" (Proverbs 4:18). Men do not come to the end of a sinful way without being warned of the result. Men who do not like the wages of sin that they are receiving must remember that God has declared plainly in his word that "the wages of sin is death." When God had determined on the destruction of the world by the flood he gave notice of it for a hundred and twenty years. Noah was his preacher of righteousness, and there was abundant opportunity for repentance and salvation. If the people of the antediluvian world had heard the message of Noah with the earnest care given to the message of Jonah by the wicked people of Nineveh, there can be no doubt that the destructive flood never would have occurred. The penitent prayer of the people would have turned aside the sentence to doom.

Noah is usually supposed to have been a very unsuccessful preacher, and yet we must not make little of the fact that he saved the people who knew him best. His wife, his sons, and their families, all came with him into the ark. He did better than Lot, for he was not able to take his wife with him, and lost a great share of his own family. There is something genuine about a man's religion when he wins to firm faith in God all the people of his own household. It must have been a great sorrow to Noah that he was not able to win his acquaintances, especially the hundreds, and possibly thousands, who must have wrought under his direction in construction the great ark which God had commanded him to build. It is well for us to reflect that God expects every one of us who have named the name of

Christ to be a preacher of righteousness. First of all, we are to be such evangelists in our own homes. It is a terrible thing for Christians to be indifferent or careless about the conversion of their own children. If the children are to grow up prayerful, and reverent, and spiritual, they must become so very largely through the fidelity of the parents. Dr. Norman Macleod says that he shall never forget the impression made upon him, during the first year of his ministry, by a mechanic whom he had visited and on whom he had urged the paramount duty of family prayer. Months passed away, when one day this same mechanic entered his study, bursting into tears as he said: "You remember that girl, sir? She was my only child. She died suddenly this morning. She has gone, I hope, to God; but, if so, she can tell him, what now breaks my heart, that she never heard a prayer in her father's house of from her father's lips! O, that she were with me but for one day again!" Let us not plant thorns in our pillows for after years by living worldly, prayerless lives in the presence of those who have a right to look to us for guidance and example.

Outside our own households there are those that come in close contact with us in a business or social way to whom we may be the preacher of righteousness more effectively than anybody else. A minister preaching in a strange place had laid emphasis on the fact that every Christian, however humble, or poor, or busy, can do some personal work for Christ if he be only willing. After the lecture a poor woman rushed up to him and said, half indignantly:

"What can I do? I am a poor widow with five children to support, and I have to work night and day to take care of my family. How can I find time to go and speak to anyone about Christ?"

"Does the milkman call at your house early in the morning?"

"Of course, he does."

"Does the baker follow him?"

"Why, yes, to be sure he does."

"Does the butcher once or twice a week visit you?"

"Yes," was the curt reply, and the woman, her face flushed with excitement and apparent vexation, flew away.

Two years after the same minister spoke in the same place. After the service a woman asked him:

"Do you know me?"

"No."

"Well, I am the person who was vexed with you, two years ago, when you asked me whether the milkman and baker and butcher visited me. But I went home to think and pray, and God helped me to do my duty. I now have to tell you that, through my humble efforts, five persons have been led to the Saviour, and they are all consistent working members of the church."

Professional men often have opportunities such as never come to a preacher in the pulpit to carry heaven's message of mercy to a needy soul. Dr. J. M. Buckley relates an incident, which recently occurred in New York City, which shows how such opportunities come sometimes to physicians. A young woman of keenest intellect, highly accomplished, had all her life sat under the teaching of so-called liberal ministers who have nothing to say except that evangelical Christianity is an outworn superstition.

She accepted their views, that Christ was a mere man and that a future life is probable, but not certain. She lived on in this way until there came a day when she was taken ill. At first there was no occasion for alarm, yet she became strangely weak as one day followed another. Her physicians were baffled and her devoted parents terrified. Conscious of the changes, and affected by the anxiety of others which it was impossible for them to conceal, the pastor who had lulled her to sleep with his skepticism concerning experimental religion called to converse with her about a musical performance which he had attended and which he much regretted that she could not have enjoyed. Suddenly she said to him: "I believe that I shall die. Cannot you tell me something to help me meet my fate?" All her blind guide could say to her was: "This is the time to test your philosophy; we must all die; everyone that ever lived has had to pass through the same valley. It is as natural to die as to live. Be courageous; be strong." There was no response from her, but gathering from his remarks that her apprehensions were just, a deep horror settled upon her face, and she said, "Where shall I go?" "That," said he, "no one knows; we can form no idea of that except by dying." Now the young lady's physician was a Christian, and as he saw the nameless dread in her countenance, he thought within himself: "Have I nothing to say? Can I see her drift unhelped to meet her fate?" And, swayed by an impulse which stimulated his memory, he whispered to her the beautiful prayers and words of promise which had often fallen upon his ears, watching her as one might watch the effect of a cordial upon the fainting. Her eye brightened a little, but not till he came to the words, "God so loved the world that he gave his only begotten Son" (John 3:16), and, "This is a faithful saying, and worthy of all acceptation, that Christ Jesus came into the world to save sinners" (1 Timothy 1:15), and, "Him that cometh to me I will in no wise cast out" (John 6:37), did she speak; then she pressed his hand and said, "Doctor, I thank you; I will trust that." What an opportunity for that physician! How well worth a lifetime of work the privilege of that one deed of Christian love!

If we could only realize the vast treasure at stake, how much more enthusiasm and devotion we should put into our search after immortal souls and into our efforts to win them from sin. If we would only give ourselves to saving souls with even the enthusiasm that men use about far less important worldly matters, great results would speedily be shown. A London literary man who is seeking after rare books and manuscripts happened to enter a little tobacconist's shop, in the East End of London, in order to ask his way to a street in the neighborhood. He was just addressing his request to the elderly Jewess who was in charge of the establishment, when he saw, to his horror, that she was tearing the pages from a black letter volume which lay on her lap, in order to wrap therein a few ounces of tobacco which she was weighing out in readiness for her customers. He snatched the volume from her hand in a frenzy of apprehension, and found that it was *The Good Huswife's Jewell*, a very rare collection of recipes published in the reign of Elizabeth. With admirable presence of mind he offered a shilling for the book, and the offer was eagerly accepted. Three leaves were missing, and the tobacconist, who explained that she had bought the treasure from a peddler of waste paper, fortunately remembered the names of the customers who had carried them wrapped round their tobacco. The literary man followed up each leaf until he found it. The fly leaf had a narrow escape, as the laboring man into whose possession it had fallen had already twisted it to make a lighter for his pipe, and was reaching it toward the fire when the gentleman entered his humble home. *The Good Huswife's Jewell* is now complete, and its rescuer from oblivion is said to be one of the happiest men in London.

Surely the follower of Jesus Christ, who has come to know in his own heart the power of Christ to forgive sins, ought to seek for immortal souls that are perishing in ignorance and sin with as much enthusiasm and earnestness as is shown by a searcher after rare books; and yet such a passion for souls on the part of every Christian in the church would revolutionize the city and cause the people to say of us, as was said of Paul and his friends when they came to Ephesus, "They that turn the world upside down have come hither" (Acts 17:6).

And yet, despite all we can do, some will refuse to heed the Gospel; and in the presence of good example, and the salvation of others, will go on in sin and be lost. It seems very strange to us that the very men who lived in Noah's community, who saw his pure and righteous life, who heard his witness to the warning which God had given, who even worked for him in building the ark, should yet have failed to turn to God in repentance and seek their own salvation. Yet, before we condemn these as the greatest sinners in the world, it is well to ask if people are not doing the same thing today. These men had been preached to, but so have you. Some of you who hear this word tonight have attended public worship, more or less frequently, all your

lives. You have heard many a sermon which had in it sufficient Gospel truth to make you know your sin and to point
out Christ as your Saviour. It will not be possible for you
to stand up at last and say, "I might have been saved, but
nobody honestly preached me the Gospel." You have heard
the Gospel again and again, and you must give an account
for it.

These people had been prayed for. Noah was a man of
the type of Abraham, who, wherever he went, built an altar
unto the Lord. They must have known that they were the
objects of Noah's prayers, and yet they hardened their
hearts against them, and would not accept Noah's God.
Who of you has not been the object of earnest and sincere
prayer on the part of Christian people? Some of you have
been prayed for by a Christian father, or mother, and by
those who are nearest to you in love and sympathy; and in
answer to their prayers the Holy Spirit has again and again
striven with your heart, and yet you have resisted him.
These prayers you must give an account for.

Again, these people, many of them, had worked for and
with a thoroughly good man. They had seen the Gospel in
its strongest presentation—incarnated in the life of an honest, sincere man. But have you never known any Christians?
There may be times when you are ready to sneer and be
cynical about the conduct of some church members, yet
there is not one of you but has known some earnest, faithful souls whose transfigured lives have put your own life
under condemnation, and you have said in your inmost
soul, "O that I were as genuine and holy in my motives and
purposes and life as that man, or that woman!" You must
give an account for the testimony of such lives.

And the reasons that kept these people from accepting Noah's message were, no doubt, the same sort of reasons that are keeping some of you from salvation. A great many were kept from joining Noah in a life of prayer because of the delight which they took in worldly things. The present life of the passions and the appetites was so near and so noisy that they gave themselves up to it and silenced the voice of conscience, which sought to tell them of the demands of the higher life of the soul. Is that not your trouble? You will not be smitten down by the paw of a lion, but your soul will be eaten up of moths. In eating and drinking, in the temporary things of life, you fritter away your interest and refuse to give ear to your soul, that hungers for worship and faith and a life of noble self-denial.

No doubt then, as now, procrastination was the cause of the destruction of many. The danger did not seem to be immediate, and so they postponed preparation. "Time enough yet," they said, until the last day of the hundred and twenty years had passed, and Noah, and every man and woman he could persuade to go with him, had gone into the ark, where the Lord shut him in, and they were shut out. Will you make that fatal mistake? You are in the same current. You are putting off your return to God. You are putting off the question of your conversion, of your immortal salvation, to some indefinite time in the future. Do not, I beg you, continue in so unwise a course. Every day of procrastination makes it easier to continue on the fatal way. Rouse yourself now to hear the word of wisdom! "Awake, thou that sleepest, and arise from the dead, and Christ shall give thee light" (Ephesians 5:14). The door will not always stand open. You are in danger of its being shut at any time. Enter in while it is still ajar, with welcome and mercy for you.

35

NOAH'S DRUNKENNESS— THE PERIL OF THE WINEGLASS

"And Noah began to be an husbandman, and he planted a vineyard: and he drank of the wine, and was drunken; and he was uncovered within his tent" (Genesis 9:20, 21).

We hear a great deal about the temptations of youth, and not much about the temptations that beset middle-aged people and those who are still farther along in the way of their life history. Yet every little while we hear of some man who has lived through youth and early manhood uprightly, with good habits, winning respect and honor on all sides, but who as he has grown older seems to have lost the pressure of restraint which once held him in check from evil ways, and shocks and astonishes the community by falling into outbreaking and disgraceful sin. It is not infrequently the case that such disaster is connected with the sin of drunkenness. I have myself known more than one man who reached the age of fifty years a total abstainer, and then, presuming on the power of will to resist undue seduction from strong drink, and persuaded perhaps in his own mind to believe that some stimulant would be valuable for his health, has been led to begin a course of moderate drinking which has ended in a few years in drunkenness and debauch. Noah seems to have been a case of that sort. All his early life was pure and strong. He was a man of upright conversation and of wholesome and noble conduct. He pleased God and was a preacher of righteousness for a hundred and twenty years. And yet, after God's signal interposition in his behalf in the preparation of the ark for his salvation, when once again the world is before him, with the rainbow of mercy and promise spanning the heavens above him, he falls under the temptation of the wine cup and is seen in a drunken debauch which shames his family and ends in the most serious consequences to some that are dear to him. The truth is that the only safe course for young or old is total abstinence from strong drink. The glass of water may not bring so suddenly the sparkle to the eye and the color to the cheek as does the glass of wine, but, on the other hand, it never brings down a man's gray hairs in disgrace to a dishonored grave. Ella Wheeler Wilcox sings a tale of a debate between these two glasses:

> "There sat two glasses, filled to the brim,
> On a rich man's table, rim to rim;
> One was ruddy, as red as blood,
> And one was clear as the crystal flood.
> Said the glass of wine to his paler brother,
> 'Let us tell tales of the past to each other,
> I can tell of banquet, and revel, and mirth,
> Where I was king, for I ruled in might,
> And the proudest and grandest souls on earth
> Fell under my touch as though struck with blight.
> From the heads of kings I have torn the crown;
> From the height of fame I have torn men down;
> I have blighted many an honored name;

I have taken virtue and given shame;
I have tempted youth with a sip, a taste,
Which has made his future a barren waste.
Far greater than any king am I,
Or than any army beneath the sky;
I have made the arm of the driver fail
And sent the train from the iron rail;
I have made good ships go down at sea,
And the shrieks of the lost were sweet to me;
For they said, "Behold, how great you be!
Fame, strength, wealth, genius, before you fall,
And your might and power are over all."
Ho! Ho! Pale brother,' laughed the wine,
'Can you boast of deeds as great as mine?'
"Said the water glass: 'I cannot boast
Of all king dethroned, or a murdered host;
But I can tell of hearts that were sad
By my crystal drops made light and glad;
Of thirst that I've quenched, and brows I have
    laved;
Of hands I have cooled, and souls I have saved.
I have leaped through the valley, dashed down
    the mountain,
Slept in the sunshine, and dripped from the
    fountain;
I have burst my cloud fetters and dropped from
    the sky,
And everywhere gladdened the landscape and eye.
I have eased the hot forehead of fever and pain,
I have made the parched meadows grow fertile
    with grain;
I can tell of the powerful wheel of the mil
That ground out the flour and turned at my will;
I can tell of manhood, debased by you,
That I have uplifted and crowned anew.
I cheer, I help, I strengthen and aid,

I gladden the heart of man and maid;
I set the chained wine-captive free,
And all are the better for knowing me.'
"These are the tales they told each other,
The glass of wine and its paler brother,
As they sat together, filled to the brim,
On a rich man's table, rim to rim."

If I speak to any man or woman who is without settled principles of total abstinence from strong drink, I would like to appeal to you as Joshua did at Shechem, "Choose you this day whom ye will serve" (Joshua 24:15).

The war between the United States and Spain has given us many striking illustrations of the peril of strong drink. The American navy, which in the course of a few months has put itself in the leading place among the navies of the world for gunnery and skill and endurance and courage, superiority of every sort, is the one branch of the United States public service where intoxicating liquors are rigidly prohibited. The fact is that we had been getting ready to do miracles with our navy by over half a century of growing sobriety. In 1831 Congress took an advance step by providing that all in the navy who voluntarily relinquished their regular ration of liquor should be paid six cents a day extra. In 1842 the ration was cut down to one gill, but the alternative of half a pint of wine was added, and if a sailor did not use it, he was allowed three cents a day. The first year of the Civil War brought a greatly increased naval force and increased trouble from strong drink. Moral sentiment has progressed, too. In July 1862 Congress revolutionized the American navy by passing the historic law providing: "That from and after the first day of September, 1862, the spirit ration in the navy of the United States shall forever cease, and thereafter no distilled spirituous liquors shall be admitted on board of vessels of war, except as medical stores, and upon order and under the control of the medical officers of such vessels, and to be used only for medical purposes. From and after the first day of September next there shall be allowed and paid to each person in the navy, now entitled to the spirit ration, five cents per day in the commutation and lieu thereof, which shall be in addition to the present pay." And since that day there has been no grog in the United States navy. This was the origin of the little couplet:

> "They've raised his pay five cents a day
> And stopped his grog forever."

It was these sober men, fed on honest food and drink, that gave them solid muscles and steady nerves and clear heads, whom Cervera undertook to fight with a mob of Spanish drunkards. There never was a better illustration of the result of water pitted against wine, sobriety pitted against drunkenness, in the history of the race. The Spanish officers sought to stimulate the sailors on their splendid modern cruisers by firing them with strong drink. They chose for their attempt at escape the hour on Sunday morning when they knew that the crews of the American ships would be at religious services. And with the command to advance came the order: "Open the stores of wine and brandy." Officers and men drank freely therefrom. The Spanish officers drew their pistols and threatened instant death to the first man who flinched or hesitated in his work. In the stoke hole, with the mercury at a hundred and twenty degrees, half-drunken officers stood near half-drunken stokers, and the first man who gave way to fatigue and heat and the effect of the liquor was shot in his tracks. On the gun decks the sun beamed down on men whose stomachs were filled with the fiery liquid, and made them half mad. They tore their clothing from off their backs, cursing and shrieking because of the strain and the liquor. Thus nerved with liquor the Spaniards prepared for the desperate struggle. The Americans went from their wholesome breakfast, with no stimulant stronger than water or coffee, followed by their Sunday prayers, and history will ever hold in wonder the result of that great naval duel between sober men and drunkards.

It is greatly to be regretted, and greatly to our discredit as a nation, that the government of the United States has not had as much wisdom in dealing with its soldiers as with its sailors. The establishment of army canteens by the government itself, and the taking of volunteers—who enlisted out of heroic spirit to fight for their country and to uphold the "Star Spangled Banner"—and degrading them to be bartenders, is a disgrace to the nation. There can be no doubt that the army canteens have during the Spanish War caused more disease and death than the wounds of the enemy. There is abundant testimony that the large death roll in our army camps, where the soldiers have not been in the face of the enemy at all, has been caused in a great degree by strong drink. As an indignant editor has recently said, the army canteen is more dangerous than the battle field. Scars upon the soldier's body are honorable, but the rotting drunkard, manufactured by consent of the government, if not by its active efforts, is a curse that disgraces both the soldier and the government long after war has ceased. It is a dishonor that the United States should betray a mother's, a wife's, or a sister's confidence by upholding a nuisance and a peril which the best citizens are fighting at home with all their strength. It is a shameful thing that the government should consent to protect and forward the canteen, and thus bring temptation and possible ruin to yong men who scorn to patronize the saloon at home. Because of these army canteens many soldiers who escaped death in the fever hospital will come back sots.

One does not have to go far for illustrations or warnings of the peril which comes from the drink. It spares neither childhood nor old age. One day, within a week, in New York City, a gray-haired man sixty-seven years old, a respectable man and fairly well-to-do, stabbed his son, twenty-six years old, to death in the presence of his horror-stricken family, simply because, while under the maddening influence of strong drink, he came home and found his son lying on the father's bed taking a nap. Had he been sober, nothing could have tempted him to do such a deed, but the drink in him made him a murderer. On the same day, in the same city and the same ward, there was found lying in the gutter, reeking with the fumes of liquor, a well-dressed little boy of seven years. He belonged to a good family. He was taken to a hospital, and when the doctors had brought him to, so that he could talk, this little boy, scarcely more than a baby, who had never tasted liquor in his life until that day, said that a saloon keeper had first given him a big drink of beer, and had then given him a glass of "something cold that burned his throat"—which those about his cot in the hospital had not difficulty in recognizing as whisky. The reporter nonchalantly closed his report of the occurrence by saying that no attempt was made to arrest the saloon keeper.

This traffic in strong drink is the horrid blight of our

time. John Ruskin says, "Drunkenness is not only the cause of crime, it is crime; and the encouragement of drunkenness for the sake of profit on the sale of drink is certainly one of the most criminal methods of assassination for money every adopted by the people of any age or country."

A physician relates that he was standing with a friend in front of a saloon in a neighboring city when a builder of his acquaintance, a man of amiable and excellent character, a first-class workman, full of business, with an interesting family, respected by everybody and bidding fair to be one of the leading men of the city, came up to them and laughingly said:

"Well, I have just done what I never did before in my life."

"What was that?"

"Why, a man has owed me a bill for work for a long time, and I dunned him for the money till I was tired; but a minute ago I caught him out here and asked him for the money. 'Well,' he said, 'I'll pay it to you if you'll step in here and get a drink with me.' 'No," said I; 'I never drink—never drank in my life.' 'Well,' he replied, 'do as you please; if you won't drink with me, I won't pay your bill, that's all!' But I told him I could not do that. However, finding he would not pay the bill, rather than lose the money I went in and got the drink." And he laughed at the strange occurrence, as he concluded.

As soon as he had finished the story the doctor's companion, an old, discreet, shrewd man, turned to him, and in a most impressive tone said, "Sir, that was the dearest drink that ever crossed your lips, and the worst bill you ever collected."

Happy would it have been for that man had he taken warning at the word of reproof, for the physician testifies that in less than twelve months that builder had become a confirmed drinker, and in three years died the death of a drunken vagabond.

I wish with all the earnestness of my soul to impress upon both men and women—for one of the saddest features of recent modern life is the increase of drunkenness among society women—that you cannot afford to depend on stimulants to build up temporarily your strength or the sparkle of your conversation. Every bit of added strength or intellectual brilliancy furnished by strong drink is fictitious and curses in the end. My good friend, Dr. Amos R. Wells, says that he once went to see an exhibition of Gustave Dore's pictures. As a boy he had been fascinated with the spirited work of this artist, as he saw it represented in engravings, and he anticipated a rich treat in seeing the glorious originals. But, alas! though a few of them met his anticipations, and were brilliant indeed, most of them were only immense sheets of dull colors; some of them mere ghosts of pictures peering out of a world of black. Dore did not use properly made colors, and so his paintings scarcely outlasted the life of the artist himself. It is said that the same is true of the widely admired work of the great Hungarian painter, Munkacsy, who painted "Christ Before Pilate," and "Christ on Calvary." He is very fond of the use of bitumen, which imparts exceeding richness to pictures, but must be used with great caution or it will turn the painting black. Munkacsy, however, uses it lavishly, and some of his most valued works are already almost indistinguishable. In working on the greater canvas of human life what multitudes are tempted to drown care, and make life sparkle and seem brighter for an hour, at the risk of ruining the whole beautiful picture! How many there are tonight in prisons and penitentiaries, in insane asylums and hospitals, in cellars and attics, while others are only human drift logs floating on the current as drunken tramps, who began the painting of a life and character with as fair and sweet a promise as is held by any one of us here, but the strong drink mixed with the colors has changed the canvas that would have been a thing of beauty into a loathsome daub that is fit only for the waste heap.

I do not dare to close without a word of hope and invitation to anyone here who is already under the grip of this evil habit, and who finds that its power has already grown upon him until his resolutions to keep away from the drink are broken again and again. I want to say to any such that for the sting of the adder, the bite of the serpent that is in the wine cup, there is only one certain cure, and that is in the Christ. Dr. Langmann read a paper not long since, before the New York Academy of Medicine, which has aroused widespread interest. It described the experiments which he has been making with snake poisons, through which he has produced an antidote which, when he has fully developed it, he believes will prove infallible. If his confidence is justified it will be a great blessing to the world, and his name will go down in history as one of the greatest benefactors of mankind. Multitudes in our own country and far greater multitudes in India and other lands would be saved from death every year though such a cure. Everyone who has the misfortune to be bitten by a poisonous snake will resort to it. How much happier the world would become if men everywhere were as wise in seeking a cure from the deadly venom of sin! But, thank

God, there is a cure which is infallible. No matter how terrible the havoc which sin has wrought in the system, God has provided a remedy which is able to bring health and peace. "As Moses lifted up the serpent in the wilderness, even so must the Son of man be lifted up: that whosoever believeth in him should not perish, but have eternal life" (John 3:14–15).

36

CAMPING ON THE ROAD TO SODOM

"Lot dwelt in the cities of the plain, and pitched his tent toward Sodom" (Genesis 13:12).

I f you want to prove the size of a man you must take a time when he is under pressure. Take a company of men who are at ease, all prosperous and contented, and they may seem to be very much alike; but put the same men under the stress of some great emergency, when you have a chance to prove the mettle that is in them, and you will be astonished to see what diversity there is in the group. One man will prove to be a hero, and another a coward; one will be generous and unselfish, while another will be stingy and mean.

Abraham and Lot, living together as uncle and nephew, seemed very much alike; but when there came to be a strife between their herders, and there was a problem on hand to be settled, Abraham looms up large and gracious and noble, while Lot become lean and shriveled under our gaze. It was a magnanimous thing for Abraham, the older man, to offer to Lot his choice of territory when it seemed wise that they should separate their flocks. And if Lot had been of the same moral stature as his uncle, he would have refused to take advantage of Abraham's generosity and have insisted on his great relative having the first choice.

But Lot was essentially a little man. He had a great greed for money. He was religiously inclined, and having been brought up to serve God, and living all his life under the shadow of Abraham's gracious influence, he purposed in a general way to be a good man; but there was a deeper, overshadowing purpose to get rich. Lot's purpose was in harmony with the advice given by the old farmer to his son: "My boy, get rich. Get rich honestly, if you can; but in any event get rich."

Lot looked out over the plain toward Sodom and he saw that it was a very well watered and fertile county, by far the richest pasture land in the entire region. One great drawback to it was that it bordered on Sodom, and Sodom was infamous throughout all the world of that day for its wickedness. To a man who had a family growing up this was no unimportant matter; but it no doubt made a good market for cattle, and Lot reasoned that it was better for him to take the risks of moral degeneration than, as a great cattle raiser, to lose the beef trade of Sodom. So Lot says, I'll take this valley, and pitch my tent toward Sodom.

Now, it is useless for us to revive this old story of a far-off past unless we apply it to ourselves; for these stories never lost their value, because the great struggles of human nature are always the same. I doubt not that some who are listening to this discourse are at the same place, where the roads diverge, and are tempted to make their camp on the road toward Sodom. Lot found it a bad choice, and so will you. Lot found that the wickedness of Sodom poisoned the air of all the plains; and so do men who thrust themselves into evil associations today.

Julia Ward Howe says that some forty years ago, in company with her husband, Dr. Samuel G. Howe, she visited Cuba. Dr. Howe there made the acquaintance of a noble Cuban advanced in age, a teacher who for years had done everything in his power to give to the youth of the country training in accordance with the progress and spirit of the time. He was closely watched by Spanish officials, but was so beloved and honored by the people that the government was reluctant to interfere with his work. Mrs. Howe one day accompanied her husband to call upon this venerable sage, whose name was Don Pepe della Luz. During the conversation the old man said, "Doctor, what we need here is that air of which you and I were speaking the other day—the air, you know." When they were by themselves she asked her husband what air it was of which Don Pepe was speaking, and he said it was the air of freedom. So there is such a thing as an atmosphere of reverence toward God and of respect for righteousness. While Lot lived with Abraham he enjoyed that sort of an atmosphere. Wherever Abraham went he built an altar to God. Angels were his visitors, and there was an atmosphere of thanksgiving and prayer pervading the life of the home. Compared to such an atmosphere Sodom was hell itself. There was no such thing as prayer, or spiritual song or conversation, in that wicked city. This explains the moral degeneration of many young men and young women who come from home, either on the farm or in some smaller town, to live in the city. They have been accustomed to a religious atmosphere. The Bible has been a respected and

loved book among the people with whom they have associated. They have been accustomed to attend public church
services, regarding the Sabbath day as sacred, and prayer
has been the daily atmosphere of life. They come to the city
and are thrown into a different air. They associate with people who do not pray, who do not read the Bible, and who
seldom go to church. It is an air poisoned with irreverence
and skepticism of sacred things. If not definitely immoral,
it is permeated with the smoke of Sodom and has the smell
of Sodom in it. A man who gives himself up to that kind
of an atmosphere has pitched his tent on the road to
Sodom; he may not have got to Sodom yet, but he is camping on the way, and it is only a question of time before he
will have settled down to live in the midst of its godlessness
and wickedness.

There is perhaps not an incident in the Bible that more
clearly suggests the danger of an evil tendency, a false current, than this story of Lot pitching his tent toward Sodom.
If you had asked Lot the next week, or the next year, if he
were going to move to Sodom to live, he, no doubt, would
have denied it. He would have declared that he had no
such intention. Perhaps one of Lot's faults was that he
lacked definite moral decision. He was getting ready to go
to Sodom all the time, though he did not know it. If you
had asked Abraham if he were going to Sodom to live, you
would have heard a "No" with such a blunt emphasis
about it that you would never have forgotten it. One of the
most dangerous things to the building up of a really successful career is the lack of a definite vital purpose to do a
noble thing. It is so in the ordinary business affairs of life.
A man without a strong and definite plan is likely to go to
the wall and to fail of worthy achievement. Owen Meredith

says of one of his characters:

> "With irresolute finger he knocked at each one
> Of the doorways of life, and abided in none.
> The man who seeks one thing in life, and but
>   one,
> May hope to achieve it before life be done;
> But he who seeks all things wherever he goes,
> Only reaps from the hopes which around him he
>   sows
> A harvest of barren regrets."

A popular novelist makes one of her young women ask of a young man:

"'Have you made any plan?'

"'Yes,' he said, the words coming in jets, with pauses between; 'I will travel first—I will see the world—then I will find work.'

"She made a little impatient movement and said: 'That is no plan; "travel, see the world, find work." If you go into the world aimless, without a definite object, dreaming, dreaming, you will be definitely defeated, bamboozled, knocked this way and that. In the end you will stand with your beautiful life all spent, and nothing to show. They talk of genius—it is nothing but this, that a man knows what he can do best; nothing else. It does not matter what you choose. Be a farmer, business man, artist—what you will—but know your aim and live for that one thing. We have only one life. The secret of success is concentration: wherever there has been a great life, or a great work, that has gone before. Taste everything a little, look at everything a little, but live for one thing. Anything is possible to a man who knows his end and moves straight for it, and for it alone.' "

And this is as true when it comes to the great questions of moral character. You are getting ready to be either a noble man, a holy, saintly woman, or a moral failure. I'm not asking what you are to-night, but on what road are you camping? Abraham went on his way, camping out and living in tents also; but while Lot pitched his tent toward Sodom, Abraham pitched his tent toward "A city which hath foundations, whose builder and make is God" (Hebrews 11:10). Every day brought each of these men toward the end of his career, and every step took them father apart. We see men making the same choices now. Two young men come from the same town to build their careers in the city. One goes at once to the church and identifies himself with the Sunday school and the prayer meeting and Christian work. He becomes acquainted with that kind of people. In a business way he may know many sorts, but he makes his fellowships and friendships among the men and women who worship God and are helping to make the world better. These friendships become like a wall about him. They commit him to a righteous life. They are his tent, which he pitches toward heaven. He is not a saint yet, but his tent is pitched on that road. Every day and every year of such a life brings him farther along the way of robust Christian character.

The other young man, while not intending or purposing to be a wicked man, thinks, perhaps, that he has been brought up too strictly, and now that he is in a new community, without the restraints of home, he can look around a little and see the world. He soon finds out that the people who are "seeing the world" are of a different class from those with whom he has been acquainted; there is about them a certain carelessness and dash, a certain freedom from responsibility—yes, a certain recklessness—

that fascinates him. The theater, the card table, the wine-glass are now, as they always have been, the favorite diversions of people who are "seeing the world." He forms his associations among such people. He is more likely to make friends with the worst of them than the best. He may or may not succeed in his business; he may or may not advance as a lawyer or doctor; but morally he steadily loses. He loses his keen reverence for the Bible. The prayer meeting and the Sunday school seem slow and heavy to him after the glamour of some play that has been spiced with a dash of wickedness—not enough to make him revolt against it, but just enough to awaken the dare-devil that is in him. He may or may not fall into outbreaking sin that will shame and disgrace him; but the very air he breathes in such association will dull the edge of his moral sensibilities, will cool his ardor for religious conversation, and will surely and steadily draw him onward on the way to Sodom.

Do not doubt that to be on the road to Sodom is to get to Sodom sooner or later, if you do not turn around and go the other way. Lot made a bad trade after all. I do not know just how much wealth he laid up—he may have become very wealthy and have retired into Sodom to live on the interest of his money; but he was finally a loser, for when Sodom was burned up because of its wickedness he lost everything he had and barely escaped with his life. Mortgages on property in Sodom are always a bad investment.

It is a bad thing to go on a path where success will mean failure. One of the saddest things one ever reads went the rounds a little while ago concerning George Du Maurier, the author of *Trilby*. While he was sick, and on his death bed, a friend referred to the success of *Trilby* as a book and as a play, whereupon Du Maurier sadly replied: "Yes, it has

been successful. But the popularity has killed me at last."
Many men are destroyed by their own success. Lot succeeded—and lost everything. Du Maurier succeeded, but
lost his life; and many men here in Cleveland are succeed-
ing—only to find remorse and ruin at the last.

I would like to say with power to any young man here
who is trading the prayer meeting in which he was brought
up for the card party or the theater, that, fascinating as the
exchange may seem, he is pitching his tent toward Sodom
and the end will be disastrous. I want to say to any youth
who is choosing his companions from among the irreverent and reckless, because they seem gayer than Christians,
that every such friendship is a tent on the road to Sodom.
Many a young woman has gone down on the road to
Sodom in such a friendship, and married a man who lived
there, and afterward found herself dragged into Sodom to
her lifelong sorrow. I want to say to every young man, or
young woman either, who is beginning to dally with the
glass of beer or the bottle of wine, You are pitching a tent
on the way to Sodom, and there are no tents that move so
rapidly as on the path of stimulant and intoxication. Have
the courage to break up every such camp while you may.
The very people who are tempting you will respect you a
great deal more for such courage.

When General Clinton B. Fish was in command of the
military district of St. Louis, it became his duty, on one occasion, officially to receive and welcome to that city an eminent major general coming to take command of the
military department. General Fish met his commander on
the east side of the river and escorted him to the hotel in
which he had engaged a suite of rooms.

As soon as they were within the parlor—at once assuming the place of host, and ready to treat the other officers as his guests—the major general ordered a servant to bring four whisky punches.

"Only three, if you please, General; excuse me," promptly and courteously spoke General Fisk.

"You'll not refuse to drink with me, will you?" said the superior officer.

"If I should drink now it would be the first time. You would not advise me to begin now, would you, General?"

"No, God bless you! Long may you wave! was the gracious and gallant response.

How I would add to the peace of hundreds of young men in this city if I could inspire them to-night to follow that courageous example.

I cannot close without urging upon any who are camping on the way to Sodom to break camp this very hour and turn the other way. True, Lot was saved when Sodom was burned up, but what a salvation! He was saved as by the skin of his teeth. He was plucked as a brand from the burning. He lost his property, he lost his wife and his children, and, old and bankrupt and broken-hearted, he crept out of that horrible desolation. Don't look forward to such a salvation as that; but no, while youth and strength are yours, break up the camp that has its tent door open toward Sodom and pitch your tent with the people of God, who, like Abraham, build an altar of worship wherever they go. Breaking camp is an open matter that everybody can see, and so the more boldly you turn about and confess your sins the happier it will be for you. "If we confess our sins, He is faithful and just to forgive us our sins, and to cleanse

us from all unrighteousness" (1 John 1:9). During the last
great plague and famine in India, many people brought
still greater horrors on themselves because they would hide
away the corpses at the back of their hovels. When the
dead-cart came around they said there were no dead in the
house, and so the decaying body was left to poison the atmosphere and kill many that would otherwise have escaped. To try to hide our sins or cover them up is like that.
They will poison all our lives. "Whoso covereth his sins
shall not prosper" (Proverbs 28:13). It is better to bring our
own sins to the light now, and have them forgiven, than to
keep them covered up for a time, and have them drag us to
judgment and doom after a while.

37

THE LADDER OF THE ANGELS, AND THE SINNER AT THE FOOT

"And he dreamed, and behold a ladder set up on the earth, and the top of it reached to heaven: and behold the angels of God ascending and descending on it. And, behold, the Lord stood above it" (Genesis 28:12, 13).

Soft sins lead to hard lodgings. It seemed a sharp, shrewd trick for Jacob to cover his hands and neck and face with the hairy goatskins, and thus deceive his father, who was old and blind, and insure for himself the blessing which belonged by birthright to Esau. But I imagine the trick seemed less cunning that night at Bethel when, tired, worn out with a forty-mile walk, he lay down on the hard ground, and with a harder stone for his pillow slept the heavy slumber of an utterly exhausted man.

Depend upon it, sin does not always wait till the end of the journey to make itself felt. It has way stations of punishment all along the path.

A very subdued looking boy of about thirteen years, with a long scratch on his nose and an air of general dejection, came to his teacher, in one of the Boston public schools, and handed her a note before taking his seat and becoming deeply absorbed in his books. The note read as follows: "Miss B——: Please excuse James for not being at school yesterday. He played truant, but I guess you don't need to lick him for it, as he and the boy he played truant with fell out and the boy licked him. Also a man they sassed caught him and licked him. The driver of a sled they hung on to licked him. Then his pa licked him, and I had to give him another for sassing me for telling his pa, so you need not lick him until next time. I guess he thinks he had better keep in school hereafter." That boy was doubtless of the opinion of Kipling, who is said to have been present at a discussion participated in by a number of literary men where the question argued was whether there was a God or not. Finally Kipling brought his fist down on the table, ending the discussion with the pertinent sentence, "I know there is somebody somewhere who gives us our licks." No man here who has come toward the years of maturity but has found that there is, back of all life, some intelligence which executes and makes real the edict of the Bible that "the way of the transgressor is hard." Jacob found it so in the old Eastern land where he dwelt, and every sinner in Cleveland is finding it so now. The sin may be soft enough, but the bed it sends you to is hard.

It may seem a far cry from this opening suggestion to the next that impresses me in our study to-night, but it is this: that heaven is not far away from earth; it is so near that its inhabitants are very much interested in the things that are going on here, and are seeking the welfare of dwellers on the earth. Jesus says that heaven is so close to this world that there is great rejoicing there over any sinner who repents of his sins and turns his feet toward that land.

I think Dr. George H. Hepworth is right in his feeling that this nearness of heaven to earth is either ignored or kept silent about a good deal more than is wise. The worst feature of that tender sorrow that bereaves us of our loved ones is the feeling that those dear to us have gone so very far away. It is that feeling which breaks the heart and clothes those who are left behind in blackest mourning. If a child out of a family goes across the sea to study in some foreign land the sense of loss is often very keen, and the separation is hard to bear, but those who remain at home are buoyed up with the thought that the young man or young woman is not only alive, but is receiving benefits which could not be obtained at home; and though those who remain are lonely and grieved, there is mingled with the sorrow something which makes them even proud of the ability to sacrifice themselves for the good of the absent member of the family. If, however, one dies out of the household flock and goes to heaven, the attitude is very different. There is then not only that sense of separation but the added sense of loss. There is usually little or no appreciation of the fact that heaven is a great deal nearer than Europe. The thought of immeasurable distance weighs down the soul into hopeless discouragement. Surely we would be very greatly comforted if we opened our hearts to receive fully the assurances of the Bible, both in the Old and New Testaments, that heaven is so near to earth that there is constant communication, and that our lives are constantly brooded over and visited on tender missions by glorious angels.

We have also suggested here the comforting truth that heaven is full of mercy and sympathy for the sinner. They do not repudiate us because we have been overborne by temptation and have been forced out into exile by our sins. Heaven is not merciful to us only when we deserve it, but when we need it. Jacob was in great need of this revelation of God's mercy and willingness to forgive him and lead him in a new way. He had made a bad start and was being driven away from home by his sins. There was every reason to fear that he would go straight to ruin; for ruin is always at the end of the sinner's path.

A young man who was converted during some special evangelistic meeting held in a mining village, desirous of doing something for God, bought some tracts. He was distributing these little booklets one day when he met some of his old companions, who derided him as he spoke to them of Jesus.

"Here," said one of the old companions; "can you tell me where hell is?"

After a moment's hesitation the young man looked up and said: "Yes, it's at the end of a Christless life."

And no man is ever in greater danger of taking the short cut to such an end than the young man whose sins have driven him away from home. He finds himself in hard circumstances, without friends, and without the constraint of the public opinion of people who have known him, to hold him up to do his best. Such a young man is tempted to say: "It makes no difference now what I do. Nobody cares; I have made a bad start, and got a bad name at home, and in this new place nobody knows me or cares what becomes of me. I might as well have my fling." Ah, how many boys have gone to ruin like that!

A man in such a state needs, more than anything else, to come face to face with God and know that God has not given him up, but loves him even now, and is willing to save him. Jacob needed nothing so much as that. No doubt he thought he needed other things more. He wanted a home; he wanted a soft bed and a square meal; he wanted friends, and employment, and a chance to make his way; but, whether he appreciated it or not, what he really needed more than anything else was to meet God.

A little boy came to his father one day and laid his hand upon his knee, looking up wistfully.

"Do you want a penny, child?"

The sweet face glowed and the answer came, "No, papa; only you."

So, my friend, it is not money, nor success, nor fame, nor fashionable pleasures, none of these things that you need most. The supreme need is to find God; to be sure of his love; to be certain that at the top of the ladder of life is God.

What a sinner needs when he has made his failure, and lost all, is a new chance. Jacob by his sins had emptied himself of home, and inheritance, and everything that he counted valuable. Is that not true of some of you? Many times people are unconscious of being in such a state until their real bankruptcy of soul comes on them as a shock.

There is an old legend about an Egyptian monarch who had his treasure-house built, as he thought, so as to be impregnable against thieves. But in one corner of the wall the architect had built a stone which revolved upon a pivot and could be pushed round, so as to give access, and when dying he left the secret to his sons. So, night after night, the sons crept in and brought away some of the hoarded wealth; and when the king, fancying his coffers to be still full, went in to count his treasures he found that they were nearly all gone. How many are being thus robbed of more important treasures! Where is the innocency which you once new as a little boy or a little girl? where is the gentle tenderness of heart? where the unselfishness? where the open-handed genuineness of character which was your treasure in your youth? where the simple confidence in God and in his word that made prayer as simple and natural as talking with your parents? Where are these treasures, worth a million times more than any gold or silver? Alas! unseen hands have stolen them away. What you need, then, is what Jacob needed: A new chance; and that is what God gave him, and what he is ready to give you. If I speak to any man her who is discouraged and disheartened, I want to say "a word in season to him that is weary." No matter if you are past middle age, and have lost what seemed to you to be the best opportunities of life; if you are yet alive God stands the new ladder of the angels down at your feet.

The whole world has recently seen a splendid illustration of what a man can sometimes do to recover lost ground in a business way even after his hair is white. Mark Twain awoke one morning a few years since to find himself utterly ruined financially; a bankrupt; a great many tens of thousands of dollars worse off than nothing. In addition to that, his health was very frail. Many a man in similar circumstances would have sat down to mope out in despair the few years left to him; but the brave-hearted humorist set himself to work, with an energy surpassing that of youth, to retrieve his fortune. He laughed at the people who said to him that he had done his best work. He belted the globe with lectures and writings, until, a little while ago, he is said to have made a dinner for his creditors and laid beside each plate, in lieu of the menu card, a check in full for the balance of his indebtedness. Someone has well said, "That is the best joke Mark Twain ever perpetrated." God gave him a new chance. But God is always doing that in a spiritual way to men. Jacob had forfeited one chance but God gave him another, and out of his despair there arose before his vision this ladder of the angels, and above them God reminding him that he was the God of his fathers, that he was his God, and that he was ready to guide him and make his life a great and splendid success.

Surely I could bring you no sweeter message than this: You may begin life over again, you may have a new chance, through God's infinite mercy. During a terrific storm, some years ago, a ship was driven far out of her course, and, helpless and disabled, was carried into a strange bay. The water supply gave out, and the crew suffered agonies of thirst yet dared not drink of the salt water in which their vessel floated. In their last extremity they lowered a bucket over the ship's side and in desperation quaffed the beverage they thought was sea water, but, to their joy and amazement, the water was fresh, cool, and life-giving. They were in a fresh-water arm of the sea and they did not know it. They had simply to reach down and accept the new life and strength for which they prayed.

My brother, weary with your sorrow and your sin, discouraged at your failure, throw a bucket over the ship's side and drink the sweet water of God's forgiving love and mercy. Start again. Do not for a moment imagine that because you have failed once you may not now succeed. Josh Billings once said, "A man who is bitten twice by the same dog is better adapted to that business than any other." The fact that you have had one failure will help you to steer clear of that failure in the future. Take heart, brother! Heaven is not far away, and God bends over you with mercy.

38

THE "SLINGS AND ARROWS" OF AN OUTRAGED CONSCIENCE

"And they said one to another, We are verily guilty concerning our brother, in that we saw the anguish of his soul, when he besought us, and we would not hear; therefore is this distress come upon us" (Genesis 42:21).

The memory is one of the most important and marvelous characteristics of the human mind. Each one of us by daily deeds is hanging pictures on the walls of memory that will make of it, in time to come, either a chamber of peace or a dungeon of torture.

There is an old Persian story of a vizier who dedicated one apartment in his palace to be a chamber of memory. In it he kept the memorials of his earlier days, before royal favor had lifted him from his lowly place to a position of honor. It was a little room with bare floor, and here he kept his crook, his wallet, his coarse dress, and his water cruse—the things which had belonged to his shepherd life. Every day he went for an hour from the splendors of his palace into this humble apartment to live again for a time amid

the memories of his happy youth. Very sweet were his rec-
ollections, and by this daily visit his heart was kept warm
and tender amid all the pomp and show, and all the trial
and sorrow, of his public life.

Whether we live in a palace or a tenement house, we
have each our chamber of memory, and we are furnishing
it after our own designs. Pictures hang there which no eye
but God's sees. And these furnishings which are daily enriching it with beautiful things that minister to comfort and
peace, or with relics and mementoes of evil that will torture
us in times of weakness and age, are our own creation; and
we should select them with the greatest care, for when once
we have them we cannot escape from them. If a man does
not like his house he may move away from it. He can sell
it or rent it and move on to another street, where the surroundings suit him better. He may even go to another town
or another city to escape unpleasant surroundings. But a
man cannot get away from the chamber of his memory in
that way. It is like his shadow; it walks with him from street
to street, from place to place, from one year into another;
lies down with him at night and rises with him in the
morning. It has the power to compel his attention when it
pleases, and ever and anon it will set its pictures before him
and insure his interest in them.

A man cannot always decide what he will remember.
The subject may be unpleasant, and to recall it may shame
and humiliate him, but he cannot, because of that, say, "I
will not think of it again." We see a signal illustration of
this in the text we are considering. Joseph's brethren were
a long way from home, in a strange land where they had
no knowledge that anyone knew anything about them. But

they are suddenly confronted with rough treatment on the part of the ruler before whom they had come begging the privilege to buy corn, in the great stress of famine which was pinching them and their families. Not a word had been said to them about Joseph, and they had perhaps not mentioned his name to each other for a long time. It was no doubt a tabooed subject between them, and it was so sad a subject to Jacob their father, that there is every reason to suppose that the name of the lost youth was never mentioned in his presence; and yet, although their wicked deed to Joseph was twenty years or more past, when they were threatened with imprisonment and misfortune to every man of them there came up that old picture of the hills of Dothan and the lad with his coat of many colors. Though the seasons of twenty years had come and gone, it all came back to them as though it were yesterday. They see the delicate, thoughtful boy coming over the hills in the distance with his message from home. They see themselves gathered together again, plotting against him as he comes with childlike trust toward them. All the old envy and jealousy that burned in their vengeful hearts comes back to them now, and seems absurd and wicked and horrible to them as they look back on it from the distance. They hear themselves saying again, "Come now therefore, and let us slay him, and cast him into some pit, and we will say, Some evil beast hath devoured him; and we shall see what will become of his dreams. Ah, what would they not give now to have that dreamer back! They see again the fear and terror on the delicate face of Joseph as they tear off his beautiful coat of many colors and fling him into the pit. And then the Egyptian caravan comes by, and they pull him up out of the pit and sell him for twenty pieces of silver, hardening their hearts against his cries and his anguish at their inhuman treatment. They have not thought of it for a long time, but to every man of them it comes back again as sharp and clear in its outlines as though it had just happened. They see that bloody coat again in their hands, which they had stained with the blood of a slain kid to deceive the poor old father. They hear again the lie on their lips when they took the bloody, torn garment to Jacob and said: This have we found: know now whether it be thy son's coat or no. And again they look in the old man's despairing face and hear his heart-broken moan: It is my son's coat; an evil beast hath devoured him; Joseph is without doubt rent in pieces" (Genesis 37:20-33). How could they ever forget that day? Jacob has never seemed like the same man since. And now these men turn one to another, and instead of talking about how they are going to escape, or how they are going to prove that they are not spies, every last man of them is thinking how he is ever going to get rid of that old sin of twenty years ago.

Marvelous is the tenacity of the memory of conscience. Forgetfulness never can be trusted. Things seem to be lost in oblivion, but they are not lost. Isaiah declares that a wicked conscience is like a troubled sea that cannot rest, and the mire and the clay that have been cast into it in years gone by are likely to come up again at any time, and be cast upon the shore only to be washed away by the returning tide and flung into sight again on some other beach a hundred miles away. Sin can never be finally hidden in God's universe, for God has not abandoned his creation and he knows how to cause a man's sin to find him out. This world is a bad place for secrets. It is a great whispering gallery. Christ said that what men think in their hearts and speak in their closets is yet to be shouted from the housetops. A little old saying, used when we have discovered somebody's secret, is often on our tongue: "A little bird told me." Like many other sayings and proverbs that have become popular in our common language, it had its source in the Bible. If you will turn to the book of Ecclesiastes you will hear the Wise Man saying: "Curse not the king, no not in thy thought: for a bird of the air shall carry the voice, and that which hath wings shall tell the matter"—a graphic way of setting forth the certainty of sin's discovering itself.

A sinner not only carries the proof of his guilt in his own heart and conscience, but he carries there the court that pronounces sentence. These men did not wait for God's judgment. Their own consciences judged them and condemned them. They said to one another: "We are verily guilty concerning our brother." Guilt of conscience turns a man against himself. Other witnesses may be all dead, or may have gone out of the country, or may be friendly to us and have no intention of accusing us, but that does not make the sinner safe; for he carries in his own breast the greatest accuser of all, one that can neither die nor run away, and one who can never be trusted to keep his guilty secret. Quaint old Doctor South says that sin will lie burning and boiling in the sinner's breast like a kind of Vesuvius of fire pent up in the bowels of the earth; which yet must, and will, in spite of all obstacles, force its way out at length; thus, in some cases of sin, the anguish of the mind grows so fierce and intolerable that it finds no rest within itself, but is even ready to burst till it is delivered of the swelling secret it labors with. There are sins which have the same effect on the conscience which some medicines have on the stomach; they are no sooner received than it is in pain and torment till it throws them out again.

No man can properly measure the force, the power, and the remorseless rage of conscience when God commissions it to call the sinner to an account. How strangely it will arouse him in an unexpected hour! How terribly it will wring and torture him, till it has bolted out the hidden guilt of which it was in search!

As a game dog will run up and down through the woods hunting out the darkest places, penetrating remote thickets, searching deep cañons until it routs the game for which it was sent and with bellowing drives it to the light, and to the master's gun, so God knows how to arouse conscience, and send it searching in the darkest corners of forgetfulness, and with the bellowing that sounds like the bell of doom drive sin from its retreat to race the glare of the judgment seat. The conscience is God's hunting dog in the sinner's breast. You cannot turn it aside with bribes of dainty morsels, but, true to its trust, it will steadily bring you to condemnation.

Reason joins with memory in bringing in the verdict against the sinning soul. When memory brought back the picture of that old wrongdoing, conscience made these men say, "We are guilty;" and their reason added, "Therefore is this distress come upon us." We talk sometimes about poetic justice; by that we mean that it is justice peculiarly adequate in punishment to the sin. All God's judgments are poetic, and the sinner himself, when conscience begins its work of judgment, is the first to admit that the judgment is poetic and just. There is a strange case related in the first chapter of Judges of an old man named Adonibezek, who lived in the land of Bezek and was a sort of an

Ishmaelite of a man in the world of his day. He was a man of great force and power, a bloodthirsty old fellow, who boasted of his genius in inventing means of torture which he administered to the great persons who were captured by him. Finally he experienced the truth of the word which says that the man who takes the sword shall perish by the sword, and was himself captured, and when he was caught his enemies cut off his thumbs and his great toes; and old Adoni-bezek in the hour of his imprisonment and despair said: "Threescore and ten kings, having their thumbs and their great toes cut off, gathered their meat under my table: as I have done, so God hath requited me" (Judges 1:7).

An aroused conscience not only cannot be thrown off the scent, but it often causes the sinner to flee when no man pursueth. At last these men had gone out with sorrow, leaving Simeon behind in the dungeon. When they made their first camp and opened their sacks they found their money, each man's money in his sack. Now Joseph had done that for love of them, but their guilty consciences made this incident only a link in the chain that seemed to be tightening about them. And the next time they came down to Egypt, when Joseph commanded that they should be brought to his own house and a feast prepared for them, although it was intended as a kindness, yet their guilty consciences made it seem like a threat and drove them wild with terror. And they said one to another, "Because of the money that was returned in our sacks at the first time are we brought in; that he may seek occasion against us, and fall upon us, and take us for bondmen" (Genesis 43:18). These men would not now be shrinking in terror for fear of becoming bondmen themselves, if they had not sold Joseph to be a bondman twenty years before.

No wild beast is more merciless and relentless than a guilty conscience. A tiger hunter in India heard his companion, who was sleeping on the veranda, scream out in agony: "Help, for God's sake! Help! the tiger's got me! Help! help!" Rushing through the darkness he found that the tiger had stolen in upon his friend without the slightest warning and had seized him by the hand, which he had raised to defend himself, and had commenced to drag him off. In his agony he arose to his feet, and after descending the steps of the bungalow was actually walking off with his hand in the tiger's mouth, to be devoured, when his friend, by his courage and presence of mind, rescued him from an awful death by stabbing the tiger through the heart. A man who has sinned against his own soul has put his hand in the mouth of a tiger that will drag him to judgment unless it is slain.

The only cure for a guilty conscience is in forgiveness of the sin that caused the guilt. How differently Joseph's brethren felt after he made himself known to them, and assured them of his forgiveness. No doubt, when they first knew who he was, they were all the more apprehensive and fearful, for they could see that he had the power to put them all to death for their sin against him. But when, one by one, he embraced them, and assured them of his forgiveness, and asked loving questions about the old home, all the bitter remorse and terror for that sin committed twenty years ago was taken away, and it no longer had the power to make them shrink and shiver and cower with dread. So, when a man is aroused by his conscience to see the horrid character of his sin against God, and to keenly appreciate his guilt, and to know the punishment which naturally belongs to his sin, and to realize that there is no escaping from God's hand, he is at first all the more apprehensive and fearful, and is ready to despair. But when he sees on the face of Christ, his Saviour, a smiling look of forgiveness, and hears his kind words: "Him that cometh to me I will in no wise cast out" (John 6:37), the bitterness is gone and the sting of guilt is taken away, and instead there is the joy and peace of conscious forgiveness. Joseph's kisses sucked all the poison out of that old wound. So the caresses of Jesus Christ suck all the poison from the memory of our sins, and bring to us a peace that passes all understanding and casts out all fear.

39

THE THREE MOST NOTORIOUS BAD BARGAINS IN HISTORY

"Esau despised his birthright" (Genesis 25:34).

"They covenanted with him for thirty pieces of silver"
(Matthew 26:15).

*"What shall it profit a man, if he shall gain the whole
world, and lose his own soul?"* (Mark 8:36).

Man is a born trader. Children begin to bargain with their toys in the nursery. From the very beginning of life to its end, man is seeking to better his condition by exchanging what he has for something else. This bargaining instinct was never more thoroughly developed than in our own time. It is peculiarly a commercial age. All parts of the world are coming under tribute to commerce. Every new island, every additional square mile of territory that comes under the dominion of the flag, is carefully investigated and measured from the trade standpoint by the merchant. In addition, things that used to be thrown away and wasted are becoming articles of commerce under the quickened inventive touch of modern science. Nothing now is wasted in many of the great departments of food product. A beef steer goes in on one side of a building as a fat steer, and comes out on the other as beefsteaks and leather and buttons and glue and brushes. Nothing is wasted. Everything has gone into bargain. Preach as you will against the bargain counter, it is always the crowded corner of the store. It is an illustration of a deep instinct in humanity.

But man's instinct is to make good bargains and not bad ones, and it is concerning the danger of bad bargains that I wish to speak to you at this time. The most notorious bad bargain that comes to us from the olden time is that of Esau, who sold his birthright to Jacob for a mess of pottage. Esau was a hunter. He liked the excitement and freedom of the chase. He liked the uncertainty and the enthusiasm of hunting for big game. No doubt the little tinge of danger there was in it spiced the joy of it for his wild and daring spirit. Many of us know how to sympathize with him in this love for the free and untrammeled and unconventional. One day he came home from the hunt having had bad luck. He had found no game, and was tired out and in low spirits. He found Jacob, his brother, a quiet, shrewd, calculating sort of fellow, making pottage of some sort of coarse vegetables (lentils perhaps), and he asked for some. Jacob, ready to drive a sharp bargain, said, "Sell me thy birthright." And so Esau, caring nothing for the birthright, having contempt for it in his heart, sold it to Jacob for a mess of pottage. The incident closes in the record by the simple statement of our text, "Esau despised his birthright" (Genesis 25:34).

The second bad bargain which has attained a like notoriety is the bargain which Judas Iscariot make when he betrayed Jesus Christ to his enemies for thirty pieces of silver. There are a great many conflicting opinions concerning Judas. Some people believe that he was thoroughly bad from the beginning; that he followed Christ and became one of his disciples purely for what he could make out of it, and was always and everywhere a scoundrel. Other people believe that Judas was, like most other folks, both good and bad, and that at first he was an honest follower of Christ, but that his besetting sin was greed. He loved money. He liked to feel its weight heavy in the bag. He like to see it slip through his fingers as he counted it in little heaps. This grew on him, and as Christ became unpopular, and Judas believed that he would be arrested anyhow, he conceived the brilliant scheme of making some money out of it and putting himself solid with the government after Christ had been condemned. I do not know which of these is right, but, as I have never found any man without some good qualities in him, I am inclined myself to this latter idea. However it may be, Judas evidently allowed his love for money to overcome his sentiments of gratitude, and deliberately made up his mind to bargain off the liberty of Jesus by betraying him into the hands of his enemies. There is something very repulsive and loathsome in the way he did it. His slipping away from the table at the last supper, where he had broken bread with Christ as one of his dearest friends, and his selecting a kiss of seeming love as the mode of betrayal, have stamped the transaction as one of the basest and most treacherous betrayals in the history of mankind.

Now, the point I wish specially to bring to your thought in regard to each of these bargains is that they turned out to be very bad bargains, and very unsatisfactory to the men who made them. Yet each man got what he had covenanted for. Esau got his pottage, and went away strong of limb from a hearty meal. Judas got his thirty pieces of silver, every one of them. No attempt was made to cheat in either case, and yet afterward both men realized that each had cheated himself and had great sorrow over his bargain.

Esau sold something he did not care for and got what he wanted at the time; his birthright was a contemptible thing in his sight, and the pottage seemed very desirable; and yet we are told in the New Testament that there came a day when he was in great agony over the trade he had made, and that he found no place for repentance, though he sought for it carefully, with bitter tears. It seems to have been not only a bad bargain, but a fatally bad bargain for Esau.

We have an equally tragic case in relation to Judas. He got thirty pieces of silver, and was at liberty to go about his business, but he was not happy. He could not find rest day or night. Esau despised his birthright while he had it. Judas despised his Lord while he was his disciple, but now that he had sold him and got good money in his pocket, Christ never seemed so beautiful and so noble to him, and the opportunity of being his disciple never appeared so precious. He went to and fro like a wild man; he could not eat, he could not sleep, and for the first time in his life the consciousness that he had money failed to give him any pleasure. Finally he seems to have had a dream of being able to rue the bargain and undo the horrible deed he had done. He went back to the priests who had made the trade with him, with the money in his hands, and wanted to trade back. He said, "I can't keep this money; I have betrayed innocent blood." But they treated him with brutal coldness and disdain. They turned on him with contempt, and said: "See thou to that. What is that to us?" Poor Judas realized then what a bad bargain he had made. Unable to undo the deed and get out of his bargain, he was determined to at least get rid of the money; and so he flung the silver pieces, that he had sold his Lord to get, down on the floor in the presence of the men who had bribed him, and went away and hanged himself.

Surely there could not be two more unsatisfactory bargains than we have outlined in these cases. There is no light on the black clouds that hang over their sky.

I have brought these two bargains before you because they are illustrations of the danger each of us is in of making a bargain of the same kind. Esau is not the only man temped to sell his birthright. Judas is not the only man in danger of betraying his Lord. The same temptation comes to every one of us. We need to be alert and watchful and on our guard, lest we make the same awful blunder and bargain away sacred and holy things for that which will only curse us in the having.

Judas associated with Christ for years, and must have been many times greatly moved by him and influenced by him, and yet finally sold him for money. Are we not in danger of allowing the love of this world's things to lead us to exchange our religious peace, and our joyous fellowship and communion with Christ, for the glitter and display of earthly things? Travelers tell us that the constant rubbing of the sand on Egyptians hieroglyphs removes every trace of color and even effaces the deep-cut characters from basalt rock. So there is great danger that the worry and hurry and competition of our everyday lives shall act on our spiritual nature as sand upon the hieroglyphs of the desert. If we are not careful they will take away the flush of fervor and the bloom of joy from our religion.

A visitor went one day into the studio of a great artist and saw on his easel some very fine gems, brilliant and sparkling. On being asked why he kept them there the painter replied: "I keep them there to tone up my eyes. The tone of the eye is brought up again, just as the musician by his tuning-fork brings his strings up to concert pitch." So if amid the sandstorms of these toilful lives of ours we are able to retain the rich radiance of the soul, and keep our spiritual eyesight toned up, we must keep before us the vision of the Christ, and not allow ourselves to make the fatal bargain of losing our own soul in exchange for the perishing treasures of the world.

A connoisseur in spiritual things says that one of the first discoveries made by some, as they look at the soul's features in the glass of Christ's perfect law of liberty, is that from some cause the once brilliant hues of their spiritual life are becoming dim, the tone of a richer, fuller experience is being lowered, and the whole temperature of their holier lives is gradually but surely going down. We are told by a recent writer that at the foot of a cliff, under the windows of the castle of Miramar, formerly the residence of the Mexican emperor, Maximilian, at a depth of eighty feet below the surface of the clear waters of the Adriatic Sea, is a kind of cage fashioned by divers in the face of the rock. In that cage are some of the most magnificent pearls in existence. Having been left unworn for a long time, the gems lost their color, and the experts were unanimous in declaring that the only means by which they could be restored to

their original brilliancy was by submitting them to a prolonged immersion in the depths of the sea. For a number
of years they have been lying in the crystal depths and are
gradually regaining their unrivaled beauty and splendor.
What a story of loss of the color of rich experience, and of
high spiritual excellency, does this incident of the famous
jewels suggest! O my brother, my sister, you cannot afford
to exchange beauty of soul, sweetness of character, true purity and gentleness of spirit, for any worldly display, however brilliant it may be. At the last you will realize that the
fatal bargains of Esau and Judas were not more tragic and
terrible than those suggested in our third Scripture—"For
what shall it profit a man, if he shall gain the whole world,
and lose his own soul" (Mark 8:36).

Every day we see men who have bargained away their
freedom and liberty of spirit for the fearful bondage of iniquity. A celebrated detective tells in his memoirs how
once, having discovered his man, he joined himself to him
as a boon companion, went with him to his haunts, secured his confidence by long friendship, until at length,
when all suspicion had been allayed, he got him, as a mere
jest, to try on a pair of handcuffs, and then, snapping the
spring that locked them, he took him, all helpless as he
was, an easy prey. So there is many a sin that captures its
poor slave in that way. It first fascinates the soul and leads
it in paths of pleasure, thus drowning a man's fears and
drugging his sense of danger, until the handcuffs of habit
slip about the wrists and the man's freedom is a thing of
the past. Many such a poor bondman will agree with me
that Esau was not a greater fool when he sold his birthright
for a mess of pottage, or Judas more desperately cheated
when he sold his Lord for thirty pieces of silver, than he

who for a few passing hours of sinful pleasure barters away noble character, peace of soul, and immortal joy.

40

THE GOLDEN CALF

"I cast it into the fire, and there came out this calf"
(Exodus 32:24).

T he chief lack in Aaron bas backbone. He was strong in his head, stronger yet in his tongue, but very weak in the back. He was one of the kind of men who are easily influenced for either good or evil. You could tell, when you saw Aaron and had talked with him five minutes, whom he had been spending the day with. If he had been with Moses he talked one way, if he had been with Miriam he talked another way, and if he had been with some cabal of grumblers, whose stomachs were hungering for the leeks and onions of Egypt, he held altogether different language. Aaron has plenty of descendants. How many people we know who are a sort of a reprint of the man or woman who had their ear last? As Christ said about the seed that was sown on stony ground and sprang up quickly, but withered away on the first hot afternoon, they have no root in themselves. I think there is not enough stress laid on this in the education of children and in the development of young manhood and womanhood. It is quite possible for parents to love children with great tenderness, and hedge them about with every safeguard that they can imagine, and yet, through lack of wisely developing the child's individuality, bring up the boy or girl to be a mere weakling. The parental influence on childhood is like scaffolding in building a house—it is useless unless a house is being built so strong and solid inside that after a while the scaffolding may be taken down and the house still stand, a thing of worth and beauty. Many people are so brought up to lean on others that they have to be propped up all their lives or fall helpless to the ground. I get a great many letters from mothers about their boys, and nothing is more common than for a mother to say: "My boy means all right, but he is so easily influenced. When he is with good people, and the influences about him are pure, he is all right. But when he gets with the other class he is led astray before he realizes his danger." That is, he is another Aaron, who so long as Moses is by, with his steadfast principles and strong purpose to do right whatever happens, is all right and can say "No!" with emphasis to temptation. But when Moses is gone, and a mob of skeptics are around with their evil prophecies and worldly lusts, he is easily won over to do their bidding.

Decision of character is one of the strongest and finest characteristics of a noble manhood. People who take hold of life with weak and nerveless fingers are sure to be scarred at every turn. If you ever pressed your way through a thicket where the wild stinging-nettles grew, you have probably learned that the way to escape being stung by them is to seize them in a quick and firm grasp, as though it were nettles that you were searching for. Then they do not sting. If you dawdle with them in a timid, fearful way, they poison your blood. It is so with the vexations and annoyances as well as the temptations to evil that often make a dense jungle through which we are compelled to force our way.

If with courage we seize hold on everything that stands in the way and thrust it aside, pressing on to do our duty, we escape the sting and we come off victorious. A man who is weak and pliable never belongs to himself, and is the plaything of many people who, in comparison, are insignificant in every other way except power of will. I would urge every young man and young woman to hold fast to that crown of will power by which they are able to say "No!" to every temptation of sin, and to hold the fort of character by the lance of truth and purpose against all comers.

Aaron's excuse to Moses seems very silly indeed to us. It could scarcely have deceived himself. He tries to throw all the blame upon the circumstances with which he was surrounded. Moses seems to have understood what sort of man he was, for he said to Aaron, "What did this people unto thee, that thou hast brought so great a sin upon them?" (Exodus 32:21). And then Aaron undertakes to throw all the blame upon the fire. He admits that he gathered the gold earrings and jewelry, but he says, "I cast it into the fire, and there came out this calf" (Exodus 32:24). He does not say anything about the mold he had made to pour the gold into, nor about the engraving tool he used to polish the image. He is strangely forgetful of all that. It was the fire that did it—the awful, wicked, idolatrous fire that turned all that jewelry into a calf to be worshiped!

But before we blame Aaron too much, or regard him to be an unusual sinner, let us reflect upon the commonness of his sin in the everyday life that we know so well. Those of you who have read George Eliot's *Adam Bede* will remember that very striking scene in which Mrs. Poyser, while scolding the clumsy Molly for her broken jog of beer, herself drops a much more precious jug from her angry fingers, and exclaims: "Did anybody ever see the like? The jugs are bewitched, I think." And then to keep herself in countenance she proceeds to argue that "There's times when the crockery seems alive, an' flies out o' your hand like a bird," and concludes with the stern philosophy that "What is to be broke will be broke." How many of us, when arraigned by the sting of our own conscience, have been ready to excuse ourselves with Mrs. Poyser's theory that we were "bewitched" by some evil influence which was beyond our power.

Bishop Phillips Brooks, commenting, with that clear vision which ever characterized him, on these deceptive but flimsy excuses for sin, pictures a man all gross and sensual, a man still young, who has already lost the freshness, glory, and purity of youth. You question him about his life. You expect him to be ashamed, repentant. But there is no sign of anything of the kind. He says: "I am the victim of circumstances. What a corrupt, licentious, profane age this is in which we live! When I was in college I got into a bad set. When I went into business I was surrounded by bad influences. When I grew rich, men flattered me. When I grew poor, men bullied me. The world has made me what I am—this fiery, passionate, wicked world. I had in my hands the gold of my boyhood which God game me. Then I cast it into the fire, and there came out this calf."

Another man is not a profligate, but is a miser or a mere business machine. He has ceased to live above the world. All the holy dreams of self-sacrifice and deeds of mercy to lift the world higher in the scale of being, to do his part in sweetening the moral atmosphere of the community in which he lives, have as the years went on been coined into gold and passed over the counter. A slot-machine, that weighs you for a penny, has as much generous brotherly sympathy for his kind as he. And yet when you talk to him about it he has the glib answer ready on his tongue: "What can you ask of me? This is a mercantile community. The business man who does not attend to his business goes to the wall. I am what this intense commercial life has made me. I put my life in there, and it came out this golden calf." And then he gazes fondly and lovingly at the yellow calf, and his knees bend under him with the old lifelong habit of worshiping it, even while he abuses and disowns it. The same thing is true of the woman of society who has frittered away the holiest ideals of womanhood in worship of the fashionable habit. "The fire made me this," she says, as an excuse for all her frivolity and pride. Here is a young college-bred man, who started out with fine dreams of public service and statesmanship, but who has yielded to the temptations of corrupt politics until he has degenerated into a time-serving party hack, and he gives, as an excuse for all his selfishness and partisanship, as a whitewash for all the black spots on his robe of political life, "I put my principles into the furnace, and this thing came out."

Parents often make the same sort of excuses for their indifference or sinfulness, which has marred and maimed and dwarfed their children in their highest nature. The father says of his profligate son, having never done one wise or vigorous thing to make him a noble and pure-minded man: "I cannot tell how it has come. It has not been my fault. I put him into the world, and this came out."

These excuses are all useless. It is the height of folly for us to attempt to throw upon circumstances, or the world, or the age in which we live, the responsibility for the characters we are forming. Circumstances will do for us just what we choose to have them do. Put an acorn in the ground, and it is not the choice of the soil what kind of tree it will develop from that acorn; no soil on earth, however fertile, could change the nature of that germ and develop there a maple, a fir, or a pine tree. There is divine will power wrapped up in that little acorn which says: "It is not for you to decide, O earth, what I shall be. Make me an oak tree, whether you will or not." And an oak tree it is. Into that same earth there falls the germ of some poisonous plant, and though the soil were ever so benevolent it could not thwart the poisonous purpose of that seed and bring forth instead some sweet and pure flower. The evil purpose will have its way. Life is like that; the world will do for us just what we want it to do. If we say to it, "Make us good, high-principled, holy-visioned," it will develop in us, despite all the seeming contradictions and cross currents which we see, a pure and noble soul. If we say to the world, "Make us mean and vulgar, with natures creeping on the earth," it will draw out of us into development every germ of meanness and vileness there is in our human nature. But it will not do for us to hold up our meanness and say, "It was my nature, and I could not help it;" or to say, "The world was so wicked it spoiled me." No; let us face the truth: if we are wicked it is because we have chosen to be wicked. Our sins are not somebody else's, they are our own sins; and the quicker we realize our definite responsibility the more hope is there that we may turn from them by confession and find forgiveness.

Let us have an earnest heart-searching to-night. What have you done with all the gold of innocency, of love, of intelligence, and of opportunity which God has bestowed upon you? As you hold it up before yourself to-night—the result of all these blessings—and see your own character in the mirror of conscience or of God's commandment, is it pleasing to you or not? You were once a little child, innocent and pure as an angel. Your hopes and your purposes unfold amid Christian influences. The first songs you remember were melodies of Christian love and mercy. And now, after twenty or thirty years have passed, what have you to show for it? If you have yielded your heart to the divine influences of Christianity, so that Christ has dwelt in fellowship with your soul, exalting your ideals, enlarging your vision, filling the veins of your thought and love with the throbbings of immortal courage, then you can in humility, but with assurance sweet and comforting, lift your life up into the presence of God and say, with Jean Paul Richter, "O my God, I have done the best I could with the material which thou hast given me."

But if you have chosen your own way, have turned away from the fellowship of Christ, have hardened your heart against his love, have refused to submit your will to him, have let your affections run on the ground, twining about the burned stumps and rotten logs of worldliness, until tonight there is in your conscience the bitter feeling of remorse, the stinging conviction that you have sinned against God and against your own soul, I come to you with the ringing challenge of Moses, and cry unto you with all the earnestness of my soul, "Who is on the Lord's side?"

Do not deceive yourself in making the answer. Do not imagine you are on the Lord's side simply because your conscience condemns you and you are conscious of a drawing toward salvation. Both Agrippa and Felix were mightily stirred under the preaching of Paul, and were conscience-stricken until they trembled under conviction of sin and expected to hear Paul again, but they never became Christians.

Do not suppose that a mere attendance on church and a nominal sympathy with the church puts you on the Lord's side. Herod liked to hear John the Baptist preach. He was greatly fascinated with John's message and his style of giving it. The record says that he heard John "gladly;" and yet, instead of coming over on the side of John and Christ, he beheaded the brave preacher and became a murderer.

No one should consider himself on the Lord's side unless he is keeping the commandments. Christ says, "He that keepeth my commandments, he it is that loveth me" (John 14:21). An open confession of Christ which all the world may see, with which the heart and life agree, is the only way of putting ourselves really on the Lord's side. An Irish gentleman, pointing to a young man, once said, "Is he an O. O.?" What do you mean by an O. O.?" "I mean," was the reply, "is he out-and-out for Christ?" That is what Christ desires of each one of us. It is not only to be sorry for sin, but to turn away from sin in heart and in conduct, that will bring us into saving relation with Christ.

Archdeacon Madden, of Liverpool, relates a curious experience with a dying gambler. He was once called out at midnight to see a dying man. He found him in a wretched and dirty back bedroom in a dingy street of Liverpool. He could not have been more than thirty years of age. He was propped up in bed and the gray look of death was upon his face.

As the minister entered the young man turned eagerly to him, and, holding out his hand, he said, "I'm dying, and I am not ready—not ready."

Just as the minister was about to speak the young man suddenly gasped out, "John, John, hand me those things on the table." John came forward and laid upon the bed a sporting paper, a pack of cards, a set of dice, a bottle of whisky, and some race lists. There was a deliberation about the whole business which convinced Dr. Madden that the matter had been talked over between the men. When all were spread out in due order, the dying man again turned to him and said: "Look, Vicar; those things have been the ruin of me; they have been a curse to me, and I want to turn my back upon them all. I want you to help me to do it."

Again he was about to speak, when suddenly stooping down he gathered them all and thrust them into the minister's hands with the words: "Shove them up my back."

The minister was so staggered by the request that he stammered out, "What—what do you mean?"

"I want you," he said, "as God's minister, to shove them up underneath my shirt. I want to turn my back upon them. I want to put them behind my back. I want God to see that I have done with them forever."

Dr. Madden did not know whether to laugh or to cry. It was all so absurd and yet so pathetic. The man was in dead earnest. He had evidently thought it over, and made it as an act of true repentance.

The minister said to him, "I will do what you wish, but I will kneel down first, and you will repeat a prayer after me." He knelt, and then solemnly and earnestly the dying man repeated after him these words: "Father, I have sinned against heaven and before thee. I renounce all my sins; from the bottom of my heart I renounce them all. Father, receive thy prodigal son, and forgive me for Jesus Christ's sake. Amen."

Dr. Madden then rose from his knees and carried out the sufferer's wishes. To all those in that chamber of death it was a most solemn sacramental rite. It was the outward and visible sign of the inward and spiritual grace of a true repentance. There the minister stood and held the things that had cursed the poor fellow's young manhood, ruined a promising career, and brought him down to poverty and a premature grave. As he held those emblems of evil behind his back he told him of that Saviour who "carried our sins," upon whom the Lord has laid the iniquities of us all.

I am sure that that strange but earnest picture ought to bear a message from God to some of you who hear me now. Do not wait until the awful emergency of death to put your sins, behind your back. Turn from them now and ask God to put them behind his back forever. King Hezekiah was in great trouble and says of his deliverance: "Behold, for peace I had great bitterness: but thou hast in love to my soul delivered it from the pit of corruption: for thou hast cast all my sins behind thy back." God is no respecter of persons. He loves your soul as much as he did Hezekiah's. If you will come to him in repentance and confession, he will cast all your sins behind his back.

41

THE COWARDS AND THE GIANTS

"And there we saw the giants, the sons of Anak,
which come of the giants: and we were in our own sight as
grasshoppers, and so we were in their sight"
(Numbers 13:33).

I t was unnecessary for these cowards to have added that last phrase, "and so we were in their sight." If a man has no self-respect he may be very sure that no one else will respect him. A man who feels like a grasshopper is pretty certain to look like a grasshopper. His cowardice will make itself evident enough to his enemies. Small men loom large when they have great courage, but giants are like grasshoppers when fear has taken possession of them.

These ten cowards brought back as enthusiastic a report about the beauty and fertility of the country as did Joshua and Caleb. They admitted that it was a land flowing with milk and honey. They came back loaded down with pomegranates and figs and grapes. Indeed, they found one vineyard in the valley of the brook of Eshcol where the grapes grew in such enormous clusters that they broke off a cluster and hung it over a staff which two men carried between them. But all the enthusiasm over the richness of the soil and the desirability of the land as a home for their people was more than overbalanced by their fears. They declared that the enemy was entrenched in walled cities, and that they were people of enormous size. The men were giants, whose fathers were giants before them, and so mighty were these men of Anak that they made the Hebrews feel like grasshoppers in their presence. Therefore it was useless, in their opinion, to undertake to go in and possess the land, even though God had promised it to them. Their conclusion was that God himself was not strong enough to whip these giants with such little men as they were.

There were two men, however, out of that dozen spies who were not of the grasshopper grade. Joshua and Caleb had taken in the size of the giants as well as the rest, but not feeling like grasshoppers themselves, but rather like the courageous men that they were, they took a different view of the outlook.

They declared that Moses and his army, under the divine leadership, were easily able to overcome these giants, and urged that they go up at once and possess the country. But the ten cowards overruled them, and succeeded in turning back the people to wander for forty years in the wilderness, suffering intolerable hardships, when they might have entered the land of promise and possessed it inside of forty days.

It is interesting to notice that these cowards were all destroyed by the plague, and the precious bodies that they were so careful of, and which they were so afraid to risk in fight under God's direction, were very shortly in their graves. The two brave men of the lot were the only ones that lived to see the final conquest of Canaan. God is not always on the side of "the strongest battalions," as Napoleon sneered; but he is ever on the side of the men of brave and noble purpose, for they are ever on his side. God has so ordered the universe that the bravest thing a man can do is also the safest, in a worldly as well as a spiritual sense.

We have here a very interesting illustration of what is going on today. Many people in Christian lands have come up so close to the promised land of a Christian life that they have become fascinated with its beauty and enjoyment. They have seen enough of the spiritual pomegranates and figs and grapes that grow in the land of Canaan, the land of forgiveness and Christian communion, to greatly attract them, and they long to enter. They will agree to anything you say about the desirability of a Christian life. They admit that it is the happiest and most secure life to live. They declare their own desires to be Christians and hope some time to enter and live and die in the midst of the joyful experiences of the Christian, but just now the difficulties are too great and the giants are too large for them to undertake such a conquest; and so, while they look longingly on the vineyards of Eshcol, they wander back into the wilderness with its stinging serpents, its deadly enemies, and its graves of lust.

I am persuaded that I speak to some here now who are exactly in this position. The Christian life seems to you, as it is, the only true and happy life for anybody to live. Some day you expect to be a Christian; but you are putting it off to some indefinite time in the future. You are like the poet who sings:

> "There are wonderful things we are going to do,
> Some other day;

And harbors we hope to drift into,
Some other day.
With folded hands and oars that trail,
We watch and wait for a favoring gale
To fill the folds of an idle sail,
Some other day.

"We know we must toil if ever we win,
Some other day;
But we say to ourselves, there's time to begin
Some other day;
And so, deferring, we loiter on,
Until at last we find withdrawn
The strength of the hope we leaned upon,
Some other day.

"And when we are old and our race is run,
Some other day,
We fret for the things that might have been done,
Some other day.
We trace the path that leads us where
The beckoning hand of grim despair
Leads us yonder out of the here,
Some other day."

No man deals wisely with any giant sin that stands in his way who does not seize hold upon it at once and throttle it. A man recovering from a debauch was moaning to himself: "I must quit! I must reform! I must stop!" "Don't say dat, boss," put in a colored men. "Dat's no good. Say, 'I am quit. I is reformed. I is done gone stopped.' Do it now, boss, an' den you won't forget it."

That colored man had good honest common sense. The sin which you are putting off to some future time to battle with is growing more giant-like every day of delay.

But in thinking of becoming a Christian, and of the difficulties that stand in the way, we must never lose sight of the divine help. That which made the difference between Caleb and Joshua and the ten cowards among the spies was that Caleb and Joshua had great faith in God, and believed that God would keep his word and make their arms victorious over the giants. All that it was necessary for them to do was to obey God and go forward doing their best. These other men would not have felt like grasshoppers in the presence of the sons of Anak if they had had the consciousness that God was with them to give them power to overcome their enemies. So you are not asked to become a Christian alone, nor to pursue the Christian life in your own strength. You are to have a mighty reinforcement in the presence of the divine Spirit strengthening you against every battle with temptation. God will take that fearful spirit out of your heart when you obey him and forsake your sins, and will give you a new heart; and the giants will seem like grasshoppers when you face them in this new courage and with this new assurance of God's alliance with you.

This power and willingness of God to change a man's heart and renew his nature is not a new thing, but is as old as God's dealings with men. Away back in the book of Job you may find this remarkable description of the transformation of the soul: "If there be a messenger with him, an interpreter, one among a thousand, to show unto man his uprightness; then he is gracious unto him, and saith, Deliver him from going down to the pit: I have found a ransom. His flesh shall be fresher than a child's: he shall return to the days of his youth: he shall pray unto God, and he will be favorable unto him: and he shall see his face with joy; for he will render unto man his righteousness" (Job 33:23–26). It is utterly futile to undertake a Christian life without this divine conversion, this surrender of yourself to the leadership of Jesus Christ, who is not only our Saviour, but our Captain in all our warfare against the giants of sin. The divine exaltation that will come to us in such fellowship will cause us to rejoice in the face of the enemy.

Spurgeon was once out riding, and was laughing, as he went, at the top of his voice. A friend met him and asked the cause of his mirth. "O," answered the great-hearted Christian, "I was just thinking about 'My grace is sufficient.' I was thinking how big grace is and how little I am."

But, after all, the initiative is in our hands. God would not give the promised land to the Hebrews unless they entered the land in obedience to him and fought for it. This is in accord with universal law. That was a remarkable scene in the life of Joan of Arc, when, as a girl of seventeen, she was brought into the presence of all the great priests and cardinals of the kingdom and submitted to a most severe and searching examination. One of the priests said: "Joan, you say that it is the will of God that the king should be crowned. If it is the will of God why, then, he will be crowned, and he needs not your help." "Aye," said Joan, "it is true that it is the will of God, and he giveth the victory; but men must fight." Garibaldi said something very much like that at Naples in 1860: "My children, liberty is from God, liberty is from heaven. But," he added, "you must all rise; you must fight for Italy." So freedom from sin, salvation from the guilt of sin, is through Jesus Christ; but we ourselves must rise and fight with him for the overthrow of every giant of evil in our hearts and in the world about us.

It need not take a long time. This Christian Canaan may be entered by you at once if you are ready to obey God. Bishop Newman tells us an interesting story of the conversion of that great citizen of Ohio, Chief Justice Chase. Bishop Newman had observed, during the time he was pastor of Metropolitan Church, Washington, that when he was administering communion Chief Justice Chase always retired. He was impressed that he ought to talk with him about the matter, so he asked him why he did not come to the sacrament, to which he replied, "I am not a Methodist and I am not good enough." Dr. Newman replied, "We will omit consideration of the former point and speak of the latter." Then he turned to the communion invitation and read: "Ye that do truly and earnestly repent of your sins—" "Stop right there," said the Chief Justice, and for an hour they talked upon repentance.

Soon after, he was administering the communion, Mr. Chase was present. After all had communed who seemed to wish to do so, Dr. Newman waited still, and said: "Is there another who wishes to come? If you feel worthy you are not fit to come. If you feel unworthy, but repent of sin and trust in Christ, come." With that the Chief Justice arose and with bowed head came to the altar; but, instead of kneeling, he fell down upon the floor. The whole congregation lingered and prayed for a soul that was seeking God. By and by the minister administered the communion to him. When he rose upon his feet he held his head erect, and the smile of forgiving grace was on his face.

Not long after, Judge Miller, on the eve of his departure for Europe, came to see Mr. Chase. The latter took him with him in his carriage to visit a sick friend. Miller turned and said to him, "How are you?" Said he, "Brother Miller, I am well in mind, feeble in body; but Christ is my satisfying portion. I have given up all to him." "Well, said Miller, "I wish I could say that. I have been trying for eighteen years to solve the problem." Said Chase, "I have solved it, and Christ is my satisfying portion." Two or three days later they went to call him in the morning and there was no answer. The Chief Justice was dead. How happy the solution of life's great problem on that Sunday morning a few weeks before!

How happy it would be for you if I could arouse you to now solve the same great problem in the same way! You are standing outside of the promised land, hesitating to enter because of difficulties that seem so giant like in their proportions that you are afraid to confront them. But, thank God, you are not asked to confront them alone, and Jesus Christ will receive you, sinful as you are, and give you a new heart of courage and love, and strengthen your arm to fight, so that you may come out conqueror over all foes that stand in your way. You will find the name of Jesus is a name before which every giant of sin will fall.

One of the magazines has a new telling, by William Converse, of an old story of the Crusades. It is the story of how Gilbert Becket was taken prisoner by a Saracen emir and was for years his slave. For a long time he was treated with great cruelty; but finally, one day when he was being beaten, Roesa, the daughter of the emir, interfered in his behalf, and afterward, through her pleading with her father, his lot was greatly improved. As time went on he came to love this young girl, and the maiden herself loved the Crusader, whose life she had saved, with even a greater devotion. The emir at length discovered his daughter's secret, and, more than that, that the young man had explained and defended to her the doctrine of the Cross. Fearful for his daughter's faith, he purposely gave the young captive a chance to escape. He sent him on horseback to a distant city. The youth determined to gain his freedom. He parted tenderly with the Saracen maid. Whatever her suspicions, she kept them quiet. She met him on horseback, as he was ready to set out, and gave him a silken purse into which she had woven some of her own hair. He laid it next his heart, and sped away to return no more.

An adventurous voyage brought him to London. He wrote to the emir that he would send him a ransom of gold. "Englishmen," he declared, "are like birds; for, though caged within gilded wires, they love freedom."

The daughter sank under the eclipse of her hope, and began to languish. Her father was anxious. The healing men were summoned, but could not minister to a mind diseased.

All at once the maiden rallied and began to gain strength and vigor. A new purpose had seized her. Her lover had not fled because he did not love her, but because freedom was a man's true life. She would go to him.

She soon set sail for England. From the port she sent a note to her father.

She knew but two English words—"Gilbert" and "London." From port to port she found her way by using the latter word. She at length reached the English metropolis. Then came the great difficulty—to find among that seething mass of humanity one man whose Christian name only she knew. Her Arabic was gibberish to those English-speaking people. To all the crowds that surrounded her, regarding her as one who seemed "crazed with some sorrow," she spoke but one word. "Gilbert! Gilbert!" she cried, as she went from street to street. "Here comes the Gilbert maiden," people would exclaim to one another as they saw her. One day she strayed to Cheapside. As usual, a crowd gathered. "It is the Gilbert Saracen maid," cried the people around.

But then a strange thing happened. Out from a house rushed a servant of Gilbert Becket, who strode along, pushing the throng aside, and came close to the maiden. "It is she!" he exclaimed, in glad recognition. "I thought I could not mistake; it is the Saracen maid!" They told him she had been calling for Gilbert. "And Gilbert she shall see, to his joy and hers, as quickly as she can cross the street and get within yon gate and door," said the servant.

The meeting was unspeakably glad. That which Gilbert had never dared to believe or ask had come to pass. Roesa had given up her father's home for him. Later she also gave up the Moslem faith and became a happy Christian. Gilbert Becket and Roesa were married. Gilbert became sheriff of London, and the Saracen maid became the mother of Thomas á Becket, the famous chancellor and martyr.

The two talismanic words that brought triumph to the Saracen maid were "Gilbert" and "London." But there are two talismanic words greater than those. They are "Jesus" and "Heaven!" I care not how far away in the desert of sin you are, nor how hopeless and despairing your present outlook for a holy and a pure life, if you will turn your face away from your sin, with these two talismanic words upon your lips and in your heart, you shall in God's good time stand before the gates of heaven, and they will open to your weary feet at the blessed name of "Jesus." Take them as your watchwords from this very hour.

42

THE ANGEL THAT BLOCKS THE WAY

*"And Balaam said unto the angel of the Lord, I have
sinned; for I knew not that thou stoodest in the way
against me: now therefore, if it displease thee I will get me
back again"* (Numbers 22:34).

BALAAM was a brilliant and ambitious man. His two weak points were his longing for money and his longing for applause. God had given him remarkable gifts, but instead of walking humbly as a prophet of God, and letting his light shine so that those who saw his good works should be led to glorify God, he sought to draw popular attention to himself, and succeeded in doing so. The people about, in surrounding countries, came to believe that Balaam had the power to curse a nation and cause it to fall to pieces in ruin, or, on the other hand, the power to bless a nation and cause it to become prosperous and triumphant. And so Balak, of the Moabites sent a message to Balaam and sought to bribe him to curse the people of Israel, and said to him: "Come now therefore, I pray thee, curse me this people; for they are too mighty for me:

peradventure I shall prevail, that we may smite them, and that I may drive them out of the land: for I wot that he whom thou blessest is blessed, and he whom thou cursest is cursed" (Numbers 22:6).

Now Balaam himself was not at all deceived. He knew that he had no power to bless or curse of himself, and that neither his blessing nor his curse would amount to anything unless he was simply the voice proclaiming God's purpose. But Balaam's eyes glistened at the rich presents that were sent and he wanted to keep the gold, and he asked of the Lord the privilege of going with the messengers and doing their bidding, but was refused. The messengers went home, but were followed by a still more honorable company of princes with a still richer bribe. And this time Balak send word to Balaam: "Let nothing, I pray thee, hinder thee from coming unto me: for I will promote thee unto very great honor, and I will do whatsoever thou sayest unto me: come therefore, I pray thee, curse me this people" (Numbers 22:16–17).

Balak was led to do this, no doubt, because of the peculiar way in which Balaam had refused the first bribe. He did not say, out and out, "It is wrong, and I cannot do it. The people of Israel are blessed of God and nothing can stand against them." But instead he had left the impression on the messengers that personally he would like to go (which was the truth), while he regretfully said to them, "The Lord refuseth to give me leave to go with you" (Numbers 22:13). Balaam was like a man who thinks it is wrong to drink wine, or to give himself up to some questionable indulgence, and when tempted does not say, out and out, "It is against my conscience and I will not do it," but hems and haws, and looks sorry, and says, "I should like to do it, but really I ought not to, for I am a church member, you know;" or, "I was not raised to do that kind of thing." Such a man has already begun to compromise with the devil, and is certain to have further trouble with that temptation. If a thing is wrong, say so straight out, and say "No!" with an emphasis that will make the devil's hair stand on end. Thus resisted he will flee from you every time. But Balaam dallied with the matter, and so, no doubt, some shrewd messenger in that first committee whispered to Balak, "Although Balaam refused, I saw his weak spot: he likes to be flattered, and he loves gold; send him a bigger bribe, and send him a committee of princes, and you will catch him sure enough." So when the new committee came back with their richer bribes we can see that Balaam is pleased to be tempted, although he blusters and says, "If Balak would give me his house full of silver and gold, I cannot go beyond the word of the Lord my God, to do less or more" (Number 22:18). He was very careful, however, not to send them away with that sort of an answer, but begged the committee to stay overnight, and let him entertain them, while he asked again permission of the Lord to accept their offer.

How many of you have made that same blunder! Instead of driving away the tempter, you have entertained him as a guest. No man can help temptation coming. The holiest people on earth have been tempted. Jesus Christ himself was grievously tempted of the devil. But there is a vast difference between saying, "Get thee behind me, Satan!" and "Come in, and stay overnight, and I will see if I cannot fix it up some way so that I can do what you want." It is a fatal mistake to thus play with the tempter. When Balaam asks permission of God the second time to do what God has told him is wrong, we are certain he is sinning against his own conscience. In matters of simple judgment about worldly things it is well to take time for reflection, but it has been well said that in matters of duty "first thoughts are best." Frederick W. Robertson says the first thoughts that come to us about a question of conscience are more fresh, more pure, and have more of God in them. There is nothing like the first glance we get at duty, before there has been any special pleading of our affections or inclinations. Duty is never uncertain at first. It is only after we have got involved in the mazes and sophistries of wishing that things were different from what they are that duty seems indistinct. Taking time to consider a duty is usually only seeking after some excuse for explaining it away. A man is usually simply juggling with his own conscience when he takes time to think over a question of direct right and wrong in conduct. Deliberation is often only dishonesty. God's guidance is plain when we are true.

Balaam knew very well what was right, but he wanted to make money and win applause without bringing on himself the curse of God. He tried to find a way to do what Balak wanted him to do, and yet not subject himself to divine punishment. He went to God to try and get his duty altered, instead of seeking to find out what his duty was. But right and wrong cannot be juggled with like that. Even God cannot say that a thing is right today and wrong tomorrow.

Am I speaking any man's heart story to him tonight? Am I uncovering any woman's soul to herself? If so, I pray God that the Holy Spirit will strengthen you in your weakness, so that you may have the courage to be honest with your own soul and turn away from the sin that is tempting you to everlasting disaster.

The principal theme, however, to which I wish to call your special attention at this time, lies farther along in the story. That night, while the second committee were lodged in Balaam's house, God told Balaam that if the men should call him in the morning, he should rise up and go with them, and should speak the word which God gave him. Balaam was then wild with greed, and, seeming to have gained his point, did not wait for the men to call him in the morning, but rose up and saddled his ass and went with the princes of Moab. And the record says, "God's anger was kindled because he went: and the angel of the Lord stood in the way for an adversary against him. Now he was riding upon his ass, and his two servants were with him. And the ass saw the angel of the Lord standing in the way, and his sword drawn in his hand; and the ass turned aside out of the way, and went into the field; and Balaam smote the ass, to turn her into the way. But the angel of the Lord stood in a path of the vineyards, a wall being on this side, and a wall on that side. And when the ass saw the angel of the Lord, she thrust herself unto the wall, and crushed Balaam's foot against the wall: and he smote her again. And the angel of the Lord went further, and stood in a narrow place, where was no way to turn either to the right hand or to the left. And when the ass saw the angel of the Lord, she fell down under Balaam: and Balaam's anger was kindled, and he smote the ass with a staff. And the Lord opened the mouth of the ass, and she said unto Balaam, What have I done unto thee, that thou hast smitten me these three times? And Balaam said unto the ass, Because thou hast mocked me: I would there were a sword in mine hand, for now would I kill thee. And the ass said unto Balaam, Am not I thine ass, upon which thou hast ridden ever since I was thine unto this day? was I ever wont to do so unto thee? And he said, Nay. Then the Lord opened the eyes of Balaam, and he saw the angel of the Lord standing in the way, and his sword drawn in his hand: and he bowed down his head, and fell flat on his face. And the angel of the Lord said unto him, Wherefore hast thou smitten thine ass these three times? Behold, I went out to withstand thee, because thy way is perverse before me: and the ass saw me, and turned from me these three times: unless she had turned from me, surely now also I had slain thee, and saved her alive. And Balaam said unto the angel of the Lord, I have sinned; for I knew not that thou stoodest in the way against me: now therefore, if it displease thee, I will get me back again" (Numbers 22:22-34).

See the tenderness and loving-kindness of God manifested in the presence of the angel standing in the way of this tempted man going into sin, and seeking to turn him from his course not only once, but twice and thrice! The first time he is turned out of the way gently, without harm; the second time his foot is crushed; the third time he is brought to the ground, and only when in that helpless condition are his eyes opened to behold God's angel blocking the way. This, then, is the message I want to put on your hearts, that God is seeking always to block our way into sin; that it is never easy to go on a path of wrongdoing. There is many a thorn in that path—thorns that are not planted there because God hates us, but because he loves us. The angel did not block the way with drawn sword because God took delight in frightening Balaam, nor was his foot crushed because God took pleasure in giving him pain, nor was he overthrown and humiliated because God was pleased at his downfall; but the infinite pity of God was blocking his way into sin, making it impossible for him to go recklessly, without knowing his danger, on the road to ruin.

The Bible is full of such illustrations of God's kindly and loving intervention in behalf of sinning souls. Even John, the beloved disciple, at one time was so filled with anger and the spirit of revenge against a town that had refused to admit Christ and his disciples, that he craved permission of Jesus to call down fire from heaven to consume the people. Jesus turned to him with severe rebuke, and said, "Ye know not what manner of spirit ye are of" (Luke 9:55). So far as we know, that is the only rebuke that John ever received from his divine Lord. He does not seem to ever have needed another. How it must have comforted John as he lay with his head on the bosom of Jesus at the last supper, or as he received the final commission from the cross to care for the Saviour's mother, that the Lord had dealt thus faithfully with him, and that that keen rebuke had come as an angel from God to block the path down which he was tempted toward a revengeful and cruel spirit! If John had not heeded that angel in the path, he never would have been known in after history as the "beloved disciple."

And on the night of Christ's arrest Peter had an experience of the angel that blocked the way. He had had one experience before, when Christ had told him of his coming crucifixion, and Peter had declared that it could never happen. Christ had blocked his way with the stern rebuke, "Get thee behind me, Satan; thou art an offense unto me" (Matthew 16:23). But on that awful night of Christ's betrayal Peter fell again into sin, and denied his Lord. Then Jesus with a single look blocked his way to utter ruin. It did not crush his foot, as in Balaam's case; but it did more—it broke his heart. That was enough for Peter, and from that bitter night be turned about to lifelong fidelity to Christ.

Paul, too, knew what it was to have the angel block his way while on the downward path. The whole world has been interested in that midday vision on the way to Damascus, when, his heart full of bigotry and cruelty, suddenly the light shone above that of the noonday sun, and the heavenly voice called to him: "Saul, Saul, why persecutest thou me? it is hard for thee to kick against the pricks" (Acts 9:5). That to Saul meant salvation. It effectually blocked the path that led to hell. He turned back, to be no longer Saul, the persecutor, but to become Paul, the triumphant Christian apostle whose life was to be poured out as an oblation before God.

God has not changed in his loving-kindness toward lost sinners. His tenderness still seeks after men and women who are tempted and led captive on the way to ruin. It is not easy, I repeat, to go that way. Not one of you can do it without kicking against the pricks; not one of you can go on in sin without facing the angel of God with his drawn sword. He will bring you easily into the kingdom if he can; if he cannot bring you gently, he will bring you in at the cost of a crushed foot or of a broken heart. He will even follow you into the throes of bankruptcy or sickness, or defeat of all your hopes or plans, if thereby he can save you from eternal hurt and destruction. There are those that hear me to-night who know what all this means. You remember when you would not obey God in days of prosperity and joy; but you did come to obey him in the face of rebuke and sorrow.

I doubt not that some of you this very night are in the narrow place of the vineyards, with the wall on either hand, and God's angel standing in the way. O that your eyes may be opened to see, and that you may have wisdom to turn from the path of danger ere it is too late!

Some of you have met with God's rebuke; you have found that the way of the transgressor is hard; you have kicked against the goad, but it has hardened your heart and made you bitter in your thoughts toward God. I want to urge upon you to-night the unwisdom of that. I want to show you that is it not reasonable. It is not hate, but love, that has impelled the Lord to make of your sinful way a way of sorrow and disappointment.

Above everything I long to do justice to my Lord and to your Saviour. I would that I had language and genius to paint before you the picture of his compassion, of his sympathy and love. I would that I could cause you to appreciate the brooding tenderness of that shepherd-spirit that hovers about you and seeks to bring you back from danger and save you from harm. I would that I could make you see with new eyes the ninety and nine gathered in the fold, and the Shepherd turning away into the darkness, going down into the deep cañon, peering into the thickets, seeking, calling longingly after you, the lost lamb. Paul Laurence Dunbar seems to have caught the real spirit of the Master's love in his little hymn;

> "O li'l' lamb out in the col',
> De Mastah call you to de fol',
> O li'l' lamb!
> He hyeah you bleatin' on de hill;
> Come hyeah an' keep yo' mou'nin' still,
> O li'l' lamb!

"De Mastah sen' de Shepud fo'f;
He wandah souf, he wandah no'f,
O li'l' lamb!
He wandah eas', he wandah wes':
De win' a-wrenchin' at his breas',
O li'l' lamb!

"O, tell de Shephud whaih you hide;
He want you walkin' by his side,
O li'l' lamb!
He know you weak, he know you so';
But come, don't stay away no mo',
O li'l' lamb!

"An' af'ah while de lamb he hyeah
De Shepud's voice a-callin' cleah—
Sweet li'l' lamb!
He answah f'om de branches thick,
O Shepud, I's a-comin' quick—
O li'l' lamb!"

43

THE MELANCHOLY FATE
OF MR. FACING-BOTH-WAYS

"Balaam also the son of Beor they slew with the sword"
(Numbers 31:8).

I t is no disgrace to be killed on the battlefield if you are fighting honorably for what you believe to be right. But Balaam died the death of a traitor. For this is our old acquaintance, the prophet whom Balak sought to bribe to curse the Israelites, and who asked God for that privilege and was refused. But here we have the last picture in Balaam's earthly life, and he is dying on the battlefield with Israel's spears in his bosom, an out-and-out foe of the people whom God had blessed. For Balaam had finally gone with the messengers from Balak, and Balak had prepared altars and offered up sacrifices, and Balaam had sought to change the mind of God in regard to the people of Israel. But every time when Balaam spoke his message, it was a blessing and not a curse that was uttered. At the very first altar, when Balak and his princes were standing about and were listening in breathless silence to the words of Balaam, we can imagine the disappointment in their faces as he began to say: "How shall I curse, whom God hath not cursed? or how shall I defy, whom the Lord hath not defied? For from the top of the rocks I see him, and from the hills I behold him....Who can count the dust of Jacob, and the number of the fourth part of Israel? Let me die the death of the righteous, and let my last end be like his!" (Numbers 23:8-10). No wonder Balak said in his disgust, "I took thee to curse mine enemies, and behold, thou hast blessed them altogether!" (Numbers 23:11).

Balak, however, had persistence worthy of a better cause. He took Balaam to another point, where he could look out over the tents of Israel, and on top of Mount Pisgah Balaam built seven altars, and offered a bullock and a ram on every altar; but when he stood up again to speak to Balak and his listening associates, this is what he said: "God is not a man, that he should lie; neither the son of man, that he should repent: hath he said, and shall he not do it? or hath he spoken, and shall he not make it good? Behold, I have received commandment to bless: and he hath blessed; and I cannot reverse it. He hath not beheld iniquity in Jacob, neither hath he seen perverseness in Israel: the Lord his God is with him, and the shout of a king is among them. God brought them out of Egypt; he hath as it were the strength of a unicorn. Surely there is no enchantment against Jacob, neither is there any divination against Israel: according to this time it shall be said of Jacob and of Israel, What hath God wrought! Behold, the people shall rise up as a great lion, and lift himself as a young lion: he shall not lie down until he eat of the prey, and drink the blood of the slain" (Numbers 23:19-24).

But Balak was determined to try once more, and he said to Balaam, "Come, I pray thee, I will bring thee unto another place; peradventure it will please God that thou mayest curse me them from thence" (Numbers 23:27). And so on the top of Mount Peor seven altars more were builded and offerings made upon them. But Balak was more crushed than ever when he heard Balaam's poetic outburst explaining the vision that came to him at the altar: "How goodly are thy tents, O Jacob, and thy tabernacles, O Israel! As the valleys are they spread forth, as gardens by the river's side, as the trees of lign-aloes which the Lord hath planted, and as cedar trees beside the waters. He shall pour the water out of his buckets, and his seed shall be in many waters, and his king shall be higher than Agag, and his kingdom shall be exalted. God brought him forth out of Egypt; he hath as it were the strength of a unicorn: he shall eat up the nations of his enemies, and shall break their bones, and pierce them through with his arrows. He couched, he lay down as a lion, and as a great lion: who shall stir him up? Blessed is he that blesseth thee, and cursed is he that curseth thee" (Numbers 24:5-9).

At last Balak gives up his hope and in his anger warns Balaam to get out of his sight: "Therefore now flee thou to thy place: I thought to promote thee unto great honor; but, lo, the Lord hath kept thee back from honor" (Numbers 24:11).

Happy for Balaam if he had really parted from Balak and his vicious temptations at that time. But the man was not at peace in his own heart. He was not a genuine man. He was not sincere. He did not want to displease God, but he wanted still more to please himself. He cared nothing for Balak, except as he could use him; but neither did he care anything for the Lord, except as he hoped to use him.

So now he enters again into negotiations with the enemy, and advises Balak to do by strategy what he could not do by direct assault. He counsels Balak to use the fascinations of the daughters of Moab to entice the Israelites into idolatry. Thus, by degrading the people of Israel and leading them into sin, he would snatch them from God's protection. God will not curse the good: therefore make them wicked, and cause them to bring the curse on their own heads. Frederick W. Robertson has well said that a more diabolical wickedness can scarcely be conceived. Yet Balaam, as the world goes, was an honorable and veracious man; nay, a man of delicate conscientiousness and unconquerable scruples—a man of lofty religious professions, highly respectable and respected.

There are men who would not play false and yet would wrongly win. There are men who would not lie and yet who would bribe a poor man to support a cause which he believes in his soul to be false. There are men who would resent at the sword's point the charge of dishonor, who would yet for selfish gratification entice the weak into sin and damn body and soul in hell. There are men who would be shocked at being called traitors, yet who in time of war will make a fortune by selling arms and ammunition and provisions to their country's foes. There are men, respectable and respected, who give liberally and support religious societies and sit in fashionable church pews, who would not swear nor do any outward, open sin, who make their wealth by crushing the lifeblood out of white slaves in stenchful sweat shops, or by renting their property for liquor saloons and gambling halls and brothels. We are all ready to curse Balaam, and he deserves it; but let us not forget that Balaam did not do one whit worse than these men, and if God damned him for doing what he did, hell yawns for the men who today are trapping the unwary that they may fatten their own greed.

We may see illustrated here the tremendous importance of the current in which a man places himself. There is a current in every community that sweeps heavenward. If a man puts himself into that current and deliberately sets out to serve God, to make his friends among Christian people, and to turn from everything that would be displeasing to God, the current of his life will gain momentum every day, and will help to sweep him onward toward the heavenly shore. On the other hand, there is a current in every community that plunges downward toward the bottomless pit; and if a man thrusts himself into that current, he is borne remorselessly on. We become like the people with whom we associate, and our thoughts and ideals, whether good or evil, have power to infuse their own quality into the very blood and fiber of our being. If you have ever read *Silas Marner* you will remember the typical miser who is described in that book. The miser had been a very dutiful man at church, and was wronged by a brother, and fled from the town and the church and buried himself in the country. He was a poor man—a weaver; and he wove and hoarded his gold, and used to go to the little spot where he had hoarded it and turn it with his hands and feel how rich he was. But one night there came a strange, sad cry, and he went out to see whence it came; and when he returned the gold had gone, and in its place he saw a little child. It was a most unwelcome exchange; but when he turned to the little child and caressed it, and it caressed him, and he fed it and grew to love it, the heart of the man was humanized, and his character was ennobled and exalted. The more he had loved the money, the more hateful he became; the more he loved the child, the lovelier he grew. Man is made by his loves. If we love mean and vulgar things we shall grow to be like them. But if we love pure, noble, holy things we shall grow to be as noble as they.

Balaam had no thought that he would finally cast in his lot with Balak and the enemies of God; but by his double-heartedness, his facing one way and then the other in order if possible to gain both the wages of righteousness and the bribe of unrighteousness, he thrust himself into this wicked current that finally forced him into the position of an open foe of God's people. Robert Louis Stevenson's book that won him his first great fame, and which has been so often discussed, with its story of Dr. Jekyll and Mr. Hyde, won because we all have in our own consciousness something which bears witness to the possibility of our being tempted to a like career. The result is always the same when the temptation is yielded to. The bad side of a man's nature will always win where a man gives himself up to live a life which faces both ways. The wicked other half may be kept in the background for a time, but in the end it will come to be *the* personality, and the good will be crushed out entirely.

There are many people like Balaam in our modern world. They have a poetic side to their nature. They have vision hours when goodness seems indescribably beautiful and a holy life greatly attracts them. They have fine sensibilities; they are wrought upon by a tale of woe, and if you talk to them of the unspeakable horrors of Turkish persecutions in Armenia, the sufferings of starving Cubans, or if their favorite novelist paints a touching picture of some fair life betrayed and debauched, they will be moved to tears and will have an hour of charitable feeling. The vulgar, loathsome, repulsive side of common sins is hateful to them. But they do not hate sin because it is a wrong against God; it is only because it offends their taste. And with all their poetic sentiment and generous impulses and occasional tearful feeling, they do not really love humanity, and their lives go on like Balaam's—seeking their own selfish interests, without real worship to God or love for mankind, until the drifting current of selfishness carries them to the camp of those "having no hope and without God in the world" (Ephesians 2:12).

I appeal to you for an open, outspoken attitude in behalf of Christ and a righteous life. It is the only right course, and it is the only safe course. I look into many of your faces to-night knowing that the one thing that you need, above everything else, is a complete cleansing of your hearts from sin; a radical transformation of your life, so that you will stand a uniformed soldier of Jesus Christ. You need not to be made better, but, by God's forgiving mercy, to be made thoroughly good.

A physician was giving earnest attention to a sick child, and encouraged the anxious mother to hope for her recovery. The mother said to the child one day, "The doctor says he thinks he will soon make mamma's little girl better."

"But why will he not make me well?" asked the child with eagerness.

Jesus Christ is able to cure us of sin. And it is not to be better only, but to be well, that we should pray.

I repeat it: This, above everything else, is your greatest want. Hugh Price Hughes relates an incident of a distinguished minister who was suddenly invited to visit a dying man. He found him with little furniture, no food, and no attendant, in the agonies of death. He was dying in the greatest destitution. "O sir," said he to the minister, "I am in great want." And the minister made the mistake we too often make, and thought he was referring to some temporal wants. He said, "Yes, I see you are in this wretched place, with no food, no medicine, no attendant. I will go and get a doctor and a nurse, and some food and nourishment." "O," he said, lifting his thin hand, "that is not what I want. What I want," he said, in the deep voice of the dying, "is to know that my sins are forgiven." When a man comes to die, he wants to know that God has forgiven him, that Christ has saved him. But if the dying need it, we need it just as certainly.

A great many make the same tragic mistake that Balaam made. Balaam longed to die the death of the righteous. There is scarcely a passage in the Bible more often quoted than Balaam's expression of desire, "Let me die the death of the righteous, and let my last end be like his!" (Numbers 23:10). That is very beautiful, and I have no doubt that for once Balaam was sincere. But he was not willing to pay the price. Everything has its cost. The cost of dying right is living right. To die the death of the righteous a man must pay the price of living the life of the righteous. Some of you who are not Christians are like Balaam in that you desire, and in some way expect, to die the death of a Christian. You read the story of triumphant Christian deathbeds, or you have stood by the side of the couch when your father or mother or some dear Christian friend met death with a smile and with the glow of heaven's joy on the face, and you have said to yourself, "Let me die the death of the righteous, and let my last end be like his!" But you are not living for it. Jesus says, "Whosoever shall deny me before men, him will I also deny before my Father" (Matthew 10:33). And yet you go on denying him—refusing to open the door of your heart at his knocking, refusing to stand on his side in the fellowship of the church, refusing to renounce your sins and bow before him in penitence, seeking his forgiveness. How can you expect that you will die the death of the Christian, and have a Christian's welcome into heaven, while you are going on living a life of selfishness and sin, and neglecting to accept Christ as your Saviour? Let Balaam, broken hearted and ruined, dying a traitor on the battlefield in disgrace and shame, bring you tonight his message of warning. He tried to life the life you are living, and you see the end. "God is not mocked. Whatsoever a man soweth, that shall he also reap" (Galatians 6:7). Balaam found it so, and every sinner against God from that day to this has found it true. The laws of the universe will not be reversed on your account. Balaam had his chance for repentance and refused it, and lost his soul. He sinned against great light and died in great darkness. You have great light. Christ speaks to you with many voices. Do not sin against him! Do not grieve the Holy Spirit! Choose now an open and honorable career as the friend and servant of Jesus Christ.

CHAPTER 44

THE FLIGHT AND ESCAPE
OF A SINNER

"Be sure your sin will find you out" (Numbers 32:23).

"There shall be six cities for refuge, which ye shall appoint
for the manslayer, that he may flee thither"
(Numbers 35:6).

"Him that cometh to me I will in no wise cast out
(John 6:37).

T here is a Scripture declaration that "The wicked flee when no man pursueth" (Proverbs 28:1). That is because there is an invisible pursuer which makes a coward of the man who is conscious that his sins pursue him and that he has no way within himself of making defense against their attack. That is the reason that many men who have been reckless in going into sin become so timid that "the sound of a shaken leaf shall chase them; and they shall flee, as fleeing from a sword; and they shall fall when none pursueth" (Leviticus 26:36). This constant threat of pursuit and punishment robs the soul of peace, and though it may be forgotten for a time, the sinner has no assurance when the pursuer will rise up to denounce him. Byron wrote out a bitter experience:

> "That pang where more than madness lies!
> The worm that will not sleep, and never dies,
> Thought of the gloomy day and ghastly night,
> That dreads the darkness, and yet loathes the
>   light;
> That winds around and tears the quivering heart,
> Ah! Wherefore not consume it and depart?"

Bryon was not the only man who has been thus haunted. We talk about haunted houses and laugh at the superstition, but a haunted soul is no superstition; it is a dread everyday reality wherever sin hangs unforgiven above a sinner's head. Heraud writes:

> "Will no remorse, will no decay,
> O Memory, soothe thee into peace?
> When life is ebbing away
> Will not thy hungry vultures cease?
> Ah, no! As weeds from fading free,
> Noxious and rank, yet verdantly,
> Twine round a ruined tower,
> So to the heart, untamed, will cling
> The memory of an evil thing
> In life's departing hour;
> Green is the week when gray the wall,
> And thistles rise while turrets fall.
>
> "Yet open Memory's book again;
> Turn o'er the lovelier pages now,
> And find that balm for present pain
> Which past enjoyment can bestow;
> Delusion all, and void of power!
> For e'en in thought's serenest hour,

When past delights are felt
And Memory shines on scenes of woe,
'Tis like the moonbeam on the snow,
That gilds, but cannot melt:
That throws a mocking luster o'er,
But leaves it cheerless as before."

If men would only believe God's word about the certainty of sin pursuing the sinner and spoiling all the sweet gladness of innocence, they would resist temptation and keep their freedom The devil deceives us with the feeling that sin is only dangerous when discovered; while the real danger in sin is not in its discovery, but in the hurt which it does to our own moral natures. And no outward evidence is required to secure our conviction at the judgment seat; the certain witness to our sin is in our own conscience. Shakespeare, in "Richard III," makes false Clarence say:

"My dream was lengthened after life:
O then began the tempest to my soul!
I passed, methought, the melancholy flood,
With that grim ferryman which poets write of,
Unto the kingdom of perpetual night.
The first that there did greet my stranger soul
Was my great father-in-law, renowned Warwick,
Who cried aloud—*What scourge for perjury*
Can this dark monarchy afford false Clarence?
And so he vanished. Then came wandering by
A shadow like an angel, with bright hair
Dabbled in blood, and he shrieked out aloud,
Clarence is come—false, fleeting, perjured
   Clarence—
That stabb'd me in the field of Tewkesbury;
Seize on him, furies, take him to your torments!
With that, methought, a legion of foul fiends

Environed me, and howled in mine ears
Such hideous cries that, with the very noise,
I trembling waked, and for a season after
Could not believe but that I was in hell;
Such terrible impression made my dream.

I have done these things
That now give evidence against my soul."

And that there is no lack of witnesses is clearly set forth farther along in Shakespeare's heart-searching tale:

"My conscience hath a thousand several tongues,
And every tongue brings in a several tale,
And every tale condemns me for a villain.
Perjury, perjury, in the high'st degeree;
Murder, stern murder, in the dir'st degree;
All several sins, all used in each degree,
Thronged to the bar, crying all—Guilty! Guilty!
I shall despair. There is no creature loves me,
And, if I die, no soul shall pity me.
Nay, wherefore should they? Since that I myself
Find in myself no pity to myself."

And these strong lines of the great poet are in perfect harmony with Scripture truth and with the testimony of human history and of our own consciences.

Happy, then, is the thought of a refuge from the pursuer of our souls. We have a glimpse, in the second verse of the text, of that mercy and love of God which ever seek to save the sinner. Under this old Hebrew arrangement certain cities were set apart as cities of refuge, to which, if one had slain another by accident or without malicious intent, he could flee, and be safe from the manslayer, or avenger. I have called your attention to it because of its suggestion of the great refuge which God has provided for the sinner in Jesus Christ, our Saviour. The roads to the cities of refuge were required to be kept open and were laid out straight, and the gates were always open, so that nothing could stand in the way of the escape of a man who was really in earnest. So Christ is accessible to every sinner who will take the straight road of obedience and enter through the open gate of repentance and confession of sin. The personal flight of the manslayer was necessary for his escape. No one could do it for him, and no amount of thinking about it, or good impulses or desires in that direction, could save him from death at the hands of the avenger. So it is true that no amount of good intention can be of any value to a sinner unless the good intentions are put into action and cause a real arousing of the man or woman to flee to Christ and enter in to him as their Saviour and Refuge.

Perhaps someone says, "I would like to be a Christian. I am ashamed and sorry on account of my sins, and the thought of them robs me of peace; but I know not how to begin to find refuge." If you will just put aside all thoughts of mystery, and ask God for forgiveness in Christ's name as simply as a little child would ask to be forgiven by his mother, your perplexity and trouble will be at an end. I have been reading an incident related by Dr. James Todd. One wintry night Dr. Todd got on the train in Chicago to return to his home in Michigan. He had shaken the sleet from his ulster, thrown it over the back of the seat, and sat down beside it, when a voice called in trembling tone, "Hello, doctor!"

He immediately sat upright, and looking forward to see who saluted him, recognized the familiar faces of two of his parishioners. He hastened to meet them, and soon learned of the serious illness of the man who at home was familiarly known as "Rob." He had been with his wife to consult a specialist in Chicago.

"I am very weak, doctor," he said, "but am gaein' home for a little and will bide there tae vote for McKinley, and then I'll come back and see the specialist, for he has helped me."

The man was a Scotchman who had been raised in a Christian home in the old country, but had been for many years religiously indifferent.

Once he had admitted to Dr. Todd, "I am gey fond o' a dram; religion is not what it once seemed tae be; I dinna like these ministers who rant in sermons, an' tell stories tae frighten the bairns, but like tae hear you preach once in a while because you are Scotch—and for the days o' auld lang syne."

In the morning, when they reached their destination, as Dr. Todd said good-bye he added, "I am coming to see you, Robert, as a man and a friend, but not as the minister."

"Well," he replied, "I'll be glad to see you. Guid morning."

A few days afterward the minister fulfilled his promise and found the sick man resting on a lounge. His cough had grown worse, and a sickly pallor hovered around his naturally ruddy cheeks.

They talked for a while about Scotland, but no reference was made to religion. Finally the sick man laughed till he coughed, as he said, "I told the neebors ye were comin' tae prepare me fur burial; but I said, 'I'm gain' tae cheat him, minister though he be.' "

On the minister's next visit he found the patient still weaker, the hacking cough more troublesome, and his manner less pleasant.

"How are you today, Robert?"

"I am not very weel, but the doctor has just left. I have been won'rin' hoo it is sick folks in this toon dinna like the minister tae see them—an' pay the doctors for comin' who fairly tire them. Na doot it is the mule in man that accounts for it."

After a pause Dr. Todd asked, "Robert, would you like me to read you a Scotch story? I've brought it along with me, believing it would interest you. It's a good one, but if it wearies you just tell me, and I will stop reading."

His eyes suddenly brightened, and his hungering nature spoke: "Read on. I'll be glad to hear it."

Dr. Todd took from his pocket a copy of *Beside the Bonnie Brier Bush*, and read from "The Doctor's Last Journey." As he read of the doctor's longing for Drumsheugh, and their friendship for each other, the sick man said in softened accents, "That's true for Scotchmen."

As the minister proceeded to read of the struggles of the doctor and Jess, Robert's eyes were moistened with tears. When he listened to the doctor's confession to his friend, he whispered huskily to himself, "That's me, that's me."

When the story was finished it was easy to see that the citadel of his heart had surrendered, and that in the inner chambers of his soul he was weeping like a sorrowing child. The minister wisely pressed his hand and slipped gently and quietly out of the room, leaving him to come to himself, with his past hanging threateningly over him, the uncertain future demanding recognition, and his soul hemmed in between.

Next day Dr. Todd visited him again and asked, "How did you like the story?"

"Ah, it was grand! Will ye read tae me again?"

The doctor opened the book again and read McClure's confession. As he finished it the sick man interrupted his further reading by an earnest confession of his own: "I have na gotten over that a' night. Doctor, I am waur than he. For I did not regard God, and I turned my back on the kirk of our fathers and my past early training. I sometimes cursed a wise Providence, and defied him. When I gaed to the church it was often tae boast hoo I knew a guid sermon, or to find fault wi' a poor one. My family has had a bad example frae me. I have been untrue tae my trust, an' unfaithful tae my God. I am kent this day as 'Reprobate Rob.' I have laughed even at deith, and it's hard for me tae seek pardon; and my sins, I remember them this day."

He turned wearily on the lounge and tried to hide his face, which reflected the inward struggle between hope and despair.

"But can ye not do as the old doctor did? He, too, was very sorry, but he trusted God would have mercy on him."

"Cud ye pray for me, doctor, an' I'll try?"

They prayed together that the entrance of the Lord's word might bring light to the one groping in the darkness, that the sick one might have the quiet and consolation of Christ's peace, and the wandering sheep be restored to the fold.

"That's better; I see it clearer noo, an' I hope in his mercy. Come again the morn'."

Some weeks passed before the death angel came, and sweet was the fellowship those two Christian Scotchmen enjoyed together. The sick man's trust was childlike in its simplicity, but it was both clear and strong. His disposition was as completely changed as the mist-covered mountain is by the rising sun. He was cheerfully patient during the remainder of his trying illness, though he had formerly been a sour and irritable man. During Dr. Todd's visits afterward he was most anxious that nothing should interfere with "oor worship," as he termed their devotions together, though, Scotchman like, he was most conservative as to verbal experiences.

One day, shortly before his death, the minister asked him, "Robert, would you not like to give some further expression concerning your changing conditions?"

His only reply to this was to repeat tremblingly, but with great feeling, the oft-quoted psalm which is, beyond all others, peculiarly the Scotchman's psalm: "The Lord is my shepherd; I shall not want. He maketh me to lie down in green pastures: he leadeth me beside the still waters. He restoreth my soul: he leadeth me in the paths of righteousness for his name's sake. Yea, though I walk through the valley of the shadow of death, I will fear no evil: for thou art with me; thy rod and thy staff they comfort me. Thou preparest a table before me in the presence of mine enemies: thou anointest my head with oil; my cup runneth over. Surely goodness and mercy shall follow me all the days of my life: and I will dwell in the house of the Lord forever" (Psalm 23:1-6).

Knowing his past life, the minister felt a little surprised at this accuracy in the recital of the psalm, and asked:

"Robert, where did you learn that?"

"In the Sabbath school in Lead Hills, when I was sax years auld. And since ye read tae me aboot Dr. McClure and showed me I was wrang, and the Lord's mercy, it has a' come back tae me. An' the things I learned frae my mither and my teachers at the schule when a laddie are my comfort today. An', doctor, some day after I hae gane hame tae them, dinna say I died a saint, but, if he think it'll dae any guid, ye might tell hoo Dr. McClure helped to save a soul."

I have told you this homely, sweet story with the hope that it might show some of you how natural and easy it is to turn to God, with the simplicity of a little child turning to father or mother, and find forgiveness.

45

THE EVOLUTION OF A SINNER

*"When I saw among the spoils a goodly Babylonish
garment, and two hundred shekels of silver, and a wedge
of gold of fifty shekels weight, then I coveted them, and
took them: and behold, they are hid in the earth in the
midst of my tent, and the silver under it"*
(Joshua 7:21).

The army of Israel had turned cowardly in battle, and
their hearts melted like water in the face of the
enemy. Never was there a braver officer on a battlefield than Joshua. He was every inch a soldier, from the sole
of his foot to the crown of his head. He was heart-broken
and in despair at the sudden cowardice of his soldiers. But
when he went to God in prayer about it he soon found out
where the trouble was. Some of his people had become
greedy and had disobeyed the commandment, which had
been very strict, that they were not to wage a war for plunder, and that none of the treasures of the enemy were to be
seized upon for private gain. So it came about that God revealed to Joshua the secret of the cowardice of Israel.

Nothing will make a people cowardly quicker than to
be given over to greed. When Christ went into the country

of the Gadarenes and found the man there who was possessed of a legion of devils, and, driving them out of the man, permitted them to go into the herd of swine, after which they drowned themselves in the sea, the hog raisers of that town immediately got up a procession to come out and petition Jesus to leave the country. They could not deny that he cast out devils, but the danger to the pork business made them cowardly. So, in one of these modern cities, if a Christian minister or a Christian church begins to agitate public opinion and arouse Christian sentiment to enforce law against the liquor sellers or drive them out of the community, every man who rents his property for saloons, or gets advertising for his newspaper from the liquor traffic, or is in any way interested in it through his pocket-book, will begin to stir up a procession to persuade the radical representative of Christ to depart out of the town. Let a minister or a church attack gambling and seek to protect the young and unwary from the traps of the gamblers, and it will not only be the thugs and professional gamblers who will cry out against him or them, but you will be astonished to see the respectable, high-toned proprietors of race tracks and pool rooms who will be arrayed against every earnest defender of the people from the gambler. The cowardly nerve of the people is ever the financial nerve. Let a man have his greed aroused, and, though liberty and humanity and righteousness may bleed and die, the greedy sinner can only gorge himself on the plunder where his heart is set.

But it is to the orderly evolution by which a sinner comes to his ruin that I wish to call special attention. Notice how logically this man Achan, for that was his name, sets forth the pivotal points in his downward career. First he says, "I saw;" next, "I coveted;" and then, "I took." Naturally, after having obtained it, and knowing that he had risked his life in breaking the law, the next step is, "I hid." And then he was discovered, and the end came in his punishment by a horrible death. Go over it again: saw, coveted, took, hid, discovered, punished. There you have it, and it is the story of sin over and over again all along down the history of the race.

Eve "saw" the tree of the knowledge of good and evil," and she "saw" that the fruit of it was pleasant to look upon, and she brooded over it, and talked with the devil about it, and then took it and ate of it and gave to Adam—and then what happened? They felt the dawn of guilt in their consciences. They were ashamed of their nakedness. They tried to make aprons out of fig leaves. They hid away in the shadows of the garden, but that did not silence the voice of God as he cried, "Where art thou?" And they went out from Eden with the flaming sword waving behind them.

Cain "saw" the prosperity of Abel; he "saw" God's pleasure in it and appreciation of his brother's goodness, and he envied his brother. He wanted his brother's blessing without paying the price in goodness. He brooded about it. The more he thought it over, the more he hated Abel. Then he went and tried to pick a quarrel with him, and, when Able would not quarrel, the very sweetness and innocence of his brother's face seemed to stab him like a dagger. Then he killed him, and became a vagabond on the face of the earth.

Joseph's brethren listened to the prattle of the young lad about his dreams of the sheaves that bowed down to him, and the stars that made obeisance, and were filled with envy and jealousy. They brooded over it, until on that day they "saw" that coat of many colors glistening in the sun as he came over the hills with his father's message. They seized upon him and sold him into slavery. They lied to the old father. They covered up their sin by an oath of secrecy. They kept it covered for twenty years, but in the counting room of Pharaoh in Egypt, when famine had driven them into a strange land, the ghost of the wronged boy came back and stared them in the face, and they cried, with anguish, "We are verily guilty concerning our brother!"

Ahab "saw" Naboth's vineyard and wanted to buy it; and when it was not for sale he still coveted it, and brooded over it until he winked at Jezebel's wicked murder of its owner. Then he entered into possession and was happy for a time; but justice did not sleep, the Nemesis was on his track, and at the very spot where Naboth was slain the arrow found its way into Ahab's body, and the dogs licked up the blood that oozed out of his war chariot.

Samson "saw" Delilah and was fascinated by her brilliancy and beauty and dash of spirit, and was lured into sin. Again and again, in contemptuous strength, he escaped out of the meshes that were laid for him; but the day came when his strength vanished, though at the time he knew it not. His eyes were put out; the great arms, that could rend a young lion as though it were a kid, were chained to grind at the mill like some poor donkey; and he who had been the hope and promise of a great people, their glory and their pride, became the slave and the laughingstock of his enemies.

You see there is a great law running through all human history, and our text is only in harmony with that law. Sin in you, if unchecked, unrepented of, unforgiven, will run the same sure and deadly career, and end in destruction.

Let us take it up for a moment, point by point. "I saw." But you say, "How could he help it?" Often a man can help it. I have no doubt that many soldiers that day were so desperately in earnest to win victory that they took no note of silver or gold or fine garments. A man is likely to see what he is looking for. Two men walk down the street, and one sees books and pictures and elevating things. They attract his attention and win his interest. The other man sees a saloon sign and snuffs the fumes of liquor through the door, or he sees something that awakens evil passion or feeds an impure thought already in his mind. And yet I do not wish to be understood as teaching that the temptation is always our own fault. Every one of us will be tempted. The disciple is not greater than his Lord, and he was cruelly tempted. The great point is how we shall treat the temptation. The fatal blunder Achan made was in permitting himself to remain gazing at those forbidden treasures, thus giving his covetousness a chance to grow and fatten until it overcame his will. The breeding place of sin is in the imagination. No man will ever commit a sin unless he first allows it to nest in his heart. People meditate on sins which fascinate them by their appearance. A man beholds with eye or thought what he knows to be wrong, to be a sin against God, contrary to the divine law, and yet it charms him. He says to himself, "If it were only right for me to do it, how great would be the joy." And then, instead of thrusting it out of his mind, he continues to think about it; he turns it over and over again, like a sweet morsel, in his imagination. He pictures himself committing the sin, and every time he does so he is the more fascinated by it. As he thinks about it the promised pleasures of the sin become more and more attractive, while the ugly, repulsive side is lost to view. And thus days may go on, possibly weeks and months, until an opportunity comes for the sin to be committed; and then, suddenly as a panther which has been crouching over a traveler's path, waiting hungrily through all the hours of the afternoon until he shall come back at night from his toil, leaps like a flash of lightning on his victim, so sin which a man has been getting ready to do, by weeks and months of thought and meditation, suddenly becomes a horrible and soul-blighting reality.

The moment the sin is committed there is born in the wicked conscience a desire to hide it, to cover it up and conceal it from view—not only from the view of the world, but from the view of the soul itself and from the view of God. But this is impossible. There are a great many things that a man has not reckoned with when he commits a sin. He has done violence to his own will. He has unleashed a violent passion or appetite. He has been conquered once, and this enemy of his soul has gained the prestige of victory and is not domineering and insolent toward him. Conscience wounded will ever and anon rise up to rebuke him, and God is never deluded for a moment.

It is said that General Kitchener, the hero of Omdurman, knows the Oriental languages almost perfectly. At one of his army camps on the Nile two Arab date-sellers were arrested as suspected spies, and were confined in the guard tent. Shortly afterward a third Arab prisoner was hastily bundled into the tent. An animated jabbering ensued between the three, and in a few minutes, much to the astonishment of the sentry, the latest arrival drew aside the doorway and stepped out, remarking, "All right, sentry; I am going to the general."

It was Kitchener. Again only a few minutes passed when an orderly hurried up and a spade was handed to each of the two Arabs, who were then marched outside the lines, made to dig their own graves, and were then shot. They were very dangerous spies and Kitchener had detected them.

So there is a traitor bundled into our own tent. Our own conscience will bear swift testimony against us if we sin against God.

But some of you are conscious of your sin and are sorry for it. Achan found no place for repentance. He died a shameful and disgraceful death. That is the natural outcome of sin. If unforgiven it always ends in that. "The wages of sin is death" (Romans 6:23). "A man is tempted when he is drawn away of his own lust and enticed. Then when lust hath conceived, it bringeth forth sin: and sin, when it is finished, bringeth forth death" (James 1:14, 15).

That is the natural logic of a sinful course. How many there are that go on to that fearful end. But, thank God, it need not be so with you! You may this very hour repent of your sins and turn from them to Christ, who is able and willing to forgive them, and give you a glad and joyous consciousness that your sins are blotted out and will be remembered against you no more forever.

Mr. Moody tells the story of a man in one of his meetings who had been brought there against his will, through some personal influence. When he got there they were singing:

> "Come! oh, come to Me!
> Weary, heavy-laden,
> Come! oh, come to Me!"

He said afterward he thought he never saw so may fools together in his life before. The idea of a number of men standing there singing, "Come! come! come!" When he started home he could not get this little word out of his head; it kept coming back all the time. He went into a saloon and ordered some whisky, thinking to drown it. But it kept coming back. He drank more whisky; but the words kept ringing in his ears. He said to himself, "What a fool I am for allowing myself to be troubled in this way!" He had another glass, and finally got home. He went off to bed, but could not sleep; it seemed as if the very pillow kept whispering, "Come! come!" "What a fool I was for ever going to that meeting at all!" he muttered. When he got up he took the little hymn book, found the hymn, and read it over. "What nonsense!" he said to himself; "the idea of a rational man being disturbed by that hymn." He set fire to the hymn book, but could not burn up the little word "Come!" He declared he would never go to another meeting; but the next night he came again. Strange to say, they were singing the same hymn. "There is that miserable old hymn again," he complained. "What a fool I am for coming." Some time afterward that man arose in a meeting of young converts and told this story. Pulling out the little hymn book—for he had bought another copy—and opening it at this hymn, he said: "I think this hymn is the sweetest and best in the English language. God blessed it to the saving of my soul."

Christ is still calling. Come to him and be saved!

46

A CAPTAIN WITH HIS FOOT ON THE NECK OF A KING

"Put your feet upon the necks of these kings"
(Joshua 10:24).

The five mountain kings, the king of Jerusalem, the king of Hebron, the king of Jarmuth, the king of Lachish, and the king of Eglon, had all gathered their armies together to fight against the men of Gibeon, in the new territory which had been allotted to them in the land of Canaan. They were threatened with destruction by this powerful coalition, and sent a most urgent appeal to Joshua to come to their relief. He did so at once, and with his accustomed valor and dash brought about a great victory that scattered the enemy in confusion. In the midst of their overwhelming defeat the five mountain kings of the Amorites, in order to save themselves from destruction, hid themselves in a cave at Makkedah. Joshua would not stop for them at the time, but ordered some of the soldiers to roll great stones into the mouth of the cave, as though they were penning up a wolf run to earth, and so he let them wait until the battle was over. When the victory was won, and the army had come back to Makkedah, he ordered the cave to be opened and the five kings to be brought out before him. The scene that was then enacted is one of the most dramatic in all history. Picture it for yourself. About are the victorious hosts, fresh from battle. Dragged out from the cave are the proud but humiliated and broken kings of the Amorites. They are led out before Joshua, and compelled to lie down upon the ground. Then Joshua called on all the captains which went with him to the battle and commanded them, saying, "Come near, put your feet upon the necks of these kings" (Joshua 10:24). And they came near, and put their feet upon the necks of them. And Joshua said unto them, "Fear not, nor be dismayed; be strong and of good courage: for thus shall the Lord do to all your enemies against whom ye fight" (Joshua 10:25). Afterward the kings were hanged on five trees, and their bodies were cast into the cave where they had his themselves, and great stones were rolled back again to the cave's mouth. Thus in selecting their hiding-place they had selected their tomb as well.

Joshua has already spiritualized this picture for us. We cannot do better than follow his example. There are other kings that make war on the sons of God, that ought to be treated in the same way that Joshua treated these. There are wicked habits, there are giant sins, the measure of whose power is so great that they may be well compared to kings. If we are to build up a good character, and live in purity and peace, we must fight these kings of evil to the death. We shall never be safe until we have trampled them underfoot. The great trouble is that men parley with their sins when they ought to kill them. No Spanish diplomat was ever so dilatory or so wily in securing advantages through parley as are the giant sins that plead in our hearts to retain some sort of standing with us.

I never shall forget an experience I had last Thanksgiving morning. I came to the church very early, but early as I was I found waiting for me a young man who asked me at the door if I had such a thing as a temperance pledge that he could sign. I told him I could soon write one, and took him into my study. He was a young man of large and splendid physique, well dressed, used excellent language, had a frank, open countenance, and gave every outward proof of being far above the average in ability and manliness. Yet he told me his story with sobs and tears. He had given way to strong drink. He had a good position as a traveling man for a commercial house, which he feared he would lose through drunkenness. He had gone out to a neighboring town a few days before, and though he had not drank for months until that day, he was persuaded to take a single glass of beer, and from that on had been drunk for a week and had not even sought to do business. He was the only son of a widowed mother that lived in a Western city. It would break her heart if he should be broken down and destroyed. His cry was, "What can I do?" " I have tried over and over again," said he, "quit for weeks and even months at a time, and then I am swept off my feet like this in a moment, and all my good resolutions go down in debauch."

I had another man come to me this week who has had a somewhat similar experience. He, too, is a big, strong, broad-shouldered, fine-looking man. He inherited a taste for strong drink. He was hedged away from it in his early youth, but in opening manhood fell into the hands of his enemies. Sorrow and misfortune came to him, and for a time he gave himself up to it and tried to drown his troubles. How many

a man has tried to drown his troubles in strong drink, but
has succeeded only in drowning himself and taking his troubles, augmented a thousandfold, with him! After a while,
however, conscience was aroused and he was awakened to
make a fight against the enemy. He vowed to himself that
he would stop his evil way and dethrone this tyrannical king.
But right here he made his great blunder. He was urged at
this time to come out openly for Christ; to confess his sins
and to throw himself completely on the Lord's side as a soldier of Jesus Christ: but the devil whispered to him and said,
"You had better wait a year or two, and see whether you are
going to be able to keep these new resolutions which you
have made. Many another man," said the tempter, "has
made the same kind of promises to himself and fallen back
in a few weeks to be worse than ever. If you join the church,
let everybody know your determination, and then should
get to drinking again, you would bring shame and disgrace
not only on yourself, but on the church. Stay out until you
are sure you can stand." Now that sounds very plausible, and
the devil has ruined thousands of men and women with that
specious philosophy.

Well, this young man I am telling you about, who came
to see me this week, took the devil's advice instead of the
preacher's, and went on trying to fight his own battles. He
succeeded in keeping sober for several months, but finally,
in an unguarded hour, he went down, and a two weeks' debauch followed. Shamed and humiliated, he came trembling back to himself, like the prodigal among the husks
of the swineherd, and tried again. This time he only went
about three months, and down again he went into the mire
and filth, trodden under foot by his sin. Then he came to
me with his tale of sorrow and despair.

I said to both these men what I have said to thousands
of men—not only in public congregations, but singly, in
heart-searching and sometimes heart-breaking conversations—that there was only one chance, and that was to
cease parleying with the tyrant who had so shamed and
disgraced them, and who held them in such cruel slavery;
to trample him underfoot, hang him to the death, bury
him out of sight, with the stones of God's promises piled
against his tomb forever. If they follow that advice they will
be saved men, and there is a future for them, bright and
glorious, as the sons of God. If they reject it they will die
in the gutter and go down to a drunkard's hell.

But that is not the only king that tyrannizes over en-
slaved souls and makes war on men who ought to be living
as the sons of God. Sin is rebellion against God; it is refusal
to keep God's law, refusal to give him loving service; and
whether it be ugly, loathsome, repulsive forms of sin, or
clothed in fashionable garments made attractive and kingly
as an angel of light, it is still the same hideous thing, and
works the same horrid results on the human soul. The skull
and the crossbones are ever the only true badge for sin; for
God's word is true, that "the wages of sin is death."

The message which I wish to bring to you with all the
power that I have is this: If you will fight against your sin,
if you will make war against it—open, earnest, aggressive
war; not war carried on in secret, but war that is avowed
and declared to all the world, war waged with sharp sword
to the very death—then you may be sure that you will soon
run your enemy to the earth, and it will be hiding like these
kings of the Amorites in the cave.

If you are going to fight your sin it is never wise to dally with it. Wisdom lies in being up and at it. Barney Barnato, the Kaffir "diamond king," gave it as his opinion that he won his great financial success because of his aggressiveness. He said: "If you are going to fight, always get in the first blow. If a man is going to hit you, hit him first, and say, 'If you try that I'll hit you again.' It is of no use for you to stand off and say, 'If you hit me I'll hit you back.' " What was policy in the diamond merchant is high wisdom on the part of the man who is going to make war on a wicked habit or a sinful appetite that threatens his moral safety. Don't quarrel or hold debate with it; stamp the neck underfoot and swing it to the first tree. Commit yourself openly before all the world as a man or woman at war with the devil.

A lady, while giving the finishing touches to a table spread for a dinner party, heard the patter of naked feet upon the stairs. Surmising that her little daughter was probably bent on plundering the dessert, she hid herself behind the window curtains and watched the proceedings. The child, in her nightdress, came into the room, climbed up on a chair, helped herself deliberately to a fine peach, and went off with her booty. The mother felt very sad, and began to consider how she should punish her little girl. Presently she again heard the same patter of feet, and hid herself as before. The child clambered into the chair, replaced the fruit, triumphantly ejaculating, "That's one on you, Mr. Devil!" and trotted off to bed in peace. She had experienced the truth of the apostle's declaration that if we resist the devil he will flee from us.

What some of you need is to be roused up to make war on your sin. You are not now fighting against it. O, I now what you would say: "I am ashamed of my sin; there are hours in which I loathe it and abominate it more than you can imagine; there are times when, if I could burn it out of my heart at the loss of a right arm or a right eye, I would not hesitate; and I have not really given up to it. I don't intend for a moment to die in my sins and give up to everlasting defeat." And yet while you feel that way about it, you are going on ever and anon yielding to sin, bearing its unholy yoke, living with God's condemnation against sin hanging over your head, living so that if sudden death should come you would be lost forever; living so that if you were suddenly cut off in your sins they would banish you from the presence of God through all eternity; and yet, conscious of this, you do not rouse yourself to fight your sin, to trample it underfoot and strangle it to death.

When the men of Gibeon had to face these five kings of the Amorites, they called for Joshua because they knew he had wisdom and courage and strength and reinforcements enough to lead them to victory. A man who is fighting his sin must call on our Joshua, the Lord Jesus Christ. He is the only one who can help you to put your foot on the neck of all the evil kings that make war on your soul. He is a leader who never gets discouraged. There never was a greater thing said about Christ than that which was foretold of him by the prophet, "He shall not fail nor be discouraged." And he never was discouraged. He came down to earth and tasted our grief and our sorrow, but no one ever found him once with "the blues." He saw mankind at its worst; he saw their hypocrisies, their ingratitude, their selfishness; but he was not discouraged in them and went on, ever seeing the vision of the day when all the devils should be overthrown and destroyed. Not Peter's denial, not even Judas's treachery, could discourage Jesus Christ. Pilate could scourge him till from loss of blood he a little later fainted under his cross; but he could not discourage him. Nailed to the cross, he suffered, he thirsted, he prayed, and died, but he was not discouraged. On Easter morning the angel descended from heaven and rolled away the stone from the mouth of the sepulcher, the Roman guard fled in terror, and the undiscouraged Christ came forth for evermore the victor over death and the grave. O my dear friends, you who have fought single-handed against your evil passions, your sinful longing, your wicked habits, and have been defeated again and again until you have become discouraged and ready to give up, call for help, I beg you, upon the Christ, who has never yet been defeated or discouraged.

When you come into touch with him you will catch his spirit, you will breathe his courage, and acquire his habit of victory. It is said that on one occasion the Duke of Wellington—whom they called the "Iron Duke"—assigned to one of his veteran soldiers a very dangerous and difficult task. The man did not shrink from danger of duty, but his reply was, "I go, sir; but first give me a grip of your conquering hand."

O my brother, my sister, discouraged and defeated by your sin, come, I beg you, and enlist under the banner of Jesus Christ. Get a grip of his conquering hand. You will feel new life running through all your moral nature. It will electrify your will; it will arouse your love and gratitude; it will clothe you with the spirit of a conqueror.

47

THE SCARLET LINE IN THE WINDOW

"And she bound the scarlet line in the window"
(Joshua 2:21).

Here is a story full of human interest. Two soldiers are spying out the land which is to be captured by their army. They are hunted, and in their emergency, when their lives hang on a thread, a woman comes to their rescue. She had been a bad woman, and her sins had not been covered up, but were known to all her little world. But she was a bright woman, and had come, in some way, to have more information about this army of Israel than most of the people in her city. She had heard enough about them and their history to believe in their God, and to have faith that he had power to give them success in taking possession of the land in which she lived. So when she saw these two spies hunted and in danger of death, she gladly risked her own life to befriend them, hoping thereby not only to do a kind deed to them, but to obtain protection for herself and for her family when the city should be taken by the enemy. She hid the men on the top of her house as long as the dared, and then tied a scarlet cord about them, one at a time, and let them down over the wall of the city. What a picture it is! I suppose that one of the spies helped her lower the first man to the ground, but when the next man's turn came Rahab alone was left to support his weight, and I can see her as she braces herself and with all her strength grips the cord in her hands until it cuts into her fingers as she lowers the spy in safety to the earth.

The men were grateful for her kindness and were glad to pledge to her protection for the future, and so they said in answer to her appeal, "When we come into the land, thou shalt bind this line of scarlet thread in the window which thou didst let us down by: and thou shalt bring thy father, and thy mother, and thy brethren, and all thy father's household, home unto thee....And whosoever shall be with thee in the house, his blood shall be on our head, if any hand be upon him" (Joshua 2:18, 19). And we are assured by the eleventh chapter of Hebrews, that wonderful roll-call of the heroes of the faith, that the army of Israel respected the pledge that had been given by these two spies, and that Rahab was saved when the city was captured.

We have suggested in this story a fact which is apparent often, that the people who seem to be the worst are sometimes the first to perceive their danger and turn away from their sins. Christ said that the publicans and sinners had a better chance of salvation in his day than the scribes and the Pharisees, and the same fact is often witnessed in our own time. No one of us will be acquitted at last by what we have done, for we have all come short of our privileges and have sins to answer for before God. If we are saved it will be because we have been forgiven of our sins through Jesus Christ. It is not justice which we want, but a pardon.

"By the deeds of the law shall no flesh be justified" (Romans 3:20). The law of God can never forgive us. Only through the pardon of God, given us because we have taken Jesus Christ as our Saviour and tied the scarlet thread of his dying blood in our window, can we ever be saved from the penalty of the law.

A Confederate soldier belonging to the army of Northern Virginia was on trial before a military court for desertion. His name was Edward Cooper, and when he rose to plead he answered, "Not guilty." The judge advocate asked, "Who is your counsel?" He replied, "I have no counsel." Supposing that it was Cooper's purpose to represent himself before the court, the judge advocate was instructed to proceed. Every charge and specification against the prisoner was sustained. The prisoner was then told to introduce his witnesses. He said, "I have none." Astonished at the calmness with which he seemed to be submitting to what he regarded as inevitable fate, the judge advocate said to him, "Have you no defense? Is it possible that you abandoned your comrades and deserted your colors in the presence of the enemy without any reason?"

He answered, "There was a reason, but it will not avail me before a military court."

The judge then said, "Perhaps you are mistaken; you are charged with the highest crime known to military law, and it is your duty to make known the causes that influenced your actions."

For the first time Cooper's manly form trembled and his eyes swarm in tears. Approaching the president of the court he presented a letter, saying as he did so, "There, general, is what did it."

General Battle opened the letter, and in a moment his eyes filled with tears. It was passed from one to another of the court until all had seen it, and those stern warriors, who had passed with Stonewall Jackson through a score of battles, wept like children. As soon as the president sufficiently recovered his self-possession he read the letter as the defense of the prisoner. It was in these words:

> "DEAR EDWARD: I have always been proud of you; since your connection with the Confederate army I have been prouder of you than ever before. I would not have you do anything wrong for the world; but, before God, Edward, unless you come home we must die: Last night I was aroused by little Eddie's crying, 'O mamma, I'm so hungry!' And Lucy, Edward, your darling Lucy, never complains, but grows thinner and thinner every day. And, before God, Edward, unless you come home we must die.
> —YOUR MARY."

Turning to the prisoner, General Battle asked, "What did you do when you received this letter?"

He replied, "I made application for a furlough, and it was rejected; I made another application, and it was rejected; a third time I made application, and it was rejected; and that night, as I wandered backward and forward in the camp thinking of my home, the wild eyes of Lucy looking up to me, the burning words of Mary sinking in my brain, I was no longer the Confederate soldier; I was the father of Lucy and the husband of Mary, and I would have passed those lines if every gun in the battery had been fired upon me.

"When I arrived home Mary ran out to meet me, and embraced me and whispered, 'O Edward, I am so happy; I am so glad you got your furlough.' She must have felt me shudder, for she turned as pale as death and, catching her breath with every word, she said, 'Have you come without your furlough? O Edward, go back! Go back! Let me and the children go down to the grave together; but for heaven's sake save the honor of your name!'

"And here I am, gentlemen; not brought here by military power, but in obedience to the command of Mary, to abide the sentence of your court."

Every officer of that court-martial felt the force of the prisoner's words. Before them stood in beatific vision the eloquent pleader for a husband's and a father's wrong; but they had been trained by the great leader, Robert E. Lee, to tread the path of duty though the lightning-flash scorched the ground beneath their feet, and each in his turn pronounced the verdict, "Guilty."

Fortunately for humanity, the proceedings of the court were reviewed by the commanding general, and upon the record was written:

> "The finding of the court approved. The prisoner
> is pardoned and will report to his company.
> —"R. E. Lee, General."

This story illustrates with great clearness how that, in strict justice, the guilty never can escape. No one here could have so good a plea to excuse his sin against God as this man had to excuse his desertion. But there was no chance for his acquittal by a just court. His only chance was the pardon of the commanding general, and our only hope, as sinners against God, is the pardon of the Great Commander. But Jesus Christ has shed his own blood on the cross as a propitiation for our sins, and wherever that scarlet thread appears above the window of the heart, God will guarantee to us forgiveness and protection.

I would like to lay emphasis on the part of a sinner in his own salvation. Rahab with her own hands let the spies down over the wall, and with those same hands she bound the scarlet cord in the window. There is a sense in which our salvation is wrought out for us, and there is another sense, equally as important, in which we may be said to "work out our own salvation." Our salvation does not hinge on the will of God, but upon our own will. God is willing to save us, and is seeking to persuade us to accept salvation. We must take hold upon it with our own hands. The Christian life is not passive or negative, but a positive seizing hold of eternal life.

In asking you to accept Christ I am not inviting you to a monotonous existence, but I am urging you to take hold on a triumphant and joyous career. I am asking you also to join hands with the very best people who live on earth, and this not only in living a good life yourself, but in seeking to lift all men up to a better life. Julia Thayer sings:

> "The hands of the world—cant' you see them
> today?
> The useless white hands, kept so shapely and
> fair;
> The hands of God's worker, one lifted to pray.
> And one reaching down for the burdens of care;
> The hardened brown hands, so deformed and
> unsightly,
> Yet beautiful still with the pathos of toil;
> And the great hands of power, used wrongly or
> rightly,
> The hands stained with sinning, from which you
> recoil;

The cultured, deft hands that are busy adorning
The unfinished temples of learning and art;
The hands in dark places that grope for the
    morning,
And the poor, stricken hands that appeal to the
    heart;
All these, if they'd clasp one another today,
Could reach 'round the world in a wonderful
    way.

"No one would be lonely, no lot wholly dreary,
The thrill of our love would, magnet-like, give
A strength to the faint and a joy to the weary,
A lightness of being and courage to live.
Then come, clasp these hands—Oh, how selfish
    to tarry
When all the world needs you this moment so
    much!
Rise with the will and a purpose to carry
The help of your presence, the warmth of your
    touch.
They want yours, the hands that drop low in
    their weakness,
Those heavy with burdens of empty with loss;
They pray you to point with the spirit of meekness
To Love's Burden-bearer who died on the cross.
We all so much need one another do-day
To girdle the globe with our hands in this way."

I appeal to the very best that is in you that you cease your ungrateful course in refusing Christ your love and your service, and that you give him, from this hour, the use of your hand and your voice, and the love of your heart, and receive from him in turn not only the forgiveness of your sins, but the uplifting of his divine fellowship.

As another has said, there are two courses open to the sinner. He may stifle or destroy for the time the thoughts and the feelings which mar his peace, or else a yearning, a longing, almost a demand, for relief shapes itself within him. Such a demand is the cry of the conscience, "What must I do to be saved?"

> "Thou who hast borne all burdens, bear our load!
> Bear thou our load, whatever load it be;
> Our guilt, our shame, our helpless misery.
> Bear thou who only canst, O God, my God;
> Seek us and find us, for we cannot thee."

If there be any soul here that has sympathy with that cry, hear the message of the Gospel, "Believe on the Lord Jesus Christ and thou shalt be saved" (Acts 16:31). "The chastisement of our peace was upon him, and with his stripes we are healed" (Isaiah 53:5). Or yet again, "He was made sin for us who knew no sin, that we might be made the righteousness of God in him" (2 Corinthians 5:21).

Sidney Watson, a converted London waif, now a popular author of Christian books in England, relates that while a prisoner in the East Indies he had as fellow-prisoner an old Scotch soldier, who after traveling over half the globe, was there dying. From a period of unconsciousness he opened his eyes and glanced around as if surprised at his surroundings, murmuring brokenly, "I thought me in my mither's cot in Perthshire." After a pause, with a quiet, fixed, peaceful look heavenward he gasped, "Nae either name—one Mediator—Jesus Christ—he is faithful—just—forgive sin." His mind wandered again for a moment, but his soldier training came back to him and he tried to raise his head as he said, short and sharp, with a dying energy, "Password? Yes! Blood of Christ—Christ cleanseth from all sin." A thrill passed through his frame, and the watchers knew that he had passed the guard into the presence of the King.

There is only one password into eternal glory, and that is the "Blood of Christ." Bind the scarlet thread in the window of your heart and be at peace.

48

POETIC JUSTICE AS ILLUSTRATED IN THE TRAGIC STORY OF ADONI-BEZEK

"As I have done, so God hath requited me" (Judges 1:7).

Adoni-bezek was a cruel old man. He lived by the sword and he perished by it. For a long time nobody could stand against him in battle. Everything went his way. Victory after victory crowned his banners. The story of the wars of Adoni-bezek have never been written. We have only the little glimpse into them from this statement of his, that seventy kings that had been captured by him had been put to torture, and had been humiliated and mortified, by having their thumbs and their great toes cut off and by being made to pick up crumbs under his table, as one might feed a hungry dog. The imagination can easily supply the long tales of war and ravage that lie in the darkness of oblivion behind those threescore and ten kings and their cruel humiliation.

But Adoni-bezek's time was coming. There came a day when the lucky star in which he boasted forsook him, and the stars in their courses seemed to fight against him. He was captured, and very naturally his captors, remembering the stories of the peculiar torture to which he had been accustomed to put his captives—stories that had given him an inglorious fame throughout all the neighboring nations—submitted him to the same humiliation.

Adoni-bezek, with all his savagery, must have had the philosophic temperament, for he recognizes at once the poetic justice in his punishment. He does not complain when he is himself brutally tortured in the same way in which he had treated others. With very clear discrimination he recognizes that his sinful life had not only been warfare against his fellow-men, but a sin against God. He sees clearly that in this punishment which comes to him at the hand of his captors they are not the chief factors. It is coming from the hand of God. "As I have done," says the despairing old king—and it seems to have been the last utterance of his life, for the next sentence tells of his death—"so God hath requited me."

I think there is something striking in the consensus of opinion that a justice which metes out punishment of the same peculiar kind as the man's sins should be called 'poetic justice." If a man in his youth has been mean and ungrateful toward his parents, and treated them harshly, and years afterward, when his own hair is getting gray, his children turn against him with hard and selfish hearts, people say it is "poetic justice." If a man is miserly and greedy and dishonest in business, gathering money without caring how he gets it, unscrupulous in but with more cunning, circumvents him, and robs him of his ill-gotten gains, people are inclined to smile and say it is "poetic justice." We say so because we recognize that poetic justice is ideal justice, and that this is a rare thing in this world among men. But justice is always poetic with God. God does not have a judgment day every week, but at last there shall be meted out poetic justice to every man and woman in the world.

This tells as truly on the side of goodness and its rewards as in the punishment of evil. God gives a man blessings in heart and soul after the kind of his deeds of righteousness. I shall never forget the glow of supreme joy and comfort I saw recently in the glistening eyes and lighted face of a man of nearly fourscore, who was telling me about his coming to this country when only a youth, leaving the dear old mother, who had been a faithful Christian mother to him, in England. He came over here and was lonesome and homesick, and in that hour of homesickness he gave his heart to Christ and became a very happy Christian. With joyous face he told me how he wrote home to his mother about it, and how happy she was, and how she prized those letters, and how proud she was of them, and how, when she came to die, she showed her great love for him and her appreciation of him by making a dying request that all the letters from her boy in the new land should be put as a pillow under her head in her coffin. And all the years since, as that man has gone on doing his work in the world, growing old like the palm tree described in the Bible, his heart has been given courage and his soul has been refreshed by the joy with which he had comforted his mother's heart.

Be sure that this is God's world, and there is no such thing as chance. It is no gambler's luck with which we are dealing. We are not throwing dice with fate in these human lives of ours. It is no haphazard at which we are playing. It is a world of cause and effect, a world where like produces like, a world where we shall receive according to our conduct. We have here a lesson for every one of us. God is no respecter of persons. He does not have one standard for the treatment of Adoni-bezek and another for us. The great principles of right and wrong run through the universe like threads through a bolt of cloth. They are the same in one age as in another. A sowing of envy and jealousy will produce strife and murder as surely now as in the days of Cain. A seedtime of hard-heartedness and stiff-necked resistance to God's commandment will still further harden the heart and prevent the day of repentance as surely in our day as in the time of Pharaoh and the plagues in Egypt. Cruelty will breed cruelty and perpetuate it as certainly in Cleveland as in the empire of Adoni-bezek.

We should remember that no sin is a separate and individual thing, having no relation to the other portions of our career. Every sin is a seed that is self-perpetuating, and produces still further evil harvest to sow still more widely the spirit of anarchy and rebellion against God.

There is this other very important thought in our text: Our sin is not merely bad policy, or mistake of judgment, or even a wrong done against our fellow-men. It is a sin against God. Sin is contempt for our Creator, our Father, our Preserver, our Judge. I think there is a vast amount of teaching in our time which rather fosters the idea that sin is more bad policy than anything else, and the keen edge is lost off the truth that sin is a crime against God that merits and requires punishment. Of course it is true that sin is unwise, that it is a bad policy; true that drunkenness wastes physical strength, unbalances the mind, depraves the heart; true that greed despoils all the finer feelings of the soul, and brutalizes the manhood and womanhood; true that lust dethrones the spiritual, and puts the reins of life into the hands of the animal; true that falsehood demoralizes all the strength of the personality, and lets loose the mental and moral nature into chaos; true that the sinner can never tell when conscience will rise up and betray him, even in this world, to destruction. But while all that is true, it is the smaller part of the ruin which sin works. Sin is crime against God, it is a wrong against the moral nature itself, it is a violation of the very law of our being, and makes necessary a judgment day and a time of punishment.

Old Adoni-bezek was thoroughly scriptural in his idea that his captors were, though entirely unconscious, no doubt, themselves, God's agents, who were requiting him according to his deeds for his evil ways. Judgment is as surely coming for the sinner today as to this hoary-headed sinner of ancient times. How strange that we should go on sinning against God as though no record were being kept of our doings. Yet there is a double record being kept. First, a record is being kept in our own memories, in the very fiber of our being. A record is being treasured up there that will be all the more legible when the body shall be left behind, like an old house, and we stand unsheltered before God. But there is another record being kept in the memory of God, a record which is absolutely perfect and from which there can be no appeal.

One day a young boy came home very angry with a schoolmate about something that had happened on the playground. He told his sister about it, and the more he thought and talked of it the angrier he grew, and he began to say terribly harsh, bitter, and unreasonable things about his comrade. Some of the things he said the sister knew were not true; but he was too angry and excited to weigh his words. She listened for a moment and then said very gently:

"Would you dare tell God that, Ralph?"

The boy paused as if someone had struck him. He felt the rebuke implied in her words, and he realized how wickedly and untruthfully he had spoken.

"No, I wouldn't tell God that," he said, with a red face.

"Then I wouldn't tell it to anybody," said the sister.

And yet we are telling God every angry, unreasonable, wicked thing we say. We are telling him every unholy purpose we form, every stubborn resistance to his will. What a cruel treasury we may gather for ourselves in this way.

We have suggested to us here that we are judged by our deeds and not by our impulses or our wishes. Some people deceive their own hearts by imagining that there is, in some vague, undefined way, virtue in their hours of daydreams when they have visions of goodness, which, alas! are never fulfilled. Many people are like the son mentioned in the Gospel parable, who, when his father commanded him to go and work in his vineyard, replied promptly, "I go, sir," but who never went. There was absolutely no value in that boy's complacent impulse to do what his father wanted, but who, when the time came for action, chose to go selfishly on his own path. So many people now are answering God, "I go, sir," but they never go. Many read a book which stirs their emotions in regard to some misery of the poor, and they seem to hear the voice of God in it saying to them, "Go, heal the heartache, relieve the distress, brighten the sky of those whose lives are dark and cheerless." And they say promptly, "I go, sir." But they wipe their tears, and their emotion passes, and their lives go on as selfishly as ever. Again, some sudden disaster, or some striking punishment following iniquity, startles the community, and many people read it with blanched faces and trembling hearts as they picture to themselves the murder, or the suicide, or the bankruptcy, or the shame and disgrace, or the heart-breaking agony that has followed like a Nemesis in the wake of some man's or some woman's sin. Conscience rises up and says, "He was no greater sinner than you. He thought his sin would never be punished; but his judgment day came and yours hastens; rise up at once and repent of your sins, and turn from your wicked ways." And the soul answers, "I go, sir," but the emotion dies away, conscience is thrust into the background, the world comes in like a flood, and no real repentance comes from it.

I know that I am not speaking in riddles to you. I am not telling you things you do not understand. Some of you, as you have listened, have seen your own portrait in the rude and simple sketches I have drawn. In God's name, do not let this appeal go the way of all the rest. You have been aroused many times before to the exceeding sinfulness of your sin, and have promised yourself to repent, only to fall the deeper into the mire. Put every good impulse into action now. Incarnate your good wishes into deeds. Rise up by the grace of God to repent of your sin and to cry out to Jesus Christ for refuge. In him is your hope, not because he can change the character of sin, but because he took your load of sin on his own shoulders and suffered in your stead, and if you accept him as your Saviour, God will impute your sin to him. He will transfer your guilt to Christ's account, and you may be pardoned and forgiven. The sense of guilt will be taken out of your soul and you will go forth, free and cleansed, to lead a new life of righteousness and peace.

No matter how hard a place you are in, Christ is able to reach you there, and lead you out of your distress.

Samuel H. Hadley, superintendent of the old Jerry McAuley Water Street Mission, New York, now one of the purest and noblest of men, was once a poor drunkard in the gutter. When he had pawned his last thing, and the alternative faced him of becoming a tramp or jumping in the river, he found his way to the mission, and this is his recollection of the prayer which Jerry McAuley offered over his bowed head: "Dear Saviour, won't you look down in pity on this poor soul? He needs your help, Lord. He can't get along without it. Blessed Jesus, this sinner has got himself into a bad hole. Won't you help him out?"

Then with Jerry's hand upon his head, Hadley tried to pray for himself: "Dear Jesus, can you help me?" The gloom that had filled him gave way to a precious feeling of safety and strength, and he has lived a glorious life ever since. There was a scriptural warrant for that prayer of McAuley's. Does not David say, "He inclined unto me, and heard my cry. He brought me up also out of a horrible pit, out of the miry clay, and set my feet upon a rock, and established my goings. And he hath put a new song in my mouth, even praise unto our God?" (Psalm 40:1-3). He will do all that for you if you will give him your hand and your heart.

49

THE SINNER'S FIGHT AGAINST THE STARS

"They fought from heaven; the stars in their courses fought against Sisera" (Judges 5:20).

The immediate cause of the utterance of this poetic and often-quoted text was probably Deborah's remembrance of a terrific thunderstorm in which the flash of the lightning and the roar of the thunder added materially to the confusion of the horses attached to the war chariots of Sisera. There is an indication of this in the twenty-second verse, where the destruction of the enemy at the river Kishon is being described, and it is said, "Then were the horsehoofs broken by the means of the prancings, the prancings of their mighty ones" (Judges 5:22). This storm, which seemed to bring the forces of the skies into the battle, is taken advantage of by Deborah and Barak in their song of victory, and is used with sublime poetic effect. There is probably not a passage in the Bible more frequently quoted by great orators dealing with the theme of the onward sweep of righteousness and the inherent weakness of a bad cause.

The text is susceptible of a very much deeper meaning than the one I have suggested as the probable cause of its utterance, and there is no doubt that in the heart of the singers there was the faith that God himself had marshaled the heavens above to fight in defense of his people and to insure the overthrow of their powerful enemy. Our theme, then, is very simple and easy to be understood. If a man is doing right he may be sure that God is on his side. So long as we are obedient to God in nature and in grace, in physical as well as in spiritual realms, we may be certain that all the forces of the universe are marshaled on our side. Paul must have had this thought in his mind when he said, "All things work together for good to them that love God" (Romans 8:28). On the other hand, if we do wrong, if we disobey God, we put ourselves out of joint, so to speak, with the universe of which we are a part. While goodness means harmony, wickedness means discord. The man who sins against God puts all the forces of the universe at war against himself. Things that seemed to be very far away from him, and to have no interest in him, become his enemies, and achieve his overthrow, when he puts himself in antagonism to the righteous laws of God's government.

The man who does right, who lives in obedience to God, finds hidden treasure laid up for him, in unexpected places all along the path of life, because everything is working for his advantage; while the man who sins against God walks a path that is ambushed by unknown enemies who are likely to spring upon him to his destruction at an unthought-of moment.

Sisera stands as a representative of those who fight against God. He seems to have been a brilliant fellow, a strong personality, a man full of vigor, and with many of those qualities which make one a leader among men. But he despised the God who had so thoroughly given evidence of his favor toward the people of Israel. Every advantage seemed to be on his side; he had military prestige, he was a great general with a famous name, he had a large army finely equipped for those days; but the people who fought against him had God on their side, and he went down in destruction before a force against which he was powerless to contend.

We may see in the death of Sisera a suggestion, also, of the great truth that the glamour which seems to surround sin in the distance is all lost in the shame and humiliation of the reality. A soldier, if he must die, longs to die on the battlefield at the head of his men, leading them to victory. How the heart of the world has caught up the death of the young and intrepid Wolfe at the capture of Quebec! The artist and the poet and the historian have made the most of those last words of the brilliant soldier who was dying, but whose spirit was recalled for a moment, seemingly, by the news of victory, and he exclaimed, "Then I die content!"

Sisera, no doubt, had gone into battle with thought of the possibility of danger to himself, and had pictured how, if death came, it would be when he was selling his life at a great price while valiantly inspiring his own troops. But how different was the end, and how humiliating to such a soldier! He was not only defeated, but routed, and finally the only hope of escape left to him was in slipping out of his carriage and running away alone, a poor refugee from the enemy. And as he ran he saw in the distance the tent of Jael, the wife of Heber the Kenite, the representative of a tribe that was supposed to be neutral to the combatants in this war. Jael saw him coming and went out to meet him;

and said to him, "Turn in, my lord, turn in to me; fear not" (Judges 4:18). And as it seemed to be the only place of refuge, and with perhaps the most absolute confidence in the woman's hospitable intention toward him, he went into her tent and she covered him over with a mantle. Sisera, greatly exhausted, and with his lips swollen and his throat parched with thirst, said as she turned to leave him, "Give me, I pray thee, a little water to drink; for I am thirsty" (Judges 4:19). And the woman took a bottle of milk, one of those old goatskin bags of that day, no doubt, and gave him a refreshing drink and covered him up again. And Sisera said to her, "Stand in the door of the tent, and it shall be, when any man doth come and inquire of thee, and say, Is there any man here? that thou shalt say, No" (Judges 4:20).

And so Sisera, tired out, utterly defeated and broken down, gave way to the prostration of his physical strength and fell asleep in fancied security. Before long Jael, standing sentinel there at the door of the tent, knows by the regular, heavy breathing of the tired man that he has forgotten his troubles and fallen asleep. In the morning when Jael saw Sisera going out to battle, his army covering the hills and his troops swarming down through the valleys, with spear and helmet and buckler, she never dreamed that Sisera would come to destruction by her weak hand. But now all is changed, the great army has melted away, the war chariots are broken in pieces, the war horses have been drowned in the river, and Sisera, stripped of all the gaudy trappings of war, lies here, a poor, helpless, sleeping man, in her tent, at her mercy. The moment she hears him breathing unconsciously she seems to have formed her purpose, if indeed she had not had that in her mind all the time, from the moment she recognized him flying toward her tent. Very quietly she takes a nail that was used in fastening down the corners of the tent, and the heavy mallet that was meant to drive it, and softly and stealthily as fate, that she may not disturb the sleeping warrior, she creeps in through the tent door, drops on one knee close to his head, and, placing the nail on the temple uppermost, with a quick savage blow of the hammer drives the sharp nail through his head and fastens him to the ground. There is a convulsive struggle, arms thrown wildly in the air, a moan, heavy breathing for a moment, and then the muscles cease to twitch, and bloody and still the warrior lies dead, pinned to the earth by a tent pin driven by a woman's hand.

Surely no soldier could ever have had a meaner end than that. But that is not too strong an illustration of the way sin deceives us into believing that at the worst it will bring us much pleasure and prosperity and honor. The glamour is all in our imagination and in the lying promises of the devil. The devil promised Eve that if she ate of the forbidden fruit she should become wise like a god. There was a fascination about that. It might be dangerous, there might be peril in it, but the glamour of that promise enthralled her imagination. What about reality? Banishment from the Garden of Eden, in shame and disgrace, to a life cursed by thorns and thistles, by pain and sorrow and tears. All the promises of happiness and peace to the sinner through sinful courses are as deceptive as that. The man who is sinning against God fondly dreams that he is going to be able to so plan, and to so execute his plans, that he shall always be able to escape the punishment of his sins: but the unexpected is always happening to the sinner. When Sisera was counting up the forces he had to meet in battle that day, he did not count on the thunderstorm and its fierce lightning that was to turn his war horses wild with panic. He did not count among his enemies Jael or her tribe; if he thought of her at all it was as a friend. But when a man wars against God he meets unexpected foes at every turn. How many passages of Scripture there are which bear out this truth! "When they shall say, Peace and safety; then sudden destruction cometh upon them" (1 Thessalonians 5:3). Or hear that word that Christ uttered about the man with the great farm, whose crops were so bountiful that he had no place to store away his harvests. Yet in that hour of abundance he had no thought of the poor who were starving, or of gratitude to God who had given him all these good things, and determined that he would build him larger barns and then comfort himself by saying, "Soul, take thine ease, for thou hast much goods laid up for many years" (Luke 12:19). Christ declares that the stinging rebuke that fell like an arrow from the skies was, "Thou fool, this night thy soul shall be required of thee" (Luke 12:20). In the story of the girls, wise and foolish, which I read for our lesson, there were five that slept in indifference and carelessness, when suddenly the cry rang out, "Behold, the Bridegroom cometh; go ye out to meet him" (Matthew 25:6). These messages tell us that we must always be at peace with God if we would be safe. The sinner has no reason for peace. In the very nature of things he is forever in danger. Hear the message to-night, and put yourself in friendship with the universe by confessing you sins against God and finding forgiveness of them in Jesus's name.

There is a most pathetic touch to this story of Sisera told in this same song of Deborah and Barak. Sisera's mother was waiting at home, expecting her son to be victorious, but watching eagerly, as a mother will. And when he did not come back as early as she expected, she began to worry about it. The writer says, "The mother of Sisera looked out at a window, and cried through the lattice, Why is his chariot so long in coming? Why tarry the wheels of his chariots?" (Judges 5:28).

Is a Christian mother or father saying that about you to-night? O, the loving, solicitous letters I get nearly every week from parents whose sons and daughters are in this city. Sisera's mother must have been heart-broken when she found he would never come again. Are you going to bring heart-break or comfort to those who love you? Give your heart to Christ to-night, and make glad the hearts that have prayed for you since your childhood.

50

THE SHIBBOLETH OF FATE

"And the Gileadites took the passages of Jordan before the Ephraimites: and it was so, that when those Ephraimites which were escaped said, Let me go over; that the men of Gilead said unto him, Art thou an Ephraimite? If he said, Nay; then said they unto him, Say now Shibboleth; and he said Sibboleth: for he could not frame to pronounce it right. Then they took him, and slew him at the passages of Jordan" (Judges 12:5, 6).

The general who devised that scheme of finding out the truth about the stragglers who were captured was, whatever else may be said about him, a very shrewd man. It seemed to have been an almost infallible test. The whole tribe or nation had lost the power to pronounce the sound of what we call the letter, "h." Little by little it had passed out of their speech, and though in general they spoke the same language as their neighbors, they spoke a language impoverished for the lack of this single sound; and this bright soldier in command of the Gileadites took advantage of this deformity of speech to prevent the escape of those who had already escaped from the battlefield. It was a test which it was impossible for them to evade. Every man born and reared among the Ephraimites had been brought up with this defect of speech, and now it betrayed him into the hands of his enemies.

This word "Shibboleth" has gone into the language of the world. It has been given, for the most part, in our time a rather unpopular and contemptible meaning, as indicating the unreasonable demand of some faction who refuse to believe in the truth or righteousness of any except those who pronounce their particular "Shibboleth" of words as representing faith in matters of religion. There is, however, it seems to me, a very great and important message which is very naturally suggested by this interesting little story— that a man must pass in the end for what he is; that a man's character, the real bed-rock principles upon which his life is built, his inner self, must finally dictate his destiny. "The Shibboleth of fate" is that a man must stand or fall by himself, his own personality. As an Ephraimite could not suddenly, at will, change the language his mother taught him; could not, if he would, at command learn the new sounds which his tongue had never known how to speak—so in the great testing emergencies of life the man you are, the woman you are, will hold your fate in its own hand. The inner self will speak out and decide where you belong.

I have been reading recently a very interesting paper, by Rev. John Hopkins Denison, which purports to give a highly scientific theory of the evolution by which the birds came to fly in the air. According to his theory, in the early days of the history of the earth, and long before man came, a queer creature poked its head out of the water at the edge of the ocean. He had an ugly snout, like a fish, only that at the end it was prolonged into a sort of horny bill with sharp little teeth set in it. His body was long and slimy and wriggly, like a fat eel, but he had two crooked, ungainly legs, with hooked claws, and at his shoulders were great flopping, awkward things that looked half like wings and half like fins. It would have been a puzzle to tell whether he was a fish or a bird. It is rather doubtful if he knew himself. He had been lying quietly enough down on the mud bottom, breathing in the cold water through his gills, when suddenly, as he had looked up with his glassy eyes toward the sunlight that was streaming in through the water, there had come over him a restless, unhappy feeling, a desire to get out of the mud and swim upward toward the light. And when his head was out of the water he found that he could draw the fresh, warm air in a new way into what was certainly the beginning of a pair of lungs; and as he sunned himself in the warmth and light there came over him a strong feeling that he belonged in this higher world, and not down in the mud at the bottom of the sea. No bird wing had yet smitten the air, and there did not seem to be much chance for a bird in this ugly, awkward, slimy creature who was beginning to feel that he was meant to be a bird. He stood on the shore and flapped his awkward stumps of wings. The thrill of the bright air was in his lungs, the glow of a new life was pulsing in his veins. His blood was no longer the cold, lifeless fluid that flows through the gills of the fish. It was warm! It was the hot, red blood that carried life from the air in the lungs to every tingling bit of the body. He seemed to feel it ready to burst forth and clothe his slimy skin with a growth of feathery plumage. It was urging him on and up into the blue sky above. He must fly. Once more he flapped the ungainly wings, one spring with the crooked legs, and he was up in the air above the sea, above the earth. How glorious it was to behold the green hills and valleys below, the radiant sun and the pure atmosphere everywhere. And just then he flew over a quiet pool, and as he passed he saw the reflection of his form in the still water. There he was, ugly, awkward, flapping his great stumpy wings, and wriggling along his slimy body with his crooked legs and huge claws sticking out in all directions. He was suddenly discouraged. What is he, ugly, awkward creature that he is, doing up there in the air and sunlight? His place is down in the mud. A few more spasmodic, tired flaps, and down he goes into the water with a great splash, and down into the ooze and slime of the ocean's bed.

But he could not stay in the water. Again he heard the call of the sunshine. Once more he crept forth into the air, and again the premonition of the bird life came back to him. He felt his lungs expand, he felt the hot blood flow, he felt again the passion for the sky. It was awkward work at first, and pitiful, to see the great ungainly thing trying to be a bird and fly. But he stayed in the air and slowly the change came. Long after, if any man had stood upon the earth, he would have seen a bird with great sweeping wings and glistening plumage soar upward from the low shore toward the sky. There is no awkwardness now, nothing ungainly in the movement. Stroke by stroke those great wings carry the glorious eagle resistlessly upward. He is at home now in the vast blue realm of the sky, bathed in the sunshine, buoyed on the air, confidently soaring above the highest mountain peaks.

Now, I have retold to you this scientific supposition because it is, I think, a very suggestive illustration of the transformation which must come to a man or a woman who has been given over to a worldly life, living without reference to God and Christ and immortality, before there may be hope of entering into the joy and glory of a spiritual life in this or any world. This creature, born to be a bird, could not more help having hot blood in the air than he could keep himself from having cold blood in the water. By remaining in the air the gills of the fish little by little disappeared, and he became a bird. If he had remained in the water all the fishy characteristics would have developed. His possible wings would have become fins, the bird life would have lost its power to charm him, and he would have settled down into the mud forever. So with the higher possibilities of man. You yourself must decide the Shibboleth of fate. It is for you to say whether you will live the worldly life of the flesh or the high and holy life of the Spirit. There are many degrees of present morality, but the great choice must be made and that will settle destiny. It is a far cry from Kipling's Filipino, "Half-devil and half-child," to Browning's tribute to his wife, whom he terms "Half-angel and half-bird;" but wherever you may be in the scale of moral quality, the final decision is in your hands, and you must utter that "Shibboleth of fate: which shall declare whether you are to sink down into the life of the appetites and passions and lusts, a mere worldly creature, or climb upward into the light and give yourself up to the sun-lit life of the Spirit.

There is no more horrible delusion of the devil than that discouraging and disheartening thing which he whispers to us, that the upper life, the life of purity and love, is impossible for us; that we have not in us the capacity to breathe that holy atmosphere, and have no powers of flight to buoy ourselves in the face of the Sun of Righteousness;

that the lower ooze and slime of base tempers and evil passions is the atmosphere, and the only atmosphere, suited for such as we are. It is a devil's slander. We were born, the poorest of us, the weakest of us, the most awkward and ungainly of us in a moral way, to be the sons of God, and that sunlight of beauty and truth that has sought us out even in the muddy atmosphere where we have lain is not meant to mock us, but to beckon us upward and onward to the glorious life which is possible for us. And if we will give ourselves a chance to breathe in God's Spirit every day, to have fellowship with the Christian graces, the warm blood of the heavenly love life will course through our veins, and our souls will rejoice to fly in the face of the sky.

The thing I want to impress on you most of all is that the Shibboleth of fate—your fate—is not in some other hands, not even the hand of God, but in your own. And we should never forget, in dealing with the most disheartened bit of humanity, that we are dealing with a kingly nature. He may be an uncrowned king, he may even be a dethroned king; but every individual is a monarch, nevertheless, over his own fate.

Robert Louis Stevenson, the novelist, was once walking with a friend when a tramp came up and begged alms. Stevenson said he would give him something if he might first give him a lecture, and thereupon he launched into a flow of oratory, brilliant, learned, humorous, and pathetic, making of the beggar before him a type of human failure, and pointing the way to rise above it; a lay sermon, in fact, broad in its charity, profound in its learning, rich in its intuition and wide philosophy. He finished rather abruptly and gave some money to the beggar, who touched his ragged cap and said: "Thank ye, sir, as much for what ye've said as for what ye've give me; I'm not very often taken to be still a man."

It is the manhood in you, that spark of divine inheritance which clings to you, to which I make my appeal. I know there is in you that which answers to the appeal to turn from your sin to a noble and spiritual life.

Dr. Bonar tells us that, in the days when the Mosque of Omar was first built over that spot of Mount Moriah where the worshiper could touch a piece of the unhewn original rock of the hill, it was customary to bring loads of incense and aromatic shrubs into the shrine, which was called Sakhrah. As a consequence, if anyone had been worshiping there he carried away with him so much of the fragrance of the place that when people passed him in the market place of Jerusalem or in the streets they used to say to each other, "He had been in the Sakhrah today!" It is our glorious possibility to so live that we may come forth daily with our garments of conversation and conduct smelling of the holy communion and fellowship we have had with God. How strange and unnatural it is that we should have in us this dream of the best things, this longing for the holiest life, and yet go for years and years making no response to it!

Mr. Moody tells of a poor mother who had an only child who was idiotic, and on the day when it was fourteen years of age a neighbor came in and found the mother weeping in the bitterness of her soul. She wanted to know what was the matter. The mother said: "For fourteen years I have cared for that child day and night; I have given up society and spent my time with her; and today she does not know me from you. If she would recognize me once it would pay me for all I have ever done for her." How many there are for whom Jesus died, and whom he has watched over and cared for and blessed, and to whom he has manifested infinite love and tenderness, who yet have never once recognized him, have never looked up into his face and said, "Thank you, dear Lord Jesus!"

51

THE MAN WITH A LOW AIM

"Abdon the son of Hillel, a Pirathonite, judged Israel.
And he had forty sons and thirty nephews, that rode on
threescore and ten ass colts" (Judges 12:13, 14).

There's a biography for you with a vengeance! Seventy young men whose father's and uncle's official position had to be recognized in a historical account, devoted themselves so assiduously and completely to the art and style of their riding of ass colts that, either by way of sarcasm, or from what other motive I know not, the writer of the book of Judges pauses in his historical narrative to mention the most notable event in the course of these young men's lives. The author is one who liked to tell a good story, who rejoiced in narrating deeds of heroism, and would have sung the glory of Judge Abdon's sons if there had been any glory to sing. But, alas! there was not. The only interesting thing about them was that there were so many of them that when they went out riding it took a herd of seventy ass colts to furnish them with a mount. Why these particular young fellows should have been selected to bear the irony of history I do not know. They are certainly not the only ones who have slighted the great opportunities of life and given themselves up to the lowest and meanest aims. As I was meditating on this little incident it occurred to me that there is not a better text in all the Bible to illustrate the folly of courting failure to one's life through entering on it with a low aim.

In the days when these men lived there were great opportunities for achievement, as there have been and are in every age. There is always a Goliath for a David to slay. There is ever a roaring lion for a young Samson to tear in pieces. A Jonathan never fails to find a friend on whom to lavish his affection. There were plenty of wrongs for these men to right, abundant opportunity for heroic service that would have given them a glorious immortality. They had the vantage ground of being of the judge's family, which in those days, before the kings of Israel, was really the royal family. But these young princes of the realm, like many modern princes, were destitute of the princely spirit. To ride an ass colt in the style of the day, and to the admiration of the crowd, was the height of their ambition. The figure of a lone mule with an empty saddle would have been a proper effigy on the tombstone of the descendants of Judge Abdon.

But I have not chosen this little story with the intention of devoting time to the heaping of contempt on these riders of ass colts in the days of the judges. It is the men like them today that I am interested in. It is their kith and kin, who live about us now, and who come to hear me preach, who arouse my interest and attention. The Bible holds its power through the ages because, more than any other book in the world, it is vital with life, human and divine. These life sketches, every one of them, have their message, full of suggestion, to the men of our day.

My message then, tonight, is that a low aim is the greatest folly, and will dictate certain failure. There is no hope for a man whose aim is so low that if he attains to it there will be no real glory in his life. The man who aims high may fail of reaching his fondest dreams, though it is an abiding faith with me that he need not fail if his dreams are noble enough to come true. But the man who aims low is doomed from the beginning, for the nearer he reaches his aim the worse he is off.

We have suggested here the folly of a person bending his chief energies toward any success which is purely frivolous and temporary, and which can confer no lasting benefit. It could be of no special permanent honor to a son of the judge of Israel that he could make a finer display on an ass colt than any other man in the nation. It was a fad, a thing to laugh at for an hour, and that was the end of it. You may see the same folly in Absalom, the favorite son of David, who came to such a contemptible end. When Absalom was a young fellow he devoted himself to his hair; it was his highest ambition in his younger days to have the finest head of curls there was in the whole city, and he used to have his curls weighed every year, and the gossip of the town was often running on the weight of Absalom's curls. Absalom seems to have doted on his looks. He was determined not only to look pretty while he was alive, but after he was dead. And so while he was yet a young fellow he selected a picturesque spot and built him a tomb, and no doubt often pictured to himself what a gorgeous funeral there would be when he died. But the end of it all was that the very curls he had spent so much time on caught in the branches of a tree when he was escaping from the battlefield, and his stubborn mule ran out from under him and left him dangling there in the air waiting for Joab's spear, and his body was afterward flung into a trench and a heap of stones piled over it, as you might bury a dog. No man whose story is spoken of in Old Testament history could have made his mark more brilliantly for the good of his race than Absalom. But his aim was low from the very beginning. It was frivolous and temporary, and he was never willing to deny himself his own way for today that there might be a better and more glorious tomorrow.

I see young men and young women every day who are making the same fatal blunder. You see young men making it financially. They get better salaries than their fathers did, who, by economy and industry and a determination to run their roots down in the land, denied themselves luxuries and saved their money, developing, in so doing, their business interests and ability until they became, and are today, the strong, reliable, well-to-do business men. But their sons and their nephews must begin where the old folks leave off. They spend as much for a suit of clothes as would have made the father respectable in his younger life for a year. They pamper their youth, that needs the discipline of self-denial in order to be its strongest, with luxuries, narcotics, and stimulants, because down at the bottom of things the chief aim of life, to them, is that they may look well in their clothes, and eat, drink, and be merry. Like the sons of Abdon, they must make a great show when they mount their ass colts. Multitudes of men came to middle life and on to old age with no strength of business character, no influence in the business community, mere driftlogs of fate, because they have frittered and fooled away all their younger years on things that were purely temporary and could be of no value when attained.

Now, if you will carry all this up to the higher realm, our illustration does not lose its value. For there the man who is wise is the one whose high aim is to so use his money and his social privileges and all the lesser ends of life that they shall be building up a character which shall shine through an immortal career. For, after all, a man may succeed in a business way and yet attain to no higher wisdom. A man may have sense enough to deny himself the present luxury that he may have the comforts of wealth in old age, and yet fail of that nobler wisdom that stores treasures up in the bank of heaven. There is many another man like the rich fool whom Jesus tells about, who in his prosperity proposed to build still greater barns to hold his goods, and then mocked his soul by saying, "Thou hast much goods laid up for many years" (Luke 12:19). That man and all men like him are, like the sons of Abdon, only riders of ass colts that shall be soon stripped of their trappings and left riderless, while the impoverished rider will hear the stinging judgment of God, "Thou fool, this night thy soul shall be required of thee: then whose shall those things be, which thou has provided?" (Luke 12:20).

Wise men are always searching for something that will last. The manufacturers of paint in this country are just now searching the country for the man who painted a sign at a railway station in Harper's Ferry twenty-five years ago. The reason they want to find him is that he so wisely mixed his paint that, though a quarter of a century has passed by and the board has warped, the words he painted, "Harper's Ferry," stand out as clear and distinct as when the work was first done. There is no man on earth, who is known, who can do that today. And these manufacturers want to find the man who can mix paint so as to make it last. There is a fortune for him if he can be found. That is the great thread that runs through the universe; it is the difference between wisdom and folly always. Deny yourself an hour that you may have a day. Deny yourself the day that you may have a week. Deny yourself in youth that you may have a glorious manhood. Refuse present dissipation that you may have long strength and power. This was what Moses did when he refused to be called the son of Pharaoh's daughter, choosing rather to suffer affliction with the people of God than to enjoy the pleasures of sin for a season. He had his eye on the greater reward, and, with the Hebrew's keen insight, refused to be cheated out of his long career of usefulness and honor for the temporary pleasures of Egypt.

You may see all this illustrated in the difference between Abraham and Lot. Lot had an eye on the present cattle market. Sodom might be wicked, but the cattle trade was good, and the pasture lands sloping that way were rich and well watered. He knew the danger to his own character and to his children, but he could not deny himself the present success; he must ride his ass colt toward Sodom. Abraham turned his face toward the desert in peace, without a cloud on his brow: why? "He beheld a city which hath foundations, whose builder and maker is God" (Hebrews 11:10). Lot lost his wealth and his home, and his family was disgraced and broken up. His failure from beginning to end was the failure of a low aim. Abraham was a success. His eyes were in the heavens. Wherever he went he built an altar unto God. Abraham had a longing for city life too, but he wanted a city that would endure. He would not put up with Sodom after he had caught a glimpse of the city in the skies.

Many of you who hear me ought to take this lesson home to your own hearts. The supreme aim of your life is too low and too frivolous. Nothing is high enough for you, nor for any man or woman, that does not take into its scope both worlds. To live a useful life here is to fit yourself for an honored life there. No life that is not useful and helpful, that does not serve the highest ends, will give you any permanent peace even in this world. And whatever success you have in this world, if it is not of a kind that works in with God's purpose, and brings you into communion and fellowship with him, it is but folly, and will bring you to contempt in the end.

A curious story comes from Madrid in explanation of the misfortunes which have afflicted the royal house of Spain. According to this superstition, the root of the mischief is a fatal ring of quite medieval deadliness. The late King Alphonso XII gave it to his cousin Mercedes when he was betrothed to her, and she wore it during the whole of her married life. On her death the king presented it to his grandmother, the Queen Christina. She died very soon after, when it was passed along to the king's sister, who at once began to sicken and in a few days breathed her last. Alphonso then handed it to his sister-in-law, but in three months she also died. His majesty now resolved to retain the fateful jewel in his own keeping, but he, too, soon fell a victim to its mysterious malignancy. By order of the widow it was suspended by a chain around the neck of the patron saint of Madrid. Alas! all intelligent people know what the fatal ring is that has led Spain from one disaster to another through all these years. It has been the fatal lack of a high aim. She has sought to amuse her people instead of educating them. She has sought the present pleasure rather than the permanent good. She has ridden her ass colt generation after generation, while other great nations have been developing their citizens in all the arts of life, and in all the strength of morality and religion. The nation is dying of a low aim. Young men, see that you do not die the same death. The present pleasure, the appealing lust, the lurking passion, all these are present and full of temptation; but it is only by denying yourself every hurtful and evil thing, only by fixing your eye upon the highest and holiest prize that God sets before you, and pressing onward toward it with untiring devotion, that you can make sure of glorious and eternal triumph. Emerson said, "If a man will but plant himself on his instincts, the great world will come round to him." But Paul said it better when he cried, "Forgetting those things which are behind, and reaching forth unto those things which are before, I press toward the mark for the prize of the high calling of God in Christ Jesus" (Philippians 3:13-14).

52

A KING IN HIDING

"And the Lord answered, Behold, he hath hid himself
among the stuff" (1 Samuel 10:22).

It was the day for Saul's ordination as king, but he was timid about it, and, driven to a panic at last, he hid himself among the camp equipage, so that when the moment arrived to ordain a king the king could not be found. Then it was that the Lord made known unto them the whereabouts of the cowardly Saul. And they went and found the foolish fellow where he was hiding and brought him forth. It wouldn't have looked so absurd if he had been a little fellow, but he was a great, tall, splendid-looking man, head and shoulders higher than any other man in all the camp, and he must have looked and felt silly enough when they brought him out from his hiding place. He looked every inch a king when once he was brought forth and the crown was on his head, but he had hidden away among the pack saddles like some silly boy.

I have recalled this picture for our study this evening because it suggests the great truth that we are constantly in danger of losing the most important things in life by hiding them among "the stuff;" concealing them among things that are of little importance compared to what is hidden. A young man comes to the city to make his life career. He had been reared in an honest, wholesome, Christian home; he has in his veins the honorable blood of a good man and a good woman who have feared God and eschewed evil. The traditions of his family, no matter how poor it may be, are all honorable, straightforward, and noble. The son comes into the great market place of the city and offers his young and vigorous manhood in the exchange in search of fortune. He thrusts himself into the thick of life, works hard, early and late, struggles, and succeeds. Ten, fifteen, twenty years go by, and people point to him and say: "What a success he has made! He came here with nothing and now he has a fortune." But I get closer to him and I begin to seek for the wholesome standard of honor which he brought to town with him years ago. I hunt for that genuineness and integrity with which he began his career; that keen sense of right and wrong which once held him to a frank and manly course, and I cannot find it. Instead I find that he has compromised with the tricks and intrigues and shady methods which men use who make haste to be rich. He has hidden his manhood among "the stuff;" a young king came to town, but he has been hidden and lost among the camp equipage.

Another man gives himself up to pleasure. How to have a good time is the one query of every day. He becomes a mere plaything, a toy in social life. Anything that tickles his fancy, that gives him a new sensation, is his attraction. It may take a hundred ways of showing itself. He may be a flirt and develop into a silly butterfly given to soft dalliance with equally silly women. He may develop into a dude and become simply a clothes-horse on which to show the changing fashions of the tailor. He may become theater-struck and give himself over to the imaginary tragedies and farces of the stage. It may be that the pleasures of the appetite attract him, and he turns toward the path of the glutton and the winebibber. Back at the first he only meant to have a good time and had no evil or malicious purpose in it. But the serious purpose to do honest work for God and man, to be of some real value to the world in which he lives, to make the best and noblest man out of himself, in order that the world may be a nobler and better place because he has lived in it—all that he has hidden among "the stuff." There was a king in him; but search for the king now, and you will find him hidden away and lost in the mere furbelows and husks of life.

What folly it is for men to hide the king in them among "the stuff!" For all these other things for which men hide their manhood are very transient and soon pass away. It is a remarkable fact that the most conspicuous examples of the men who have been preeminent in those characteristics that men count most to be desired have come to notable inglorious ends. Men struggle to attain strength, and are full of admiration for it; and yet Samson, the strong man who could rend a lion in his hands, who could slay three thousand of the enemies of his country with a bludgeon in his naked hand, hid his strength amid the mere "stuff" of folly and sin, and came to a miserable old age and a pitiful death. Absalom, who was famous as the most handsome man of his age, and whose beauty and brilliant qualities stole away the hearts of the people of a great city and nation, died the death of a dog. Ahithophel, the diplomat of Jerusalem in the brilliant days of King David, hid his honor amid "the stuff" of timeserving and policy, and hanged himself with his own hand. Alexander the Great made conquest of the earth, but died by poison at the end of a career which had mastered everything but himself. He had made himself king of the world, but lost the inner kingdom of his own manhood. When men come to the end of life they find that everything is "stuff" except the quality of the manhood itself. Then, if a man has traded off or covered up manhood for money or power or pleasure, he realizes how he has been cheated. All the things that men struggle for that are outward are but "stuff" when the great emergencies of life come.

In the reign of King Henry VI there is mention made of Henry Beaufort, a rich and wretched cardinal, who, lying on his death-bed and perceiving his time to be but short, expostulated with himself thus: "Wherefore should I die, being thus rich? If the whole world were able to save my life, I am able either by policy to get it, or by riches to buy it. Fie, Fie! will not death be hired? Will money and power do nothing?" But he found that they could not do anything. Such is the impartiality of death that unlimited money will do nothing: there is no protection against the arrest of death. In such an hour how like "stuff" seems everything that has interfered with the development of the kingly qualities of the soul.

There is a suggestion, I think, of great encouragement in the statement here that it was the Lord who kept track of Saul, knew where he was hidden, and told them were to go and get him that they might bring him forth to his crowning. So, my brother, you that are hidden away among "the stuff," making a failure of the best things of life in the great kingly qualities of the soul, God has not forgotten you, he has not lost track of you, he has not lost his interest in you, he watches over you where you are hidden, and he inspires our hearts with courage and with sympathy to seek after you and bring you forth, if possible, to be crowned again as the son of God.

And we who are seeking to save men must never forget that, however repulsive and discouraging the pile of "stuff" that may be heaped upon a sinful soul, there is a king in hiding there, and if we can but arouse the nobler self into action we may save him.

Colonel Richard Hinton relates a very interesting little story of how he was walking once in Boston with Walt Whitman, the poet. It was at night, and as they passed along they saw a figure slouching toward them as if half afraid. The poet threw a massive arm out, as if startled, when he caught the fellow's face in the shadows. "Why, Jack," he cried, and drew him close with a kiss on the forehead. The man was evidently "a hard case." His dress was disordered and his face haggard. Colonel Hinton instinctively drew away to a seat nearby. Evidently in bitter trouble, the man almost clung to the stalwart arm that was about his shoulder. Some money passed and words were whispered. Then he noticed the man straighten his figure as Whitman again kissed his forehead, and he walked away quickly, saying firmly as he did so, "I will, Walt, I will!"

They passed on. They did not talk about him that night, but the next morning the poet briefly said at breakfast that "Jack" was a Long Island boy whom he had known in his youth. Jack had been reckless, and was fleeing from officers who were after him for stabbing a companion in a drunken brawl. The wounded man was recovering.

Years afterward Colonel Hinton was mustered out of the volunteer army and went to live in Washington. Whitman was one of the noted personalities there and they renewed their friendship. One day, in the Department of Justice, where Whitman was records clerk, Hinton was sitting by his desk, when the poet looked up suddenly and handed him a faded tintype of a private soldier, and said, "Do you think you have ever seen that face?" It was a shrewd, sharp visage, coarse but strong in outline, and with something of a hunted look in the eyes. He shook his head and the poet remarked: "That's Jack. Boston Common, you know. He was killed at Peach Orchard—a good soldier, too." It is Christ's assurance that there is the making of a good soldier for the great battle of life in any poor sinful man if he be only willing to surrender at the cross and enlist in the army of the Lord. Christ knows how to find the king hidden under all "the stuff" of sin and bring him out to a new chance.

I fear that we often gather so much form and ceremony and outward show about our Christian churches and our Christian service that we lose sight of the great fact that the one thing for which all these things exist is to save lost men and women.

Thirty years ago a business man in Peoria, Ill., met a friend, William Reynolds, also a prominent business man in that city, and said to him, "Mr. Reynolds, how long have we known each other?"

"About fifteen years."

"Do you believe that it is necessary for me to believe on the Lord Jesus Christ if I am to be saved?"

"Yes."

"Do you care whether or not I am saved?"

"Certainly."

"Pardon my frankness; I do not want to hurt your feelings, but I do not believe that you care at all whether I am saved or lost."

"What do you mean?"

"You are a professing Christian, an officer in the church. We have met frequently during the last fifteen years. I have heard you speak on many topics. We have had many conversations. I would have listened gladly to you if you had spoken to me on the subject of religion, and yet in fifteen years you have never said one word about my salvation. You have never tried to win my soul to Christ. I cannot believe that you care whether I am saved or lost."

Mr. Reynolds with shame confessed that he had neglected his opportunities, and then said to his friend, "What has wrought this change in you?"

"I was in Chicago yesterday, and when I started to come home a young man asked if he might share my seat. As soon as the train began to move, the conversation, started by him, ran something like this:'Pleasant day.' 'Yes.' 'Good crops this year.' 'Yes, pretty good.' 'We ought to be thankful to the Lord for sending good crops.' 'Yes, I suppose we should.' 'My friend, are you a Christian?' 'Well, I have a high regard for religion. I think churches are a good thing in a community.' 'Are you a Christian?' 'Well, I cannot say that I am, now that you ask the direct question.' 'Do you think it wise for a thoughtful man to go on for years without giving thought to this subject?' 'No, honestly, I do not think it wise.' 'My friend, may I pray with you?' 'Why, if we are ever where there is a good opportunity, and you desire to do so, I do not think I would object.' 'There never will be a better opportunity than the present. Let us bow our heads here behind this car seat.' And with the train speeding through the suburbs of Chicago and across the prairie this man prayed for my salvation. I never saw a man so much in earnest. I know that he cared whether I was saved or lost. Just as he finished his prayer the brakeman called out the name of a station and my new-made friend was off. He had reached the door when it occurred to me that I did not even know who he was. I rushed after him and asked his name, and he replied, 'D. L. Moody.' I am going back to Chicago to find him and to have him show me the way of life."

Before Mr. Reynolds left his friend that morning he had led him to Christ, and then Mr. Reynolds said: "I am going to Chicago myself to find Mr. Moody. There is something wrong with my life."

A gentleman who had heard of this incident was on the Pacific coast years after that, and meeting a man from Peoria, Ill., inquired of him, "Do you know William Reynolds of your city?" "I know him well." "What is his business?" "The people who know him best say that his business is to serve the Lord Jesus Christ, and that he packs pork to pay expenses." Mr. Reynolds himself had become a great soul saver, and he has given his life to pull into the light kings whom he has found hidden amid "the stuff" of sin and folly.

I am sure there are some who hear me at this time who are in just such a case as Saul. God has called you to a noble manhood, or a holy womanhood, but you have turned a deaf ear to the call, and have hidden yourself amid the trumpery of the world. I come as God's messenger to call you back to your high destiny. God has not forgotten you, Christ has died to redeem you, the Holy Spirit will comfort and inspire you, Christian friends will give you fellowship. Shake off the follies that have covered you and come forth with earnest purpose to fill the great and worthy place to which God has called you as his child.

CHAPTER 53

THE DIFFERENCE BETWEEN SELF-CONCEIT AND SELF-RESPECT

"Seest thou a man wise in his own conceit? there is more hope of a fool than of him" (Proverbs 26:12).

"Should such as man as I flee? And who is there, that, being as I am, would go into the temple to save his life? I will not go in: (Nehemiah 6:11).

Between self-conceit and self-respect there is in reality a great gulf fixed; but the chasm is not always discerned, and the two are often confused in the mind and are sometimes taken the one for the other. Paul undertakes to distinguish between them in a careful way in the twelfth chapter of his letter to the Romans, where he says, "For I say, through the grace given unto me, to every man that is among you, not to think of himself more highly than he ought to think; but to think soberly, according as God hath dealt to every man the measure of faith" (Romans 12:3). And from that Paul sets out to show that we have, every one of us, our own rightful place to work in the

world, and our own important work; that there is no reason for our envying anybody else, and no cause for anyone
to think of our place or talents with contempt.

The fatal folly and sin of self-conceit lies in the fact that
the conceited man expects to win on the principle of his
own shrewdness or cunning or lucky star, instead of earn-
ing fairly and squarely his success by living a righteous life
and giving an honest return in labor for the reward he expects. He thinks that somehow or other he is going to escape that great law of God which girdles the earth as
completely as the law of gravitation, and which says, "God
is not mocked: for whatsoever a man soweth, that shall he
also reap" (Galatians 6:7). But the self-conceited man
thinks that it is possible for him to cheat God, and, though
he sow wild oats, reap a useful crop into the garner of old
age. He will admit that other men have tried to do the same
thing and come out bankrupt and impoverished in every
way, but his self-conceit causes him to believe that he will
be able to do what others have always failed to do—to live
a life of sin and yet in some way obtain the wages of righteousness. No wonder the wise man said of such an illogical
and unreasonable creature, "Seest thou a man wise in his
own conceit? there is more hope of a fool than of him"
(Proverbs 26:12).

In the great cities, where young men gathered from all
the little towns and villages throughout the country congregate by the thousand, self-conceit works its awful ravage
of destruction. Here is a young man who has just come to
town from his village home with a curiosity to see the
sights, and with a large idea of his own ability to take care
of himself under all circumstances. And he is able to take
care of himself until he begins to thrust himself into the

ways of folly. The bird is able to take care of itself so long as it keeps out of the trap, and the writer of Proverbs says that it is in vain to set a trap in the open sight of a bird; but a self-conceited man will see the trap set, and know that it is a trap in which other men are constantly being caught and plucked of everything of value, and yet will walk straight on to his destruction. This young man has heard about gambling houses in the city; he has heard, of course, that they are dangerous places, where it is the rule and not the exception for men to come to disgrace and sorrow. But he thinks that these young men that have been caught were not so sharp as he is, and so, like the green goose that he is, he goes into the gambling saloon. He has been warned against it by his father and mother, and by wise friends, and yet so enormous is his self-conceit that he goes into the trap to pit himself against an old, trained gambler who is a match for five hundred such young men as he is. Anybody that has been behind the scene knows that with all his experience, with all his craft, with all his secret arrangements, with all his organized knavery, it is impossible for anybody from the outside to make head against him. As Mr. Beecher once said, a man may have some chance in a game of chance, but in gambling saloons chances are not allowed. A man who gambles for a living is nothing but an incarnate thief, a cunning thief, a perpetual thief—first, last, and all the time a thief—and his business is to steal. He has made stealing a profession, and is practiced in it. He is acquainted with men's dispositions, and knows how to take them. And here comes in this green young man. He is exactly like a little fly exploring a great big black-bellied spider's web, that says, "It does not look as though there was very much to be afraid of here; I do not see anything that I cannot manage; at any rate, I will try," and pitches in. And after he is once in—you hear one faint buzz, and that is the end of him.

Here is another young fellow, with a little rotten spot of self-indulgence in him, who thinks that because he is away from home, where his mother will not know and his sisters are not likely to hear about it, he can afford to glut his idle curiosity, or give vent to his evil passion in the dark places of the city that have held for him an unholy fascination. He has heard about other men being ruined there, but his overweening self-conceit bolsters him up and makes him believe that he can go, and come out whole, where others have lost their manhood and their lives. And so he goes to the brothel, and is flattered and intoxicated by drugged wines and drugged pleasure, until the dart strikes through his liver. Poor fool, to think that he could handle pitch and not be defiled! When it is too late he wakes up to know that God's word is true when it says, "The lips of a strange woman drop as an honeycomb, and her mouth is smoother than oil" (Proverbs 5:3), and that the other part of the warning is also true, that the end of her career is bitter as wormwood, and that "her feet go down to death, her steps take hold on hell" (Proverbs 5:5). If the self-conceited and deluded youth who is beginning to go in that dark way could only have wisdom to see "the ghastly skeletons, the pallid cheeks, the leaden eyes, the rotting bones, the consuming marrow, the hideous outcome of such a life! But ten thousand men perish because they deem themselves so smart; because they are confident that, however many may have perished, they are not going to perish." "Seest thou a man wise in his own conceit? there is more hope of a fool than of him" (Proverbs 26:12).

Here is another young man, brought up on the farm to drink cold water, and eat plain and simple food, and shun strong drink. He has heard of the sting of the adder, of the danger of drunkenness, and all that; but now that he is away from home influences he finds himself surrounded by people who sneer at those safe and quiet ways of life in which he has hitherto walked. And so he begins to reason that men have come to be drunkards because they were weak and had not much will power. The young man's self-conceit causes him to boast that he himself has an iron will and that he can always stop drinking when he wants to, and so he begins with the wine cup, and the taste grows until it becomes his master and ruins him body and soul. Other men look on and see him ruined and walk straight into the trap themselves, with their eyes open, because their bloated self-conceit flatters them that they are a little stronger than he was. "Seest thou a man wise in his own conceit? there is more hope of a fool than of him" (Proverbs 26:12).

Now, self-respect is a very different thing. Nehemiah, who uttered this second text, was a man who had genuine self-respect. Nehemiah had had a good place in the palace of the king of Persia and was a great favorite of the king. If he had been a selfish man he would have settled himself down there and feathered his own nest, and given himself no trouble about the said condition of his native city. But Nehemiah was an unselfish and noble soul. It was impossible for him to be happy while, though living in a palace, he knew that his relatives and friends were in trouble and that the walls of his native city had been torn down. And so he betook himself to prayer, and prayed most earnestly that God would in some way open the way for him to help in bringing prosperity again to his people. The next day, when he came into the presence of the king, the monarch at once detected the sorrow that was mirrored in the sensitive face of the young man. He saw that some trouble was gnawing at his heart, and required of him an explanation. The king became interested in his story, and sent him away to restore the walls of Jerusalem and build up again the prosperity of his people. Nehemiah returned to a discouraged and disappointed people, but his own faith in God was so strong, and his own magnetic personality so irresistible, that he soon put new heart into them, and had them all at work rebuilding the broken wall. So great was his success that the enemies of his people saw that the Hebrews would soon be independent of them unless Nehemiah could in some way be frightened from his great work. At first they wanted him to come and have a council with them, but Nehemiah sent them word, saying, "I am doing a great work, so that I cannot come down: why should the work cease while I leave it and come down to you?" They tried four times to get him off with them into some sort of council where they would have a chance to fall upon him and kill him. But Nehemiah steadfastly went on with his work. Then they undertook to scare him. They told him that there was a lot of evil gossip going about, to the effect that he was planning treachery and rebellion, thinking in this way to frighten the brave young leader and dishearten him in his work. They did not frighten him, but they did succeed in alarming some of his friends, and one of them said to him, "Let us meet together in the house of God, within the temple, and let us shut the doors of the temple: for they will come to slay thee; yea, in the night will they come to slay thee" (Nehemiah 6:10). "Should such a man as I flee?" shouted Nehemiah. "Who is there, that, being as I am, would go into the temple to save his life? I will not go in" (Nehemiah 6:11). It turned out that this was a false friend, who had been hired by Nehemiah's enemies to entice him, if possible, to show cowardice by hiding in the temple.

Nehemiah's self-respect was not founded on any self-conceit or any overgrown idea of his own strength of greatness. It was built on the solid rock of his belief that God had called him to do a great work, and that because of that his life was dear to God, and it was his place to go on doing the work given him, leaving himself in the Lord's hands. That is the foundation of all true self-respect. No man can really respect himself unless he feels that he is doing right, that his life is justified in God's sight, and that he is doing the noble work which God would have him do. To make a man feel that he is fulfilling his mission is to dignify him with a noble and royal self-respect.

> "Just where you stand in the conflict,
> There is your place!
> Just where you think you are useless
> Hide not your face!
> God placed you there for a purpose,
> Whate'er it be;
> Think he had chosen you for it;
> Work loyally.
>
> "Gird on your armor!
> At toil or rest,
> Whiche'er it be, never doubting
> God's way is best.
> Out in the fight, or on picket,
> Stand firm and true;

This is the work which your Master
Gives you to do."

To give your heart to Christ and become a Christian cannot help but give you a more wholesome self-respect. The fact that Christ loves you, that he has chosen you for his friend, and that he daily holds communion with your heart, will make you feel differently about yourself.

A lady prominent in society in an eastern city wears a ring which has a very romantic history. It is an old-fashioned ring containing a lock of faded brown hair covered by a glass setting. Nearly forty years ago the white-haired lady who now wears the ring cut that tress of hair from her own curls and gave it to a jeweler to be enclosed in a ring which she gave to her soldier lover when he was setting out for the war. It can be imagined how he prized this memento of the girl he loved. Through many a weary month, in many a sad scene, it remained on the finger on which she had placed it. One day, after one of the fierce battles of the Wilderness, the young officer was carried, wounded, to the field hospital. He was insensible, but the surgeons saw that there was life in him and thought it might be preserved by amputating his arm. There was no time to be lost and they cut through the sleeve, and, having done their work, set the limb away with the sleeve and gauntlet still on it. A friend was beside his bed when the young officer recovered his senses, and gently told him what had been done. His first thought was of his treasured ring; it was dearer to him than the lost hand. His friend went and found the arm, removed the gauntlet and saw the ring, which he took back to the sufferer. It was put on the only hand he had left, and his mind was relieved. This is the ring that his wife now wears. To her it is endeared by the affection in which her husband held it for her sake. Its intrinsic value is probably small, but as the symbol of a love which manifested itself in that trying hour it is precious beyond price. It is such a love that gives Christ a claim on his followers. "Having loved his own which were in the world, he loved them unto the end" (John 13:1). No good woman could be loved like that by a noble man without an increased self-respect, without feeling dignified and ennobled by such love. So Christ ennobles and dignifies and glorifies us by the great love wherewith he loves us.

54

THE STORY OF A MAN WHO WAS CAUGHT IN HIS OWN TRAP

"So they hanged Haman on the gallows that he had prepared for Mordecai" (Esther 7:10).

Haman furnishes a very graphic illustration of the way sin, when yielded to, can take a man who is seemingly hedged about until he is impregnable to misfortune, and utterly destroy him. If Haman had been willing to let well enough alone, and live honestly and decently, he might have had a long and conspicuous career at the Persian court. He was a brilliant adventurer from the broken-down nation of the Amalekites and had captured the fancy of King Ahasuerus. The king was so greatly pleased with him that he honored him above all the other courtiers in his realm, and he came to be known as the power behind the throne in that kingdom. So great became his power and majesty that whenever he walked in the streets the proudest of the nobility bowed to him with as much reverence as if he were the king himself. Haman was a proud man and a vain one, and nothing made him quite so happy as to have people bow to him in public. It thrilled him through and through with delight when some powerful noble did him princely honor before the eyes of the crowd.

But there was one man in town that didn't bow. He permitted the great Haman to go by without the slightest nodding of his stubborn head. This was Mordecai, a relative of Esther, the beautiful young queen. This stubbornness on the part of Mordecai was a source of the greatest chagrin and mortification to Haman. But Haman was proud, and thought Mordecai alone was scarcely big enough game for his gun. On learning that Mordecai was a Jew, he concluded that he would not only rid himself of Mordecai, but would exterminate the Jews from the country.

Haman was himself an exile because of the power of the Jewish people, and to get a chance to not only destroy Mordecai, but wreak vengeance on thousands of Jews throughout the empire, made his wicked little heart dance for joy. So the first time he had a good chance to talk with the king he told him that he had discovered a large number of people scattered throughout his empire who were disloyal to the government. They worshiped a strange God, and were especially disrespectful to King Ahasuerus himself. These people were wealthy people, and he, Haman, loved the king so tenderly that it just broke his heart to see these people, who were traitors to the king, fattening on the good things of his realm. If the king would only give him a chance, nothing would make him happier than to clear the kingdom of this vile race.

Ahasuerus was a hot-headed sort of fellow, always going off half primed, and he fell into the trap very neatly. He took his signet ring off his finger and gave it to Haman, and told him to work his will with them; though, as for enriching the public treasury from the spoils of these Jews who were to be murdered, Haman might keep all that to himself. Haman went home walking on air. He lost no time in sending out the edict all over the kingdom that, from the palace to the hovel, it should be no crime to kill a Jew on certain days. This brought even Queen Esther into danger of her life.

Mordecai lost no time in making the queen acquainted with this horrible plot of Haman's, and reverently assured her that it was no doubt providential that she had come to her high place for such a time as this, and that not only the fate of her race and her relatives, but her own life depended on her immediate action. Esther was put in a hard place. King Ahasuerus was not the most gentle husband in the world; he had deposed one queen because she would not come to the dining room when he and this lords were drunk, and he had made a strict rule that anybody, even the queen, who should come into his presence without being invited, unless he graciously held out the scepter, was to be punished with death. The king had not seemed to care about sending for her for a long time, and he might not think of her again until it was too late; so she sent Mordecai word that, if he would call a prayer meeting among all their people on the outside, she would have a prayer meeting with her maids in the palace, and then on a certain day she would go to the king, whether she lived or died, and trust the result to God. There is romantic heroism in her words, "So will I go in unto the king, which is not according to the law: and if I perish, I perish" (Esther 4:16).

Well, it turned out all right. As Esther came in timidly, his majesty, happening to be in a good humor, held out the scepter to her with gracious pleasure, and wanted to know her desires. Esther had the matter all arranged in her mind. She knew the king's weak spot. He was very fond of a good dinner, and greatly delighted in Haman's conversation and society; so she expressed her desire that the king and his friend Haman should come that day to a banquet which she had prepared. This pleased the king, and he sent word to Haman to hurry up and come to the feast.

When the king was mellow with his wine after dinner, he again asked the queen what was at the bottom of all this. Man like, he couldn't get it out of his head that Esther wanted something out of the ordinary, to cause her to get him up such an unusually fine dinner. And the queen replied that if she had found favor in the sight of the king, she would like to have him come to a banquet again tomorrow, and let Haman come also, and then she would make known her request.

There was, no doubt, method in Esther's delay. She had found out that it was a good thing to pique the king's curiosity. By her making so much of it he would gradually get his mind made up to yield to a large request. The king gladly granted her petition, and Haman went out bubbling over with vanity and happiness. But as he went down the steps of the palace he saw something that ironed all the smiles out of his face. There was Mordecai, with a neck as stiff as if it had an iron ramrod in it, and he never bowed or paid the slightest reverence to him. Haman wanted to choke him, but he clinched his fists and went on in silence.

That was a notable night in Haman's house. Everything seemed to be going his way. He sent out for all his friends to come in, and he had a great time boasting to them about how rich he was and what a nice lot of children he had, now smart his boys were and how beautiful his girls, and what great honor the king had bestowed upon him. And now, he says, Queen Esther has taken as great a fancy to me as the king, and I was the only man invited to her banquet today with the king, and as a special mark of favor I am to be at a banquet again tomorrow with the king alone. And then Haman made a wry face: "Yet all this availeth me nothing, so long as I see Mordecai the Jew sitting at the king's gate" (Esther 5:13). Poor Haman, he was one bow short, and that one old stiff-necked Jew was the fly in the ointment which robbed him of all his pleasure. But his wife and his friends advised him not to worry about Mordecai. "Let a gallows be made of fifty cubits high," they said, "and tomorrow speak thou unto the king that Mordecai may be hanged thereon" (Esther 5:14).That pleased Haman, and he ordered the gallows built.

Just here an interesting thing happened in the palace. Ahasuerus was troubled with insomnia, and that very night he could not sleep. He had hit upon the ingenious plan of having himself read to sleep, and he found that nothing would work so well as having his own writings read to him. I never tried it, but I have heard of preachers having their own sermons read to them on such occasions with great profit. Well, this night the king had one of his servants reading to him out of his diary. And, reading along, they came to the place which told how Mordecai had once discovered a plot against the king's life and by loyally making it known had saved him. The king immediately inquired, "Has any honor ever been paid to Mordecai for that kindness?" (Esther 6:3). And he found that nothing had been done. He felt very much ashamed about it, and had it still on his mind when the courtiers began to gather in the outer room the next morning. He turned to his steward and said, "Who is in the court?" Now Haman was there, an early comer, in order to ask the privilege of hanging Mordecai. But the moment he was admitted, before he got a chance to speak, the king turned and said, "Haman, is that you? I am glad to see you; I was just wanting your advice about a case. What shall be done unto the man whom the king delighteth to honor?" (Esther 6:4-6).

Haman very naturally supposed that he was the man that was to receive this honor, so he fixed the thing up in great shape, with this idea as the basis of his proceedings. He advised that the royal apparel be brought, and the king's horse, and the crown royal for his head; and counseled that the man be appareled by the noblest princes of the realm as his servants, and that one of these princes lead the horse through the streets with this favored man on its back, and let it be shouted everywhere, "Thus shall it be done to the man whom the king delighteth to honor" (Esther 6:9).

"All right," said the king; "that will do. Haman, you go and treat Mordecai that way." Can you imagine a bitterer thing than that? If there was ever poetic justice done on earth it was done then. There are some historic scenes that I should like to have witnessed, and one of them would be the dressing of Mordecai by Haman. But all things pass, and the bitter hour was over, and Human went home crestfallen and broken-hearted to tell his wife and his friends the horrible shame that had fallen on him. His wife and friends were evidently very much alarmed themselves, and were very poor comforters, for they prophesied that this was probably the beginning of the end. But while they were talking, one of the king's chamberlains came to hurry him away to the banquet. Poor Haman went, with a heart like lead, because he had to. It was not appetite that dragged him thither.

As the second banquet drew near its close the king again inquired of Esther her petition, and then she told him that her relatives and friends, as well as her own life, had been plotted against, and were in immediate danger. The king, aroused and angry, said, "Who is he, and where is he, that durst presume in his heart to do so?" (Esther 7:5) Then I can imagine Esther leaping to her feet from the banquet, and pointing the accusing finger at the shrinking, trembling scoundrel shaking like a man with the palsy at the table, as she shouts, "The adversary and enemy is this wicked Haman" (Esther 7:6). One of the servants threw a cloth over Haman's head, hiding his face from the king's anger, and Harbonah, the chamberlain who had been at Haman's house to hurry him to the banquet, and who had seen the peculiar preparations that had been made there, said, "Haman has a gallows fifty cubits high, which he made for Mordecai, the king's friend, standing in his house." Then said the king, "Hang him thereon" (Esther 7:9). And so the gallows which Haman had built for Mordecai was all ready for himself.

The sermon has preached itself as the story has gone on, and there remains little for me to say. "Whatsoever a man soweth, that shall he also reap" (Galatians 6:7). The man who goes through the world full of hatred and vengeance, building a gallows for the man he hates, is only preparing for his own disaster. "With what measure ye

mete it shall be measured unto you again" (Matthew 7:2).
The man who is full of forgiveness and kindness and love
toward his fellow-men sows the seeds of all that is gracious
and beautiful, that shall make fragrance to bless the path
of his declining years. He who goes through the world
with bitterness and meanness is sowing dragons' teeth that
will be a hard pillow to lie on when he is old. Wickedness
may succeed for a while, but every iniquitous plot has
within it the elements of its own disintegration. Righteousness that will not bow its head to a sin because it is successful or popular may be threatened and plotted against,
and for a time clouded with defeat, but in the end its enemies hang on the gallows they have built for it.

55

THE HANDWRITING ON THE WALL

"Then the king's countenance was changed, and his thoughts troubled him" (Daniel 5:6).

"Then was Daniel brought in before the king" (Daniel 5:13).

The theme we are to study is one that has been used by artist and poet and orator for hundreds of years. It is one of those strong and splendid pictures so replete with instruction, of such universal application, that its teaching is as valuable in one age as in another and finds something that echoes back a response in every human breast.

I have brought these two Scriptures together in this contrast in order to suggest the striking difference that exists between a man who depends for his power on his own inherent personality and a man who is dependent entirely upon the position which he holds or the circumstances which surround him. A few hours before this scene is opened, Belshazzar would have seemed to be by far the most splendid and important personage in all Babylon; he was king over a rich and powerful nation, which had in Babylon the most magnificent capital in the world. Compared to him, Daniel was small indeed. But a few hours pass by, and a great emergency arrives which calls not for position or office, but for manhood; and in that hour Belshazzar shrinks and shrivels, and Daniel looms up large. So it will ever be on the great occasions of life. Office, wealth, fame—these are only the scabbards; manhood is the sword, which is infinitely more important.

A good deal of comment has been made concerning the sword presented recently to Commodore Schley by the people of Philadelphia. The sword cost several thousand dollars, and by far the greater part of this money was spent on the jewels and decorations on the scabbard. This fact has revived a story told of General Winfield Scott many years ago, who had received a beautiful sword from the State of Louisiana and was asked how it pleased him.

"It is a very fine sword, indeed," he said, "but there is one thing about it I should have preferred different. The inscription should be on the blade, not on the scabbard. The scabbard may be taken from us; the sword never."

An eastern editor, reflecting on this incident, brings out very pertinently the great fact that the world spends too much time, money, and energy on the scabbard of life; too little on the sword. The scabbard represents outside show, vanity, and display; the sword, intrinsic worth. The scabbard is ever the semblance; the sword is the reality. The scabbard is the temporal; the sword is the eternal. The scabbard is the body; the sword is the soul. The scabbard represents the material side of life; the sword represents the true, the spiritual, the ideal.

Now, Belshazzar had a very much more brilliant scabbard than Daniel, but when it came to the sword of real manhood the young man from Jewry outclassed him entirely. Belshazzar had the title of king, but Daniel was far more like a king as they stood there facing each other in that time of peril and alarm.

Let us keep our story and our sermon together as we go along. We have here the story of that evolution which goes on, in a sinful life, just as surely in a bookkeeper or a trolley car conductor or a drug clerk as it does in a king. The first step in most downward careers is the step of dissipation or wastefulness of the forces of life. If you will think over most of the men and women you have known who have come to moral disaster, you will find that this is correct. Not always the same kind of dissipation, but a failure to hold one's self keenly responsible to God for the careful and noble use of the talents committed to us. The story we have in hand is like that. Belshazzar, the king of Babylon, went the way of dissipation. We have not seen all the steps that come up to this climax. We see him after he is ripe in wickedness. He has gone the path of the drunkard. He talked the language of those modern silly fools who say, "A short life and a merry one, for we will be a long time dead." Dissipation has bred in him, as it does in men and women everywhere, irreverence and recklessness. Ten years before Belshazzar never would have dreamed of the blasphemy and reckless conduct of this hour which is portrayed to us. But sin must, in the very nature of things, grow more reckless and wicked as the time goes on. So there came a day when Belshazzar determined to make a feast such as Babylon never saw; one that should be talked of for many years to come. Alas! he little dreamed how long it would be talked of and what an immortality of ignominy it would give him. And so, "Belshazzar the king made a great feast to a thousand of his lords, and drank wine before the thousand. Belshazzar, whiles he tasted the wine, commanded to bring the golden and silver vessels which his father Nebuchadnezzar had taken out of the temple which was in Jerusalem; that the king, and his princes, his wives, and his concubines, might drink therein. Then they brought the golden vessels that were taken out of the temple of the house of God which was at Jerusalem; and the king, and his princes, his wives, and his concubines, drank in them. They drank wine, and praised the gods of gold, and of silver, of brass, of iron, of wood, and of stone" (Daniel 5:4).

It was a brilliant scene of revelry and drunkenness. All hearts were full of gayety; fears were thrust aside; reason and conscience were crushed under foot; and yet judgment waited on the wicked throng. Belshazzar might be rich and powerful, but he could not measure arms with God. In the midst of the revelry, "in the same hour came forth fingers of a man's hand, and wrote over against the candlestick upon the plaster of the wall of the king's palace: and the king saw the part of the hand that wrote. Then the king's countenance was changed, and his thoughts troubled him, so that the joints and his loins were loosed, and his knees smote one against another" (Daniel 5:5, 6).

Often it is true that the most reckless man in sin is the greatest coward when his sin overtakes him in judgment. What a pitiful spectacle Belshazzar is as he stands there staring at the ominous sentence on the wall, with his knees smiting together, his hands trembling, and his teeth chattering, like a man with the ague. Where is all his bravado now? Where is all his blasphemous recklessness? It is gone like froth, and the bitter dregs at the bottom of the cup remain to be swallowed to the very last. Pride and recklessness are poor foundations to build on; they will not stand when the storm comes. When the rain of affliction and death beats upon such a house it falls, because it is built upon the sand. Kings may come and go in Babylon, but Daniel abides, for his character is built upon the solid rock. How is it with you? Can you stand the storm, or not? Only the reverent soul, living in humble fellowship with God, can have composure in the day of reckoning.

There is something suggestive in the fact that it was not in the first hour of his fright that Belshazzar was wise enough to turn to Daniel. No; the astrologers, the Chaldeans, and the soothsayers—every humbug of a fortune-teller in Babylon—all had their turn before he was wise enough to go to the man of God. Finally the queen sent to him and reminded him of the presence of Daniel in the city. She said, "There is a man in thy kingdom, in whom is the spirit of the holy gods: and in the days of thy father light and understanding and wisdom, like the wisdom of the gods, was found in him" (Daniel 5:11). So Daniel was called, and it was found that the wisdom which cometh from God still abode in that noble man.

How may men overtaken by their sin, in our own day, turn everywhere for relief before they turn to Christ and the house of God. A man tries to drown his grief in drink, or forget his sorrow in cards, or lose his restlessness in speculation—only to sink himself the deeper in his misery—before he turns with humble heart to confess his sin and find forgiveness at the mercy-seat.

It is a very sad note which I am compelled to strike in conclusion: that one may go too far on the path of sin, and call when it is too late. The day of probation had passed for Belshazzar; judgment had overtaken him. The handwriting on the wall was not a warning; it was a sentence. The warning had been coming again and again, but he would not heed it. Daniel said to him: "O thou king, the most high God gave Nebuchadnezzar they father a kingdom, and majesty, and glory, and honor: and for the majesty that he gave him, all people, nations, and languages, trembled and feared before him: whom he would he slew; and whom he would he kept alive; and whom he would he set up; and whom he would he put down. But when his heart was lifted up, and his mind hardened in pride, he was deposed from his kingly throne, and they took his glory from him: and he was driven from the sons of men; and his heart was made like the beasts, and his dwelling was with the wild asses: they fed him with grass like oxen, and his body was wet with the dew of heaven; till he knew that the most high God ruled in the kingdom of men, and that he appointeth over it whomsoever he will. And thou his son, O Belshazzar, hast not humbled thine heart, though thou knewest all this; but hast lifted up thyself against the Lord of heaven; and they have brought the vessels of his house before thee, and thou, and thy lords, thy wives, and thy concubines, have drunk wine in them; and thou hast praised the gods of silver, and gold, of brass, iron, wood, and stone, which see not, nor hear, nor know: and the God in whose hand thy breath is, and whose are all thy ways, hast thou not glorified: then was the part of the hand sent from him; and this writing was written...
.God hath numbered thy kingdom, and finished it...

Thou art weighed in the balances, and art found wanting…
Thy kingdom is divided, and given to the Medes and Persians" (Daniel 5:18-28) And that night Belshazzar was slain.

I bring this solemn message to you tonight, glad in my heart to know that you who hear me are still in the day of probation and warning; that if you will you may hearken unto God, and by turning from your sins to Christ may find forgiveness and eternal life. Hear his message to-night, and be saved!

56

THE VALLEY OF DECISION

*"Multitudes, multitudes in the valley of decision: for the
day of the Lord is near in the valley of decision"*
(Joel 3:14).

I do not care to enter into a discussion of the prophecy
of this book, or to inquire into the relation of the text
to its setting. It is the simple statement of fact that there
are multitudes of people who are in the place where they
must decide one way or the other, and where the judgment
of God will follow fast upon their decision, to which I wish
to call your attention.

There is nothing so important as a decision. To choose
while one has the power to choose, rather than to drift with
the current until the power of choice is taken away, is one
of the important characteristics of a strong and noble manhood or womanhood. Things are so arranged that when we
will not decide for ourselves a decision is made for us, and
it is ever against us. A boy passing through the years of his
youth has the power to choose, oftentimes, whether he will
have a good education or not. But if he delays, and does
not decide, the years soon tell the tale and the power to

choose is taken from him; the time has passed by when school days are possible for him. We are assured that life is like that in other things. We have the opportunity now to choose Jesus Christ as our Saviour, to choose the Christian character as our own, to choose the Christian life as our career; but life is steadily passing on, and if we do not choose Christ it will not be long before the opportunity will have passed by forever, and our decision will be registered against him.

To-night I offer you Jesus Christ as your Saviour. You have the power, by God's grace, to accept him tonight and to begin this very hour to lead a Christian life. If you do not accept him definitely, and obey him by an open confession, then you reject him. There cannot be any neutrality in this matter, for Christ asks for your open friendship. He declares that the man that is not with him is against him. If you accept him to-night you enlist under his banner. The white flag of the cross becomes your life. You have put yourself with his friends and you have the promise of his friendship and guidance. Will you decide for him tonight? God says to us, in his word, "I have set before you life and death" (Deuteronomy 30:19); he entreats us in every conceivable way to choose life, and you will choose one or the other by your own action. You say, "I do not choose." But your very conduct is a rejection of Jesus unless you accept him. As Dr. Cuyler says, people do not usually set success and happiness on the one hand, and ruin on the other hand, and then willfully choose to be ruined. No man voluntarily chooses the disease, disgrace, and horrors of drunkenness. Yet thousands do choose to tamper with the seductive, intoxicating glass, and their own free choice brings them to the drunkard's self-damnation. In like manner, when you decide to refuse the loving Saviour who is knocking at the door of your heart, you choose to risk the consequences. When you choose to continue on in sin, to follow the devices and desires of an unconverted heart, and to refuse to be all that Christ would make you, you are deliberately choosing the path that separates you from Christ and heaven.

No man can serve two masters. You cannot go toward Chicago and toward Buffalo from Cleveland at the same time. Every day you spend away from Christ you are getting farther from the Christian life, and the harder it will be for you to become a strong and happy Christian.

It is not more meditation, more thinking, more theorizing, that you need; it is more decision. Dr. Newman Hall, the great English preacher, relates in his autobiography two very interesting incidents showing how people came to a decision at unexpected times and were saved. One was when he undertook to climb Mount Snowdon. He slept on a plank in a wretched little hut on the mountaintop. A large number of workingmen, quarrymen, were also waiting to see the sun rise in the morning. It was the most beautiful sunrise he ever saw. No words could describe the reddening sky, the first level rays goldening a hundred peaks, the shadow of the mountain they were on creeping over the lakes and valleys below. There were about one hundred Welshmen and a dozen Englishmen on the mountain with him. They asked him to speak to them—someone recognizing who we was—but he replied that God was preaching to them and they had better hear his voice. But he offered prayer, and when he closed he noticed that several men were shedding tears. A year afterward he was taking a walking trip through that same country when a man pulled up the cart he was driving, containing cheeses and a live pig, and asked if he might give him a lift. Dr. Hall felt that it was a good opportunity for conversation. The countryman had recognized him, and, speaking of that sunrise, said it resulted in the conversion of fifty people. Dr. Hall said that he had only offered prayer. But the man replied that some had decided for Christ that morning, though they had not understood a word he said, they being Welsh, but the effect of their conversion was a revival in the village churches near.

The other story is of a very different circumstance. One Sunday evening, in his own church, Dr. Hall was delivering a written sermon on temptation, and suddenly felt that his address was unlike his usual style, and too argumentative for may of the people. He suddenly paused, looked away from his manuscript, and, appealing with a loud voice to the more distant of his audience, said: "Perhaps among those pressing in at the door there may be someone so miserable as to think of throwing himself over yonder bridge, saying, perhaps, 'It's too late to tell me not to enter into temptation. I have done it; I am in it. There's no hope for me.' Stop! Stop! There is hope. Christ died for thee. He will pardon, he will save, even thee!" A few weeks afterward one of the members of his church told him that he had called to see a woman who had made up her mind to throw herself over Blackfriars Bridge, one Sunday evening, but she thought it was too light and a policeman might stop her; so in order to wait for the darkness she went into the church and stood in the crowd inside the door. Standing there it seemed to her that Dr. Hall had called directly to her to stop, and come to Christ, and she went back to her home to pray, and became a true and happy Christian.

What saved these people was that, though the call of salvation came unexpectedly and in an unusual way, they at once decided and accepted Christ as their Saviour. In their immediate decision was their salvation. I wish I knew what I might say to win everyone here to-night to the safe refuge under the shadow of the cross of Jesus Christ.

A young traveler, who was making a pedestrian tour through the Alps, tells a beautiful story of Swiss honesty. The Swiss friend who was with the foreign sightseers, observing that they were weary after a six hours' march from the Monastery of St. Bernard, said, "We shall soon reach my brother's house, and you shall all have a cup of hot coffee and some food." But when they reached the farmhouse it was closed—doors locked, shutters shut—and the whole place deserted, for it was the time of vintage and everyone was in the vineyard. Our young traveler was much disappointed, but the good Swiss friend said, "You will get your refreshment just the same." And reaching up toward a cross made of gay mountain flowers which hung on the door, according to the pretty Valais custom, he pulled down a great door key, and in another minute the door was open. A blazing fire of logs was quickly kindled, and in a short time they were refreshed with food and drink. All this seemed so strange to the tourists that that they made inquiry as to how people would dare go away and leave the key in such a convenient place. "O," said the Swiss, in quite a shocked tone, "there's no fear of any of our people entering a house which does not belong to them. If the key is put under the cross it is always safe there."

But the key under the cross on a Swiss door is not so safe as your soul will be, both in time and in eternity, if you put it under the shadow of Christ's cross, by choosing him this day as your Saviour and Lord. No one can pluck us out of that refuge.

57

THE VILLAIN IN THE FIRST CHRISTMAS DRAMA

"Herod will seek the young child to destroy him"
(Matthew 2:13).

Herod is preeminently the villain in the plot of the first Christmas story which has fascinated the heart of mankind for so many hundreds of years. All the others that appear in the story are most attractive characters. The wise men who come from across the desert following the star in the East, bringing their rich gifts and ready to worship the Christ, are altogether winning and splendid in their suggestion of nobility and largeness of character and life. The shepherds out in the fields keeping watch over their flocks by night, who, when they have heard the good news, come into the little town of Bethlehem full of curiosity and reverent awe, and who go back again to their flocks to praise God, win out hearts by their honesty and simplicity. The angels who bore the good tidings of peace and good will, and all that mighty company of the heavenly host which sang their praises to God and their anthems to the newborn Christ, have made all human life richer and sweeter ever since by the glimpse they gave into the beauty and glory of the inhabitants of the upper skies. They have filled the background of all our lives with singing angels, and put a prophecy of peace and brotherhood on human lips wherever the story of the Christ has gone. The little manger itself and the stable and the cattle have captured the fancy of the world. And pure-minded, honest Joseph, and sweet-faced, glory-crowned Mary, with the holy glow of motherhood resting on her innocent face as she kisses the newborn child—all these are attractive. There is only one villain in the plot, and that is Herod.

Herod desired to slay Jesus because he feared the overthrow of his government. He had no idea of a spiritual kingdom, and there was no basework in the man for such a belief. He was a brutal, sensual, wicked man, to whom only brute force appealed, and he supposed that this new Messiah, prophesied about, and whom the wise men of the East had come so far to seek, was the birth of a new kingdom which was to be a threat against his temporal power. The Herods, all of them, knew the truth of the proverb, "Uneasy lies the head that wears a crown." This Herod, like the rest, was all the time looking for danger, and so he was determined to crush it out while the promised king was only a child. When the wise men were led of God to return to their home without seeing Herod, he determined to make sure of his wicked purpose by killing every child under two years old in the entire region. This cruel edict was carried out, and the land was filled with the graves of little children. But the child he sought escaped his malice.

I have not selected this picture for our study with the intention of taking the time for a discussion of the sins of

Herod, who has long since gone to his judgment; but to try to bring clearly before your mind the fact that Satan and sin are ever trying to destroy the Christ in our time as persistently and wickedly as in the days of Herod. All that is wicked in the world is warring against Jesus, and is seeking to take him out of the heart and lives of men. You who are Christians could bear testimony to the truth of this. You know that to maintain a Christian life and to keep a happy communion with Jesus in your soul require that you shall war against the world and the flesh and the devil.

And you who have never become Christians, but who were reared in Christian homes and were brought up to look forward to Christmas as a time of love and good will, will bear witness as to how persistently the evil spirit has wrought in his attempt to destroy entirely that old spirit of love and reverence toward Christ and his Church which you knew something about in your childhood. It may be that I speak to some out of whom the Christ-thought and the Christ-life have almost entirely disappeared. The memory of the prayers that were taught you in boyhood or girlhood is like a shadowy dream that has no longer any power to influence your daily conduct. Even the habit of church-going has ceased to be anything more than an empty form. Its true function in bringing you into relation to Christ, which had something real and genuine in blessing in your youth, has now vanished. Your indifference or your sinfulness has driven Christ out of your life. Other things have come in and filled your thought and affection until, like the little inn in Bethlehem on the first Christmas Eve, there is no room for Christ in your soul. If this is so, you have met with the most terrible loss that can come to any human life.

Henry Van Dyke, who has given us a number of supremely beautiful Christmas Stories, has given one of rare interest this year, in which he tells the story of the "Lost Word." It is the story of a young man who lived in Antioch some fifteen hundred years ago. This young man was the son of Demetrius, a very proud and wealthy old pagan. The son, however, came under the influence of the great Christian preacher, John of Antioch, and though it cost him his father's home and all the prospects of wealth and power as his father's son, he accepted Christ and for two years lived with the Christians. But he fell, at last, into a gloomy mood, and lost the sweetness and joy out of his Christian faith. While he was in this depressed and unhappy condition Christmas morning came, and having no joy with the Christians in their festivities, Hermas wandered away by himself to the Grove of Daphne, in which there was a heathen temple. He sat down beside a gushing spring and gave himself up to gloom and sadness. While he sat there, feeling that his Christian life was a failure, an old pagan priest came upon him, and tempted him to renounce Christ. Although he refused to do that, he opened his heart to the old priest and admitted his longing for worldly pleasure.

"Well," said the old man soothingly, as he plucked a leaf from the laurel tree above them, and dipped it in the spring, "let us dismiss the riddles of belief. I like them as little as you do. You know this is a Castalian fountain. The Emperor Hadrian once read his fortune here from a leaf dipped in the water. Let us see what this leaf tells us. It is already turning yellow. How do you read that?"

"Wealth," said Hermas, laughing as he looked at his mean garment.

"And here is a bud on the stem that seems to be swelling. What is that?"

"Pleasure," answered Hermas bitterly.

"And here is a tracing of wreaths upon the surface. What do you make of that?"

"What you will," said Hermas, not even looking. "Suppose we say success and fame."

"Yes," said the tempting priest; "it is all written here. I promise that you shall enjoy it all. This is the season that you Christians call the Christmas, and you have taken up the pagan custom of exchanging gifts. Well, if I give to you, you must give to me. It is a small thing, and really the thing you can best afford to part with: a single word—the name of Him you profess to worship. Let me take that word and all that belongs to it entirely out of your life, so that you shall never need to hear or speak it again. You will be richer without it. I promise you everything, and this is all I ask in return. Do you consent?"

"Yes, I consent," said Hermas, mocking. "If you can take your price, a word, you can keep you promise, a dream."

The old priest laid the long, cool, wet leaf softly across the young man's eyes, and an icicle of pain darted through them; every nerve in his body was drawn together there in a knot of agony. Then all the tangle of pain seemed to be lifted out of him, and he fell into a deep sleep.

When Hermas awoke he had gone back again to his worldly life. He left the grove and walked toward his father's house. As he drew near he saw a confusion of servants in the porch, and the old steward ran down to meet him at the gate, saying," The master is at point of death, and has sent for you."

Hermas hurried to his father's side and found him dying. The feeble old man said, "It is good that you have come back to me. I have missed you. I was wrong to send you away. You shall never leave me again. You are my son, my heir. I have changed everything. Hermas, my son, come nearer—close beside me. Take my hand, my son!"

The young man obeyed and, kneeling by the couch, gathered his father's cold, twitching fingers in his firm, warm grasp.

"Hermas, life is passing—the last sands, I cannot stay them. My soul is empty—nothing beyond—very dark. I am afraid. But you know something better. You found something that made you willing to give up your life for it—it must have been almost like dying—yet you were happy. What was it you found? See, I am giving you everything. I have forgiven you. Now forgive me. Tell me, what is it? Your secret, your faith—give it to me before I go."

At the sound of this broken pleading a strange passion of pity and love took the young man by the throat. His voice shook a little as he answered eagerly:

"Father, there is nothing to forgive. I am your son. I will gladly tell you all that I know. I will give you the secret of faith. Father, you must believe with all your heart and soul and strength in——"

Where was the word? The word that he had been used to utter night and morning, the word that meant to him more than anything he had ever known—what had become of it?

He groped for it in the dark room of his mind. He had thought he could lay his hand upon it in a moment, but it was gone. Someone had taken it away. Everything else was most clear to him: the terror of death; the lonely soul appealing from his father's eyes; the instant need of comfort and help. But at the one point where he looked for help he could find nothing; only an empty space. The word of hope had vanished. He felt for it blindly and in desperate haste.

"Father, wait! I have forgotten something—it has slipped away from me. I shall find it in a moment. There is hope—I will tell you presently—O, wait!"

The bony hand gripped his like a vise; the glazed eyes opened wider. "Tell me," whispered the old man; "tell me quickly, for I must go."

The voice sank into a dull rattle. The fingers closed once more, and relaxed. The light behind the eyes went out. Hermas was kneeling, full of agony, beside the dead.

One would have thought this would have sent him back again to the Christians and the holy faith, but he had bargained away the name of God and Christ for worldliness and pleasure, and so he went forward. He was not very wealthy and powerful. He married a beautiful woman, Athenais. A son was born to them who was the idol of their hearts. Yet all their wealth and power did not give them peace; they longed for something, they knew not what. To try and find peace Hermas thrust himself into the world's excitement and glory. He built palaces, he patronized art, he gave banquets to kings, he sent grain ships across the seas; but peace did not come. One day he entered the great chariot races at Antioch, and his black Numidian horses won the victory over a score of rivals. Hermas received the prize carelessly from the judge's hands, and turned to drive once more around the circus, to show himself to the people. He lifted his eager son into the chariot beside him to share his triumph.

Here, indeed, was the glory of his life—this matchless son. As the horses pranced around the ring, a great shout of applause filled the amphitheater and thousands of spectators waved their salutations of praise: "Hail, fortunate Hermas, master of success! Hail, little Hermas, prince of good luck!"

The great acclamation and the fluttering of garments in the air startled the horses. They plunged violently forward, a rein broke, a wheel of the chariot caught against a stone parapet, and the boy was tossed into the air, his head striking the wall. When Hermas turned to look for him he was lying like a broken flower on the sand.

Some of you know the agony of the days that followed; know, as I do, by personal experience, what it means to have a son, who holds all your heart, trembling in the darkness between life and death. Hermas tried to pray, but he could not, for the name he used to pray to was lost. His wife begged him to pray, but he could only say, "Long ago I knew something. It would have helped us. But I have forgotten it. It is all gone. But I would give all that I have if I could bring it back again now at this hour, in this time of our bitter trouble."

A servant entered the room and told him that John of Antioch was waiting to see him, and also Marcion, the old pagan priest. Hermas and his wife, broken-hearted, went together to meet them. The good Christian looked the young man tenderly in the face and said, "My son, I have come to you because I have heard that you are in trouble."

"It is true," answered Hermas passionately. "We are in

trouble; desperate trouble, trouble accursed. Our child is dying. We are poor, we are destitute, we are afflicted. In all this house, in all the world, there is no one that can help us. I knew something long ago, when I was with you—a word, a name—in which we might have found hope. But I have lost it. I gave it to this man. He has taken it away from me forever."

He pointed to Marcion, the old pagan priest. The old man's lips curled scornfully. "A word! a name!" he sneered. "I promised him wealth and pleasure and fame. What did he give in return? An empty name."

"Servant of demons, be still!" The voice of John of Antioch rang clear, like a trumpet, through the hall. There is a name which none can lose without being lost. There is a name at which the devils tremble. Depart quickly, before I speak it!'

Marcion had shrunk into the shadow of one of the pillars. A bright lamp near him tottered on it pedestal and fell with a crash. In the confusion he vanished like a shadow.

John turned to Hermas, and his tone softened as he said, "My son, you have sinned deeper than you know. The word with which you parted so lightly is the key-word of all life and joy and peace. Without it the world has no meaning, existence no rest, and death no refuge. It is the word that purifies love, and comforts grief, and keeps hope alive forever. It is the most precious thing that ever ear has heard, or mind has known, or heart has conceived. It is the name of Him who has given us life and breath and all things richly to enjoy; the name of Him, who, though we may forget Him, never forgets us; the name of Him who pities us as you pity your suffering child; the name of Him who, though we wander far from Him, seeks us in the wilderness, and sent His Son, even as His Son has sent me this night to breathe again that forgotten name in the heart that is perishing without it. Listen, my son, listen with all your soul to the blessed name of God our Father."

The cold agony in the breast of Hermas melted away. A sense of sweet release spread through him from head to foot. The lost was found. The dew of a divine peace fell on this parched soul, and the withering flower of human love lifted its head again. The light of a new hope shone on his face. He lifted his hands above his head and words of prayer were on his lips: "Out of the depths have I cried unto thee, O Lord! O my God, be merciful to me, for my soul trusteth in thee. My God, thou hast given; take not thy gift away from me, O my God! Spare the life of this my child, O thou God, my Father, my Father!" A deep hush followed the prayer. "Listen!" whispered his wife breathlessly.

Was it an echo? It could not be, for it came again! The voice of the child, clear and low, waking from sleep and calling: "My father, my father!"

It was no echo; the prayer of Hermas was answered.

I have brought this story to you because I know that to many of you it is your own story. You have lost out of your heart all that personal and real conception of God which made your prayer and your faith a comforting reality in which you could trust. You are wandering in the darkness without God and without hope in the world. God help me to bring back the lost word to you! Open your heart and let him come back to you again with all the old tenderness of sympathy and love.

58

THE EASTER CONSPIRACY

*"Some of the watch came into the city, and shewed unto
the chief priests all the things that were done. And when
they were assembled with the elders, and had taken counsel, they gave large money unto the soldiers, saying, Say ye,
His disciples came by night, and stole him away while we
slept. And if this come to the governor's ears, we will
persuade him, and secure you. So they took the money and
did as they were taught"* (Matthew 28:11-15).

Modern cities have not gained so many points in
deviltry after all. It is very easy to read between
the lines here and see the skeleton of a whole political machine. The governor was the city boss in politics;
he was a carpet bagger from Rome, and though he was independent of these fellows in a certain way, he found it
necessary, in order to keep his fences up and hold himself
solid in the saddle, to keep a strong political machine
among the local politicians at Jerusalem. These elders and
chief priests talk a language that is very well known in our
modern towns today. It is the language of the man with a
"pull." The soldiers, scared out of their wits, came hurrying
as fast as their legs could carry them into the city with the

marvelous story that, while they watched the sealed tomb in Joseph's garden, suddenly the earth rocked to and fro under their feet and a great being clothed with lightning came down from the sky and rolled away the huge stone door from the tomb they were guarding. What could they do but flee? And fortunate they considered themselves to have escaped with their lives. Something had to be done at once to quiet the town. If this true story of the resurrection of Christ went abroad among the people, if these soldiers went about blurting out the simple truth, the whole town would believe in Christ and accept him as the Messiah, and the ecclesiastical politicians in Jerusalem would, every one of them, find himself "a statesman out of a job" in short meter.

In their excitement they send out messengers and gather in the chiefs of the ring to decide on a course of action. It does not seem to have occurred to them to accept the truth as it was, admit that they had been deceived and had been in the wrong; they would risk their souls by continuing in the wrong rather than lose their political control of the city. And so they devise this scheme. They reason: These soldiers are poor fellows, they get barely enough to keep body and soul together, and a little money will go a long way with them; so we will just draw on the boodle fund and bribe them to keep still, for we shall have the whole city about our ears unless they are silenced.

The moment, however, they began to talk to the soldiers about keeping still, new difficulties arose. The soldiers said, "We are willing enough to take your money and keep still, but we have got to have something to tell. We were left to guard a tomb with a dead man in it, and the seal of the Roman government was put on the tomb; and now the seal had been broken, the great stone door has been rolled away, and the man is gone. The grave is empty. What are we going to say about that?"

To this the schemers replied, "You shall say, His disciples came by night and took him."

At that the soldiers laughed in scorn, and replied, "Nobody would believe that. Have you seen those disciples? You know who they are; twelve ignorant, untrained fellows; there is not more than one of them, that fellow Peter, that has a spark of fight in him—and when this Jesus was waiting for trial he swore he never knew him, and went back on him entirely. Beside these men there are three of four women that have been crying all the time since the crucifixion. We never could make anybody believe that that crowd of weaklings came and overpowered a company of hardened veterans like us, when there was nothing to gain by it but to get a dead body."

Then some more cunning man among the plotters said, "Tell the people that you fell asleep, and while you were sleeping these fanatical friends of his came and stole his body."

"Yes," say the soldiers, "that will put us in a pretty pickle! We shall lose our necks that way. You know what it means for a Roman soldier to get caught sleeping on guard; his body goes to feed the vultures inside of twenty-four hours."

Then up spoke a sly old elder, with a leer and a wink in one eye, "Don't you worry about your necks. That sleepy story is the best yet. You tell that, and if it comes to the governor's ears, and he shows any disposition to make any trouble for you, I have a pull with the governor and I'll stand between you and all danger."

And so the soldiers were finally persuaded and went out, carrying the money in their pockets and with their parrot-like lie on their lips, to explain away the resurrection of Christ.

It is very interesting and suggestive to note what a diverse group of people will sometimes be gathered in defense of a bad cause. Shakespeare makes one of his characters say, "Misery doth acquaint a man with strange bedfellows," and politics in defense of a bad cause many times illustrates the same fact.

A gentleman in southern California went out to look for some of his stock that were in danger because of widespread forest fires. When he came upon them he was astonished to find not only his cattle and horses, but a deer, three wildcats, a coyote, and several rabbits, all alive, and apparently in no fear of him. They watched his approach with indifference, the timidity gone from the big-eyed deer, fear taking the place of venom in the wildcat's purr, and a professed honesty shining in the gray coyote's face. The rabbits sat on their haunches, as meek as the pets of children. The rancher drove the stock through the smoldering brush, the deer going along with the cattle, the rabbits hopping along at the rancher's heels, and the coyote and the wildcats keeping pace with the rest. But when the burning field was passed and the danger of immediate destruction no longer threatened, the deer broke into a run for the distant hills, the rabbits were away like a flash, and the old defiance and snarling leer came back to the wildcats, while the coyote plainly showed that he was the same old cowardly, slouching thief as of yore. How often we see that illustrated when, to save the domination of some corrupt and wicked political machine in a city, saloon keepers and gamblers and prize fighters and thugs and deacons and elders, and even an occasional preacher, will flock together rather than see the corrupt machine go to pieces.

We have here another suggestion which deserves the greatest emphasis, and that is the crime of leading another man to sin. These soldiers were an ignorant type and poor, with but little opportunity for intellectual or moral cultivation, while the men who were bribing them were men of education and culture and wealth. Yet they deliberately bought these men up as they would purchase so many calves in the market, and sent them away with the hired lie on their lips. And, no doubt, if you had approached them about it they would have had some plausible excuse on their tongues, and would have claimed that the end justified the means. But, according to Jesus Christ, to cause another man to sin is just as wicked and damning as to go and do the sin yourself. Do you remember that heart-searching declaration of Jesus when he was setting forth the value of a little child and said, "But whoso shall offend one of these little ones which believe in me, it were better for him that a millstone were hanged about his neck, and that he were drowned in the depths of the sea?" (Matthew 18:6). In that day the mills were hand mills, and the grinding was done in stone basins with another stone worked by hand. That sort of a millstone was just about heavy enough, if it were tied about a man's neck, to sink his head under water and drown him. A great many people condemned to death were executed in that way, so that Christ by this illustration must have meant to teach that to cause another person to do wrong is a capital offense.

This is susceptible of very wide application. Down at the heart of things it means that our attitude toward our fellow-men must be one that shall, in so far as we have the power, lead them in the right way. We cannot draw back with Cain's question on our lips, "Am I my brother's keeper?" and expect to escape condemnation when we stand at the judgment seat of Jesus Christ.

There is an old story of Edward the Confessor which tells how he spent thirty years of his life in poverty and exile while the cruel and rapacious Danes ruled in England. At last, after the death of the most powerful of the Danish kings, the English people, high and low, recalled Edward to the throne of his father. And when he had been welcomed back by the people, and had been crowned and anointed as king, and had been honored by all the kings of Europe, his treasurer and his courtiers, thinking to gladden the heart of their king who had known so much poverty, wished to show him the riches of which he would now be the royal possessor. And so they took him into his treasury, and showed him large barrels filled with the yellow gold and the white silver treasure that had been raised by cruel and oppressive taxes from the English people. They thought their new king would be charmed and delighted at the sight, but they soon learned their mistake. The old story says that the king saw a sight they did not see. He saw a fiend, or demon, or evil spirit, sitting on the treasures, mocking and sporting at the miseries of the people. He seemed to see the blood of his poor subjects on the money which had been extorted under the name of the "Danegeld;" a tax that was supposed to be used to get rid of Danish pirates, but which was really put into the coffers of the king. The king's heart was sore to think of his people, so dear to him, who had been pillaged an despoiled; so he caused the treasures to be returned and no more to be raised in that cruel way.

No man can look over modern life, even in our own country, under the Stars and Stripes, and see money brought into the treasury by licensing the liquor traffic, the stains of blood upon every piece of it—the blood of drunkards, the red heart's blood of drunkard's wives, the blood of little children—and behold the corrupt political machines that in our modern cities sell the law for so much a statute as at auction, that protect gamblers for a reward, that use the police force not to enforce righteous laws or to protect the interests of the people, but as a threat by which to extort tens of thousands of dollars through blackmail, and know this money is used to fatten the creatures of political rings, and to bribe the base and ignorant and so perpetuate the brutal rule of the political boss, without praying God that in every one of our great cities there may be leaders like Edward the Confessor, who shall rise up in the majesty of manhood to scorn the blood-money wrung from the sins and sorrows of the poor.

But, as every question of reform resolves itself back to the question of personal righteousness, it remains for every one of us to smite, with all the power we have, these vicious influences in modern society which degrade and ruin manhood and womanhood. It is better to fail, while doing the best one can for the right, than to shout with the victorious party at the loss of self-respect through having compromised with the wrong. We can stand by with fidelity and share the fate of righteousness in the community.

A ship arrived at San Francisco recently which had been two hundred and ninety-six days from Newcastle, Australia. She had been in great peril in a storm at sea and had had long delays. One night, when she was in great danger, the captain asked the captain of another ship to "stand by" through the night, and the captain did so at great risk to his own vessel and his own life, but finally was the cause of the salvation of the other vessel. As soon as he was safe in harbor, the captain of the ship that had been threatened with wreck gave his first attention to show his appreciation of the other captains' assistance and sent him a gold watch, and went before the council of the city of Sydney and told the story of his heroism. On learning of it the Sydney authorities presented to the noble captain a medal bearing his name on one side, and on the other the simple inscription, "The man that did stand by."

In the midst of the campaign for righteousness that is going on in our modern life, when the liquor traffic, the gamblers, the plunderers, the thieves, and the political demagogues club together to debauch the courts, to entrap the unwary, to brutalize the poor, to stir the passions of the people, so that the poor shall hate the rich and the rich shall be suspicious of the poor—and all this for selfish aims and purposes—in such a fight I want to share the fate of righteousness; to be no more popular than Jesus Christ would be if he stood in this place and sought, as of old, to make it easy for men to do right and hard for them to do wrong. Rather than anything else I would have Christ look down upon me and say, "The man that did stand by."